Because, Soferim Bebel, if it goes to that, (and dormerwindow gossip will cry it from the housetops no surelier than the writing on the wall will hue it to the mod of men that mote in the main street) every person, place and thing in the chaosmos of Alle anyway connected with the gobblydumped turkery was moving and changing every part of the time: the travelling inkhorn (possibly pot), the hare and turtle pen and paper, the continually more and less intermisunderstanding minds of the anticollaborators, the as time went on as it will variously inflected, differently pronounced, otherwise spelled, changeably meaning vocable scriptsigns.

James Joyce, *Finnegans Wake*

JAMES JOYCE'S 'WORK IN PROGRESS'

The text of *Finnegans Wake* is not as monolithic as it might seem. It grew out of a set of short vignettes, sections and fragments. Several of these sections, which James Joyce confidently claimed would 'fuse of themselves', are still recognizable in the text of *Finnegans Wake*. And while they are undeniably integrated very skill-fully, they also function separately. In this publication history, Dirk Van Hulle examines the interaction between the private composition process and the public life of Joyce's 'Work in Progress', from the creation of the separate sections through their publication in periodicals and as separately published sections. Van Hulle highlights the beautifully crafted editions published by fine arts presses and Joyce's encouragement of his daughter's creative talents, even as his own creative process was slowing down in the 1930s. All of these pre-book publications were 'alive' in both bibliographic and textual terms, as Joyce continually changed the texts in order to prepare the book publication of *Finnegans Wake*. Van Hulle's book offers a fresh perspective on these texts, showing that they are not just preparatory versions of *Finnegans Wake* but a 'Work in Progress' in their own right.

Dirk Van Hulle is Professor of Literature in English at the University of Antwerp. He is the author of *Modern Manuscripts: The Extended Mind and Creative Undoing* (2014) and co-director of the Beckett Digital Manuscript Project. He recently edited the *New Cambridge Companion to Samuel Beckett* (2015).

Studies in Publishing History: Manuscript, Print, Digital
Edited by Ann R. Hawkins and Maura Ives

Exploring the intersection of publishing history, book history, and literary and cultural studies, this series supports innovative work on the cultural significance and creative impact of printing and publishing history, including reception, distribution, and translation or adaptation into other media.

James Joyce's 'Work in Progress'

Pre-Book Publications of *Finnegans Wake* Fragments

DIRK VAN HULLE

Routledge
Taylor & Francis Group

LONDON AND NEW YORK

First published 2016
by Routledge

2 Park Square, Milton Park, Abingdon, Oxfordshire OX14 4RN
52 Vanderbilt Avenue, New York, NY 10017

Routledge is an imprint of the Taylor & Francis Group, an informa business

First issued in paperback 2019

British Library Cataloguing in Publication Data
A catalogue record for this book is available from the British Library

Library of Congress Cataloging-in-Publication Data
Hulle, Dirk van.
   James Joyce's 'work in progress' : pre-book publications of Finnegans
wake fragments / by Dirk Van Hulle.
       pages cm. — (Ashgate studies in publishing history: manuscript, print, digital)
   Includes bibliographical references and index.
   ISBN 978-1-4094-6595-9 (hardcover)
   1. Joyce, James, 1882–1941. Finnegans wake.   2. Joyce, James,
1882–1941. — Relations with publishers.   3. Literature publishing–
England–History–20th century.   4. Authors and publishers–England–
History–20th century.   I. Title.
   PR6019.O9F593535 2016
   821′.912—dc23
   2015033110

ISBN: 978-1-4094-6595-9 (hbk)
ISBN: 978-0-367-34662-1 (pbk)

Typeset in Times New Roman and Gill Sans
by Apex CoVantage, LLC

For Geert Lernout

Contents

Acknowledgements

The research for this book was made possible thanks to an ERC grant (European Research Council) for a project called 'Creative Undoing and Textual Scholarship' (CUTS) and thanks to a TOP BOF project of the University of Antwerp. Several archivists, Joyce scholars and friends have greatly helped me during the writing of this book. My first debt of gratitude is to Luca Crispi and Ronan Crowley, whose invaluable help has been instrumental in filling particular lacunae in this publication history. I would also especially like to thank James Maynard at the University at Buffalo for all his help with the press clippings and other documents in the James Joyce Collection. I owe a debt of gratitude to Michael Basinsky, Tim Conley, Tom De Keyser, Wout Dillen, Ann Donahue, Daniel Ferrer, Michael Groden, Cheryl Herr, Wim Van Mierlo, Nicholas Morris, Sam Slote, J. Eric Smith at Salisbury House and to the editors of *European Joyce Studies* and the *Dublin James Joyce Journal* for their willingness to include a version of two sections of this book in their publications.

Most importantly, I would like to seize this opportunity to thank one man in particular. In the past 20 years, he has been my *Doktorvater*, elder brother, mentor and friend. I don't think I will ever be able to pay proper credit to all the things he has made possible, all the help, all the encouragement, all the friendship, all the critical advice – and all of this on a daily basis. I therefore dedicate this book to Geert Lernout.

The research leading to these results has received funding from the European Research Council under the European Union's Seventh Framework Programme (FP7/2007-2013) / ERC grant agreement no 313609 and from the University of Antwerp (TOP BOF).

European Research Council
Established by the European Commission

Universiteit
Antwerpen

Abbreviations

ALP	*Anna Livia Plurabelle*, with a Preface by Padraic Colum, New York: Crosby Gaige, 1928.
BL	British Library, followed by the call number and folio number.
Cr	'Fragment of an Unpublished Work', *The Criterion*, London, III.12 (July 1925), 498–510.
FDV	*A First-Draft Version of 'Finnegans Wake'*, edited by David Hayman, Austin, TX: University of Texas Press, 1963.
FW	James Joyce, *Finnegans Wake*, London: Faber and Faber, 1939.
HCE	*Haveth Childers Everywhere: Fragment from* Work in Progress, by James Joyce, Paris and New York: Henry Babou and Jack Kahane / The Fountain Pess, 1930.
HRC	Harry Ransom Humanities Research Center, The University of Texas at Austin.
JJA	James Joyce, *The James Joyce Archive*, edited by Michael Groden et al., New York: Garland, 1978–79.
JJSB	*James Joyce's Letters to Sylvia Beach*, edited by Melissa Banta and Oscar A. Silverman, Oxford: Plantin Publishers, 1987.
LI	*Letters of James Joyce, vol. I*, edited by Stuart Gilbert, London: Faber and Faber, 1957.
LIII	*Letters of James Joyce, vol. III*, edited by Richard Ellmann, London: Faber and Faber, 1966.
Mime	*The Mime of Mick Nick and the Maggies: A Fragment from Work in Progress*, The Hague: The Servire Press, 1933.
Nd'A	'From Work in Progress' in *Navire d'Argent*, Paris, II.5 (October 1925), 59–74.
S	*Storiella As She Is Syung: A Section of 'Work in Progress'*, by James Joyce, s.l.: Corvinus Press, 1937.
SL	*Selected Letters of James Joyce*, edited by Richard Ellmann, London: Faber and Faber, 1992.
t	*transition* (followed by the issue number).
TQ	'Extract from Work in Progress', *This Quarter*, Milan, I.2 (Autumn–Winter 1925–26), 108–23.
TR	'From Work in Progress', *transatlantic review*, Paris, 1.4 (April 1924), 215–23.
TT	*Tales Told of Shem and Shaun: Three Fragments from Work in Progress*, by James Joyce, Paris: The Black Sun Press, 1929.
TW	*Two Worlds: A Literary Quarterly Devoted to the Increase of the Gaiety of Nations* (followed by the issue number).
U	*Ulysses*, edited by Hans Walter Gabler with Wolfhard Steppe and Claus Melchior, London: The Bodley Head, 1986.

UB JJC   University at Buffalo, James Joyce Collection (Poetry Collection),
          described and annotated by Luca Crispi.
UBC   University at Buffalo Clippings, James Joyce Collection (Poetry
          Collection), uncatalogued newspaper clippings, preserved in brown
          envelopes; the abbreviation UBC is followed by the number of the
          envelope and the handwritten number (in red crayon) on the clipping.

Note on Transcriptions

The transcription method applied in this study tries to represent the quoted passages from manuscripts with as few diacritical signs as possible, crossing out ~~deletions~~ and using superscript for additions. The manuscripts' catalogue number is followed by the folio number, 'r' or 'v' indicating the recto or verso side. Bold typeface is used to highlight particular words in the transcriptions.

Illustrations

Colour Plates

Illustrations

Introduction
Joyce and the Enacted Mind

In 1919, the mind became an issue in the battle between two generations of writers. Virginia Woolf tried to make a clean break with the generation of Arnold Bennett, John Galsworthy and H.G. Wells. While the content of her essay 'Modern Fiction' accords with Ezra Pound's motto 'Make It New', it makes use of the classic 'They say, I say' structure. Woolf's rhetorical strategy to distinguish her generation from the previous one centres around the mind. The traditional novel, according to Woolf, 'more and more ceases to resemble the vision in our minds' (Woolf 1994, 160):

> *Look within* and life, it seems, is very far from being 'like this'. Examine for a moment an ordinary mind on an ordinary day. The mind receives a myriad impressions – trivial, fantastic, evanescent, or engraved with the sharpness of steel. From all sides they come, an incessant shower of innumerable atoms; and as they fall, as they shape themselves into the life of Monday or Tuesday, the accent falls differently from of old; the moment of importance came not here but there; so that, if a writer were a free man and not a slave, if he could write what he chose, not what he must, if he could base his work upon his own feeling and not upon convention, there would be no plot, no comedy, no tragedy, no love interest or catastrophe in the accepted style, and perhaps not a single button sewn on as the Bond Street tailors would have it. [. . .] *Let us record the atoms as they fall upon the mind* in the order in which they fall, let us trace the pattern, however disconnected and incoherent in appearance, which each sight or incident *scores upon the consciousness*.

> (Woolf 1994, 160–1; emphasis added)

The imperative 'Look within' opening this paragraph has functioned as an order in modernism studies, which have consequently been characterized in terms of a 'journey within' (Guerard 1958, 326), an 'inward turn' (von Kahler 1973) or a 'shift from outside to inside' (Meisel 2006, 79). More recently, however, this 'critical commonplace' (Herman 2011, 249) is being questioned by cognitive narratologists. The evocation of fictional minds is not necessarily a matter of 'looking within', and Woolf's image of the mind as some kind of surface upon which 'the atoms [. . .] fall' is perhaps not the most appropriate metaphor.[1] But her appeal to her

---

[1] In *Modern Manuscripts: The Extended Mind and Creative Undoing from Darwin to Beckett and Beyond* (London: Bloomsbury, 2014) I have made a brief analysis of Woolf's use of this metaphor.

co-modernists certainly had an impact. With the activating 'Let us', Woolf mobilizes her generation and in the same paragraph she refers to Joyce as an exponent of this new movement:

> Let us not take it for granted that life exists more fully in what is commonly thought big than in what is commonly thought small. Any one who has read *The Portrait of the Artist as a Young Man* or, what promises to be a far more interesting work, *Ulysses*, now appearing in the *Little Review*, will have hazarded some theory of this nature as to Mr. Joyce's intention. On our part, with such a fragment before us, it is hazarded rather than affirmed; but whatever the intention of the whole, there can be no question but that it is of the utmost sincerity and that the result, difficult or unpleasant as we may judge it, is undeniably important. In contrast with those whom we have called materialists, *Mr. Joyce is spiritual*; he is concerned at all costs to reveal the flickerings of that innermost flame which flashes its messages through the brain, and in order to preserve it he disregards with complete courage whatever seems to him adventitious.
>
> (Woolf 1994, 161; emphasis added)

The question is to what extent Woolf was projecting her own programme onto Joyce's work, and to what extent Joyce felt comfortable with this appropriation. Richard Ellmann has drawn attention to Woolf's much more negative reaction in *A Writer's Diary*: 'After *Ulysses* was published he [T.S. Eliot] came to tea with Virginia Woolf at Hogarth House, and in discussing *Ulysses* was for the first time in her experience "rapt, enthusiastic". "How could anyone write again after achieving the immense prodigy of the last chapter?" he asked. To her it was "underbred", "the book of a self taught working man", of "a queasy undergraduate scratching his pimples", but Eliot insisted that Joyce had killed the nineteenth century' (Ellmann 1983, 528). A few years later, in 1927, Wyndham Lewis called Joyce 'the poet of the shabby-genteel, impoverished intellectualism of Dublin', treating him as 'an Irish parvenu' (Ellmann 1983, 595). 'His world is the small middle-class one', Lewis wrote in *Time and Western Man* (1993 [1927], 75). Lewis's attitude towards the 'smallness' of this world and Woolf's private opinion on the 'self taught working man' contrast sharply with her magnanimous, outwardly unprejudiced gesture towards 'what is commonly thought small'. Both of them 'could not resist judgement by social class', Ellmann suggests (595).

Joyce and the Extended Mind

This social context is only a small part of the environment in which 'Work in Progress' took shape. What I would like to show in this book is that modernist evocations of the human mind – which were so important to Woolf and which Joyce is equally famous for – are not confined to a spiritual interior. If Joyce is to be called 'spiritual'– as Woolf suggests – he is just as much of a 'materialist' at the same time. If his evocations of fictional minds are famous, it is because they present the human mind as what David Herman has called an interaction between intelligent agents and their cultural and material circumstances (Herman 2011, 266). In this sense, Joyce intuited much of what in the last few decades has come to be known as 'distributed cognition' (Hutchins 2000, 2068) or what Mark Rowlands has dubbed '4e cognition', encompassing the Embodied, Embedded, Enactive and Extended Mind theories.[2] This so-called 'post-cognitivist' paradigm of enacted cognition[3] is anti-Cartesian in that it focuses on the 'inextricable tangles of feedback, feedforward, and feedaround loops that continuously criss-cross the boundaries of brain, body and world', and thus works with a 'porous' model (as opposed to a 'brainbound' model) of the mind (Clark 2012, 277). This 'post-cognitivist' model opposes the Cartesian dualism underlying the 'cognitivist' approach to cognition, which works with representational models to explain the workings of the mind, notably the human mind. Various models of distributed cognition start from the assumption that cognition is situated and that action plays a crucial role in cognitive processes. Hutchins also refers to the notion of 'cognitive artefacts',[4] which David Herman defines as 'objects – mental and cultural as well as material – that *scaffold* sense-making activities' (Herman 2013, 272; emphasis added).

This notion of 'scaffolding' is an important element in Daniel Hutto and Erik Myin's 'radical enactivism',[5] which makes a difference between 'basic minds' and 'scaffolded minds', and claims that 'Basic cognition is not contentful; basic minds

---

[2]   In his chapter 'Mind Embodied, Embedd, Enacted, Extended', in *The New Science of the Mind: From Extended Mind to Embodie Phenomenology*, Rowlands explains the subtle differences between these forms of cognition: 'The thesis of the *extended mind* is, first and foremost, a thesis of the composition or constitution of cognitive processes: some cognitive processes are partly composed of environmental processes. As such, the extended mind parallels [. . .] the thesis of the *embodied mind*, according to which some cognitive processes are partly composed of wider bodily structures and processes' (Rowlands 2010, 67); 'the thesis of the *embedded mind* is a very different thesis – far weaker and less interesting. According to the *embedded mind*, cognitive processes are often (and on some versions essentially) embedded in the environment' (68).

[3]   'Enactivism' works with the hypothesis that basic minds 'do not operate on the basis of internal representations in the subjectivist/objectivist sense. Instead of internally representing an external world in some Cartesian sense, they *enact* an environment inseparable from their own structure and actions' (Thompson 2007, 59; emphasis added).

[4]   From Don Norman's *The Things that Make Us Smart*, 1993.

[5]   Daniel Hutto and Erik Myin suggest that basic minds are not just 'extended' but 'extensive'. They abbreviate their hypothesis as 'REC' for 'Radical Enactive (or Embodied) Cognition' (2013, xii). This paradigm is presented in opposition to 'The Default Internal Mind assumption', which 'takes it for granted that, in their basic state, minds are unextended and brain-bound. If that is the case, then they become extended only when external resources are needed to complete certain cognitive tasks. On that model, what is fundamentally internal occasionally becomes extended' (Hutto and Myin 2013, 137–8). The so-called 'radical' version of enactivism inverts this assumption: 'Basic minds are fundamentally extensive,

are fundamentally, constitutively already world-involving. They are, as we say, extensive' (Hutto and Myin 2013, 137). The notion of 'enaction' (in relation to cognition) was first suggested by Francisco J. Varela, Evan Thompson and Eleanor Rosch in 1991 in their book *The Embodied Mind*, which 'questions the centrality of the notion that cognition is fundamentally representation' (9).[6] They propose the notion of 'enaction' to denote the idea that 'cognition is not the representation of a pregiven world by a pregiven mind but is rather the *enactment* of a world and a mind on the basis of a history of the variety of actions that a being in the world performs' (Varela, Thompson and Rosch 1991, 9; emphasis added).

These philosophical paradigms (embodied, embedded, enactive, extended mind) are marked by subtle differences, but they have an 'externalist' focus in common. For the purposes of this book, the notion of the 'extended mind' is the most suitable paradigm because, unlike enactivism and radical enactivism, it does not concentrate on 'basic minds' and basic sensorimotor activity. Joyce's mind and the fictional minds he evokes in his works are not 'basic' but 'scaffolded', and representation cannot be downplayed since language plays such a crucial role in the genesis of *Finnegans Wake*. Moreover, when the 'extended mind' theory was introduced by Andy Clark and David J. Chalmers in 1998, their key example was a notebook – which makes it directly applicable to Joyce's writing practice. With 'Otto's notebook', Clark and Chalmers demonstrated that an Alzheimer's patient ('Otto') has a mind that interacts with tools such as a notebook. This notebook plays the role of a memory. The only difference with a biological memory is that it 'lies beyond the skin'.[7] His mind is simply 'extended'. This obviously does not imply that only the mind of Alzheimer's patients is

---

whereas special kinds of scaffolded practices must be mastered before anything resembling internalized [. . .] mentality appears on the scene' (138).

[6]   As Varela, Thompson and Rosch argue, the notion that cognition is fundamentally representation is based on three assumptions: 'The first is that we inhabit a world with particular properties, such as length, color, movement, sound, etc. The second is that we pick up or recover these properties by internally representing them. The third is that there is a separate subjective "we" who does these things' (9). In contrast with this view, Varela, Thompson and Rosch define cognition as 'embodied action': 'By using the term *embodied* we mean to highlight two points: first, that cognition depends upon the kinds of experience that come from having a body with various sensorimotor capacities, and second, that these individual sensorimotor capacities are themselves embedded in a more encompassing biological, psychological, and cultural context. By using the word *action* we mean to emphasize once again that sensory and motor processes, perception and action, are fundamentally inseparable in lived cognition' (172–3).

[7]   'Now consider Otto. Otto suffers from Alzheimer's disease, and like many Alzheimer's patients, he relies on information in the environment to help structure his life. Otto carries a notebook around with him everywhere he goes. When he learns new information, he writes it down. When he needs some old information, he looks it up. For Otto, his notebook plays the role usually played by a biological memory. [. . .] The information in the

'extended'. The 50 notebooks for *Finnegans Wake* are a case in point. Joyce made frequent use of notebooks and copybooks to give shape to his 'Work in Progress'. And the extended mind theory not only applies to Joyce's own daily practice as a writer. It also applies to many of his characters, as the pre-book publications discussed in this book suggest.

A good example of the extended mind at work can be found in the notes Joyce took while he was reading Virginia Woolf's essay 'Modern Fiction' in its original form, published in the *Times Literary Supplement* (10 April 1919, 189–90) under the title 'Modern Novels'. As mentioned above, Woolf presents the mind as some kind of surface onto which the impressions of outside reality are 'falling':

> we seek to define the element which distinguishes the work of several young writers, among whom Mr. James Joyce is most able, from that of their predecessors. [. . .] Let us record the *atoms* as they fall upon the mind in the order in which they fall, let us trace the pattern, however disconnected and *incoherent* in appearance, which each sight or incident scores upon the consciousness.
>
> (qtd in Joyce 2002b, 132; emphasis added)

From this passage, Joyce excerpted and combined the words 'incoherent atoms' (*Finnegans Wake* notebook VI.B.06: 116). There was one other passage in Woolf's essay that caught his attention, especially the words 'poverty of [. . .] mind':

> A work of such originality yet fails to compare [. . .] with *Youth* or *Jude the Obscure*. It fails, one might say, simply because of the comparative *poverty of* the writer's *mind*.
>
> (qtd in Joyce 2002b, 132; emphasis added)

Whenever Joyce inserted a note from the notebooks in his drafts, he crossed it out with a colour crayon, a system he devised in order not to use any note twice. When he was writing the portrait of Shem the Penman (*Finnegans Wake*, chapter 7) in his 'Guiltless' copybook,[8] he crossed out and used only the critical note, 'poverty of mind': the first draft reads 'your terrible poverty of mind' (*BL* 47471b-72) – which eventually became 'your horrible awful poverty of mind' in the published version (*FW* 192.10). But also the *undeleted* entries are of interest, as they show what caught Joyce's attention in the first instance. The undeleted entry 'incoherent atoms' can shed some light on the development from *Ulysses* to *Finnegans Wake*, which is in many ways a radicalization of the atomic method observed by Virginia

---

notebook functions just like the information constituting an ordinary non-occurrent belief; it just happens that this information lies beyond the skin' (Clark and Chalmers 2010, 33–4).

[8] The British Library holds a red-backed notebook, containing early drafts of chapters 2, 3, 4, 5, 7 and 8. Unlike the *Finnegans Wake* notebooks at Buffalo, this document does not contain loose jottings, but drafts of the texts. The first draft opens with the word 'Guiltless'. Hereafter, this document will be referred to as the 'Guiltless' copybook.

Woolf. Actually, Woolf's metaphor of the atoms applies to the very words Joyce excerpted and recorded 'as they fall upon the mind in the order in which they fall'. If we take Joyce's notes into account, we treat his notebooks as part and parcel of his extended mind, not unlike the notebook that features in Clark and Chalmers's article. Joyce's use of his notebooks is paradigmatic of enactive cognition and extends, as it were, the 'extended mind' theory: the example of Otto's notebook related to an exceptional brain (the brain of an Alzheimer's patient), but perhaps extension is the rule rather than an exception. 'Work in Progress' / *Finnegans Wake* could not have been written if Joyce had not borrowed all the brains that he could – to paraphrase Louise Barrett (2001, ix) – distributed in other books, articles, pamphlets and encyclopaedia. Joyce's mind is not a pre-given; nor are the minds of his characters or character amalgams (see chapter 1). Similarly, the 'incoherent atoms', the chaotic jottings in his notebooks, serve as extensions of the writer's mind.

Joyce's 'Stuff'

This 'incoherent' aspect of cognition recurs elsewhere in Virginia Woolf's essay, when she refers to the scene in the cemetery in *Ulysses*, with 'its incoherence, its sudden lightning flashes of significance'. The images of light and visual impressions are developed in the following famous passage, focusing on the mind's complexity as 'the proper stuff of fiction':

> Life is not a series of gig lamps symmetrically arranged; life is a luminous halo, a semi-transparent envelope surrounding us from the beginning of consciousness to the end. Is it not the task of the novelist to convey this varying, this unknown and uncircumscribed spirit, whatever aberration or *complexity* it may display, with as little mixture of the alien and external as possible? We are not pleading merely for courage and sincerity; we are suggesting that *the proper stuff of fiction* is a little other than custom would have us believe it.
>
> (Woolf 1994, 160–1; emphasis added)

Woolf advocates a literary approach that 'conveys' the mind in all its complexity, but preferably in isolation, 'with as little mixture of the alien and external as possible'. If that is the 'proper stuff of fiction', the passage reads as a criticism of Joyce's method, with its constant mixture of 'the alien and external'. Against the backdrop of Woolf's definition of 'the task of the novelist', Joyce's 'stuff' is not the 'proper stuff of fiction'. This distinction between Joyce's 'stuff' and the 'proper stuff' comes close to the point Wyndham Lewis makes in his 'Analysis of the Mind of James Joyce' in *Time and Western Man*:

> At the end of a long reading of *Ulysses* you feel that it is the very nightmare of the naturalistic method that you have been experiencing. Much as you may

cherish the merely physical enthusiasm that expresses itself in this stupendous oupouring of *matter*, or *stuff*, you wish, on the spot, to be transported to some more abstract region for a time, where the dates of the various toothpastes, the brewery and laundry receipts, the growing pile of punched 'bus-tickets, the growing holes in the baby's socks and the darn that repairs them, assume less importance.

(Lewis 1993 [1927], 89)

Lewis's criticism applied to *Ulysses*, but it was undoubtedly also informed by his reading of the pre-book publications of 'Work in Progress' and by the manuscript of 'The Muddest Thick That Was Ever Heard Dump', which Joyce had written for Lewis's new magazine, *The Enemy*.

In this book, I would like to investigate how this 'stuff' informs the process of thinking and writing (the 'extended mind' at work), and how 'Work in Progress' develops from *Ulysses*. This interaction with 'stuff' works on three levels: the level of the text, the level of its reception and the level of its production.

On the level of the text, the evocations of fictional minds show the extended mind at work. Whereas the ficional minds in *Ulysses* were embedded renditions of a character's thought process with techniques such as interior monologue and stream of consciousness, 'Work in Progress'*is* that process itself. Beckett's famous characterisation of 'Work in Progress' – 'Here, form *is* content, content *is* form [. . .] His writing is not *about* something; *it is that something itself*' (Beckett 1972 [1929], 14; original emphasis) – is also applicable to Joyce's literary evocation of cognition. This does not imply that Joyce had a systematic, philosophical model in mind to give shape to his characters, but the text of 'Work in Progress' enacts ways of thinking, which cognitive philosophy would now – with hindsight – categorize as forms of the 'extended mind'.

On the level of the reception of the text, the minds of the reviewers and journalists were clearly extended as well. It is remarkable how few of the contemporary articles referring to 'Work in Progress' are actually based on a direct reading of Joyce's texts, as evidenced by the misquotations that lead a life of their own in the newspapers. Journalists make use of other journalists' impressions, thus creating a 'Chinese whispers' effect that is – in its turn – thematized by Joyce in his 'Work in Progress'.

On the level of the production of the text, Joyce's 'stuff' – all the books he read, all the hassle with journals and publishing houses, all the material aspects of his pre-book publications, all the reactions from his direct environment, all the reviews and the clippings from newpapers – was part and parcel of the extended mind at work.

Any writer who makes use of notes and drafts is an example of the extended mind according to the paradigm of cognitive integration (see Richard Menary's 'Writing as Thinking', 2007). Joyce clearly was a writer who 'thought on paper'. He was also sensitive to whatever happened to offer itself as potential material for his work. He was able to incorporate enormous amounts of external material by means of a process that became thematic in *Finnegans Wake*, when he described it as 'decomposition' for the purpose of subsequent 'recombination' (*FW* 614.34–5). Not unlike Shem the 'notesnatcher', he snatched words and excerpts from numerous books in his notebooks, thus decomposing others' texts and recombining them in his drafts. Evidently, these impressions were processed in the writer's mind, but this mind was not limited to the writer's physical brain; it included the interplay with his environment, and the process of conscious recombination proceeded according to what Daniel C. Dennett has described as the 'multiple drafts model' (Dennett 1991, 111–43; see also chapter 3), which he also referred to as a 'Joycean machine in our brains' (Dennett 2006, 171–2). This 'machine' is not only predicated on Joyce's stream-of-consciousness technique, as Tim Conley notes, but is also akin to 'textual-genetic methods of re-reading Joyce' (Conley 2014, 34–5), and *Finnegans Wake* in particular. Quoting the Wakean phrase 'to isolate i from my multiple Mes' (*FW* 410.12), Conley argues that 'consciousness is not so much a quality as a process, not a given but a work in progress' (Conley 2014, 32).

In the 'Guiltless' copybook, this process becomes palpable as it shows the creative and generative potential of Joyce's interaction with the material environment of this copybook.[9] In the study of writing processes this interaction is known as the impact of the 'text produced so far' or TPSF (Flower and Hayes 1981, 370; Leijten, de Maeyer, van Waes 2011, 331) on the writing process, since the writer is simultaneously his own reader and this re-reading of the text produced so far keeps informing and colouring the rest of the text that is still to be written.

If enactive cognition can be charactized by means of the nexus or interplay with cultural and material circumstances (Herman 2011, 266; see above), Joyce's immediate environment certainly also included the material and cultural circumstances of his work's publication history – which brings me to the core of this book's subject matter. My research hypothesis is that the immediate circumstances in which Joyce was working – including the fierce criticism of Wyndham Lewis, Ezra Pound, Harriet Shaw Weaver, but also the massive number of negative reviews in newspapers – played a considerable role in the workings of the extended mind that shaped 'Work in Progress'. John Nashe's *James Joyce and the Act of Reception* does not discuss *Finnegans Wake*, but his characterisation of Joyce's work as a 'writing of reception' (Nashe 2006, 3) is also applicable to 'Work in Progress'. Readers' often vehement and heated responses had an impact on Joyce's writing method, his 'writing as thinking' (Menary 2007). It is interesting to revisit Wyndham Lewis's criticism from this cognitive perspective, for it is largely thanks to Lewis's criticism that Joyce was prompted to write the episode of Dave the Dancekerl; similarly, the fable of the Mookse and the Gripes was created as a reaction to reading Lewis; and the fable of the Ondt and the Gracehoper had not been planned either. By reacting to criticism from his cultural environment, Joyce was

---

[9] For a reconstruction of this interaction, see Van Hulle 2009, www. antwerpjamesjoycecenter.com/guiltless/index.html

able to proceed with his work, and in this regard 'Work in Progress' did not differ from his other works, as Stacey Herbert notes: 'The works' composition and publishing histories were also shaped by editors, printers, publishers and other authorities and by Joyce's reaction to the influence they exercised' (Herbert 2009, 3). Readers also belong to this group of agents. As Finn Fordham notes with reference to the 'Circe' episode in *Ulysses*, 'events around [Joyce] affected his method' and 'these events included the strong responses of readers' (Fordham 2010, 214). How strong these responses could be, and how deeply they affected Joyce's method becomes evident in 'Work in Progress', whose reception is an inherent part of its genesis and publication history.

Newspaper Clippings

The present publishing history therefore tries to give an impression of the immediate reception of 'Work in Progress' in the press, by making use of the newspaper clippings that are preserved at the University at Buffalo (hereafter referred to as UB, followed by a C for 'Clippings', the number of the brown envelope in which they are preserved, and the number of the actual clipping).[10] To gather these reactions in the press, Joyce's *entourage* employed various clipping services, such as Durrant's Press Cuttings (St Andrew's House, 32–34 Holborn Viaduct, London); Romeike & Curtice Ltd. (35 Shoe Lane, London);[11] The Original Henry Romeike Press Clipping Bureau (220 West 19th St, New York); Le Courrier de la presse[12] (directeur Ch. Demogeot, 21 Boulevard Montmartre, Paris); The Reliable Press Clipping Bureau;[13] International Press Cutting Bureau (329 High Holborn, London). Considered separately, most of these notices, announcements and short reviews may not be particularly insightful in and of themselves, but as a whole they do give an adequate impression of the way the world at large responded to 'Work in Progress'. By charting this immediate reception, it is possible to reconstruct – to

---

[10] The envelopes containing newspaper clippings relevant to 'Work in Progress' are UBC 1: 'Anna Livia, Critical / cf. 72–2210'; UBC 14: 'Haveth Childers, Critical (773–2185)'; UBC 23: 'Tales Told of Shem and Shaun, Critical (584–2004)'; UBC 32: 'Ulysses, Piracy (676–837)'; UBC 33: 'Work in Progress, Critical (39–2003)'; UBC 34: 'Work in Progress, Critical (2005–2225)'; UBC 35: 'Anna Livia, Critical, Group (483–2213)'; UBC 36: 'Anna Livia, Miscellany, Group (36–2216)'; UBC 46: 'Haveth Childers, Critical Group (912–2164)'; UBC 47: 'Haveth Childers, Miscellany Group (884–2182)'; UBC 68: 'Work in Progress, Critical, Group (32–2206)'; UBC 69: 'Work in Progress, Miscellany Group (20–2196)'

[11] 'Romeike & Curtice' used to send its clippings to Harriet Shaw Weaver.

[12] This press-cutting service's slogan was: 'Lit tout'; 'Renseigne sur tout ce qui est publié dans les Journeaux et Publications de toute nature et en fournit les Extraits sur tous Sujets et Personnalités'.

[13] 'The Reliable Press Clipping Bureau' used to send its clippings to Sylvia Beach.

some extent – the cultural environment with which Joyce interacted to give shape to his work.

As part of a series called Studies in Publishing History, this is not a publishing history of *Finnegans Wake*, but of 'Work in Progress', that is, of the pre-book publications that appeared in the 17-year period between *Ulysses* (1922) and *Finnegans Wake* (1939). The publication history of *Finnegans Wake* is a story of its own, and Geert Lernout has recently written an account of this publication process (Lernout 2013). While Joyce was designing the overall architecture of his work, however, he was also publishing fragments of it. This implied exposure to the public's reactions, which created a dialectic that contributed considerably to the dynamics of 'Work in Progress'. It also implied that these fragments were supposed to be able to function on their own, as separate publications, not just as instalments or 'continuations of a Work in Progress' in magazines, but also as separately published books. Whereas the instalments are the subject of *Part I: 'Work in Progress'* (consisting of three chapters, devoted to respectively the early scattered instalments; the pirated versions by Samuel Roth; and the instalments in the magazine *transition*), *Part II: 'Work in Press'* is devoted to the separate publications by Fine Arts presses and other publishers:

> *Anna Livia Plurabelle*, published in October 1928 (Crosby Gaige) and June 1930 (Faber and Faber);
> *Tales Told of Shem and Shaun*, published in August 1929 (Black Sun Press), and *Two Tales of Shem and Shaun* in December 1932 (Faber and Faber);
> *Haveth Childers Everywhere*, published in June 1930 (Babou and Kahane / Fountain Press) and May 1931 (Faber and Faber);
> *The Mime of Mick, Nick and the Maggies*, published in June 1934 (Servire Press);
> *Storiella as She Is Syung*, published in October 1937 (Corvinus Press).

Each chapter closes with a review of reactions in the press, based on the newspaper clippings. The first Appendix at the back of the book gives a survey of all the pre-book publications, arranged according to: (1) the chronology and material aspect (separate books and contributions to books or periodicals); (2) the place in the narrative sequence of *Finnegans Wake*. The rest of the Appendices provide a survey of the textual variants between the pre-book publications and the text of *Finnegans Wake* (New York: Viking, 1939; London: Faber and Faber, 1939).

PART I
Work in Progress

Chapter 1
Before *transition*

In late September 1926, while Joyce was in Brussels, he wrote to Harriet Shaw Weaver that he wanted fragments of his 'Work in Progress''to appear slowly and regularly in a prominent place' (*LI* 245). Finding such a place proved to be harder than expected, though. Eventually, *transition* was to become this 'prominent place', but no matter how appropriate this magazine's name may have been for a 'Work in Progress', the real years of transition were the ones between the publication of *Ulysses* in 1922 and the first instalment in *transition*, when Joyce did not find a place that could offer the slow regularity of publication he was looking for. At the same time, the restlessness of this period of transition also reflects the spirit of the age. In order to map the publication history of 'Work in Progress' it is useful to focus on the various magazines in which Joyce tried to get fragments of his new work published, taking Sylvia Beach's advice: 'The best way of following the literary movement in the twenties is through the little reviews, often short-lived, alas! But always interesting. Shakespeare and Company never published one. We had enough to do taking care of those published by our friends'(Beach 1980, 137).

On a sheet of paper, preserved in Buffalo, Sylvia Beach once made a list of the early publication history of 'Work in Progress', starting with the 'First extracts in reviews'. The first section ('*Reviews*') does not mention *transition*, as it apparently represented a category of its own (see Chapter 3). It does mention *The Calendar*, though, but without number and with the parenthetic note '(not able to print a part of it *ALP*)':

Work in Progress
First extracts in reviews

Reviews

1   Transatlantic Review april 1924
    Four Old Masters
2   (anthology) Contact Collection June 1925
    Earwicker
3   The Criterion July 1925
    The document

The Calendar (not able to print a part of it *ALP*)

4   Le Navire d'Argent 1er Oct 1925
    Anna LiviaPlurabelle
5   This Quarter 1925–6 Autumn-Winter
    Shem the Penman (UB JJC XVIII.G, folder 20)

This sketchy list only represents what Sylvia Beach remembered of this early period of 'Work in Progress'. T.S. Eliot was the first to solicit a fragment (McMillan 1975, 180), but Joyce failed to comply with this initial request for an instalment in *The Criterion* as he did not consider the fragments ready for publication (Crispi and Herbert 2003, 64). He did offer an instalment somewhat later, for *The Criterion* III, after having tried out several other magazines – *transatlantic review, This Quarter* and *Le Navire d'Argent*.

transatlantic review

'From Work in Progress', *transatlantic review*, Paris, 1.4 (April 1924), 215–23 [FW 383–398.30] (Slocum and Cahoon 1953, 100; C.62)[1]

After having established himself in Paris, in October 1923, former editor of the *English Review* Ford Madox Ford asked Joyce for a contribution to his new journal, the *transatlantic review*. Joyce explained his hesitation to Harriet Shaw Weaver on 2 November, as he thought the fragments he had already written were not quite ready to be published. The *transatlantic review* was not exactly the prominent place he was looking for. As Luca Crispi and Stacey Herbert note, 'with its plain white covers and letters of welcome and praise by H.G. Wells and Joseph Conrad, the only thing that could be construed as *avant-garde* were the all lowercase letters of the title in the Paris and London editions, but even then the New York edition maintained the title in its more conventional typography' (18). The first issues had contained 'nothing aggressive, incisive, or even slightly eccentric', according to Bernard Poli (Poli 1967, 56). Still, Joyce did prepare the 'Mamalujo' vignette (first drafted in September 1923; *LI* 205; *FDV* 213) for publication in Ford's magazine (corresponding with Book II chapter 4 of *Finnegans Wake*, *FW* 383.01–398.28). In *Finnegans Wake*, this passage contains many elements of the 'Tristan and Isolde' sketch he had made in 1923, in which the love scene between Tristan and 'the belle of Chapelizod' is described as a soccer attack, Tristan (a 'rugger and soccer champion') driving 'the advance messenger of love [. . .] into the goal of her gullet' (*FDV* 209), while the seaswans sing: 'Three quarks for Muster Mark' (*FDV* 212). This is

---

[1]   Throughout the narrative of the publishing history, the bibliographical references to pre-book publications will be indicated by means of this sans-serif typeface.

one of five sketches centred around the kiss of Tristan and Isolde, which Daniel Ferrer beautifully dubbed 'brouillons d'un baiser' ['drafts of a kiss'].[2]

As Jed Deppman has shown, Joyce 'actively pulverized and recombined his textual elements, notably shattering "Tristan" and scattering *its* pieces into "Mamalujo"' (Deppman 2007, 309). But this happened much later, in 1938. In the version of the *transatlantic review*, the 'Tristan and Isolde' sketch had not yet been merged. The piece in the *transatlantic review*, the first pre-book publication of 'Work in Progress', opens with the conjunction 'And' and introduces Matthew, Mark, Luke and John or the Four Masters/annalists/historians: 'And there they were too listening in as hard as they could to the solans and sycamores and the wild geese and gannets and the migratories and mistlethrushes and the auspices and all the birds of the sea, all four of them, all sighing and sobbing, and listening. They were the big four, the four master waves of Erin' (*TR* 215)

The piece ends with the so-called 'Anno Domini' poem, introduced as follows: 'Hear, O hear, Iseult la belle! Tristan, sad hero, hear! *Anno Domini nostri sancti Jesu Christi*' (*TR* 223). The verses are personalized and composed according to a scheme, which was sent to Miss Weaver on 12 October 1923 (*SL* 296–7). In this scheme, each of the Evangelists is connected with one of the Four Masters (Peregrine O'Clery, Michael O'Clery, Farfassa O'Mulconry, Peregrine O'Duignan), with a pronoun (thou, she, you, I, respectively), with the four provinces of Ireland (Ulster, Munster, Leinster, Connacht), with their respective evangelist symbols, with a specific Irish accent and so on. Later on, Joyce also added references to Blake's four Zoas on the separately revised pages of the *transatlantic review* (*JJA* 56: 125–33).[3] The version

---

[2]   James Joyce, *Brouillons d'un baiser: Premiers pas vers* Finnegans Wake, réunis et présentés par Daniel Ferrer, préface et traduction de l'anglais par Marie Darrieussecq, Paris: Gallimard, 2014. The five sketches are preserved partially at the National Library of Ireland in Dublin and partially at the British Library in London. They have been given the following titles: A) [*Portrait of Isolde*], B) [*Tristan & Isolde*], C) [*Tristan & Isolde, the kiss*], D) [*The Four Old Men and the kiss of Tristan & Isolde*], E) [*Mamalujo*]. While in the first part of sketch B (NLI), Isolde 'kissed him' and Tristan ('being an inborn gentleman') 'counterkissed', the 'physiological moment' (86) of the kiss is much more elaborately described in the third sketch (84–5) and 'the detonation of the osculation' (96–7) in sketch D is observed by the Four Old Men, who become the protagonists of sketch E, 'Mamalujo', 'spraining their ears listening and listening to all the kissening with their eyes glistening all the four' (104).

[3]   'From the urizen of speeches' (*JJA* 56: 126; BL MS 47481–63v);
    'Tharmaz syphon Mark' (*JJA* 56: 127; BL MS 47481–64r);
    'For the luvah the lauds Lucas' (*JJA* 56: 129; BL MS 47481–65r);
    'the grand old Urthonian' (*JJA* 56: 130; BL MS 47481–65v).

Geert Lernout and Vincent Deane traced these references to Darrell Figgis, *The Paintings of William Blake*. See Vincent Deane and Geert Lernout, 'O'Casey and Blake: Two VI.B.13 Indexes', *A Finnegans Wake Circular* 4.2 (1988): 21–31.

in *transatlantic review* closes with the lines about 'a wet good Friday', followed by 'an allnight eiderdown bed picnic' and the lady, who gets the last word:

> *By the cross of Cong*, says she, rising up Saturday in the twilight from under me,
> *Mick whatever your name is you're the most likable lad that's come my ways yet*
> *from the barony of Bohermore.*

(TR 223)

Dougald McMillan notes that 'Ford's *transatlantic review* had given him [Joyce] proofs so "grotesque" that he asked for a delay while the printer learned his trade' (McMillan 1975, 179). Still, Ford had facilitated the first public appearance of a fragment 'From Work in Progress' and the title he suggested for the fragment in his review was adopted in subsequent publications. Thus, for instance, 'Here Comes Everybody' was introduced to the literary world as a fragment 'From Work in Progress' in the next instalment, published in the *Contact Collection of Contemporary Writers* (see Figure 1.1).

Contact Collection of Contemporary Writers

'From Work in Progress', in *Contact Collection of Contemporary Writers* (Paris: Contact Editions / Three Mountains Press, 1925): 133–6 [FW 30–4]

Contact Editions was run by Robert McAlmon, one of the typists of *Ulysses* and the author of *A Hasty Bunch* (1922). In the first issue of the *transatlantic review*, Robert McAlmon announced his plans to found the Contact Publishing Company: 'At intervals of two weeks to six months, or six years, we will bring out books by various writers who seem not likely to be published by other publishers, for commercial or legistlative reasons' (qtd in Beach 1980, 130). The announcement contained the following invitation to potential contributors: 'Anybody interested may communicate with Contact Publishing Co., 12 rue de l'Odéon, Paris'. One of these authors who – at that moment at least – seemed not likely to be published elsewhere was the then relatively unknown Ernest Hemingway. Contact published his *Three Stories and Ten Poems*.

According to Neil Pearson, Hemingway referred to McAlmon as 'McAlimony', because he 'used the money he had come into on marrying the heiress Winifred Ellerman (who wrote under the pseudonym Bryher) to bankroll a Paris imprint called Contact Editions. Without his wife's money the small print runs and even smaller sales of Contact's unbendingly highbrow list – combined with McAlmon's innate lassitude and lack of business sense – would have seen the enterprise fail almost before it began' (Pearson 2007, 3). McAlmon's marriage not only enabled him to establish Contact Editions; as he was homosexual, Pearson suggests, it also enabled his wife to 'break away from her family and pursue her relationship with the poet Hilda Doolittle' (Pearson 2007, 6).

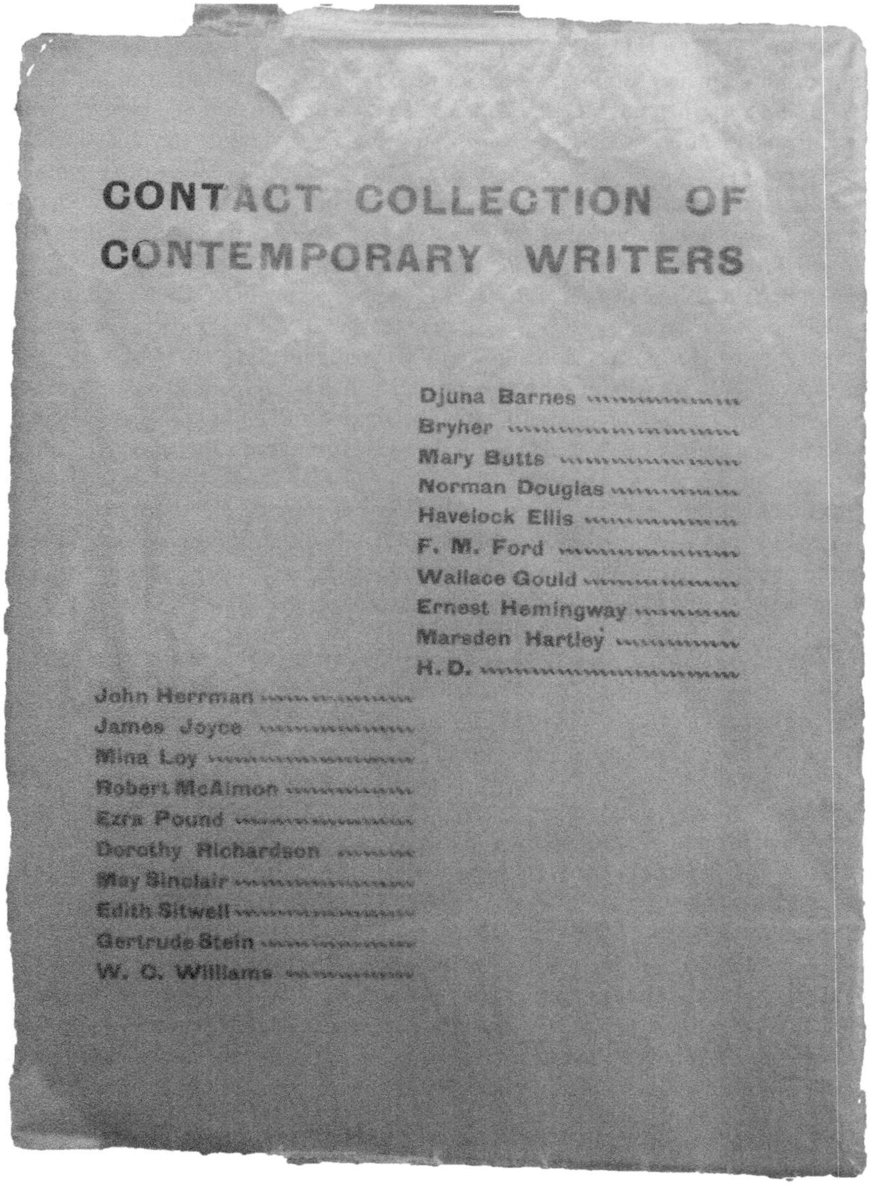

CONTACT COLLECTION OF CONTEMPORARY WRITERS

Djuna Barnes ~~~~~~~~~~~~~~
Bryher ~~~~~~~~~~~~~~~~~~~
Mary Butts ~~~~~~~~~~~~~~~~
Norman Douglas ~~~~~~~~~~~~
Havelock Ellis ~~~~~~~~~~~~~
F. M. Ford ~~~~~~~~~~~~~~~~
Wallace Gould ~~~~~~~~~~~~~~
Ernest Hemingway ~~~~~~~~~~
Marsden Hartley ~~~~~~~~~~~~
H. D. ~~~~~~~~~~~~~~~~~~~~~

John Herrman ~~~~~~~~~~~~~~
James Joyce ~~~~~~~~~~~~~~~
Mina Loy ~~~~~~~~~~~~~~~~~~
Robert McAlmon ~~~~~~~~~~~~
Ezra Pound ~~~~~~~~~~~~~~~~
Dorothy Richardson ~~~~~~~~~
May Sinclair ~~~~~~~~~~~~~~~
Edith Sitwell ~~~~~~~~~~~~~~~
Gertrude Stein ~~~~~~~~~~~~~~
W. C. Williams ~~~~~~~~~~~~~

Figure 1.1   Cover of *Contact Collections of Contemporary Writers*

The contributors – including such authors as Djuna Barnes, Ford Madox Ford, Ernest Hemingway, H.D., John Herrmann, Mina Loy, Ezra Pound, Dorothy Richardson, May Sinclair, Edith Sitwell, Gertrude Stein and William Carlos Williams, in addition to Bryher and McAlmon themselves – dedicated the collection to Sylvia Beach, who mentions it in *Shakespeare and Company*, calling it 'the most interesting book of scraps' she had ever seen (131). These 'scraps' were fragments of whatever the contributors happened to be working on, which explains why Joyce's contribution is not the only piece referred to as an extract 'From Work in Progress' (John Herrmann's and Dorothy Richardson's pieces had the same title). On 21 November 1924, Joyce wrote to Robert McAlmon, asking him: 'By what date (latest) do you want my copy and on what date (earliest) will the book [*Contact Collection*] be out' (*LI* 23). The collection would eventually come out in May 1925. In the same letter to McAlmon, Joyce mentioned he had to be operated on for cataract. It was not until after Christmas 1924 that his sight returned in his 'occluded' eye. In a missing notebook (VI.D.3, partially reconstructed on the basis of France Raphael's transcription in notebook VI.C.4), Joyce made notes between December 1924 and February 1925 on Hester Travers Smith's *Psychic Messages from Oscar Wilde* (London: T. Werner Laurie, 1923).[4] In this book on spiritual messages sent by the ghost of Oscar Wilde to his mediums through automatic writing with the Ouija board, Joyce read what 'Wilde's spirit' thought of *Ulysses*:

> Yes, I have smeared my fingers with that vast work. It has given me one exquisite moment of amusement. I gathered that if I hoped to retain my reputation as an intelligent shade, open to new ideas, I must peruse this volume. It is a singular matter that a countryman of mine should have produced this great bulk of **filth**.
>
> (Travers Smith 1925, 17; emphasis added)

Joyce used the words of the attack ('this great bulk of filth') for HCE's defence in a draft of *Haveth Childers Everywhere*: 'Who accuses me. My adversary, ~~the~~ ʰᵉ is the first liar ~~in his~~ ᵒᶠ ᵗʰⁱˢ land. Shucks! Such ᵇᵘᵍʰᵒᵘˢᵉ **filth** as I cannot ᵇᵃʳᵉˡʸ conceive ᵒᶠ' (British Library MS 47482b-113v; *JJA* 58:094). Wilde's ghost felt that 'even I, who am a shade, and I who have tasted the fullness of life and its meed of bitterness, should cry aloud: "**Shame upon Joyce, shame on his work, shame on his lying soul**"' (Travers Smith 1925, 17). Joyce incorporated this criticism of his previous book (*Ulysses*) in his new work, notably in the fair copy of *Haveth Childers Everywhere*: 'It is truly most amusin. There is not one teaspoonspill of evidence to my

---

4   I owe a debt of gratitude to Viviana Braslasu for drawing my attention to this source text. In *The Textual Diaries of James Joyce*, Danis Rose suggested this book could be the source of the notes (including 'ouidja board') on page 186 of notebook VI.B.14. Mikio Fuse discovered that these notes probably derive from another source text, relating to Hester Travers Smith's transcript: Herbert Thurston's article 'The "Oscar Wilde" Script in its Baring on Survival', *Studies: An Irish Quarterly Review*, vol. 13, Nr. 49 (March 1924): 14–28.

~~bad~~ ^{baad as you shall see as this is} and I can take off my coats here before those in heaven to enter into my ~~process~~ ^{protestant} *caveat* against the pupup publication of libel by any Ticks Tipsylon to that hightest personage at moments holding down the throne. **Shames upon pipip private M – ! Shames on his foulsomeness! Shames on his lulul lying sowel!'** (MS 47484a-27; *JJA* 58: 128).

In a letter of 27 January 1925, Joyce told Harriet Shaw Weaver that Sylvia Beach was going to send her 'a book of spirit talks with Oscar Wilde' – adding in the simplest terms: 'He does not like *Ulysses*' (*LI* 225). So Joyce tried to neutralize the ghostly criticism by means of his vaccination technique, incorporating a bit of the harmful matter to strengthen the immune system of his 'Work in Progress'.

On 4 April 1925, he wrote to McAlmon: 'I have had a relapse since I saw you but am now better so if you have received the proofs of the book, I should like very much to revise my contribution now that I am between two operations' (*LI* 226). One month later, the collection was ready, printed in Dijon by the printer of *Ulysses*, Maurice Darantière, and published by Contact Editions / Three Mountains Press (29, Quai d'Anjou, Île Saint-Louis, Paris).

Immediate Reception: Press Clippings

A few press clippings, preserved at the University af Buffalo's Poetry Collection, give an impression of how Joyce's new work was received at this early stage of 'Work in Progress'. In the *New York Times Book Review* of 23 May 1926, Naomi Royde-Smith wrote it was 'a shock to find the capital of Bohemia capitalizing the methods of Philistia', trying to attract 'the shekels of the Philistines' by presenting 'a catalogue of [authors'] wares' like 'a Sears-Roebuck or a Butterick' (UBC 69: 744). The capitalist approach was inconsistent with the Parisian image of 'the perennial centre of the literary underworld of England and America', 'the setting for la vie de Bohème, without experience of which no young writer dare write about Life'. Joyce is of course presented as one of the major 'exponents of literary revolt', but it is remarkable that his new experimental work is regarded as more of the same: 'Joyce's literary technique has not altered since the oftmentioned tour de force [*Ulysses*]' (UBC 69: 744).

A closer look, however, shows that his technique had altered noticeably. The language is not yet full-blown Wakese, but here and there the linguistic distortions do indicate a new direction. To determine the degree of distortion, it may be useful to have a detailed look at the language of this piece as published in the *Contact Collection*. Under the title 'From Work in Progress', Joyce's four-page contribution opens with the same word as the first line of Shakespeare's *Richard III*, drawing attention to the present situation and what preceded it: 'Now, concerning the genesis of Harold or Humphrey Chimpden's occupational agnomen and discarding once for all those theories from older sources which would link him back with such pivotal ancestors as the Glues, the Gravys, the Northeasts, the Ankers and the Earwickers of Sidlesham in the hundred of manhood or proclaim him offsprout of Vikings who had founded wapentake and seddled hem in Herrick or Eric, the best authenticated version has it that it was this way' (133). The narrative keeps stressing the mediated nature of this account of his 'genesis':

> We are told how in the beginning it came to pass that like cabbaging Cincinnatus the grand old gardener was saving daylight one sultry Sabbath afternoon in pre-fall paradise peace by following his plough for rootles in the rere garden of ye olde marine hotel when royalty was announced by runner to have been pleased to have halted itself on the highroad along which a leisureloving dogfox had cast followed, also at walking pace, by a lady pack of cocker spaniels.
>
> (133)

On the next page, words like 'andrewpomurphyc' would have alerted contemporary readers to the experimental nature of Joyce's new literary project: 'Comes the question are these the facts as recorded in both or either of the collateral andrewpomurphyc narratives. We shall perhaps not so soon see. The great fact emerges that after that historic date all holographs so far exhumed initialled by Haromphrey bear the sigla H.C.E.' (134), which gave him 'the nickname Here Comes Everybody' (134–5). He is first introduced as a respectable man and 'an imposing everybody', 'constantly the same as and equal to himself and magnificently well worthy of any and all such universalisation' (135), but then the text starts mentioning bad rumours: 'It has been blurtingly bruited by certain wisecracks that he suffered from a vile disease' and his detractors also insinuate that 'he lay at one time under the ludicrous imputation of annoying Welsh fusiliers in the people's park' (135). The narrator suggests that this is 'particularly preposterous' given 'the christlikeness of the big cleanminded giant H.C. Earwicker' (136). The gravest impropriety he is accused of by the slanderers is that of 'having behaved in an ungentlemanly manner opposite a pair of dainty maidservants' (136), whom 'dame nature' had sent into 'the rushy hollow' for a stop of an 'intimate nature', involving 'partial exposure' (136).

That is where the fragment in the *Contact Collection* (I.2, section 1; *FW* 30–34.29) ends. The next section (I.2, section 2; *FW* 34.30–44.21) originally opened with the sentence 'Guiltless he was clearly'.[5] It was also the opening sentence of the 'Guiltless' copybook (see Introduction). The idea of opening a new notebook with the word 'Guiltless' marks an important moment in the development of the writing process. Reading the word 'Guiltless' has the same paradoxical effect as the command 'Don't think of an elephant'. The constant attempt to deny the slander only makes HCE more suspicious, and the same goes for his

---

[5]   The sentence actually reads 'Guiltless he was clearely'; the extra e in 'clearely' is probably a misspelling by Nora Joyce, who took Joyce's dictation for the first version of this section (Lernout 1999).

wife's attempts to counter the accusations by writing a letter, also drafted in the same red-backed 'Guiltless' copybook. The first draft of the letter is one of the very first performances of ALP. Joyce had not yet introduced this new character. He lets her introduce herself, as it were, by means of this letter. In Sylvia Beach's list (see above), this fragment is mentioned as 'The document' under the item 'The Criterion'.

The Criterion

'Fragment of an Unpublished Work', *The Criterion*, London, III.12 (July 1925), 498–510 [*FW* 104–125] (Slocum and Cahoon 1971 [1953], 100; C.64)

To some extent, Joyce's method of working with his notebooks and manuscripts as an instrumental 'extension' of his own mind during the creative process informed the evocation of *fictional* minds, the minds of his characters. His 'Work in Progress' offers an interesting example of this process, illustrating how a simple 'environmental vehicle'[6] such as a notebook can play a role in the construction of a new fictional mind. In reply to the rumours about HCE's alleged crime in the park,[7] his wife Anna Livia Plurabelle (ALP) writes a letter, which ends up doing more harm than good. One of the reasons for this unwitting effect is a strange turn in the letter's compositional structure. At the least expected moment, when ALP is already closing the letter, she suddenly introduces a completely unrelated memory regarding an 'experience' of hers with a 'clerical friend'. This *non sequitur*, which does not exactly contribute to the defense of her husband against the allegations, was already present in the first draft of the letter:[8]

> Well, revered Majesty, I tender you heartest thanks & regrets for lettering you and I shall ᶰᵒʷ close hoping you are in the best of~~ health~~. I ~~don't~~ care that for him and lies about an experience of mine ᵃˢ ᵃ ᵍⁱʳˡ with a clerical friend.[9]

What seems to be a sudden association 'inside' ALP's mind (a reminiscence of an 'experience' with a clerical friend) is itself the result of a remarkable writing process. To give shape to ALP as the fictional writer of the letter, the actual writer,

---

[6] According to Richard Menary, the 'extended mind' theory focuses on 'how the manipulation of environmental vehicles constitutes cognitive processes' (Menary 2010,21).
[7] The idea of the alleged crime in the park is prefigured in *Ulysses*, when Bloom ruminates 'Must be careful about women. Catch them once with their pants down. Never forgive you after' (*U* 6.484–5).
[8] In the following transcriptions, additions are rendered in superscript, deletions are crossed out.
[9] BL MS 47471b-32–3; *JJA* 46, 257–9.

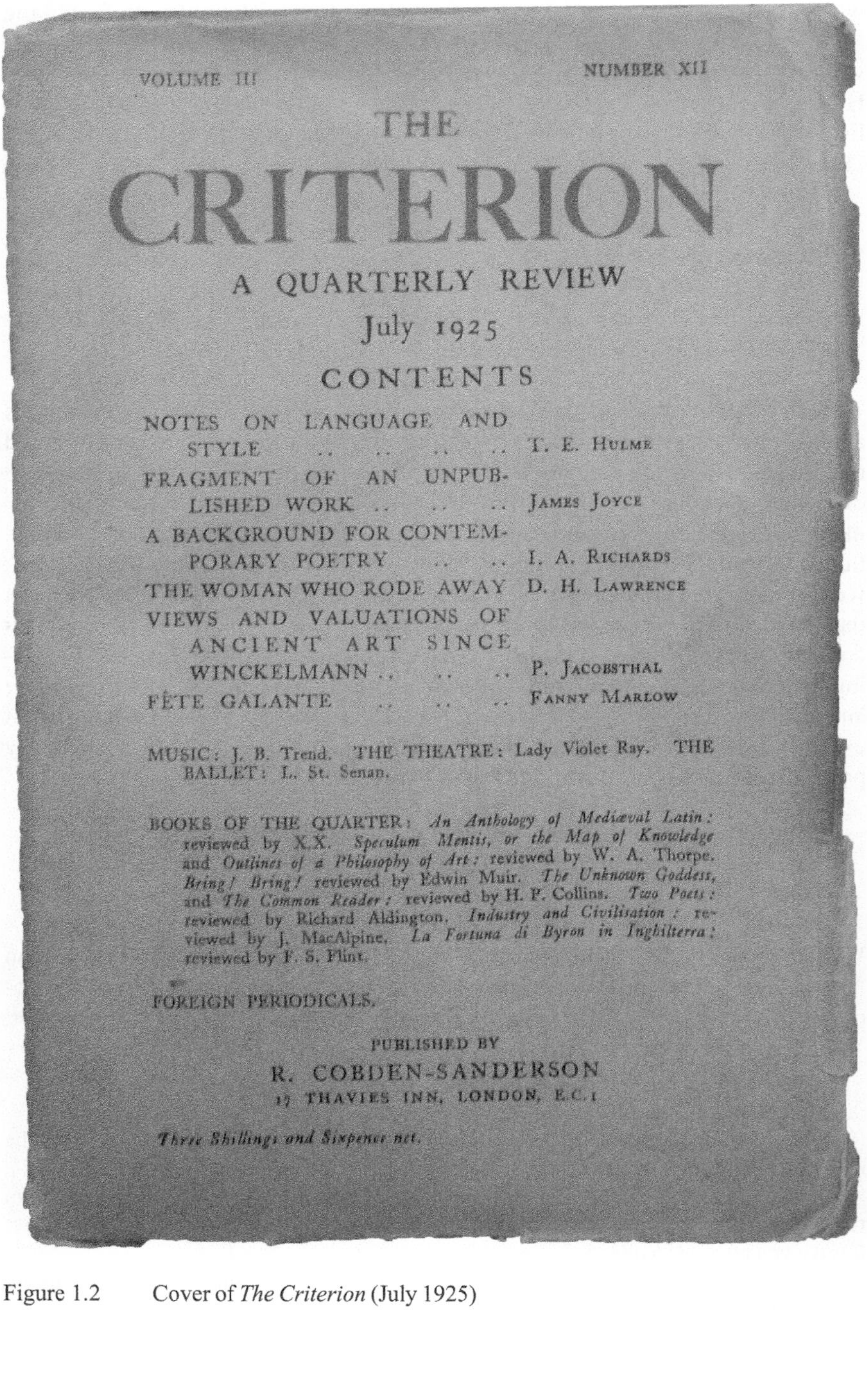

VOLUME III NUMBER XII

THE

CRITERION

A QUARTERLY REVIEW

July 1925

CONTENTS

NOTES ON LANGUAGE AND STYLE	T. E. HULME
FRAGMENT OF AN UNPUBLISHED WORK	JAMES JOYCE
A BACKGROUND FOR CONTEMPORARY POETRY	I. A. RICHARDS
THE WOMAN WHO RODE AWAY	D. H. LAWRENCE
VIEWS AND VALUATIONS OF ANCIENT ART SINCE WINCKELMANN	P. JACOBSTHAL
FÊTE GALANTE	FANNY MARLOW

MUSIC: J. B. Trend. THE THEATRE: Lady Violet Ray. THE BALLET: L. St. Senan.

BOOKS OF THE QUARTER: *An Anthology of Mediæval Latin*: reviewed by X.X. *Speculum Mentis, or the Map of Knowledge* and *Outlines of a Philosophy of Art*: reviewed by W. A. Thorpe. *Bring! Bring!* reviewed by Edwin Muir. *The Unknown Goddess*, and *The Common Reader*: reviewed by H. P. Collins. *Two Poets*: reviewed by Richard Aldington. *Industry and Civilisation*: reviewed by J. MacAlpine. *La Fortuna di Byron in Inghilterra*: reviewed by F. S. Flint.

FOREIGN PERIODICALS.

PUBLISHED BY

R. COBDEN-SANDERSON

17 THAVIES INN, LONDON, E.C.1

Three Shillings and Sixpence net.

Figure 1.2 Cover of *The Criterion* (July 1925)

James Joyce, was using a notebook[10] for the epistolary composition. The letter's closing formula is based on three jottings on one of the last pages in the notebook:

> **lettering you**
> **I shall close** with
> **in the best (health)**

(notebook VI.B.2, page 178).

With these items he wrote the first sentence in the above quotation from the 'Guiltless' copybook: 'I tender you heartest thanks & regrets for **lettering you** and **I shall** ᵖᵒʷ **close** hoping you are **in the best** of **health**' (*JJA* 46: 257–9). At that moment in the writing process, this could have been the end of the letter. There is no indication that Joyce deliberately planned this closing formula to be followed by an associative digression. But one of the remarkable characteristics of the genesis of *Finnegans Wake* is its openness to contingencies.[11] After having combined the three jottings from page 178, Joyce only had to turn one page to arrive at the end of the notebook. The inside of the back cover featured the notes:

> **an experience of** her[s]
> **clerical friend**

(notebook VI.B.2, inside back cover)

With these two notes that drew his attention he then composed the subsequent sentence 'I ~~don't~~ care that for him and lies about **an experience of** mine ᵃˢ ᵃ ᵍⁱʳˡ with a **clerical friend**' (*JJA* 46: 259; *FDV* 82).

In other words, a material contingency triggered the composition of the associative digression. This textual coincidence may not be that remarkable in itself, but it does have consequences for the literary evocation of ALP's mind. At this moment in the composition history, ALP was a new character. The first draft of her letter is one of her very first appearances in the manuscript record of *Finnegans Wake*. So Joyce chose the act of writing (ALP writing a letter) as the starting point for the invention of a new character and the way she thinks. At first sight, ALP's associative reminiscence is an involuntary memory. Not entirely unlike the case of the

---

[10]   The notebook is preserved at the Poetry/Rare Books Collection in Buffalo, NY, and is known as *Finnegans Wake* notebook VI.B.02.

[11]   During the 2012 Joyce Symposium in Dublin, in the panel on Joyce's library (14 June 2012), Daniel Ferrer drew attention to a jotting in Joyce's notebook VI.B.14 (page 32) that emphasizes this openness: '~~SD~~ JJ no gambler / his style gambles / infinitely probable' (SD standing for Stephen Dedalus). See *The Finnegans Wake Notebooks at Buffalo: VI.B.14*, p. 65; Daniel Ferrer, 'The Possible Worlds of Joycean Genetics', in: *Praharfeast: James Joyce in Prague*, eds David Vichnar, David Spurr and Michael Groden (Prague: Litteraria Pragensia, 2012), 40.

Proustian madeleine, the reminiscence is triggered by an *external* element. Here the interaction with her own handwriting and the 'text produced so far' during the act of writing reminds her of the 'experience' with the 'clerical friend'. Joyce fully exploited his own openness to compositional contingencies to evoke the workings of a fictional mind. And this fictional mind is not presented as a place within a skull, but as an interaction with an environment. When the letter was ready, Joyce made a second and a third draft in the same 'Guiltless' copybook (BL MS 47471b).

It is remarkable that Joyce kept writing in the same copybook, even when there was hardly any space left. The notebook's role as a so-called 'environmental vehicle' (Menary 2007, 21) was considerable. The 'Guiltless' copybook is the material trace of one of the most creative periods in the genesis of 'Work in Progress' and the confined creative space of the notebook seems to have contributed to the intensity of this writing process. Chapter I.5 (sections 1 and 4) – the fragment published in *The Criterion* (see Figure 1.2) – is a good example. As the visualization of the sections'entanglement shows,[12] Joyce wrote section 1 literally *around* section 2 (the letter, first draft, written on pages 31r, 32r, 33r), starting on page 33r, continuing in the margin of 34r, then jumping backward to the open spaces on the pages preceding the Letter (29v-30r) and continuing in retrograde direction to page 25v on the pages that were not filled yet (between and among the first draft of I.4 section 2 and the second draft of I.4 section 1).[13]

The Letter opens with the word 'Revered' and is therefore often referred to as the 'Revered' Letter. In its first version, the first sentence does not have apostrophes, as in Molly Bloom's monologue in the last chapter of *Ulysses*: 'Majesty well, Ive heard all those birds what theyre ~~saying~~ bringing it about him ~~but~~ and welcome for they will come to no good. The Honourable Mr Earwicker, my devout husband, is a true gentleman' (*FDV* 81). But even while she angrily states that she 'will not have a reptile the like of McGrath Bros [. . .] to be spreading his dirty lies all round where we live', she herself starts slandering the two girls, suggesting that 'those two hussies neither of them was virtuous after the public doctor's declaration' (*FDV* 82).

The letter (I.5, section 2) was the object of analysis in the surrounding sections 1 and 4. Once the letter and its delivery (sections 2 and 3) were extracted and put aside, the analysis stood on its own, without its object of research. This analysis (sections 1 plus 4) is what Joyce sent to T.S. Eliot. On 2 February 1925, he was

---

[12] See Introduction; Van Hulle 2009, www.antwerpjamesjoycecenter.com/guiltless/index.html

[13] The Centre for Manuscript Genetics at the University of Antwerp is working on a digital edition that visualizes this role of the 'Guiltless' copybook as a creative space. This project is part of the project 'Literature and the Extended Mind: A Reassessment of Modernism' (TOP BOF project, funded by the University of Antwerp; principal investigator: Dirk Van Hulle).

trying, in spite of his eye problems, 'to revise the piece for Mr Eliot'.[14] On 26 February, Eliot wrote to Lucia Joyce that he hoped he could expect the manuscript 'as soon as possible for the June number, as the April number has already gone to press'. He gently insisted that Joyce would finish the manuscript 'immediately he is able to work again' so that he could send it 'to the printers at once and allow him plenty of time to deal with the proof' (Eliot 2011, 595). Lucia notified Harriet Shaw Weaver on 25 March that Joyce had finished the revision for *The Criterion*, but that the changes needed to be copied again as no 'typist would make it out' (*LIII* 117). On 15 April, T.S. Eliot thanked Sylvia Beach for the typescript from Sylvia Beach, asking her to convey his 'deep sympathy' to Joyce and informing her that the 'next *Criterion* should appear toward the end of June' (Eliot 2011, 650–1). It appeared in the July number under the title 'Fragment of an Unpublished Work'.[15] Perhaps it is telling that Eliot did not solicit a second instalment for his journal,[16] although he did remain supportive of 'Work in Progress', which he would end up publishing in 1939.

The analysis of the letter, written 'around' this document's first draft (in the 'Guiltless' copybook), originally opened with the words: 'The proteiform graph itself is a polyexigetical piece of scripture' (*FDV* 84). The opening paragraph as it appears in *The Criterion* grew out of an addition on page 33v: 'Untitled as her memorial it has ~~been named~~ gone by many names in many times' (*FDV* 84). One of the names is 'An Apology for a Husband, Can you excuse him'; another one can serve as a concise summary of the book and how it works *through* its discourse:

> The only true account [. . .] by an honest woman of the world who can only tell the **naked truth** about a dear man and all his conspirators how they tried to fall him by putting it all around Lucalizod by a mean sneak about E – and a dirty pair of sluts, showing to all the unmentionableness falsely accused about the redcoats.
>
> (*FDV* 84)

Joyce added the adverb 'only' to the 'true account', emphasizing the nakedness of the truth to such a degree that it becomes suspicious. By the time the piece was

---

[14] Letter to Harriet Shaw Weaver, British Library, Archives and Manuscripts, *Harriet Shaw Weaver Papers, Vols I–VIII*. Add. MS 57347, 2 February 1925.

[15] This publication is the result of what Mikio Fuse categorizes as Stage I in the writing process of chapter I.5 of *Finnegans Wake*: 'Stage I began with the writing of the first drafts of the four sections in December 1923-January 1924. Then, in spring 1924 Joyce abandoned the second and third sections, had the remaining two sections typed (now in the extant diptych format) in early 1924 (level 3), and ended with the publication of *The Criterion* 3.12 in July 1925 (level 6)' (Fuse 2007, 99).

[16] *The Criterion* was not unique in this respect. As Katherine Mullin notes with regard to the first five pre-book publications in periodicals, 'none of these journals cared to repeat the experiment' (Mullin 2008, 384).

published in *The Criterion*, this title had become the '*First and Last Only True Account all about the Honorary Mr. Earwicker, L.S.D., and the Snake by a Woman of the World who only can tell Naked Truths*' (*Cr* 498). The summary of what HCE is being accused of does not change dramatically, although ALP's own tendency to start slandering whilst writing against the slander already shows through (thus, for instance, the 'sluts' become 'Sloppy Sluts'): '*about a Dear Man and all his Conspirators how they all tried to fall him putting it all around Lucalizod about Earwicker and a Pair of Sloppy Sluts plainly showing all the Unmentionability falsaly* [sic] *accusing about the Redcoats*'. Most importantly, after a few drafts, the 'naked truth' has already become plural, '*Naked Truths*', suggesting the ease with which it multiplies.

The author of the account is presented as 'an honest woman of the world', but 'Closer inspection of the *bordereau* would reveal a multiplicity of personalities inflicted on the document' (*Cr* 498) and the question arises 'who in hell wrote the durn thing anyhow?' – a 'whittlewit laden with the loot of learning?' (*Cr* 499).[17]

Before the question of authorship can be dealt with, the fragment suggests that the research method needs to be discussed first. Not only the content, but also the form of the document is important. As one of the earliest pre-book publications of *Finnegans Wake*, this paragraph can be read as a statement of Joyce's poetics at this stage of his career. The text suggests we look 'sufficiently longly' at the 'envelope', instead of showing only an interest in its content. 'Admittedly it is an outer husk: its face is its fortune: it exhibits only the civil or military clothing of whatever passionpallid nudity or plaguepurple nakedness may happen to tuck itself under its flap' (500). This metaphor is then fully developed:

> to concentrate solely on the literal sense or even the psychological content of any document to the sore neglect of the enveloping facts themselves circumstantiating it is as hurtful to sound sense [. . .] as were some fellow in the act of perhaps getting an intro from another fellow [. . .] to a lady of the latter's acquaintance straightway to run off and vision her plump and plain in her natural altogether.
>
> (*Cr* 500)

This would be an approach that closes its eyes to the enveloping 'definite articles of clothing [. . .] full of local colour and personal perfume and suggestive, too, of so much more' (500). What one is to think of this approach is suggested by means of a rhetorical question:

---

[17]   In the early 1930s, Samuel Beckett referred to his pseudo-Joycean method of notesnatching (see *FW* 125.21–22) as a form of gathering '*butin verbal*', verbal loot; and in his poem 'Gnome' he turned the Joycean 'loot of learning' into a criticism of the 'loutishness of learning', Samuel Beckett, *Collected Poems*, ed. by Seán Lawlor and John Pilling (London: Faber and Faber, 2012), 55.

Who in his heart doubts either that the facts of feminine clothing are there all the time or that the feminine fiction, stranger than the facts, is there also at the same time, only a little to the rere?

(500)

Less rhetorical, however, is the question how to interpret the metaphor. What are the facts, what is the fiction? If we zoom in: (1) on a narrative microlevel, HCE's incident with the two 'sluts' in Phoenix Park could be seen as a fiction, and the rumours as the facts; (2) on another level, however, the 'skeleton key' or the 'first draft version' of 'Work in Progress' / *Finnegans Wake* can be regarded as the 'plaguepurple nakedness', while the readers are invited to look 'sufficiently closely' at the wordy Wakese, the verbal distortions 'circumstantiating it'; (3) on the macrolevel, the text of the *Wake* is the fiction, 'stranger than the facts', and the reader is invited to take the bibliographical 'enveloping facts' of its publication history into account. Fiction and the facts, 'both may then be contemplated simultaneously' or 'one may be separated from the other' and 'each may be taken up and considered in turn apart from the other' (*Cr* 500). All these options are suggested by the text in *The Criterion*. Probably it is the combination of all these approaches on all different levels that works best to make us appreciate the 'Silks appeal' (*FW* 508.29) of 'Work in Progress' as 'she stripped teasily for binocular man' (*FW* 68.01–02).

In the first draft, the first section ends with a sentence that was never copied and was lost in the subsequent writing stages: 'Wonderfully well this explains the double nature of this gryphonic script and while its ingredients stand out with stereoptican relief we can see ~~peep~~ tour beyond the figure of the scriptor into the subconscious editor's mind' (BL MS 47471b, 25v). If the 'scriptor' is ALP, the 'editor' might be Shem the Penman, the one who is actually behind the writing of the letter. As to the question of the authorship of the letter, the examination of the document results in the following hypothesis: 'in addition to the original sand [. . .] it has acquired accretions of terricious matter whilst loitering in the past' (*Cr* 503) and the 'teastain' in the first-draft version (*FDV* 87), which has become a 'teatimestained terminal' in *The Criterion* (503), is said to be important in establishing the identities of the 'writer complexus' (503). In the first draft, the **'identity'** was still singular; the *Criterion* version speaks of plural **'identities'**. For, in addition to the teastain, 'every word, letter, penstroke, space is a perfect signature of its own' (503).

The common-sense approach – 'Anyhow, somehow and somewhere somebody [. . .] wrote it all down, and there you are, full stop' (504–5) – is immediately nuanced ('yes, but . . .'), for one has to take a few circumstances into account, such as 'the continually more and less intermisunderstanding minds of the anticollaborators' (*Cr* 505). Among the special features of the document, 'the toomuchness, the fartoomanyness of all those fourlegged ems', 'the cut and dry aks and wise form of the semifinal' and 'lastly when all is zed and done, the penelopean patience of its last paraphe' allude to *Ulysses*. Thus, to contemporary readers (readers of the piece as published in *The Criterion*), 'Work in Progress' must have made a metafictional, self-reflexive impression.

Eventually, the 'unmistaken identity' of the writer is established by examining the 'numerous stabs and foliated gashes' or 'paper wounds' (*Cr* 509). According to the first draft, 'investigation showed that they were provoked by the fork of a professor at the breakfast table ^{professionally} ~~trying~~ ^{piqued to introduce tempo into a plane surface by making holes in space}' (*FDV* 89).[18] Joyce revised 'the piece for Mr Eliot' toward the end of February 1925 (see *LIII* 114) and in a handwritten note he replaced the above quotation by the following passage, full of diacritical signs and punctuation marks:

> following up their one true clue, the ^{circumflexuous} wall of a singleminded men's
> asylum, accentuated by bi tso fb rok engl a ssan dspl itch ina, – Yard enquiries
> pointed out → that they ~~ád~~ ȧd bîn 'provòked' by ∧ fork, ŏf ă grave Profèssòr;
> ăth é's Brèak – fast – table ; ; acùtely profèssionally piquéd, to = introdùçe ă
> nòtïȍn ŏf tīmē [ŭpòn ă plãñe (?) sù ''rfaiç'e'] by pùnct ! ingh òles (sic) in
> iSpåce?!
>
>   (*JJA* 46: 355–6; transcribed by Tekla Mecsnóber)

The idea of introducing a 'notion of time' or 'tempo into a plane surface by making holes in space' is applied relatively traditionally by Joyce. For instance, the diacritics in 'ŭpòn ă plãñe' seem to indicate the metre by accentuating the unstressed and stressed syllables. As Tekla Mecsnóber points out (2014), this version features 20 diacritics more than the 16 diacritics in the 1939 text of *Finnegans Wake* (*FW* 124). And some of the original diacritics, notably the breves (for short or unstressed vowels), were already misinterpreted by the typist (for instance, breves were misread as grave accents) and by the printers of *The Criterion*, as early as 1925 (*JJA* 46: 427–8). As a result, whereas Joyce's notation served as an attempt to introduce time into space or tempo into a plane surface, 'the most "realistic" facets of Joyce's quasi-phonetic notation were blurred, and the original rhythm of accents (as in "ŭpòn ă plãñe") was reduced to a meaningless uniformity ("ùpòn à plãñe")' (Mecsnóber 2014). Still, the printers of *The Criterion* were more courageous than those of *The Calendar of Modern Letters* (cf. infra). They did try to take all the typographical, 'enveloping facts' of the text into account and the *Criterion* version does add quite some local colour to the naked straightforwardness of the first draft ('the fork of a professor at the breakfast table'). And finally, whereas in the first draft the letter's author was presented as the 'notetaker, Jim the Penman' (MS 47471b, 43v; *FDV* 89), the *Criterion* version described him as 'that odious and still today insufficiently malestimated notesnatcher, Shem the Penman' (510).

---

[18]   *The Professor at the Breakfast Table* was a book Joyce took excerpts from. As Viviana Braslasu has shown, the combination of the Professor's pomposity and the stuttering Lewis Carroll's love of little girls constituted a basis for the characterisation of the stammering HCE and his incestuous relationship with his daughter.

The Calendar of Modern Letters

As the previous section has shown, the fragment in the *The Criterion* was originally based on the letter ALP wrote to defend her husband against the slander. After this brief introduction of ALP, as defender of HCE, she deserved a more detailed description, at least as extensive as HCE's introduction in *Contact Collection of Contemporary Writers*. Joyce devoted a separate fragment to her, which eventually became chapter I.8 of *Finnegans Wake*. The piece was first published in *Le Navire d'Argent*, but it was originally planned to appear in *The Calendar of Modern Letters*. This magazine, edited by Edgell Rickword and Douglas Garman, was going to publish an early version of *Anna Livia Plurabelle* in the Summer of 1925. *The Calendar of Modern Letters* had already serialized works by such authors as D.H. Lawrence and Wyndham Lewis before (Crispi and Herbert 2003, 65). On 27 July 1925, Joyce sent a short note to Sylvia Beach, asking her to make a few emendations to the piece.[19] Towards the end of July and on 22 August, Joyce sent her more emendations. He expected the piece to appear in 'the September *Calendar*' (*LIII* 121); by mid-August he thought it would be the October issue (*LIII* 125). *The Calendar* itself announced it in its September number (see Figure 1.3):

We shall publish in October:

JAMES JOYCE: Section from Work in Progress
WYNDHAM LEWIS: The Foxes' Case
LAURA GOTTSCHALK: Poems
LEONID MASSINE: A Note on Ballet
CECIL GRAY: The Notes on Music, begun in September, will be published each month.

In the end, however, the piece did not appear in *The Calendar*. The cautious English printers of the magazine refused to set the text of *Anna Livia Plurabelle* without excisions, as Joyce informed Harriet Shaw Weaver on 6 September 1925: 'the Calendar printers flatly refuse to compose Madame Anna Livia' (*LIII* 127; see also Crispi and Herbert 2003, 65; McMillan 1975, 180), even though they did set up 'a partial set of galley proofs' (BL 47474, fs. 204–206; *JJA* 48.153–5),[20] as Luca Crispi notes in the invaluable catalogue of the Joyce material at Buffalo. Three

---

[19]   Second carbon copy of the typescript, BL 47474, fs. 186r–202r; see *JJSB* 56–8.BU Joyce VI.I.19, emendations for a duplicate copy of the third typescript intended for *The Calendar of Modern Letters* I.8 (1925).

[20]   The Special Collections Research Center at Southern Illinois University holds the 'Galley proofs of part of Anna Livia Plurabelle which should have appeared in the London *The Calendar*', SIU MS 1/8/975, http://archives.lib.siu.edu/index.php?p=collections/controlcard&id=2688&q=Joyce

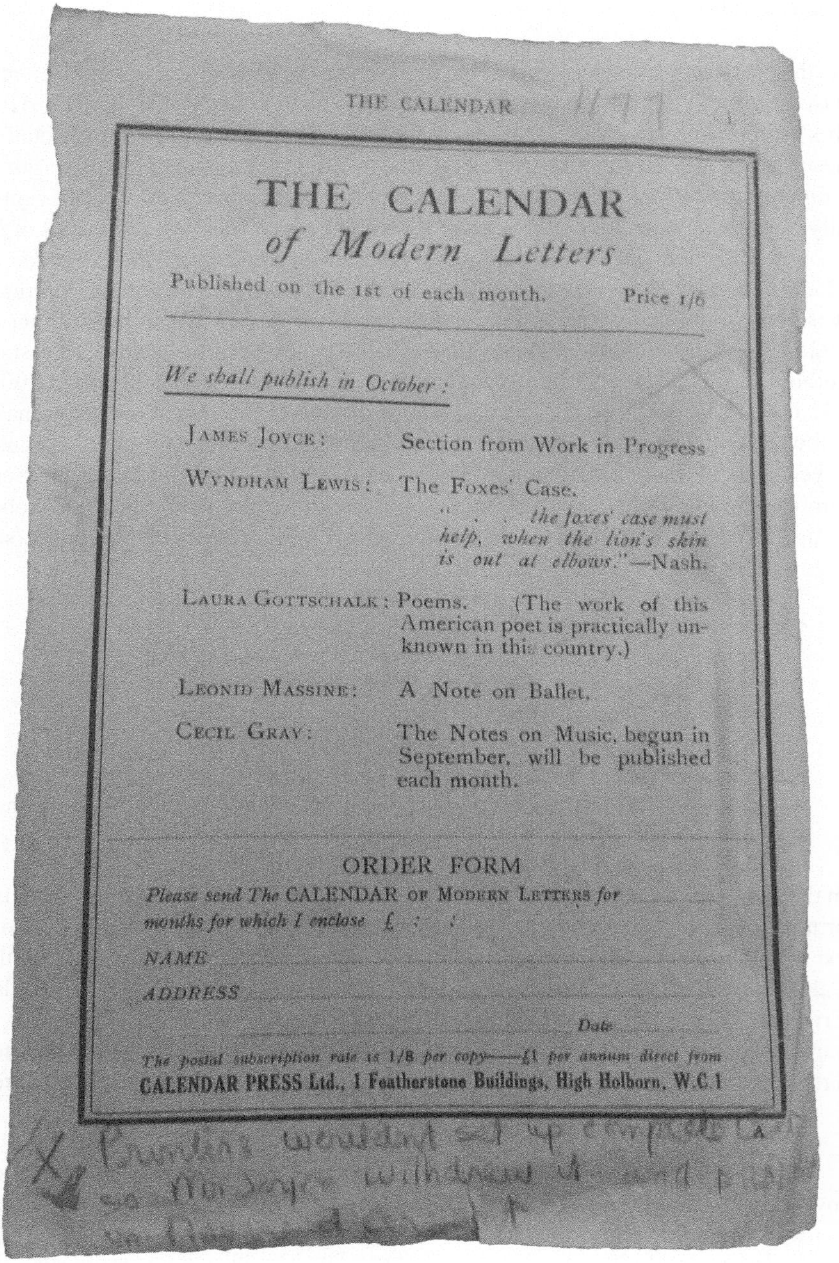

THE CALENDAR
of Modern Letters

Published on the 1st of each month.   Price 1/6

We shall publish in October :

JAMES JOYCE :	Section from Work in Progress
WYNDHAM LEWIS :	The Foxes' Case.
	" . . . *the foxes' case must help, when the lion's skin is out at elbows.*"—Nash.
LAURA GOTTSCHALK :	Poems. (The work of this American poet is practically unknown in this country.)
LEONID MASSINE :	A Note on Ballet.
CECIL GRAY :	The Notes on Music, begun in September, will be published each month.

ORDER FORM

Please send The CALENDAR OF MODERN LETTERS *for*
months for which I enclose £ : :

NAME

ADDRESS

                                                        Date

The postal subscription rate is 1/8 per copy——£1 per annum direct from
CALENDAR PRESS Ltd., 1 Featherstone Buildings, High Holborn, W.C.1

Figure 1.3   Announcement for the October issue in *The Calendar* (September 1925) (The Poetry Collection, Buffalo)

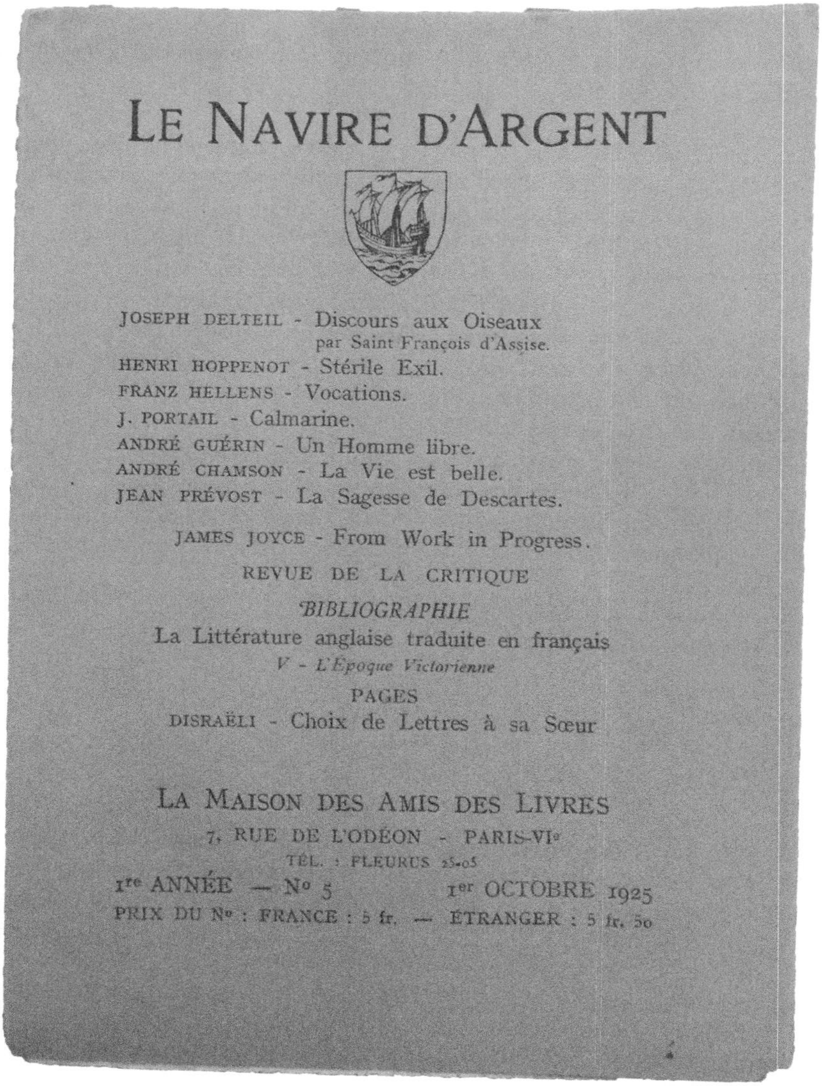

LE NAVIRE D'ARGENT

JOSEPH DELTEIL - Discours aux Oiseaux
par Saint François d'Assise.
HENRI HOPPENOT - Stérile Exil.
FRANZ HELLENS - Vocations.
J. PORTAIL - Calmarine.
ANDRÉ GUÉRIN - Un Homme libre.
ANDRÉ CHAMSON - La Vie est belle.
JEAN PRÉVOST - La Sagesse de Descartes.

JAMES JOYCE - From Work in Progress.

REVUE DE LA CRITIQUE

BIBLIOGRAPHIE

La Littérature anglaise traduite en français
V - L'Époque Victorienne

PAGES
DISRAËLI - Choix de Lettres à sa Sœur

LA MAISON DES AMIS DES LIVRES

7, RUE DE L'ODÉON - PARIS-VIᵉ
TÉL. : FLEURUS 25-05

Iʳᵉ ANNÉE — Nᵒ 5   Iᵉʳ OCTOBRE 1925
PRIX DU Nᵒ : FRANCE : 5 fr. — ÉTRANGER : 5 fr. 50

Figure 1.4   Cover of *Le Navire d'Argent* (October 1925)

weeks later, Joyce had already arranged to publish the piece in *Le Navire d'Argent* (see Figure 1.4), as he indicated in a letter to his brother Stanislaus on 28 September 1925: 'The English printer of *The Calendar* refuses to set up a piece of my new book. It comes out therefore complete (the piece) on Wednesday in a Paris review' (*LIII* 128).

Le Navire d'Argent

'From Work in Progress' in *Navire d'Argent*, Paris, II.5 (October 1925), 59–74 [FW 196–216] (C.66)

That the piece on Anna Livia Plurabelle quickly found another magazine was the work of Adrienne Monnier and Sylvia Beach. Monnier's magazine *Le Navire d'Argent* tried to introduce recent Anglo-American literature to a French audience. In June 1925, it had published T.S. Eliot's 'Love Song of J. Alfred Prufrock' (in a translation by Beach and Monnier). In the October issue, four months after the translation of Prufrock and the women who 'come and go / Talking of Michelangelo', the journal gave the floor to Joyce's washerwomen, talking of Anna Livia. Valery Larbaud, who edited the magazine for Monnier, did have second thoughts and privately expressed his doubts about what he called a 'divertissement philologique' (McMillan 1975, 180). But Monnier and Beach fully supported Joyce's work and it is only fitting that advertisements for Adrienne Monnier's 'La Maison des amis des livres' and Sylvia Beach's 'Shakespeare and Company' (respectively 7 and 12, rue de l'Odéon) are printed side by side on the back of the volume that welcomed 'Anna Livia Plurabelle' (see Plate 1).

The text as it appeared in *Le Navire d'Argent* opens without any typographical fancywork, only an indentation of two spaces before the opening 'O':

> O tell me all about Anna Livia! I want to hear all
> about Anna Livia. Well, you know Anna Livia? Yes,
> of course, we all know Anna Livia. Tell me all. Tell me
> now.

(Nd'A 61; see Figure 1.5)

The gossip about ALP and HCE by the two washerwomen on the banks of the Liffey keeps swelling. Anna Livia, upset about the gossip, decides to distribute presents to all of her children. 'Her Pandora's box contains the ills flesh is heir to', Joyce wrote to Harriet Weaver (7 March 1924; *LI* 213). When she slowly reaches the delta, a new cycle of evaporation, pouring down and welling up is predicted by means of the theme 'The same anew' – which will later be followed by numerous variations throughout 'Work in Progress': 'Then all that was was fair. In Elvenland? Teems of times and happy returns. The same anew. Ordovico or viricordo. Anna was, Livia is, Plurabelle's to be' (*Nd'A* 73). At dusk, as Anna Livia approaches the sea and the distance between her banks widens, the two gossiping washerwomen hardly understand each other anymore, eventually turning into a tree and a stone.

Le Navire d'Argent made publicity for this fragment of 'Work in Progress', notably by means of small posters and flyers. The French magazine interestingly presented Joyce, not as the author of *Ulysses*, but as 'censored in England':

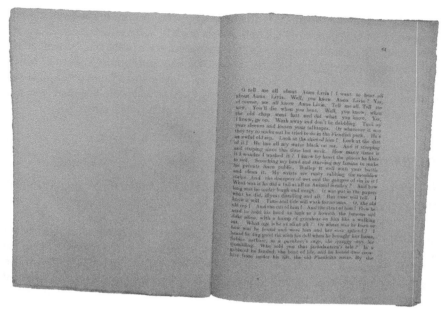

Figure 1.5   Opening page of 'From Work in Progress' in *Le Navire d'argent* (October 1925)

WORK IN PROGRESS

BY

JAMES JOYCE

CENSORED IN ENGLAND

LE NAVIRE D'ARGENT

OCTOBER NR.

FIVE FRANCS.[21]

Immediate Reception: Press Clippings

The French press was generally positive about the heroic role played by Adrienne Monnier, sometimes almost styled as the Jeanne d'Arc of contemporary literatures who defended ALP against the bad English printers. It is remarkable how often the

---

[21]   UB JJC XVIII.G: Miscellaneous Material Related to 'Work in Progress' / *Finnegans Wake*, Folder 1: Torn fragment of poster for 'Work in Progress' in *Navire d'Argent*; October [1925].

adjective 'anglais' or 'English' is stressed in reviews to refer to the overcautious printers. In *Vient de paraître*, 'les imprimeurs anglais' were said to have refused to print the text in its entirety, whereupon 'le manuscrit revint à Paris le 20 septembre' and the text appeared 'sans mutilation' on 1 October in Monnier's journal, which was explicitly identified as a 'revue française'. Joyce's treatment of English 'en matière plastique' is compared to Rabelais's French, when the language was not yet solidified ['solidifié'], and the result is described in lyrical terms.[22]

This Quarter

'Extract from Work in Progress', *This Quarter*, Milan, I.2 (Autumn–Winter 1925–26), 108–23 [FW 169–95] (C.67)

In the meantime, Joyce and Beach had been preparing another publication, introducing a new character of 'Work in Progress', the first of HCE and ALP's children: Shem the Penman. The piece was to be published in *This Quarter*, established by Ernest Walsh and the Scottish poetess Ethel Moorhead. The 'vagabond review', as Luca Crispi and Stacey Herbert call it (65), published contributions by what Sylvia Beach describes as writers 'who were about' in 'that exciting "Paris period" of America's literary history' (Beach 1980, 140), but *This Quarter* was not yet the 'prominent place' where Joyce wished his fragments to appear 'regularly' (*LI* 245; cf. supra). Ernest Walsh was dying of consumption (McMillan 1975, 179), and as Sylvia Beach explains, he 'knew that he had only a few months to live and he had decided to come to Paris to spend the time remaining to him among the writers he admired' (Beach 1980, 140).

The first number was dedicated to Ezra Pound; the second contained the fragment on Shem the Penman from Joyce's 'Work in Progress'. The last line of the fragment in *The Criterion* had revealed the identity of 'Shem the Penman' as the author of the letter. In the 'Guiltless' copybook, the second draft of this section ended in the middle of a page, and was immediately followed by the first draft of what eventually became chapter I.7 (devoted entirely to Shem the Penman): 'Shem is as short for Shemus as Jim is [jokey] for Jacob' (BL MS 47471b, 49v; *FDV* 108).[23] In this first draft, Shem's penmanship was presented not as unambiguously negative as in the eventually published version: 'Who knows *how many unsigned first copies of original masterpieces, how many* pseudostylous shamiana, how few of the most venerated public impostures, how very many palimpsests slipped from that

---

[22] 'Ces quatorze grandes pages forment une puissante symphonie aux ondes tour à tour élargies et précipitées et s'achèvent en liquides sonorités nocturnes' (UBC 1: 983).

[23] To write this negative portrait of Shem by his biased brother Shaun, Joyce made use of several negative reviews of *Ulysses* (Landuyt 1999). One of the reviews he used, was Virginia Woolf's essay 'Modern Novels' (*Times Literary Supplement* 899, 10 April 1919, pp. 189–190) (see Introduction; Van Hulle 2008, 87).

plagiarist pen?' (*FDV* 117; emphasis added). The line '*how many unsigned first copies of original masterpieces*' was omitted along the way and did not appear in *This Quarter*: 'Who can say how many pseudostylic shamiana, how few or how many of the most venerated public impostures, how very many piously forged palimpsests slipped in the first place by this morbid process from his pelagiarist pen?' (*TQ* 115; emphasis added).[24]

The typescript prepared for the printer of *This Quarter* still contains the passage 'how many unsigned first copies of original masterpieces' (and 'plagiarist pen' is not yet 'pelagiarist pen'; *JJA* 47, 459–60; BL MS 47474–47). The proofs for *This Quarter* are unfortunately missing (*JJA* 47, 397). Unless Joyce cancelled the passage on these missing proofs (chapter I.7, level 1.6/2.6), the missing line may be one of the many cases of homoeoteleuton causing a *saut du même au même*[25] in the genesis of 'Work in Progress' – the eyes of the typesetter having jumped from the first 'how many' to the second 'how many' on the next line. If that is the case, Joyce never cared to restore the lost line. The passage remained unchanged until the publication of *Finnegans Wake* in 1939 (*FW* 181.36–182.03).

The biased characterisation culminates in the Latin description of how Shem the 'pelagiarist' penman produces ink from his excrements. In the second section of chapter I.7 (*FW* 187.24–195), Mercius (or Shem) is accused by Justius (or Shaun) of the so-called Improperia (*FDV* 120), listed in the first draft: 1. Hell (he has become 'a doubter of all known gods'); 2. Progeny; 3. Prophecy; 4. Shirking (refusing to work); 5. Sin (more specifically fratricide); 6. Doles (being wasteful); and finally he is accused of forswearing his 7. Mother. Shem's only defense is that 'gossipaceous' Anna Livia will speak through him (*FDV* 122).[26]

Immediate Reception: Press Clippings

The New Criterion (April 1926) devoted a short review (by 'H.R.') to *This Quarter* No. 2, noting that it was a 'massive periodical of nearly 350 pages, all of it very

---

[24] Robbert-Jan Henkes and Erik Bindervoet mention the line in their list of transmissional departures (Joyce 2002, 639).

[25] See for instance Sam Slote ('Sound-Bite against the Restoration'. *Genetic Joyce Studies* 1 (2001)) with reference to the long conditional clause 'Or, if he was always striking up funny funereels with Besterfarther Zeuts [. . .]' (*FW* 414.35–6), which is not followed by an apodosis: 'In its initial draft, this sentence was itself the apodosis: "If **he** was not doing that **he** was always getting up funny funeralls with Besterfather Zeuts . . ." (*JJA* 57: 294). The sentence remained in this format through the publication of *Tales Told of Shem and Shaun* in 1932. When the galleys were prepared for *Finnegans Wake* in 1938, the protasis was omitted (*JJA* 62: 17). On the pages of *Tales Told of Shem and Shaun*, the second "he" lies almost directly under the first (*JJA* 57: 325). Evidently, the typesetter skipped the clause following the first "he" and jumped to the second. Scholars of Mediæval manuscripts call this kind of copyist's error haplography'.

[26] See letter to Harriet Weaver, 16 January 1924; *LI* 208.

experimental' and that 'There is an instalment from work in progress by James Joyce: it has all the merits and defects of *Ulysses*, but nothing more'. Although in theory *The Criterion* was 'not the place to discourage any kind of literary experiment', the overall verdict on *This Quarter* was quite reactionary: 'In general the atmosphere of the magazine is tiresomely adolescent'. And the review concluded with a patronizing and grandiloquent generalization: 'literature is something more than the expression of an individuality. It is a component element of a society, and only subsists in relation to some common ethos or national development. It must work within a tradition, with some lien on the dominant institutions of a race. All art is indigenous; otherwise it is in danger of being merely impudent' (UBC 68: 2025).

In the meantime, Joyce had other fish to fry. After having spent several months working on the Shem fragment, Joyce wrote to Sylvia Beach on 19 October 1925: 'For goodness' sake will you please take charge of this fellow. I cannot stand any more of him. I don't know if I have corrected all his errors and omissions. Anyhow please keep him in the cage till called for' (*JJSB* 66). On 5 November, Joyce told Herbert Gorman that he would 'forward [him] in the next week or so, a copy of *This Quarter* containing another piece'. And in the same breath, he went on, jumping to a seemingly divergent topic: 'As since the death of Mr. John Quinn, I have no agents in America, I should be very glad if you could give me any information concerning a quarterly review entitled "Two Worlds" edited by Mr Samuel Roth' (*LIII* 132). This was a magazine of an entirely different kind, which will be the subject of the next chapter.

Chapter 2

Pirates and Critics

'A New Unnamed Work', *Two Worlds*, New York, I.1 (September 1925), 45–54 [*FW* 104–125] (C.65)

'A New Unnamed Work', *Two Worlds*, New York, I.2 (December 1925), 111–14 [*FW* 30–4] (C.65)

'A New Unnamed Work', *Two Worlds*, New York, I.3 (March 1926), 347–60 [*FW* 196–216] (C.65)

'A New Unnamed Work', *Two Worlds*, New York, I.4 (June 1926), 545–60 [*FW* 169–95] (C.65)

'A New Unnamed Work', *Two Worlds*, New York, II.5 (September 1926), 35–40 [*FW* 383–99] (C.65)

Joyce was especially alerted to the dangers of his fragments' exposure to public life in November 1925. On the same 5th of November 1925, when he asked Herbert Gorman if he knew anything about the *Two Worlds* magazine (see Plate 2), he also wrote to Harriet Shaw Weaver that he was having 'queer experiences with editors. New press opinions of Δ are: "all Greek to us" "unfortunately I can't read it" "is it a puzzle?" "has anybody had the courage to ask J. how many misprints are in it" "those French printers!" "how is your eyesight?" "charming!" – This last from Mrs Nutting, who, however, heard me read it and indeed suggested my voice should be dished (misprint for "disced")' (*LIII* 131). And of course, the really 'queer experience' was the matter of Samuel Roth's magazine *Two Worlds: A Literary Quarterly Devoted to the Increase of the Gaiety of Nations* (see Plate 2). Joyce's mood does not seem to have been particularly gay when he explained the situation to Weaver:

> Nobody here, not even Mr Ford, can solve the problem of Two Worlds. Huge advertisements have appeared in several big American and English reviews, the former costing, I am told, $1000 each! I never wrote a letter or sent any MS to Mr Roth. He wrote (or roth) to me in 1921. I did not answer, I think. He also wrote to me on 25 September asking me to give him something and said he would buy the forests of Hudson Bay for paper etc. I did not answer. And yet number 1 apparently came out on 15 with a piece of mine in it.
>
> (*LIII* 131)

Joyce's fragment in the first issue of *Two Worlds* was the piece on ALP's letter (aka the Mamafesta, or 'The document' as it was called in Sylvia Beach's list), which had appeared in Eliot's *The Criterion*.

When he wrote his letter on 5 November, Joyce does not seem to have actually seen a copy of the pirate edition. It would have struck him immediately that the text was anything but carefully typeset. Luca Crispi and Stacey Herbert note that the very first paragraph already contains four typographical errors. Thus, for instance, 'the Allhighest' (*Cr* 498) becomes 'the All highest' (*TW1* 46), and the long title (see above, Chapter 1) lacks 14 words: '*about a Dear Man and all his Conspirators|*' *and a Pair of Sloppy Slutts plainly showing all the Unmentionability falsely accusing about the Redcoats*'. The | indicates a lacuna where Roth failed to print the following clause, which does appear in the text of *The Criterion* edition: '*how they all tried to fall him putting it all around Lucalizod about Earwicker*' (see Crispi and Herbert 2003, 66). The '*Sloppy Sluts*' became '*Sloppy Slutts*' with double tt. Admittedly, the text in *The Criterion* had not been flawless either, but *Two Worlds*' correction of '*falsaly accusing*' into '*falsely accusing*' could hardly make up for the numerous errors it introduced.

Joyce seems to have been so eager to publish the fragments of his new 'Work in Progress' that he even considered letting Roth publish the first three of the four watches of Shaun. When he 'wanted to revise ∧abc for Mr Roth', it was only fatigue that had prevented him from it, as he told Harriet Shaw Weaver on 5 March 1926 (*LIII* 139). By then, Roth had already published a second instalment ('Here Comes Everybody', which had appeared in the *Contact Collection of Contemporary Writers*).

The third issue of *Two Worlds* (March 1926) contained 'Anna Livia Plurabelle'. As in *Le Navire d'Argent* the text did not yet open with the typographical triangle, but it did open with an opening O in a much larger font size (see Figure 2.1).

The fourth issue (June 1926) was to contain a republication of the piece on Shem the Penman (published in *This Quarter*). Since Shem and his parents were thus being introduced across the Atlantic, it somehow made sense that Joyce considered revising the first three of Shaun's watches and work towards a completion of the picture of the nuclear family.

But then Roth started yet another magazine, the *Two Worlds Monthly*, in which he republished *Ulysses* in instalments from July 1926 onwards. This was an entirely different matter for Joyce. To his brother Stanislaus, he wrote on 5 November 1926: 'Roth is pirating *Ulysses* (bowdlerized) in a new monthly magazine of which he sells 50,000 copies a month. I have tried to enjoin the publication but there seems to be no remedy' (*LIII* 145). By 15 December, he had found out that 'American lawyers refused to take up this case' while 'The American press [. . .] continues to print Roth's full-page advertisements, knowing them to be a swindle' (*LIII* 148). According to Joyce, Roth was 'pocketing at least 1,000,000 francs a month' (*LIII* 148), which had a direct effect on the market, even in Europe: 'Roth has killed the sales here, too [. . .] Not a single daily or weekly in U.S. published our cabled denial. I am engaged in a very costly law suit, but will go on even if I lose it. I have organised an international protest to make this a test case for the reform of U.S. law' (*LIII* 149). This international protest took shape in a 'Statement regarding the piracy of *Ulysses*', issued on Joyce's birthday, 2 February 1927. As Robert Spoo

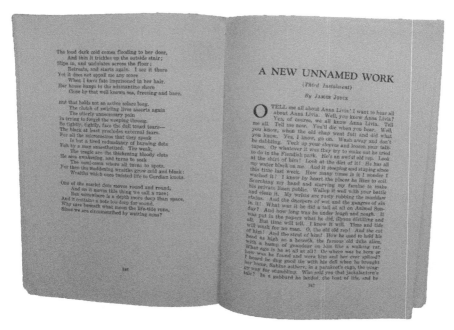

Figure 2.1   Opening page of 'A New Unnamed Work' (Third Instalment: 'Anna Livia Plurabelle') in *Two Worlds* I.3 (March 1926)

explains, the remarkable legal situation was based on the so-called 'manufacturing clause': 'The 1909 U.S. Copyright Act, which determined what was and what was not protected within the borders of the United States, specified that, to enjoy full copyright, foreign works written in English had to be reset, printed, and bound on American soil within a fixed number of days after they had been published abroad'. Authors with a dubious reputation such as Joyce – the author of a 'banned' book – often 'failed to find a legitimate publisher in time to safisfy these requirements, known collectively as "the manufacturing clause"' (Spoo 2013, 2). As the 'bad boy of magazine publishing' (11), Roth cynically took pragmatic advantage of the manufacturing clause, 'the cheap reprinter's best friend' (Spoo 2013, 86), to sell a sort of sweetened, *salonfähig* avant-garde as a form of 'gaiety', bringing together 'two worlds', Europe and America, but also – as Robert Spoo points out – the heterogeneous worlds of 'literary ambition and bawdy entertainment' (168). These 'two worlds' intertwined in the most bizarre ways, which is even reflected in the typography, as the fourth instalment of 'Work in Progress' in *Two Worlds* shows (the fragment that corresponds with chapter 7 of *Finnegans Wake*).

The opening line immediately indicates that this fragment is a portrait of Shem: 'Shem is as short for Shemus as Jem is joky for Jacob'. The initial 'S'

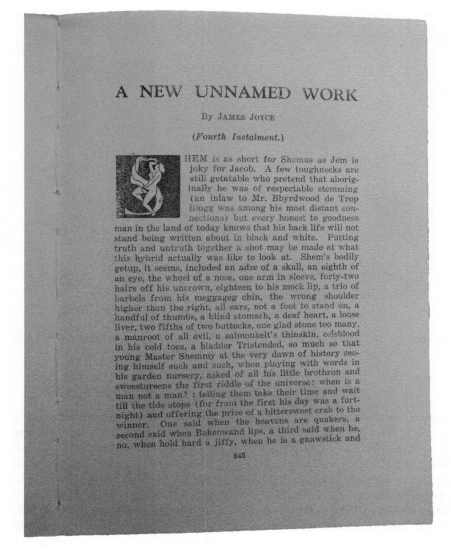

HEM is as short for Shemus as Jem is joky for Jacob. A few toughnecks are still getatable who pretend that aboriginally he was of respectable stemming (an inlaw to Mr. Bbyrdwood de Trop Blogg was among his most distant connections) but every honest to goodness man in the land of today knows that his back life will not stand being written about in black and white. Putting truth and untruth together a shot may be made at what this hybrid actually was like to look at. Shem's bodily getup, it seems, included an adze of a skull, an eighth of an eye, the whoel of a nose, one arm in sleeve, forty-two hairs off his uncrown, eighteen to his mock lip, a trio of barbels from his meggageg chin, the wrong shoulder higher than the right, all ears, not a foot to stand on, a handful of thumbs, a blind stomach, a deaf heart, a loose liver, two fifths of two buttocks, one glad stone too many, a manroot of all evil, a salmonkelt's thinskin, eelsblood in his cold toes, a bladder Tristended, so much so that young Master Shemmy at the very dawn of history seeing himself such and such, when playing with words in his garden nursery, asked of all his little brothron and sweestureens the first riddle of the universe: when is a man not a man? : telling them take their time and wait till the tide stops (for from the first his day was a fortnight) and offering the prize of a bittersweet crab to the winner. One said when the heavens are quakers, a second said when Bohemeand lips, a third said when he, no, when hold hard a jiffy, when he is a gnawstick and

545

Figure 2.2   Opening page of 'A New Unnamed Work' (Fourth Instalment: 'Shem the Penman') in *Two Worlds* I.4 (June 1926)

(see Figure 2.2) is illuminated, but there is no connection with the content of the fragment. Luca Crispi and Stacey Herbert describe the initial as 'a woodcut illustration of a naked woman provocatively entwined with the letters [. . .] astride the snake-like "S"' (Crispi and Herbert 2003, 67). In a study of 'Sexy Punctuation in American Magazines', Amanda Sigler calls this 'S' 'Arguably

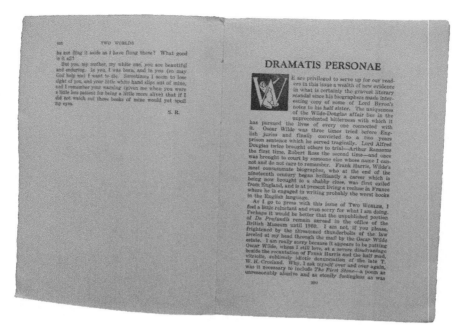

Figure 2.3   Decorated initial letter, immediately following after Samuel Roth's editorial in *Two Worlds* I.4 (June 1926)

the most titillating initial letter in the magazine' (Sigler 2014, 62). Sigler suggests that the content of the issue, devoted primarily to Oscar Wilde 'and his sexual scandals' (62), might be a reason for the introduction of several other 'sexually provocative initial letters' in the volume, described in vivid terms: 'In the initial "A" [. . .] a naked lady [. . .] peers out at the audience from within the letter's frame, apparently unabashed by her full frontal nudity'; 'a naked woman boldly sticks her breasts through the middle of an initial "W"' (see Figure 2.3), 'and a pole dancer spins around an initial "I"' (62).

It may be argued that the impact of an initial letter on the text's reception is relatively small, but it did play a role in the publishing history and no matter how superficial these typographical circumstances may seem, they 'also shaped readers' experience of *Work in Progress* in *Two Worlds*' (Sigler 2014, 63).

The last fragment of 'A New Unnamed Work by James Joyce' that appeared in *Two Worlds* (II.5, see Figure 2.4) was a reprint, preceded by a woodcut by Cecil French, of the piece that had appeared in *transatlantic review*.

Roth did try – albeit only for a brief period – to position himself as a respectable publisher and become the 'authorized' publisher of 'Work in Progress'. As Robert Spoo notes, he expressed his admiration to Joyce in late September 1925 (*after* reprinting the first fragment in *Two Worlds*); he sent a cheque for 100 dollars

Figure 2.4   Cover of *Two Worlds* II.5 (September 1926)

to Sylvia Beach on 2 January 1926; another cheque for 100 dollars on 18 March; and he offered 300 dollars for the Shaun chapters (Book III of *Finnegans Wake*). That was his 'bid to rise above his status as a parasitic reprinter' (Spoo 2013, 171). But it was not enough. On 12 July 1926, Joyce – through Sylvia Beach – offered the Shaun chapters to Marianne Moore, editor of *The Dial*, noting that the price offered so far was too low and that this 'certain review' was not a suitable place

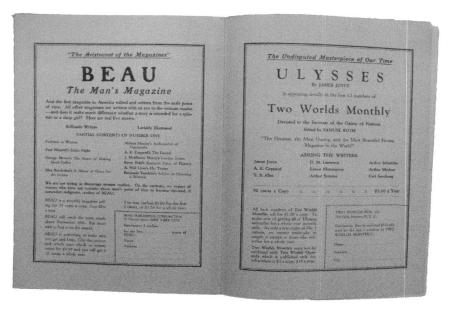

Figure 2.5   Advertisement for the serialization of *Ulysses* in *Two Worlds Monthly* at the back of *Two Worlds* II.5 (September 1926)

for Joyce's 'Work in Progress' (Beach 2010, 110). That was as far as Roth's attempt to become the authorized publisher of 'Work in Progress' went. The same month, he launched his new magazine called *Two Worlds Monthly* and started publishing *Ulysses* (as announced in an advertisement at the back of *Two Worlds* II.5; see Figure 2.5).

Since *Ulysses* was 'not protected by copyright in the United States' (*LIII* 151), Joyce could only try to gather support for a 'protest against Mr. Roth's conduct' and 'appeal to the American public in the name of that security of works of the intellect and the imagination without which art cannot live, to oppose to Mr. Roth's enterprise the full power of honorable and fair opinion' (*LIII* 152).

In the meantime, Roth's other magazine *Two Worlds* had ceased to exist. The last issue appeared in September 1926 and contained the only fragment of 'Work in Progress' that was still left to be reprinted at that moment: the Mamalujo piece, which had appeared in *The Transatlantic Review* as the first of the pre-book publications. According to Slocum and Cahoon, this was in fact the reason of the cessation: publication 'ceased because no further fragments of Work in Progress were available for Roth to reprint' (Slocum and Cahoon 1971 [1953], 99 [C 65]). In the third issue of *This Quarter* (Spring 1927), a letter from Sylvia Beach to the editor, Ethel Moorhead, explained that the fragments of 'Work in Progress' in *Two Worlds* had been reprinted 'without permission' and that, after having protested to Samuel Roth, she received 'two hundred dollars and a promise of more which never came' (qtd in Banta and Silverman 1987, 110).

Immediate Reception: Press Clippings

The New York *Evening Post* of 30 April 1927 devoted a short article to the Roth affair ('As the Case May Be', signed by H.E.D.), which deserves closer attention. It offers a perspicacious, contemporary insight into this matter of 'the recent protest, which has about 170 noteworthy signatures, against the unauthorised serialization', including Wells, Yeats, Galsworthy, Bennett and Einstein: 'the protest is headed "Stop, Thief!" and is outspoken in the extreme'. The background is sketched concisely: 'Ordinarily in publishing a foreign novel without permission Mr. Roth would have infringed on copyright [. . .] But it happened that in this country "Ulysses" was outlawed [. . .] Therefore, Mr. Roth could publish it, outside Mr. Joyce's *legal* rights'. An interesting parenthesis follows, regarding the so-called 'obscenity' the book was charged with: '(The grossness or "obscenity" is undeniable, but is not the thing here in question. It is not Mr. Joyce or our "censorship" that is up for judgment, but Mr. Roth.)' The details of the case are preceded by Webster's definition of 'piracy (figurative)' as 'Willfull infringement of copyright, *or the publication of the literary property of another without his consent*', highlighting the second part of the definition to assess Roth's public letter:

> It has moved Mr. Roth to write a circular letter, attempting self-defense. 'As the impression created is', he says, 'that I have done Mr. Joyce a grave injustice, I beg that you will consider the facts as they relate to me'.

According to Roth

(1) 'Ulysses' was given, without request for payment, by Mr. Joyce to America for serial publication in the *Little Review*, which ceased publication.

(2) Not to make money, but to popularize a work of art, I resumed the publication of 'Ulysses' and offered Mr. Joyce $1,000 compensation. When some time had gone by and I did not hear from Mr. Joyce, I deposited that sum of money with his American attorney. [. . .]

(3) I did not, as charged, bowdlerize 'Ulysses'. About a dozen words were left out in the first two instalments by a subeditor, who was discharged [. . .]

(4) I also offered Mr. Joyce $2,000 a year for the rest of his natural life if he would consent to turn over to me all his future work – in spite of the fact that the appearance of 'Ulysses' in my *Two Worlds Monthly* cost me considerable money.

The comments to these four points are level-headed and effective. The melodramatic suggestion that *Ulysses* was given 'to America' was immediately undercut and Roth's protest against the bowldlerization charge assessed as utterly grotesque: '(1) The gift of "Ulysses" to the *Little Review* has nothing to do with the case. The *Little Review* was not America, and neither is Mr. Roth. (2) and (4) Mr. Roth's motives make no real difference. (3) The "bowdlerizing" charged in the protest is a relatively inconsequential offense. The picture of an editor publishing "a work of art" with no moral right to it, and then loftily firing a subeditor for leaving a few words out of it, is in its way as amusing as the picture that rises to mind of the good Thomas Bowdler, back on earth and sitting down to "Ulysses" to blue-pencil "those words and expressions which cannot with propriety be read aloud in a family"'. Roth's subsequent rhetorical question, asking 'plaintively' 'Have I done Mr. Joyce an injustice?' and his willingness to submit to any decision arrived at 'by my literary peers' is undermined with an exemplary economy of words; 'H.E.D.' simply points out that the decision had already been arrived at, not by Roth's peers but 'by his literary superiors' (UBC 32: 837).

Another decision that was arrived at in the wake of the Roth case was that the pre-book publications in *transition* (see Chapter 3) needed to be protected. To safeguard the copyright in the US, the first instalment of 'Work in Progress' in *transition* was printed separately and sent to the Library of Congress. Among the clippings preserved at Buffalo University, there is a list of 'New Books Received by Library of Congress' (UBC 46: 2174), published by the Washington *U.S. Daily* (13 February 1928), which features the entry:

Joyce, James. . . . Work in progress. 1 v. N. Y., D. Friede, 1927. 28–1908

Later on, other fragments that appeared in *transition* (nrs 11, 12, 13, 15 and 18) would similarly be printed for US copyright purposes.

In all this hubbub one would almost forget that Joyce was trying to write a book. In the Fall of 1926 he suggested to Harriet Shaw Weaver that she place an order for him to execute. Weaver played along and Joyce thus wrote the first chapter of *Finnegans Wake* (see Lernout 2007). He also tried to finish the four watches of Shaun, which he had already been working on for quite a while. The letter of 5 November 1925, in which he informed Harriet Shaw Weaver about Roth and the bad press opinions of *Anna Livia Plurabelle* (see above), actually opens with his report on the progress he was making. The first thing he wanted to tell her was that he had 'been working very laboriously these last few weeks and ha[d] almost made a first draft of ∧d [*Finnegans Wake*, Book III, chapter 4]' (*LIII* 131). In the following months, he tried to find a suitable magazine to publish them, but by the summer of 1926 Joyce had still not found the 'prominent place' in which he wished his fragments 'to appear slowly and regularly' (*LI* 245). Of all the attempts that eventually did not result in publication, Sylvia Beach's list (see Chapter 1) only mentions *The Calendar*, but there were many more. In this period Joyce submitted fragments of 'Work in Progress' to *The Dial*, *Exile* and the *Enemy* – in each case without success.

The Dial: In July of 1926, he offered a fragment to Marianne Moore, editor of *The Dial*. The piece on the four watches of Shaun (later Book III of *Finnegans Wake*) had been typed by Lily Bollach in May 1926 (*LIII* 141), revised and sent to Harriet Shaw Weaver in the first week of June. On 12 July, Sylvia Beach sent her initial letter of inquiry to Marianne Moore, promising 'exclusive periodical rights in

America and Europe' (Beach 2010, 110).[1] The letter also suggests that this was the prominent place Joyce had in mind: 'Your review occupies the highest place among reviews and is the most appropriate one to bring out Mr Joyce's work' (110). After *The Dial* had cabled that they paid 2 cents per word but had to see the manuscript first (20 July; Wasserstrom 1963, 120–121; Crowley 2015),[2] Beach sent it by registered post on 21 July (Beach 2010, 111). On 25 July 1926, Joyce confirmed to Weaver that the piece had been sent to *The Dial* and confided that he felt 'about as diffident as a young lady of 19 at her first coming-out' (*LI* 243).[3] On 10 September, Sylvia Beach received an acceptance letter from Marianne Moore (dated 26 August). She immediately informed Joyce[4] and forwarded the acceptance letter, which requested 'some slight biographical data about Mr Joyce' (Wasserstrom 1963, 121). Moore had also asked if 'abcd' was to be the title, so Joyce informed Beach the next day (11 September) that 'Λabcd is a titlesign or private mark for myself like the others, for reference. She may use some such title as Ford or Walsh or The Criterion used' (*JJSB* 70–71). So on 16 September, Beach wrote to Moore: 'I am very glad to hear that Mr Joyce's work is going to appear in the "Dial". It has no title yet and he says anything will do. The fragments that were published by the "Criterion", "Le Navire d'Argent" etc., were called "From Work in Progress", "Work in Progress", "Extract from Work in Progress" so you may give it some such name' (*JJSB* 112). And as for the biographical notes, she referred Moore to *Who's Who* or Herbert Gorman's book *James Joyce: His First Forty Years*.

What Beach could not know, however, was that the day before (15 September), Moore had contacted James Sibley Watson, Jr, the joint-owner – together with Scofield Thayer – of *The Dial*. She had been discussing payment for Joyce's contribution with Lincoln MacVeagh and they had found quite a few objections to publication in the piece (Crowley 2015). The next day, Watson cabled that he appreciated MacVeagh's advice, but that the objections were probably not insuperable. He suggested 'using asterisks for omissions of words or short phrases' (Wasserstrom 1963, 121). And as to his partner's opinion, he wrote: 'Scofield probably not vitally interested either way' (121). In spite of Watson's mild, conciliatory and positive attitude, Beach received a forbidding telegram from *The Dial* on 17 September: 'Unpermissible to publish Joyce verbatim' (Crowley 2015, 11). Moore explained the situation in a longer letter, which she sent the same day:

---

[1]   Beach added the word 'periodical' above 'exclusive rights'. For a survey of the correspondence regarding Joyce's submissions to *The Dial*, see Crowley 2015.

[2]   Joyce wrote to Harriet Shaw Weaver on 25 July: 'The Dial telegraphed it would pay ½d a word for Λabcd but must see my text first' (*LI* 243).

[3]   For a discussion of this submission to *The Dial* from the perspective of Moore criticism, see Wasserstrom 1963, 154; Bazin 2013, 59.

[4]   A telegram and letter enclosing the acceptance letter is preserved as part of the Hans E. Jahnke Bequest at the Zurich James Joyce Foundation.

We find that it would not be possible to publish the Joyce manuscript verbatim. We should be obliged if we are to publish it, to omit pages and parts of pages, reducing it by one third – perhaps a half. We are very much distressed that this discovery was not made before I had written to you. Do you feel that you must withdraw the manuscript?

(Wasserstrom 1963, 121)

There seems to be quite a difference in tone between Watson's constructive suggestion to use asterisks for omissions and Moore's suggestive question 'Do you feel that you must withdraw the manuscript?' Joyce's reaction (two days later) was quite laconic: 'Dear Miss Beach: All safely received. So that closes temporarily my financial stabilisation scheme. Will you please cable them: Joyce requests return typescript with corrections?' (*JJSB* 72) – which Beach did, 'verbatim', the very same day (19 September; Wasserstrom 1963,121). After this reply, Moore contacted Watson, who had wished to publish Joyce's text, if necessary with asterisks for omissions. Moore now wrote that she was 'acutely desirous' of publishing in *The Dial* 'what it is your wish to publish' and that is was 'sickeningly ironic' to her to refuse a text by 'one in whose technique I have such delight',[5] but she must have realized by that time that the 'verbatim' telegram and letter had already made publication impossible, for Joyce had clearly interpreted them as a rejection. On 23 September he instructed Beach: 'As regards Λabcd when it comes back you may dispose of it to anyone who will print it gratis for if *The Dial* will not even pay that modest sum no other review will' (*JJSB* 73).

From the Astoria hotel in Brussels, Joyce first notified Weaver on 24 September 1926 that 'Λabcd was accepted by *The Dial* for 600 dollars'; he also added the parenthesis '(I enclose it in four pictures from the G.P.O. vestibule here.)' (*LI* 245). The four enclosed picture postcards from the post office vestibule in Brussels represent a miniature history of postal services, starting with Charlemagne (Λa) and followed by Charles-Quint, in 1520, swearing in J.B. Tour & Taxis, grand master of the empire's postal service (Λb), a postcard of the universal postal union (Λc)

---

5   See letter from Moore to Watson, 22 September 1926: 'Miss Beach cabled September 19th "Joyce requests return typescript with corrections". In going over the chapters, understanding the content as I did not when I first read the manuscript in Maine, I do not see how we could use more than the first section – 12 pages – and another section – pages 24–9. You think we might count on Scofield's co-operating more, I fear, than I think we really could. I remember his indignation against the censors of *Ulysses*, but just before he went away he happened to speak to me emphatically of his disbelief in the present Joyce. I suppose you know without my saying it that I am acutely desirous of our having for *The Dial*, what it is your wish to publish and it is sickeningly ironic to me to refuse the work of one in whose technique I have such delight. I am also distressed to involve us in the disgrace of modifying an affirmative letter. Of course I should, if you could countenance our offering to publish but two sections, concentrate in myself in so far as I could, the whole blame and responsibility' (Wasserstrom 1963, 121–2).

and finally a postal steamer from Congo, arriving in the port of Antwerp in 1895 (∧d) (*JJSB* 75). But then Joyce gave the full report of the course of events: 'a week later they cabled, declining to print it as it stood whereupon I recalled it' (*LI* 245). Joyce implies that this did not really upset him; he just continued writing: 'I then set to work, in spite of moving about, to finish the Δ piece for Wyndham Lewis who wrote to me from Spain that he was coming to Paris to see me. I finished it and sent it to Paris to be typed and hope to correct it tomorrow and send it to you with the MS' (*LI* 245).

This is the same letter in which Joyce, 'devoured' by Antwerp gnats, came up with the idea that Weaver might order a piece and told her 'I am sorry the *Dial* has rejected the pieces' (*LI* 245). And two days later, he told Sylvia Beach he was 'sorry to have lost the strategic position in the *Dial*'s pages and the not excessive booty of 600 \$', adding: 'I suppose it is the fault of my "bourgeoisisme" again' (26 September 1926,[6] *JJSB* 74).

Exile: After the *Dial* refused the four watches of Shaun, Joyce repeated to Harriet Shaw Weaver what he had told Sylvia Beach the day before: 'I suppose no other review will take ∧abcd but I will give it to anyone who will print it' (*LI* 245). On 8 November 1926, he told Weaver that he gave ∧abcd to the American writer and playwright Lewis Galantière 'to sell in the U.S.A.' (*LI* 246). As Dougald McMillan notes, Pound was also planning a new literary review, the *Exile*, and asked Joyce in early November 1926 for the typescript of a new fragment (McMillan 1975, 181). Joyce sent him the four watches of Shaun (8 November 1926, *LI* 247). Pound received the manuscript on 15 November and immediately replied. His critical reaction hit home: 'Nothing short of divine vision or a new cure for the clapp can possibly be worth all the circumambient peripherization' (15 November 1926, *LIII* 145).

The American Caravan: Just before he received Pound's reply, Joyce wrote to him (postmark 14 November) that ∧abcd 'has now been accepted for publication in an annual which a number of American writers bring out in February for \$200. It is the whole of part 3 of the book' (*LIII* 144). As Ronan Crowley suggests, this annual was probably *The American Caravan: A Yearbook of American Literature*, edited by Van Wyck Brooks, Alfred Kreymborg, Lewis Mumford, and Paul Rosenfeld (New York: The Macaulay Company, 1927). But eventually the piece did not appear in this publication either. Thus, Crowley concludes, 'The North American trail for Book III grew cold early in 1927, concluding with the typescript being deposited with Eric Pinker, Joyce's literary agent' (Crowley 2015). In late January, Lewis Galantière acknowledged the arrival in New York of another typescript (of 'The Triangle'), but he told Sylvia Beach that he could no longer place this piece with *The American Caravan*, 'as its first annual had already gone to press'

---

[6]   On the same 26th of September 1926, Joyce wrote to Weaver: 'The *Dial* proposed to delete one third of ∧abcd! Lewis, it seems, has been to Paris and asked for the MS and is coming here as he wants to see me' (*LIII* 142).

(Crowley 2015). That the typescript of 'The Triangle' was sent to Galantière was a result of yet another refusal, this time involving Wyndham Lewis.

The Enemy: In May 1926, Wyndham Lewis had asked Joyce for a contribution to his new review, which he planned to start publishing in 1927. After a few phone calls, Joyce reported to Harriet Shaw Weaver on 21 May: 'Wyndham Lewis rang me up twice last week. I arranged to meet him at the clinic and we went to a café. He told me he wanted to meet me because he is to bring out a critical review (6 times yearly) The Tyrocritic (I hope he will correct the misspelling). It is to be all critical and philosophic and contain no creative work. But he wanted to make an exception in my case and asked me would I give him something. I said I would with great pleasure' (*SL* 313). Joyce sent him 'The Triangle' (aka 'The Muddest Thick That Was Ever Heard Dump'), which he finished on 25 July 1926.[7] On 22 September 1926, Joyce wrote to Sylvia Beach that he 'spent a great deal of time on the piece of Lewis', who had informed him he would call on her: 'I suppose he wants his piece. I have been working at [sic] for the past few weeks again. Here it is. Can you have it ~~copied~~ typed for me in very legible type, double spaced, original and three copies?' She was to send it to Joyce to check, and 'Lewis can have it then' (*JJSB* 72). A few days later, Joyce received the typescript and copies in Brussels: 'All safely arrived. Thanks. Here are three copies, for you, for Lewis and my own (all of them initialled) I have not corrected it. Perhaps if you have time these next days and are reading the piece again you could do it as it strains my eyes. Goodbye now, geometry!' (*JJSB* 73–4). Joyce also instructed her to sign the typescript: 'If I have not signed his copy please forge my signature, printed' (26 September 1926; *JJSB* 74). The typescript that was sent to Wyndham Lewis and that is still present among Lewis's papers is indeed signed in capitals.[8] When the first issue of the *Enemy: A Review of Art and Literature* was published, it turned out that instead of this fragment of 'Work in Progress' Lewis had published his own essay 'The Revolutionary Simpleton', criticizing Joyce (see Chapter 5, *Tales Told of Shem and Shaun*). This first issue was to have come out in January, as Paul O'Keeffe notes. January 1927 was also what is indicated on its cover, but a note inside explained that 'it is appearing in February instead', 'owing to miscalculation as to the time required to prepare it' (qtd in O'Keeffe 2000, 268). Lewis's essay (later republished as 'An Analysis of the Mind of James Joyce' in *Time and Western Man*) dismissed *Ulysses* as 'a monument like a record diarrhoea' (Lewis 1993, 90) and 'Work in Progress' as 'literary horseplay on the one side, and Steinesque child-play on the other' (103). Joyce was not indifferent to Lewis's critique,[9] which he called an

---

[7]   Letter to Harriet Shaw Weaver: 'I finished the Euclid lesson but will not attempt anything more for the present' (*LI* 243).

[8]   Preserved at Cornell University's Department of Rare Books (included in *JJA*).

[9]   For a comparative analysis of Joyce and Lewis, see Klein (1994), who sees them as 'anticollaborators' (*FW* 118.25), that is, not collaborators in the traditional sense; they never co-authored a text, but they 'mined similar veins of aesthetic ideas and structural forms,

'attack',[10] and he regretted that Lewis had not given 'Work in Progress' more time to prove itself.

The Dial (again): Whether or not Joyce was informed about the non-publication of 'The Muddest Thick' in the first issue of the *Enemy* and of its replacement by Lewis's critical essay, Joyce does not seem to have waited until the issue was out to start looking for another place to publish the Euclid lesson. In September 1926, when he had asked Sylvia Beach to forward it to Lewis – 'Goodbye now, geometry' (see above; *JJSB* 74) – he added a postscript: 'If Lewis does not accept the piece I shall be glad if he will let me know within a few weeks so that you may offer it elsewhere' (*JJSB* 74). By 16 January 1927, while Joyce was preoccupied with collecting signatures for his protest against Roth, he had still not heard from Lewis. He realized he could not undertake any legal action against piracy if his works were not protected by copyright and decided not to wait for Lewis's reply before sending it to the US: 'It is impossible to get a reply from Lewis (who was so anxious to have something of mine in his new review) so I have sent the piece to New York to try to get American copyright' (*LIII* 150). By 26 January 1927, the piece had indeed been sent to Lewis Galantière,[11] who was with the International Chamber of Commerce in Paris 1920–27 (*LIII* 140n2) and at that moment acted as a liaison between Joyce and his agent James B. Pinker & Sons. In early February, Galantière asked Sylvia Beach whether he could place 'The Triangle' with *The Dial*, as he felt sure they would be glad to have it.[12] Apparently, he had had a conversation with Marianne Moore on 8 February 1927, during which she had expressed an interest in the mechanics of Joyce's writing. So the next day, referring to their conversation, he sent the piece to Marianne Moore, explaining that the subject was the third proposition of Euclid.[13] A few days later (14 February) Marianne Moore sent 'The Triangle' to Watson, immediately adding that they

---

separately at first but later taking one another's work as implicit and explicit subjects into their fictions' (Klein 1994, 19).

[10] On 20 September 1928, shortly before publication of the Crosby Gaige edition of *Anna Livia Plurabelle*, he wrote to Harriet Shaw Weaver: 'A.L.P. has not yet arrived but I expect her every day. It is a pity that W.L. did not wait for its publication too as it would probably have much mollified his attack' (*SL* 336–7).

[11] A letter from Lewis Galantière to Sylvia Beach, dated 26 January 1927 and enclosed in a letter sent to Beach in early February 1927 (preserved at the University at Buffalo's Poetry Collection), mentions that he had turned over the long manuscript (the four watches of Shaun) to Pinker as directed and that he received the typescript of 'The Triangle'. He wrote that he could not place it any longer in *The American Caravan*, because the first yearbook had already gone to press, but he promised he would try to place it elsewhere.

[12] UB JJC XIII: Correspondence Galantière to Sylvia Beach. I wish to thank Ronan Crowley for sharing his discovery of the submission of a second piece of 'Work in Progress' to *The Dial*. For a discussion of this second submission, see Crowley 2015.

[13] Correspondence held at the Beinecke Library (*Dial*/Scofield Thayer Papers (YCAL MSS 34), Yale Collection of American Literature, Beinecke Rare Book and Manuscript

seemed to her beyond consideration. Nonetheless, she mentions she told Galan-tière she would be happy if the new fragment were found acceptable (Crowley 2015). She even sent a holding letter to Galantière on 26 February, telling him she was sorry they were not yet ready to give an official answer (Crowley 2015). On 3 March, she sent another letter to Watson, asking for his 'final impression of our obligation with regard to the Joyce manuscript': 'I still feel that the manuscript is bad material intrinsically, but I feel also very strongly that your wish in the matter ought to be pre-eminent' (Moore 1997, 229–30). Eventually, Joyce's second attempt to get a fragment of 'Work in Progress' published in the *Dial* was as unsuc-cessful as the first. For Moore's initial verdict remained unchanged, against Wat-son's wish – as she was well aware, writing to Watson on 10 March: 'To argue against taking the article seems contradictory to my assertion that your wish was to decide the matter. My reason for writing is that you may know specifically what has influenced me' (Moore 1997, 230).

One of the arguments in Moore's long explanation to Watson[14] is that Joyce 'is no longer in financial straits' (Moore 1997, 230). But that was a misinterpretation. For financial distress was precisely the most down-to-earth reason for Joyce's eagerness to publish the fragments of 'Work in Progress'. If he did not ask Sylvia Beach for money directly, he tried to do so indirectly by complaining about the dearness of his life as a 'genius': 'It is a hard thing, so I am told, to be a "genius" but I do not think I have the right to plague and pester you night, noon and morning for money, money, and money' (*JJSB* 116). And yet, he kept asking her for favours and services, usually in short messages which typically open with 'Will you please send . . .'. As Noel Riley Fitch notes, the Roth piracy of *Ulysses* and all the stress that ensued (combined with a death in the Beach family) 'opened a fissure in the Beach-Joyce partnership that in five years would widen irreparably' (1985, 243). In April 1927, Sylvia Beach was fed up and wrote a letter, which she never sent (Banta and Silverman 1987, 110):

> I am afraid I and my little shop will not be able to stand the struggle to keep you and your family going from now till June, and to finance the trip of Mrs Joyce and yourself to London 'with money jingling in your pocket'. It is a very

---

Library, Yale University). I owe a debt of gratitude to Ronan Crowley for drawing my atten-tion to this and the following letters.

[14] 'We have elected to exclude obscenity when it was dull, and even the advance guard couldn't think that we consider this piece brilliant. You permitted me to oppose Scofield when he fell below what we felt to be his own standard; so for us to like this would be exceedingly grievous to him, the more that he resists Joyce's present method. When Mr. Joyce has written what would make a magazine illustrious and yet chooses to coerce us, showing even for an author, exaggerated unconcern in the matter of reciprocal consideration, – we refraining from self interested requests – our position is, I feel, the more judicial, our liberty being emphasized by the fact that he is no longer in financial straits' (Moore 1997, 230).

terrifying prospect for me. I have already many expenses for you that you do not dream of, and everything I have I give you freely. Sometimes I think you don't realize it, as when you said to Miss Weaver that my work was 'easing off'. The truth is that as my affection and admiration for you are unlimited, so is the work you pile on my shoulders. When you are absent, every word I receive from you is an order. The reward for my unceasing labour on your behalf is to see you tie yourself into a bowknot and hear you complain. (I am poor and tired too.)

(*JJSB* 209)

The way Sylvia Beach puts herself in parentheses – '(I am poor and tired too)' – is emblematic of how she saw her role in Joyce's life. It is perhaps characteristic that she did not send her letter to Joyce, but then again it is also telling that she wrote it in the first place and that she carefully kept it instead of throwing it away after she decided not to send it. She really must have had enough, but she may also have been aware of the bad timing, for after all these years of looking for a home for his fragments, Joyce had finally found one.

Chapter 3

transition (1927–38)

The Dial was the magazine Joyce had in mind when he said he wanted his fragments 'to appear slowly and regularly in a prominent place' (*LI* 245). According to Dougald McMillan, the magazine 'was by the mid-twenties busy trying to secure imagism as part of the established tradition. And as T.S. Eliot himself remarked, it seemed a little tired by 1927' (McMillan 1975, 16). When Joyce sensed that *Dial* editor Marianne Moore was not exactly enthusiastic about his new work, and erstwhile supporters like Ezra Pound, Valery Larbaud and Harriet Shaw Weaver openly expressed their criticism, Joyce found encouragement in a circle of new friends, whom he invited on 12 December 1926 to hear him read the opening of his 'Work in Progress'. Apart from Sylvia Beach and Adrienne Monnier, the new friends listening to his reading were Elliot Paul, Maria and Eugene Jolas, Myron and Helen Nutting (Fitch 1985, 250). To Helen Nutting, who had sent him flowers afterwards, he expressed in disarmingly simple terms what must have been a genuine feeling of happiness that he had found a supportive audience: 'I am glad you liked the piece I read' (*LIII* 148). And a few days later (21 December 1926), he wrote to Weaver, enclosing 'her' piece. As if to convince her that her doubts were unjustified, he mentioned the reading and emphasized that 'it seems to have made an impression' (*LIII* 149). A second reading was organized on 26 January 1927 and the circle of friends reached an agreement to publish the piece in a new magazine and to reprint the fragments that had already appeared in various journals, this time in the order of their narrative sequence in the projected book, the structure of which was now more or less clear to Joyce (on 21 May 1926 he had written to Harriet Shaw Weaver: 'I have the book now fairly well planned out in my head'; *LI* 241). But it was clear only to Joyce, 'who is so good that nobody ever seems to know just what he is trying to say', according *McNaught*'s (New York, December 1926; UBC 68: 992). On 14 December 1926, *Il Piccolo* in Trieste announced that James Joyce, 'lo stranissimo e stravangantissimo scrittore irlendese' ['the strange and most extravagant Irish writer'] was writing 'un lavoro dal titolo "Un romanzo senza nomi"' ['a work called "An Unnamed Novel"'] (UBC 69: 373), without however mentioning where it was going to be published.

The new magazine was to be called *transition*. Eugene Jolas, a book reviewer and local news editor of the Paris edition of the Chicago *Tribune* who had settled in Paris in the 1920s, had already been making plans for the first issue when he was listening to Joyce's reading. In the autumn of 1926, a few weeks after the death of *This Quarter* editor Ernest Walsh, Jolas had written to Kay Boyle, who had been with Walsh in Monaco during his last days (McMillan 1975, 17). Jolas

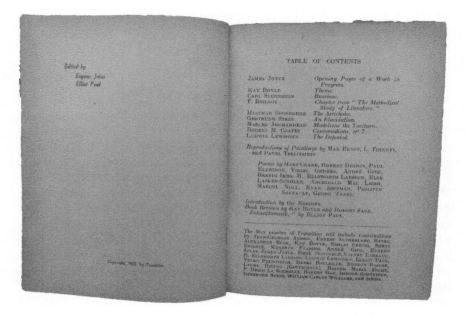

Figure 3.1   Table of Contents in the first issue of *transition* (April 1927)

told her that he wanted to carry on what Walsh had begun and invited her to contribute a story to his new magazine. The first issue came out in April 1927 (see Figure 3.2), and its table of contents indeed features Kay Boyle's story 'Theme' as the second item. Joyce's 'Opening Pages of a Work in Progress' had pride of place (see Figure 3.1).

Since *transition* was the publication in which, for the first time, the fragments of 'Work in Progress' appeared on a regular basis, this was also the place where readers taking an interest in Joyce's writings first got a real sense of the content of his 'Work in Progress'. As the early reviews indicated, the first reactions were – understandably – related to the prominence of the form to the alleged detriment of the content. Some readers did appreciate the way form and content were inextricably linked up with each other, but to an audience reading for the plot, the linguistic and stylistic experiment seemed to be so pre-eminent that it prevented them from finding out what the text 'was about'. With hindsight, it is easy to look back at early searches for a continuous narrative, a plot or a 'skeleton key' and to denounce them as forms of reductive reading, but these attempts were necessary at the time. The same goes for David Hayman's *A First-Draft Version of 'Finnegans Wake'*, which implicitly presented itself as a more straightforward narrative, 'revealing the basic plan', 'the root ideas' and 'the rationale behind the book's form' (*FDV* 3). It may have been criticized for its teleological approach to the organization of the various sections' first drafts (arranged according to the final structure of *Finnegans Wake*, rather than for instance in the chronological order of composition), but the entire

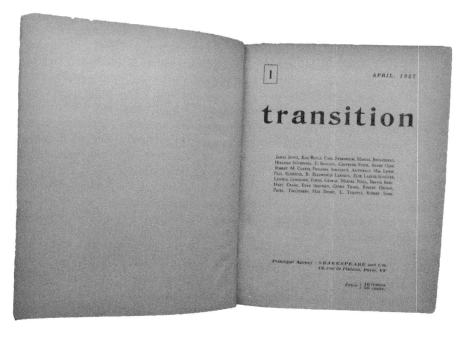

Figure 3.2   Title page of *transition* 1 (April 1927)

community of researchers interested in genetic Joyce studies owes a debt of gratitude to this pioneering work. Not only did Hayman do the hard work of deciphering
Joyce's sometimes near-illegible drafts; he also invited his readers to juxtapose
these early drafts 'with the printed version' and discover 'how simple concepts
have ramified' (*FDV* 3). The following sections therefore make use of the *First-
Draft Version* to highlight and summarize narrative elements, some of which were
already present in the early versions, and briefly explore their ramifications in the
fragments published in *transition*.

transition 1

'Opening Pages of a Work in Progress', *transition* 1 (April 1927), 9–30 [FW 3–29]
(Slocum and Cahoon 1971 [1953], 101, C.70)

Under the heading 'Opening Pages of a Work in Progress' by James Joyce, the first
line ('riverrun brings us back to') was indented several centimetres, so that the
word 'riverrun' appeared almost in the middle of the line. The overture (cf. *FW*
3.01–10.23), written in response to Harriet Shaw Weaver's 'order',[1] introduces

---

[1]   *LI* 245–6, 24 September and 8 November 1926; *LIII* 144, 16 October 1926.

Finnegan and his fall, followed by the thunder of the first 100-letter word (*tl* 9). It tells the story of how Finnegan, 'of the Stuttering Hand' (10), 'stottered from the latter' and 'was dud' (11). His body – lying alongside the river Liffey – is recognizable in the landscape, where the Willingdone Museyroom (13) is located. The guide in the Museyroom mentions 'the three lipoleums' who have allegedly seen a crime, in which 'the Willingdone' and two girls were involved: 'This is the jinnies with their legahorns feinting to read in their handmade's book of stralegy while making their war undisides the Willingdone' (14). With the 'undisides', the early readers on this guided tour got a fair impression of the way Joyce's 'Work in Progress' worked – (1) first of all on the microlevel, with all its '*undecided*' conflicts and the aporetic ambiguities of the mind; (2) on the level of the plot – the design of the text as a model of cognition, the making up of a mind regarding the '*undies*' of the two girls who are involved in the alleged crime, which is the topic of the endless rumours that constitute (3) the macrolevel, the mechanism behind the history of the world – the official history as well as its '*underside*'.

After the guided tour through memory and through history as a landscape sculpted by layers and layers of war casualties and 'Canon Futter' (15), bodies and battlefields, inspired by Joyce's holiday in Flanders' fields and Waterloo – 'This is me Belchum' (15) – a gnarlybird (*FDV* 52) or hen (an incarnation of ALP) collects all the litter of the past in her 'nabsack' – possibly the same bag from which ALP later distributes presents to her children in the 'Anna Livia Plurabelle' chapter, I.8. The 'Annals' passage (*FW* 13.30–14.27) discusses the dates 566 and 1132, associated with the fall (the law of falling bodies, 32 feet per second per second) and renewal. It is followed by the 'Mutt and Jute' dialogue (*FW* 15.29–18.16), in which the invader and the native swap hats (*FDV* 55) and talk about the Battle of Clontarf.

The second section (*FW* 18.17–21.04) tells the story of the alphabet and suggests that 'the world, *mind*, is, was and will be writing its own wrunes forever' (*tl* 25; cf. *FW* 19.36; emphasis added). The combination of runes and ruins in human history appropriately follows after the 'Museyroom' passage on memory as a mental battlefield. The insertion of 'mind' between 'the world' and 'is, was and will be writing' was already in place in the first draft (*FDV* 57). By interjecting this verb, Joyce emphasizes the link between the 'mind' and 'all matters that fall under the ban of our senses' (*FDV* 57). The 'matters' can be all the stuff that history is made of, but here it is also very literally the material onto which human beings have written their 'wrunes', from a bone to a ramskin, 'for that is what papyr is meed of, made of, hides and hints and misses in prints [. . .] Till we finally (though not yet endlike) meet with the acquaintance of Mister Typus, Mistress Tope and all the little typtopies. ~~Fillstop~~ ᶠⁱˡˡˢᵗᵃᵖ' (57). The next sentence originally read (in the first writing layer of its first-draft version): 'So you need hardly tell me that every word will carry 3 score & ten readings through the book of life' (*FDV* 57; BL MS 47482a, 78v). The explicit suggestion to read 'Work in Progress' as a 'book of life' was immediately veiled ('~~life~~ ᴮᵃˡˡʸˡⁱᵛⁱⁿᵍ ᵈᵘᵇˡᵉ ᵘⁿᵈˢ ᵒᵘᵗ'; *FDV* 57) and in *transition* 1 the sentence reads: 'So you need hardly spell me how every word will be bound over to carry three score and ten toptypsical readings throughout the book of Doublends Jined till Daleth, who oped it, closeth thereof the dor' (*t1* 25). The latter part of the sentence was inspired by Joyce's reading of J.-C. Mardrus's translation of 'the essential Suras' of the Koran (Lernout 2007, 58), which ends in the form of a triangle. Joyce noted down 'delta at end' (in notebook VI.B.12:137) and at the bottom of the page (BL MS 47482a, 78v), underneath the 'Daleth' and the 'book of life', he arranged ALP's initials in a typographical triangle, prefiguring Anna Livia Plurabelle's delta as the end of book I, as the subject of Shem and Shaun's geometry lesson in chapter II.2 and as the end of the book:

p | | p
l l
a

The last part of the first chapter (*FW* 21.05–29) is the tale of the Jarl van Hoother and the Prankquean, based on Grace O'Malley, who is refused entrance at the Earl of Howth's castle when the Jarl was at dinner. She therefore presents him with a riddle and kidnaps Tristopher, one of his twin sons. The other son, Hilary, is kidnapped when the Prankquean arrives a second time. The third time, she wants to take the earl's daughter, but at that moment a thunderclap is heard and eventually 'they all drank free' (*FDV* 59; *t1* 28). Finnegan wakes up, but is told to lie down again and 'Finn no more' (30), for he will be replaced by the hero of the so-called democratic period (according to Vico's cyclic view on history), HCE, 'who will be ultimendly respunchable for the hubbub caused in Edenborough' (*t1* 30).

At the back of the first issue of *transition*, an entire page was devoted to a four-line note, explaining that 'The complete text of Mr James Joyce's work, the opening pages of which appear in this issue, will be printed consecutively in Transition from month to month' (*t1* 159).

Immediate Reception: Press Clippings[2]

Even before the first number came out, *L'Intransigeant* announced that *transition* ('revue américaine [. . .] qui paraît à Paris') was on the verge of publishing the opening pages of Joyce's new work, 'intitulé: *Pages d'ouverture d'un ouvrage en cours d'exécution*' (17 March 1927) (UBC 69: 867). On Sunday, 20 March 1927, Robert Sage prepared the ground in the European edition of the Chicago *Tribune*, describing Joyce's 'never-static genius' in terms of the 'superb progress in his development' as a writer in general, and his multiplication of the 'force of words' by 'telescoping them' in particular (UBC 34: 2201). On 28 March 1927, the

---

[2]   The title of *transition* is spelled in various ways in the press, often with capital T and sometimes without italics. Hereafter, the quotations from the clipping respect the original spelling and layout.

correspondent of the London *Daily News* called Joyce 'A Literary Bolshevik', who
was 'making a big stir' in the Latin Quarter. The 'Opening Pages of a Work in
Progress' revealed 'Tendencies noticed in his earlier works', but 'developed [. . .]
to an astonishing pitch', resulting in 'jazz English' (UBC 69: 748). The same
announcement appeared on 7 May 1927 in the Australian *Adelaide Advertiser*; only
the title was changed to 'Bolshevik or Lunatic?' (UBC 68: 748a). The term 'jazz
English'also appeared in a belated review in the Atlanta *Journal* (22 May 1927;
UBC 69: 988). In Melbourne, it took *The Age* more than a month (7 May 1927,
when the second number of *transition* had already been out for more than a week)
to report about the first number: 'Mr. Joyce has a streak of genius perhaps, but it is
singularly akin to madness. Nevertheless, he is sufficiently outré for people to fall
down and worship. Others will possibly think that, if this is literature, thank God
for journalese' (UBC 68: 975).

The *London Weekly* (2 April 1927) quoted the first sentence of 'Work in Progress', suggesting it was not bad as an opening, but 'It might make an even better
ending' (UBC 755: 68). The New York *Evening Post* (20 April 1927) reported – in
the section 'Foreign Intelligence' – about 'The appearance of two new magazines
edited by Americans', *transition* and *Exile* by Ezra Pound. Even though the piece
is not much more than an announcement, it does indicate the special status Joyce
had in 1927: 'no new type of writing [. . .] was ever invented out of hand, unless,
perhaps, it be the new method of Mr. Joyce' (UBC 69: 251).

Harry Hansen, 'The First Reader' in the *New York World* (8 April 1927), only
quotes the sentence with the first thunder word to give his readers 'an idea of what
is going on inside Joyce's head' (UBC 68: 786). The same thunder word was quoted
by the *Daily Herald* (8 April 1927) as a sample of Joyce's 'eccentricities of phrasing and spelling that would make even Gertrude Stein gasp' (UBC 68: 743). The
Saturday Review of Literature (New York, 16 April 1927) also quoted the thunder
word, predicting 'a big printers' strike over in Paris' and referring to the separate
version of Gertrude Stein's 'An Elucidation', folded into the first number of transition (which already contains another version of 'An Elucidation'). Elliot Paul
explained that the version printed in *transition*, 'while containing the correct words,
presented them in the wrong order (through an inadvertence in the printing estab-
lishment)'; the text had therefore been 'rearranged' in the supplement – much to
the jollity of the *Saturday Review*: 'So you certainly have a treat! [. . .] If the matter
isn't completely elucidated to you, it's your own fault' (UBC 68: 1001).

The Boston *Transcript* announced the publication of *transition* 1 as if *le nouveau beaujolais* were *arrivé*: 'transition (sic) at last is here!' Unlike the royal 'We
are not amused', but with the same *pluralis maiestatis*, the review claimed to be
'not very excited, but we are amused'. Having received two versions of Stein's 'An
Elucidation', and 'Feeling it our duty to read both, we did so, then we cut the
supplement and the magazine into little pieces, and pasted them in another order.
This failed to make any sense either'. Similarly, 'we seriously went to work on
"The Opening Pages of a Work in Progress" by the "master" and were getting along
nicely until we came to the following word'– the thunder word again. But this time

no ridicule; simply a warning about 'what you're up against when you read *transition*'. The anonymous review somehow intuited the lots of fun at *Finnegans Wake*, long before the title had been divulged: 'Perhaps you will like it. We did. Even if we didn't find out what it was all about' (UBC 68: 318).

Two weeks after Robert Sage's promising announcement of *transition* in the Chicago *Tribune*, the same newspaper published a less enthusiastic review by Alex Small (10 April 1927), characterizing the new magazine as 'A Transitional Phenomenon' and 'roughly divid[ing] the prose [presented in the first number] into the intelligible and the unintelligible'. Joyce, according to Small, had 'deliberately chosen to break the ordinary social contract between author and reader', thus neglecting the 'fundamental concept of the old esthetic code'. As a consequence, his writing was doomed to remain 'an ephemeral phenomenon', 'an eddy in the current'. 'The idea of communication is flouted', according to Small, and yet it seemed very evident to him what Joyce wished to communicate: 'His obvious aim is to reproduce the flux of consciousness through the human mind'. Small's analysis is negative but subtle and it recognizes the merits of Joyce's text: 'Here is figured, to some extent, that which makes of every man who is ever so little self-conscious, a criminal and a philanthropist, a sadist and a masochist, and a thousand other personalitites at one and the same time'. But the result was 'dull' and 'futile'. And Joyce's admiring 'thurifers' were either 'preposterously naïf' or simply 'poseurs', according to Small (UBC 34: 2204).

No matter how 'transitional' the phenomenon was called, even reviewers who thought the first number of *transition* was unintelligible immediately recognized its value, if only as a curiosity or as an investment: 'it is Greek to us', but 'we wouldn't for worlds want to lose our copy', the Philadelphia *Public Ledger* observed (16 April 1927), for it 'will be an interesting collector's item' (UBC 69: 818). The same day, *The Irish Stateman* (16 April 1927; 136–8) published a darker, more perturbed review by the so-called 'Querist', querying: 'is consciousness really so chaotic? Is it not rather that Joyce has his mental eye so close to the content of consciousness that there comes a distortion of vision?' This distorted image is described in terms of a thousand, thousand slimy things: 'after I have fished in Joyce's obscure chaos, I discover nothing except the writhings and wrigglings of words as eels might writhe or wriggle in a pond'. Which leads to more queries: 'Is literature tending to this? I cannot believe it. I think this *Transition* is to decay' (UBC 34: 2200).

In the New York *Herald Tribune* (Sunday, 24 April 1927), Mary M. Colum wondered whether the editors of *transition* published the opening pages of Work in Progress 'entirely on the reputation of Mr. Joyce' or 'their admiration of his genius, without knowing what it meant' (UBC 34: 2065). *Truth* (20 April 1927; 775–6) felt 'like Alice when, after reading "Jabberwocky", she said: "Somehow it seems to fill my head with ideas – only I don't exactly know what they are!"' But the 'almost voluptuous devotion to all that is dreadful and unhealthy' turned this 'attitudinising' in *transition* into a disease, called 'Jabberwockitis' (UBC 68: 980). It is interesting that the link with Lewis Carroll was pointed out immediately after the first instalment in *transition*, for as late as 31 May 1927, Joyce claimed he had 'never read' Lewis Carroll's work until a few weeks earlier.[3] Nonetheless, whatever Joyce claimed in his letters, he did take a greater interest in Carroll's work than he cared to acknowledge as he took dozens of notes on Belle Moses's *Lewis Carroll in Wonderland and at Home* (New York and London: D. Appleton & Co., 1910), probably as early as the Fall of 1923.[4] Another anonymous reviewer of *transition* 1 in the *Saturday Review of Literature* (New York City, 30 April 1927) was also reminded of Lewis Carroll. The review is called 'Gyring and Gimblin (Or Lewis Carroll in Paris)' and complains about 'the half mythical James Joyce and that lesser mistress of experimental prose', 'the mother founder of the school, Miss Stein', whose work was an 'onslaught and ravage upon the English language'. *transition* had only just started appearing, but the general verdict was already clear: 'Language was made for men, not men for language, but these Parisian expatriates would turn over the age-old structure in order to get new effects' (UBC 33: 986).

transition 2

'Continuation of a Work in Progress', *transition* 2 (May 1927), 94–107 [FW 30–47] (Slocum and Cahoon 1971 [1953], 101, C.70)

The next month (May 1927), HCE was introduced, again, after his first appearance in the *Contact Collection of Contemporary Writers*, together with the rumours of his 'having behaved in an ungentlemanly manner' (*t2* 97). As Bill Cadbury points out, the text of this passage is ambiguous as to where these rumours come from and the accusations 'always seem also to be projections' (Cadbury 2007, 68). HCE's sense of himself is characterized by complacency and this complacent self-image is constantly in conflict with others' impressions of him. Cadbury reads this tension or interplay as a metaphor of 'intrapersonal conflict' (68). This suggests that the mind at work in 'Work in Progress' is Everybody's mind, and that its mechanisms are the mechanisms of the human mind in general.

The first word of the chapter's next section – 'Guiltless' – encapsulates much of the tension of that intrapersonal conflict. HCE is tautologically without guilt because he said so himself: 'Guiltless of much laid to him he was clearly for so

---

[3]   'Another (or rather many) says he is imitating Lewis Carroll. I never read him till Mrs Nutting gave me a book, not *Alice*, a few weeks ago – though, of course, I heard bits and scraps' (*LI* 255). Apart from that, Joyce only mentions Carroll briefly in a letter to Harriet Shaw Weaver of 28 March 1928.

[4]   Source discovered by Viviana Mirela Braslasu, Centre for Manuscript Genetics, University of Antwerp. According to Braslasu, Joyce excerpted passages from Moses's book in the missing notebook VI.X.2, which was compiled in December 1923 according to Danis Rose's dating (Rose 1995, 26).

once at least he clearly expressed himself as being' (*t2* 97). In Phoenix Park, HCE 'met a cad with a pipe' (98) who simply asks him what time it is – 'how much a clock it was that the clock struck' (98). HCE tells him that it is 12 o'clock, but feels the urge to add, for no good reason, that the accusation against him had been made by a creature 'in youman form' but several degrees lower than a snake (98), stressing: 'I am woowoo willing to take my stand, sir, [. . .] that there is not one tittle of truth [. . .] in that purest of fibfib fabrications' (99). The stammering was possibly inspired by Joyce's reading (in the Fall of 1923)[5] of Belle Moses's *Lewis Carroll in Wonderland and at Home* (see above). Moses mentions that Carroll 'stammered, not on all occasions' but 'enough to make steady speaking an effort' (Moses 1910, 75). The hagiographic rhetoric of Moses's discourse lent itself easily to parody: 'He was so truly good and religious, his faith was so simple, his desire to do right was so unfailing, that in spite of the slight drawback in his speech he had the gift of impressing his hearers deeply' (77). The overemphasis on the goodness of his character ('Such was the character of Lewis Carroll') easily creates the impression that it is a form of overcompensation to hide some darker side, which in HCE's case is directly linked to the two girls in Phoenix Park and to the hints of an incestuous relationship with his daughter Issy. In the case of Lewis Carroll, a similar link with girls (not just Alice Liddell, but also Isa Bowman) is made by Belle Moses, but without the hint of a crime: 'most of all he loved to preach to children, to see the earnest young faces upturned to him, to feel that they were following each word. It was then that he put his whole heart into the task before him; the light grew in his eyes, he forgot to stammer' (77).

When Joyce added the stammering to the typescript, this was a new element vis-à-vis the first draft, which read (in the first writing layer): 'I am prepared to stand on the monument any day at this hour and to declare before the deity and my fellows that there is not ᵒⁿᵉ tittle of truth in that purest of fabrications' (*FDV* 64). After mishearing the Cad, HCE stammers out a protest of his innocence, which – as Chris Eagle notes – is 'one of the most condensed moments of disordered speech in all of the *Wake*' (Eagle 2014, 85).

It is interesting that, according to the dating in the *James Joyce Archive*, the stammering in this section was added fairly late – in Febrary and March 1927 (*JJA* 45: 45) – to a typescript that was probably prepared much earlier (December 1923; *JJA* 45: 55; BL MS 47472, 139). In the meantime, Wyndham Lewis's critical remarks in the chapter 'Mr. Jingle and Mr. Bloom' had appeared in *The Art of Being Ruled* (1926), including his characterisation of Gertrude Stein and Joyce's methods as 'a literary system that consists in a sort of gargantuan mental stutter' (Lewis 1989 [1926], 346). On 23 March 1926, Joyce had mentioned *The Art of Being Ruled* to Harriet Shaw Weaver, noting 'a very determined onslaught on my offending work if I am to judge by some of the epithets', such as 'demented', 'stuttering' and

---

[5]   After filling *Finnegans Wake* notebook VI.B.11 (dated 'late Sep–late Nov 1923' by Danis Rose) and before notebook VI.B.6 (dated 'Jan–Feb 1924'; Rose 1995, 25–6).

'squinting'. The 'demented' and 'squinting' refer to the sentence: 'Under the heading of *the Demented* you get Miss Gertrude Stein and the various stammering, squinting punning group who follow her' (Lewis 1989 [1926], 344). The category of the 'Demented' was one of four types that, according to Lewis, constituted the current 'anti-intellect campaign' (344).

When Joyce added the stammer to the 'Guiltless' section (February–March 1927 according to the *JJA*), Lewis's essay 'The Revolutionary Simpleton' in the first issue of the *Enemy* had just been published (February 1927; see Chapter 2) and Pound's skepticism about 'all the circumambient peripherization' (15 November 1926; *LIII* 145) was followed by Harriet Shaw Weaver's doubts about the piece Joyce had written to order, to which he replied on 1 February: 'Your letter gave me a nice little attack of brainache. I conclude you do not like the piece I did?' Joyce told her it was 'the best [he] could do' and 'the editors of *Transition* liked the piece so well that they asked [him] to follow it up and [he] agreed to finish off the part between the end of *Contact* and *The Criterion* for the second number' (*LI* 249). After revising the parts on HCE and reading them to the editors of *transition*, Joyce again emphasized to Weaver that 'They liked it so much that they want the suite for the April number' (*LI* 250). Although the idea of giving HCE a stammer had already been introduced in January 1925 (Eagle 2014, 90), it is quite appropriate that the stuttering in HCE's defensive encounter with the cad is added at the moment Joyce had to defend himself against Lewis's charges of creating 'a sort of gargantuan mental stutter'. Joyce must have been painfully aware of the impossibility to react appropriately to these charges. Any attempt to deny it would be construed as a confirmation. So the best reaction was to emphasize the mental stuttering by worsening HCE's physical stutter, performatively enacting the interaction with a critical environment.

Judging by HCE's stammering overreaction, the cad obviously thinks something fishy must be going on. He mentions it to his wife, who speaks of the matter to an 'overspoiled priest' (*t2* 100), who is overheard telling 'a slightly varied version' to a layteacher of rural science (100). The rumour spreads to other characters such as Treacle Tom and Frisky Shorty, reaching the poet Hosty, who writes a ballad about it: the 'Ballad of Persse O'Reilly' (104–7).

Immediate Reception: Press Clippings

On 18 April 1927, the publication of *transition* 2 was announced in the European edition of the Chicago *Tribune*: 'The May issue of *Transition* will appear tomorrow morning [. . .] A most satisfactory presentation of work by *Surrealistes*, consisting of reproductions of paintings and poems, including a Surrealiste text, by Paul Eluard, is one of the chief interests in a book of varied attractions. [. . .] James Joyce is again represented by an extract from his new work, continued from the April issue' (UBC 69: 1094). *Paris-Midi* announced the publication of the second number on 30 April (UBC 69: 20); a week later, reviews started appearing elsewhere. *The Irish Statesman* (7 May 1927, p. 217) reported that 'The second number of Transition (Paris) is more varied and intelligible than the first. We find an explanation of James Joyce's later manner in one of the articles, which says: "His new work is proof enough that he no longer considers the English tongue – or, in fact, any other *single* tongue – sufficiently rich, flexible, colourful and sonorous to express what he has to say. A new Rabelais, he has tumbled no less than thirteen languages into a smouldering crucible, and we are witnessing the birth of a new literary idiom, which being brought into the world by a thorough artist, stands a much better chance of vitality than esperanto or volapuck'". Without a glossary, however, it seemed more like 'a subtle way of getting past the customs barriers': 'Must one know thirteen languages to read the later Joyce? If so, it will no longer be necessary to prohibit the importation of his books' (UBC 68: 581). The next month, the editorial of the *Catholic Bulletin* (June 1927) reacted to this reaction, unwittingly mimicking the gossip factory that drives 'Work in Progress': 'Thus wrote the *Irish Statesman* of May 7, 1927, giving to an obscure Paris journal more than half of its notice-space for current magazines. Thus can it get in a pleasant gibe at any censorship of obscene literature. [. . .] Some of the Associated Æsthetes, Dublin Wigwam, did manage to get the muck-heap past the Customs Barriers, for all its obscenity'. Joyce must have appreciated this inadvertent echo of the 'muck-heap' in 'Work in Progress', which the *Catholic Bulletin* refers to as 'The new plan of thirteen languages at once' and 'the later manner': 'The prospect of "the later manner" of the Parisian Pillar of Putridity will have a worse effect on their [the Associated Æsthetes'] weak literary nerves than was produced even by Samuel Bowdler Roth of New York, N.Y., U.S.A., when he put *Ulysses* through sewage treatment last winter and spring, while the one hundred and fifty Associated Æsthetes roared aloud, stricken with sympathetic pains' (UBC 32: 676).

In reaction to the second number of *transition*, *The New Statesman* published an article by 'Affable Hawk' (Desmond MacCarthy; 14 May 1927),[6] which opens with an entry from the diary of a man suffering from aphasia, trying to convey that he 'took out the dog this morning; took him out again – had a good night's rest':

Took out the dog this mirughing;
Took out the dog this mirghng;
Took out the dog agagalling;
Took out the dog agallaagnn;
Took out the dog alallaagen;
Hoat a all good nighest ling.

---

[6] Three years earlier, 'Affable Hawk' MacCarthy had already written in the *New Statesman* that *Ulysses* was 'an obscene book' and that Joyce was 'a man of prodigious talent without a clear sense of direction': 'The net result of the great part of his work is to show what is *not* worth doing in fiction – by going one better in the directions in which the modern novel is moving. Is the object to put life under a magnifying glass and show its very texture, the stuff it is made of? Mr. Joyce employs a far stronger glass and writes a vast book about twenty-four hours; one sees the carpet from the point of view of a beetle' ('Books in General', *New Statesman* 20.520 (31 March 1923), 751 [UBC:1131]).

This quote is then compared to a passage from Joyce's second instalment in *transition*: "'Here say figurines billycoose arming and mounting. Mounting and arming bellicose figurines see here. [. . .] When a part so ptee does duty for the holos we soon grow to use of an allforabit'". The passage then passes moral judgement: 'The taste which inspired it is taste for cretinism of speech, akin to finding exhilaration in the slobberings and mouthings of an idiot'. The indignant and outraged conclusion about the fragment from 'Work in Progess' could not be more concise: 'It should disgust' (UBC 34: 2052).

The *Chicago Post* (20 May 1927) informed its readers that 'The magazine has a local representative, George MacGovern, the Studio bookshop, 611 North State street' and that 'the magazine is to be taken seriously', wishing the new venture success *in spite of* Joyce's 'Work in Progress': 'indeed we can imagine it appealing to a fairly large audience, even if the "Continuation of a Work in Progress", by James Joyce, which it is publishing serially, is as much more obscure than "Ulysses" as "Ulysses" was more obscure than "Mother Goose"' (UBC 69: 416).

transition 3

'Continuation of a Work in Progress', *transition* 3 (June 1927), 32–50 [*FW* 48–74] (Slocum and Cahoon 1971 [1953], 101, C.70)

Who caused the fall of HCE is the central question in the third fragment published in *transition*. To answer it, however, the data are 'too few':

> The data, did we possess them are too few to warrant certitude, the testifiers too irreperible but certain it is that ere winter turned the leaves of the book of nature the shade of the great outlander had stood at the bar of the hundred tribunals [. . . The heroic *shade* looms up big, human, erring, forgivable *behind the varied speeches of his fellow men & women.*
>
> (*FDV* 71; emphasis added)

This passage makes the book's structural concept of the rumours explicit. Sylvia Beach mentions in *Shakespeare and Company* that Joyce compared history to 'that parlour game where someone whispers something to the person next to him, who repeats it not very distinctly to the next person, and so on until, by the time the last person hears it, it comes out completely transformed' (Beach 1980 [1956], 185). The idea to work with the 'shade' of a character, which looms 'behind the varied speeches of his fellow men & women' was inspired by Joyce's notes on a series of street interviews in the *Daily Sketch* of 14 December 1922, a source discovered by Vincent Deane. The interviews were part of a petition regarding the trial of Frederick Bywaters, who murdered the husband of his beloved Edith Thompson. He received the death penalty on 9 January 1923, and so did Edith Thompson, as an accessory to the murder. One of the street interviews in the *Daily Sketch* suggests that she was actually more to blame than Bywaters himself: 'Three soldiers were walking together in Fleetstreet: one gave an opinion in which all concurred. It was the *woman* who was to blame. Bywaters played a bad part in the crime, but he was coerced. He *proved* himself a man afterwards' (qtd in Deane, Ferrer and Lernout 2001, 10). After Joyce had excerpted this passage in his notebook (VI.B.10, 71), it took him a year to discover its potential and develop it in his draft of chapter I.3 (in the 'Guiltless' copybook): 'Three soldiers of the Coldstream Guards were walking in Montgomery street. One gave an opinion in which all concurred. It was the *women*, they said; he *showed* himself a man afterwards' (*FDV* 71; BL MS 47471b, 3r; emphasis added). The 'woman' (singular) became 'women' (plural) and whereas Bywaters 'proved' himself a man in the text of the *Daily Sketch*, HCE 'showed' himself a man. In the first typescript, he first showed himself a 'man'; then, 'man' was crossed out and replaced by 'private'; and eventually the whole sentence 'He showed himself a private afterwards' was crossed out (BL MS 47472, 150; *JJA* 45: 189). If HCE's crime was that he exposed himself to two girls in Phoenix Park, it is significant that Joyce decided to undo this sentence alluding to how HCE 'showed himself a man' (Van Hulle 2013, 235) and to the ambiguous 'private' part. This would imply that the cancellation was an instance of creative undoing: the hesitation (first making the crime explicit, then undoing it) resulted in a cancellation that created the 'void' upon which Joyce built the *Wake* – which is what Shem is being accused of in chapter I.7: 'you have reared your kingdom upon the void of your ~~very~~ more than doubtful soul' (*FDV* 120) / 'you have reared your disunited kingdom on the vacuum of your own most intensely doubtful soul' (*FW* 188).

By creating this gap of indeterminacy, Joyce fully exploited the narrative device which Wolfgang Iser called '*Leerstelle*'. The *Wake*'s motto 'In the buginning is the woid' (*FW* 378.29) is evidently much more than a mere pun. From the perspective of cognitive narratology, it is the very engine of fiction, the narrative drive that mobilizes readers' knowledge and experience to supplement what is left unsaid: 'narratives come into being through the interaction between minds and narrative gaps' (Bernaerts et al. 2013, 3). In 'Work in Progress' Joyce thematizes this gap-filling activity undertaken not only by readers, but also by fictional minds. What applies to history – the Chinese-whispers mechanism of the 'parlour game' mentioned by Sylvia Beach – simultaneously applies to the notion of the mind: Joyce's history of 'the world' is also, at the same time, a story of 'a world', the '*Umwelt*'[7] of a fictional mind. It consists of all the experiences of its environment (the

---

[7] '*Umwelt*' in the sense of an organism's perception of its environment is a term coined by the biologist Jakob von Uexküll and re-employed in the context of literary modernism by David Herman in his essay 'Re-Minding Modernism'. Herman regards 'storyworlds' as a staging ground for 'procedures of *Umwelt* construction' and modernist writers as '*Umwelt* researchers in von Uexküll's sense – explorers of the lived, phenomenal worlds that emerge from, or are enacted through, the interplay between intelligent agents and their cultural as well as material circumstances' (Herman 2011, 266).

surroundings, the landscape, the rumours, . . .) and it constantly changes, is evalu-
ated, reevaluated, revised. The mind continuously tries to fill the gaps, possibly
according to the principle which Alva Noë calls 'presence in absence', using a
classic example from sense-data theory (an example he borrows from H.H. Price):
when examining a tomato, you can observe it from various points of view. During
the examination of the tomato, the senses receive new information, but there is
always a part of the tomato that is out of sight. The senses only perceive parts of
the object, and yet it looks as though its occluded parts are present, too. The world
is thus experienced as 'presence in absence' (Noë 2006, 413–4; Blakemore 2013, 40).
The inquiry into minds and narrative often implies a search for gaps, or what
Gérard Genette has termed 'paralipsis' (information that is necessary to make sense
of a story, but is absent in the narration; Genette 1980, 194). One of the fascinating
aspects of Joyce's 'Work in Progress' is that he thematizes this cognitive search.
The mental activity in 'Work in Progress' revolves around this central gap: what
happened in the park? Or what caused HCE to fall? – the question at the heart of
the third fragment in *transition*.

In this third issue, Elliot Paul replied to the tendency of linking Joyce and Gertrude Stein together 'as the leaders of a cult of "unintelligibility"' (McMillan 1975,
204). In the essay 'K.O.R.A.A.' ('Kiss Our Royal American Ass', by analogy with
the heading 'KMRIA', 'Kiss My Royal Irish Ass', in *Ulysses*) he tried to make a
distinction between Stein's approach and Joyce's. His statement, defending Joyce
and Stein against the misunderstandings in the press, was immediately picked up
by the same press.

Immediate Reception: Press Clippings

On 27 May 1927, the *Morning Post* (London) reported that 'The third number of
"Transition" is issued to-day'. Again Joyce and Stein were presented together, this
time as 'two literary Quixotes' who 'address their fellow mortals in language which
only their fellow immortals can comprehend' (UBC 68: 746). The day after the
publication of *transition* 3, the European edition of the Chicago *Tribune* (28 May
1927) reported that it was 'due to reach America June 1' and that 'James Joyce's
new book, which has already caused a furore in New York, is continued, with a
rollicking episode in which "caveman chase and sahara sex" is justified and the
droll and composite hero, H.C. Earwicker, undergoes a siege during which he is
called a list of abusive names' (UBC 69: 1116).

Harry Hansen, 'The First Reader' in the *Virginian Pilot* (Norfolk, VA; 9 June
1927; UBC 59: 1006B), *Greensboro News* (10 June 1927; UBC 69: 1006) and the
Tacoma Ledger (26 June 1927; UBC 69: 1006C), explained that the lower case *t*
in *transition* was to express the editors' belief 'that our age of transition is not
important': 'The third number, just arrived, is full of meat, but we find that the best
results are obtained by writers who use the language in the orderly manner established by long usage'. Judging from the reactions in the press, Elliot Paul's apologia
came across as an arrogant provocation: 'The editors have endeavored to allay the

qualms of simple-minded reviewers (like the undersigned) by explaining the inexplicable. Hence an essay on James Joyce and Gertrude Stein, in the course of which we read: "So many reviewers were terrified by the long word on the first page of Mr. Joyce's new work in Transition No. 1 that it may be well to explain it so they can get on with the story'". The cynical press of course just welcomed this patronizing pass, laying the ball on beautifully for any reviewer to score his next goal. The long pass was an extensive quotation about what a 'reader's pleasure' was supposed to consist of, followed by Hansen's carefully placed header:

> We read that: 'A reader's pleasure does not consist exclusively in being reminded of things he already has noticed or in having familiar ideas restated. Mr. Joyce transcends the informatory function by combining so many references and associations that they shed their topical limitations. [. . .]' This deprives reading of its utilitarian values – its usefulness for communicating ideas, emotions or expressions. [. . .] we'll wager ten to one that even the editors of Transition get their principal pleasure out of being reminded of things and ideas with which they are familiar or to which they are hospitable.
>
> (UBC 69: 1006)

The Sioux City *Journal* (15 June 1927) had the same reaction to the editorial apologia in *transition*: 'The editors are evidently worried as to how unsophisticated people (like the Book Chatterer) will take these cryptic authors [. . .] They may be right, of course. But since a writer presumably writes to be read, it seems to us the sensible and the courteous thing for him is to make his writing as clear as his subject – and his ability – will permit. After all, Joyce or no Joyce, this doesn't pick over the strawberries, does it?' (UBC 68: 1005). The Louisville *Journal Courier* (12 June 1927) also makes grateful use of the editors' explanation 'in their present manifestations' to define the distinction between Joyce and Stein: 'Their methods with words are exactly opposite it seems. Miss Stein strips them of all meaning; Joyce "brings out simultaneously and harmoniously all the meanings (the word) ever had"'. But the purpose appeared to be similar:

> In the light of a concluding short and earnest editorial headed 'Suggestions for a New Magic', it seems clear that whatever means these two 'revolutionaries' employ their end is the same – to dismiss what we know as intelligence and by playing upon the senses to awaken other and deeped [sic] senses in the subconscious.

The 'new magic' the editors of *transition* had in mind was compared to a new mysticism, with an emphasis on their rhetoric: '"We who live in this chaotic age, are we not aware that living itself is an inferno? And having experienced it, can we not express it by seeking new outlets and new regions of probability?"' The quotation goes on for several lines and what follows is a concise and not entirely unjust rhetorical analysis: 'Thus do mystics teach their disciples' (UBC 68: 996).

As Joyce wrote to Claud W. Sykes (on a postcard from the Krasnapolsky hotel in Amsterdam), he received 'threats, denunciations, jokes etc. by every sending of press clippings' (10 June 1927; *LIII* 160). Samuel Dashiell in the New York *Evening Post* (2 July 1927) had 'been studiously reading the third number of the newest English language magazine in Paris, called Transition' and notes about the 'earnest thinkers among the expatriot colony of Montparnasse' that 'Perhaps it really isn't fair to quote them right out in the public prints'. But then he does so anyway. He refers to 'their own undersigned credo' and duly draws attention to its rousing rhetoric: '"Transition will attempt to present the quintessence of the modern spirit in evolution. [. . .] We believe in the ideology of revolt against all diluted and synthetic poetry [. . .] we prefer to skyscraper spirituality, the immense lyricism and madness of illogic"'. Dashiell suggests it would be 'charitable to endow a home for printers and copy readers who have gone crazy and blind producing this Transition literature', and to illustrate his point he quotes a sentence from 'Work in Progress' under the subheading 'Tabloiditis Meek Beside Transition' (UBC 68: 1008).

The reactions to *transition* became a topic in and of themselves. The Minneapolis *Journal* (31 July 1927) reported that 'the new Joyce masterpiece' was different from *Ulysses* and was 'inclined to take up with the Gertrude Stein slant away from language': 'Copies of it have reached this Country and are in the hands of the critics of the literary reviews. These critics quote from it, though they appear to be far from excited about it' (UBC 1: 2162).

transition 4

'Continuation of a Work in Progress', *transition* 4 (July 1927), 46–65 [FW 75–103] (Slocum and Cahoon 1971 [1953], 101, C.70)

In the meantime, the fourth instalment of 'Work in Progress' had appeared in *transition* 4 (July 1927), continuing the stories about HCE. If HCE is not dead, he seems at least to be 'hibernating' (*t4* 49). 'Widow Strong' (49) makes a statement, which reads that she left a 'filthdump near the Serpentine' in Phoenix Park, showing all kinds of footprints, bootmarks and fingersigns 'of a most envolving description' (50). On this spot, an assault seems to have taken place; a suspect called Festy King is arrested. Four judges preside at the trial regarding the assault, but they have to remain noncommittal since the evidence is inconclusive.

In the second section of this chapter, 'HCE's struggles with the public are rendered as a fox hunt, which suggests identification with Parnell' (Cadbury 2007, 83). The rumours keep spreading. 'Who, but who [. . .] was then the scourge of the parts about folkrich Lucalizod it was wont to be asked' (*t4* 64), until one person 'stood forth' (65), 'one nearer him, dearer than all', ALP, 'first warming creature of his early morn, bondwoman of the man of the house' (64).

In Joyce's own case, the ones 'nearer him, dearer than all' tried to defend him in their own way. After Elliot Paul's editorial statement in 'K.O.R.A.A.', Eugene

Jolas, Elliot Paul and Robert Sage jointly wrote a 'First Aid to the Enemy'. It was a direct response to Wyndham Lewis's criticism of *transition*, suggesting an identity of aims with communism and surrealism. The three editors denied any such conspiracy. Strangely enough, this denial was exactly the kind of mechanism that was the engine of 'Work in Progress', concisely summarized in the first word of the 'Guiltless' copybook. No matter how forceful the denial is ('-less'), it does give pride of place to the 'Guilt-' (see above). And indeed, to Wyndham Lewis, the three editors' forceful denial in itself proved exactly his point, as he did not fail to emphasize in the third issue of *The Enemy*.

What this craftsmanship also shows is a form of what Lambros Malafouris calls 'material agency'. According to Malafouris, 'Material signs do not represent; they enact. They do not stand for reality; they bring forth reality' (2013, 118). This 'material agency' has an impact on the mind, which Malafouris regards as 'an emergent product of complex ecological relationships and flexible incorporative forms of material engagement' (239). Applied to Joyce's notebooks and drafts, this material engagement accords with Richard Menary's suggestion that the 'manipulation of environmental vehicles constitutes cognitive processes' (2007, 621). Malafouris's 'material engagement theory', however, is not based on the study of such complex cultural objects as literary manuscripts. It is actually based on some of the most primitive tools as signs of the earliest forms of human culture: knapped stones (Malafouris 2013, 175). Perhaps one could object that knapped stones are hardly comparable to Joyce's intricate, multilingual notes and drafts. And yet, the way Joyce was consciously 'hammering' at his verbal matter, in his notebooks, is not that radically different from the knapper's manipulation[8] of a stone as an 'enactive cognitive prosthesis' (175): 'The knapper first thinks through, with, and about the stone (as in the case of Oldowan tool making) before developing a metaperspective that enables thinking about thinking' (175). Joyce's source texts, reading notes and even the bad criticism, which he recycled in his work, constituted a more sophisticated 'enactive cognitive prosthesis' for the craftsman. But that was not the way the press saw it. Whereas Lewis tried to present Joyce the craftsman as a simpleton, the majority of reviewers perceived Joyce's craft as a form of scorn for 'the ordinary citizen' and 'the plain man'.

Immediate Reception: Press Clippings

The press generally reacted negatively, but not always for the same reasons. While the Paris *Times* reported on 18 June 1927 that 'The July number of *Transition* came to hand yesterday' (and 'James Joyce is represented by another instalment of "work in progress"'), Joyce was being depicted as 'almost a monster' by Shaun Bullock

---

[8] There is something in the way Joyce was 'hammering' at his texts that willingly acknowledged Lewis's *Analysis of the Mind of James Joyce* in terms of craftsmanship and manipulation of 'stuff' (see Introduction).

in his London Letter in the Chicago *Post* (24 June 1927; UBC 68: 252). The next week (1 July 1927) an anonymous reaction was published, disagreeing with Bullock's dislike for Sean O'Casey and Liam O'Flaherty, but agreeing that 'if James Joyce has reached a point where he needs a hybrid of all tongues in which to express the sort of thing that he is expressing – in *Transition* – there is need for some forthright and destructive criticism' (UBC 68: 994). 'The Phœnician' in the New York *Saturday Review of Literature* briefly noted (9 July 1927), as if bored to tears: '*transition* (sic) again comes to us from Paris, containing, as usual, more *Joyce* and *Gertrude Stein*' (UBC 68: 1002).

transition 5

'Continuation of a Work in Progress', *transition* 5 (August 1927), 15–31 [FW 104–25] (Slocum and Cahoon 1971 [1953], 101, C.70)

The fifth fragment (dealing with the 'Mamafesta') had already appeared in *The Criterion*, so it did not require too much work,[9] but while it was being published in *transition* 5, Joyce was preparing a literary response to Wyndham Lewis, which had to be part of the next instalment. To Harriet Shaw Weaver he wrote on 26 July 1927: 'I am working night and day at a piece I have to insert between the last [chapter 5] and [chapter 7]. It must be ready by Friday evening. I never worked against time before. It is very racking' (*LIII* 163). In April, he had suggested to Harriet Shaw Weaver that she try to guess the title of his book; in the same letter of 26 July, he told her that 'The piece I am hammering at ought to reveal it' (*LIII* 163). The answer to the first of the 12 questions that make up chapter 6 is 'Finn MacCool', which was indeed a hint. But what is perhaps more revealing is Joyce's word choice ('hammering at') as it emphasizes Wyndham Lewis's criticism that Joyce was 'essentially the craftsman' (Lewis 1993 [1927], 88). According to Lewis, Joyce did not have any 'special point of view, or none worth mentioning' (88):

> What stimulates him is ways of doing things, and technical processes, and not things to be done. Between the various things to be done he shows a true craftsman's impartiality. He is become so much a writing-specialist that it matters very little to him *what* he writes, or what idea or world-view he expresses, so long as he is trying his hand at this manner and that, and displaying his enjoyable virtuosity.
>
> (Lewis 1993 [1927], 88)

When, during his holiday in Belgium, Joyce had suggested to Harriet Shaw Weaver that she 'might "order" a piece' and he would 'do it' (*LI* 245), he added that 'The

---

[9]   Levels 7 and 8 in the *James Joyce Archive*; 'stage II' in Mikio Fuse's scheme (Fuse 2007, 99).

gentlemen of the brush and hammer seem to have worked that way' (*LI* 245) – according to the method of the Flemish primitives and the medieval guilds. Now he was hammering at another piece, thus 'piecing' his book together. Although Lewis's criticism that Joyce did not have a special point of view is quite unfair (his view on history as rumour-mongering, for instance, is certainly 'worth mentioning'), his observation that Joyce was a craftsman was perspicacious, and Joyce may not even have objected to it. To some extent, his way of reacting proved Lewis's point. By taking Lewis's attack as an implicit 'order' for another 'piece', he confirmed that the way he functioned best was in the manner of the medieval associations of craftsmen. And he had found a great medieval example in the work of Dante Alighieri. 'Like Dante in *The Divine Comedy*', Noel Riley Fitch notes, 'Joyce repaid old grudges and settled scores by scattering his enemies throughout his work' (264).

Immediate Reception: Press Clippings

When *transition* 5 came out, the Chicago *Tribune* reported about it under the heading 'Boston Bans Transition': 'With the May and June issues of *Transition* already banned in Boston and Philadelphia up in arms over the July number, speculation is now rife as to what will be the fate of Number Five which has just appeared' (UBC 69: 241). 'It is as difficult to treat these things any more seriously than the ordinary citizen, who pays his taxes and supports the Constitution of the United States, treats the work of the Modernists in painting with which he has been afflicted of late', was the *Minneapolis Journal*'s opinion about Joyce's 'New Masterpiece' (31 July 1937; UBC 1: 2162). Marjorie Peters in the *New York World* (14 August 1927) drew attention to the way *transition* announced itself 'a little pompously' as being of the *avant-garde* and for it, characterizing the journal's content as 'A New Tongue for Literary Snobs' (UBC 33: 576). In Australia, the Sydney *Daily Telegraph* (7 August 1927) invited its readers to decide 'which of the two is the sillier', Joyce or Stein, concluding that it did not matter how much scorn they felt: 'the scorn the plain man has for this school is as nothing compared with the scorn this school has for the plain man' (UBC 68: 2161).

transition 6

'Continuation of a Work in Progress', *transition* 6 (September 1927), 87–106 f. [*FW* 126–68] (Slocum and Cahoon 1971 [1953], 101, C.70)

On 14 August 1927, Joyce announced the completion of the sixth fragment to Harriet Shaw Weaver: 'At last I finished the piece for t.6 and had the MS sent you in two parcels. Please let me know if you get it. No 11 [question 11 in the questionnaire] is ∧[Shaun] in his know-all profoundly impressive role for which an "ever devoted friend" (so his letters are signed) unrequestedly consented to pose' (*LI*

257–8). The same day, he told Sylvia Beach: 'In question 11 I have allowed Shaun to speak with the voice of The Enemy'. And in the same breath, he mentioned the hostile reception of his work: 'The opposition to my book is now so acute and general (even Miss Weaver in a letter yesterday speaks of "wallowing in its verbiage") that it would seem to me almost a good policy to take a 6 months holiday and rest' (*JJSB* 129). Weaver's comment ('wallowing in its verbiage') goes some way to explain the length of his letter to her of the same date, in which he also complains about the 'indignant hostility' against his work, which he calls an 'experiment in interpreting "the dark night of the soul"' (*LI* 258).

Wyndham Lewis's criticism is indeed recognizable in the answer to question 11 in the questionnaire (*FW* 126–149.10), each item of which discusses another cluster of characters. These are enumerated in a list of sigla preceding the first draft.[10] The title of the book itself (represented by a square) appears among the characters, HCE, ALP, the four old men (here the four capital cities of Ireland), Sigurdsen, Kate, the 12 customers, the 29 Maggies or leap-year girls, Issy, Shaun and Shem. The last question is by far the shortest, and is preceded by the longest one, concerning Shaun. His answer to the question whether he would help his brother in times of need is simply no, but it takes him about 20 pages to explain the difference between him and his brother.

The controversy between Lewis (interested in the notion of space) and Joyce (who, according to Lewis, was too preoccupied with the notion of time) is reflected in the so-called 'dime-cash' problem (*FW* 149.11–150.14), considered from the point of view of a 'spatialist'. In the first draft, the 'dime' was originally spelled 'time': 'my disposals of the same ~~time~~-dime-cash problem elsewhere, *naturalistically*, of course, from the blinkpoint of a spatialist' (*FDV* 99; emphasis added). In *The Art of Being Ruled* (1926), the 'spatialist' Wyndham Lewis had already criticized the 'considerable degree of *naturalism* aimed at' in *Ulysses*, suggesting a correspondence between Leopold Bloom's stream of consciousness and the conversation of Mr Jingle in Charles Dickens's *The Pickwick Papers*. His conclusion was that 'by the devious route of a fashionable naturalist device – that usually described as "presenting the character from the *inside*" – [. . .] Mr. Joyce reaches the half-demented *crank* figure of traditional English humour' (Lewis 1989, 346; original emphasis). And in *Time and Western Man*, he quoted himself extensively on this topic, adding that Joyce's method 'is based upon a flaubertian naturalism' (102) and that 'Work in Progress' is 'still in the manner of [*Ulysses*]' (103).

If this implies that it is also a naturalistic form of 'telling from the inside' (102), it has interesting consequences for the notion of Modernism. As discussed in the Introduction, Virginia Woolf's 'Look within' as a motto of literary Modernism was part of the rhetorical strategy in her essay 'Modern Novels' to distinguish her generation of writers from the previous ones. Presenting the method of 'telling from within' as a form of naturalism punctures the 'Make it new' rhetoric. In *Ulysses*,

---

[10]   BL 47473–150v; *JJA* 47: 2; cf. also BL 47473–132v; *JJA* 47: 28.

Joyce – according to Lewis – 'had to pretend that we were really surprising the private thought of a real and average human creature', but for an average human being 'Mr. Bloom was abnormally *wordy*. He *thought in words*, not images, for our benefit, in a fashion as unreal, from the point of view of the strictest naturalist dogma, as a Hamlet soliloquy' (Lewis 1989 [1926], 347).

If Bloom is 'wordy', the thought process at work in *Finnegans Wake* is even more so. The question however is: who is doing the thinking. This makes 'Work in Progress' interesting from the point of view of cognitive narratology. One can only speak of 'telling from the inside' if – within the fictional world – there is an outside from which it is to be distinguished. In *Ulysses*, the first scene with Bloom as main focalizer presents him first 'from the outside' as he is making breakfast for Molly and gradually, by means of his sensory perception of the cat's presence, his empathetic attempt to figure out how the cat must see him is told 'from the inside'. In *Finnegans Wake*, however, there is no such gradual process of entering. Readers 'enter' the mind at work as soon as they open the book. No narrator guides them from an 'outside' narrative universe to an 'inside'. You become part of a stream of consciousness as soon as you read the first word, 'riverrun'.

As to the question *whose* consciousness, a possible answer might be H.C.Everybody's – which would imply a generic human mind, regarded as a 'work in progress'. The work's title is being asked for in the third item of the questionnaire, and has a siglum of its own (the square), like the other character amalgams of *Finnegans Wake*. From a traditional Cartesian perspective the *res extensa* of the book, wrapped in the container of its cover can easily be allegorized as the skull, containing the 'wordy' thoughts, separating them from the material world according to the Cartesian dualism of mind and body. If one works with this stream-of-consciousness interpretation, readers of the book *Finnegans Wake* – opening *in medias res* (in the middle of *res cogitans*, as it were), with a direct hint that the reader is in a 'riverrun' of consciousness from the first word onwards – have an advantage over the readers of the pre-book publications (except for the fragment in *transition* 1), who had to do without that hint. But this does not need to be a disadvantage. For the shorter pre-book publications present fragments of this fictional mind as a work in progress in a way that is less protected, less contained, but presented instead as 'A continuation', in direct contact with the outside world. David Herman's definition of literary modernism in terms of '*Umwelt* research' (Herman 2011, 266) thus acquires an extra dimension. The pre-book publications play an enactive role in a model of the mind that is more extensive than the Cartesian internalism (with its *res cogitans* versus *res extensa*).

The instalment of 'Work in Progress' in *transition* 6 is a good example. What Joyce did is more complex than a straightforward autobiographical approach; it comes closer to what H. Porter Abbott called 'autography', with its fragile and semi-permeable borders between the cognitive-narratological levels of [1] the imaginative production of the storyworld, [2] the storyworld itself and [3] the reception. Joyce (level [1]) is confronted with serious criticism (level [3]) of his work such as the analyses by Wyndham Lewis. As a Modernist writer he has a special interest in evocations of fictional minds (level [2]). In order to evoke such a cognitive process he takes recourse to the cognitive process he is most familiar with: his own mind (level [1]). His experience, reading Lewis's criticism (level [3]), has a creative effect on him. It triggers his imagination. What he then writes is a simulation[11] of this triggering, a 'fictive imagination' as Fred Higginson called it (see also Chapter 4). The result is not a 'telling from the inside', because that would maintain the Cartesian body/mind split of the 'inside' and the 'outside'. Instead, what Joyce presents might be thought of as the enactment of an 'extended' mind at work.

The instalment in *transition* 6 involves the simulation of extensive interaction with a cultural environment. This environment is evoked by means of references to T.S. Eliot at Faber and Faber, *The Criterion* ('Talis and Talis [. . .] who is on at the *Craterium*; *FDV* 99) and Lewis's vorticism ('At a recent postvortex'; *FDV* 99). Joyce's reaction to Wyndham Lewis is modelled after stimulus-response behaviourism, which is one of the schools of thought that are criticized by Lewis in *The Art of Being Ruled*. After having ridiculed Bergson as a 'fashionable, unskeletal, feminine philospher of the flux' (338), Lewis starts railing at 'Professor Watson', 'the greatest exponent of behaviorism, and the king of *testers*' (339). The stammer (like HCE's) is the element that connects the philosopher and the behaviourist according to Lewis: 'Hatred of *the word* goes hand in hand with hatred of the intellect, for *the word* is, of course, its sign. Language is one of the things to be broken up – a stammer, a hiatus, an ellipsis, a syncope, a hiccup, is installed in the midst of the verb, and the mind attacked through its instrument' (339; original emphasis). In the schools of American psychology, 'deriving from William James', this war against words was being waged more 'epically' than elsewhere, according to Lewis. It was in the laboratories of the Watsons of the world that the word was being 'annihilated' (339). Watson, the 'tester', suggested there were two categories of behaviour, 'implicit' and 'explicit'; apart from the word 'tester', Joyce noted down the adjectives 'implicit' and 'explicit' (notebook VI.B.20, page 72), based on the following description by Lewis:

> These two forms of behaviour are the big and the little; or; as he puts it, those affecting the large musculature of the animal, and those affecting the small. The former, the big, he calls *explicit* behaviour. The lesser, the small, he calls *implicit* behaviour. [. . .] A man hits you on the head. Either (1) you respond by striking him back: in which you are giving an example of *explicit behaviour*; or (2) you go away and think it over, and perhaps ten years after you approach him again, and return the blow. His blow is *a stimulus* whose response, your blow, will then

---

[11] Patrick Colm Hogan argues that 'simulation is closely related to what literary writers refer to as "imagination"' and that one can even 'identify the literary process of imagination with the quotidian process of simulation' (3). He defines simulation as 'our ordinary cognitive process of following out counterfactual or hypothetical trajectories of actions and events in imagination' (Hogan 2013, xiii).

be ten years overdue. Where explicit behaviour is delayed (i.e. where deliberation ensues) the intervening time between simulus and response is given over to implicit behaviour (to 'thought processes').

(340)

Of these two types, the implicit behaviour is 'claimed' by what Watson calls 'the introspectist'. From Watson's point of view the 'introspectist' thus 'denies to us' this implicit behaviour by placing it inside a so-called 'mind': 'When the psychologist threw away the soul he compromised his conscience by setting up a "mind" which was to remain always hidden and difficult of access' (Watson qtd in Lewis 1989 [1926], 340). This topic is echoed in more recent debates relating to embodied, enactive[12] or situated cognition. Louise Barrett, for instance, argues that 'to contrast "cognitive processes" with "noncognitive" stimulus-response machines[13] or "automatons" is to generate a false dichotomy [. . .] because, broadly speaking, any process by which sensory input is transformed into behavioral output can be considered "cognitive", and so a stimulus-response mechanism is a legitimate "cognitive" process' (Barrett 2011, 10).

After reading Lewis's rant against behaviourism, Joyce responded 'behavioristically' (*t6* 98), employing this adverb in the first draft of chapter 6, in which 'Professor Levis-Brueller' (99) tries to explain the 'dime-cash problem' and starts with the question '*Why am I not born like a Gentilman*' (99), alluding to Lewis's discussion of Bloom's 'gentleman-complex – the Is he or isn't he a gentleman? – the phantom index-finger of the old shabby-genteel' (Lewis 1993 [1927], 105). But soon enough the Professor notices that his message is not getting across: 'As my explanations here are probably above your understandings I shall revert to a more expletive method which I frequently use when I have to sermo with muddleclass pupils' (*t6* 100). To illustrate his point he tells the fable of 'The Mookse and the Gripes' (101), followed by a second illustration, the Burrus and Caseous episode, alluding to Brutus (Shaun) and Cassius (Shem), who killed Julius Caesar. The illustrations to his 'muddleclass pupils' were drafted very shortly before the publication in *transition* 6, as David Hayman notes: 'It was sent to Miss Weaver in August [1927]. The author appears to have worked on this chapter until the very last moment. In order to include this new material the printer added five extra pages to the chapter taking the discrepancy into account by numbering the last five pages 106 a-f' (*FDV* 101). Five years later, in his 'Homage to James Joyce' (published in *transition* 21, March 1932), Eugene Jolas recalled this moment 'when a four-page

---

[12] Enactivist philosophers are fully aware of 'the standard charge that any enactivism that rejects representationalism – and hence cognitivism – in an uncompromising manner must reduce to some kind of behaviorism' (Hutto and Myin 2013, 17).

[13] According to Louise Barrett 'the real "problem-solving machine" is not the brain alone, but the brain, the body, and the environmental structures that we use to augment, enhance, and support internal cognitive processes' (Barrett 2011, 219).

addition had to be made after the first four hundred copies of the review had already been stitched':

> Everything was held up. The addition that had been announced by telephone came by the early mail and was rushed to the composing-room. During the day the completed copies were ripped apart, and by evening a sufficiently clean proof of the new text had been obtained for us to feel we could call it a day.
>
> (252)

The number of extra pages was actually six. The fable of the Mookse and the Gripes ends at the bottom of page 105 ('*I no canna stay!*'). Page 106 opens with the Professor's smug recapitulation ('As I have now successfully explained to you . . .'); on the next page (106 *a*; see Figure 3.3) he reminds his audience: 'My heeders well recoil with a great leisure how at the outbreak before trespassing on the space question [. . .] I proved to mindself as to your sotisfiction how his abject all through [. . .] is nothing so much more than a mere cashdime however genteel he may want ours' (106 *a*) – another allusion to what Lewis called the 'gentleman-complex' of the 'shabby-genteel' (Lewis 1993, 105).

This is immediately followed by the Professor's second illustration, the Burrus and Caseous episode: 'Burrus, let us like to imagine, is a genuine prime, the real choice, full of natural greace [. . .] whereat Caseous is oversely the revise of him' (106 *a*).

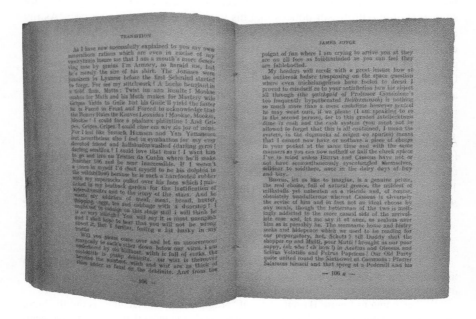

Figure 3.3   'Continuation of a Work in Progress' in *transition* 6, pages 106 and 106a

In the chapter 'Hatred of Language and the Behaviorist "Word-Habit"' (*The Art of Being Ruled*), just before discussing Watson's behaviourism and the 'war of words, or against words' in American psychology, Lewis had argued that 'without the control of the intellect, words have tended to go over into music' (Lewis 1989 [1926], 339). Joyce alludes to this theme on page 106 *d* when he introduces 'Margareen': 'We now romp through a period of pure lyricism of shamebred music evidenced by such words in distress as *I cream for thee, Sweet Margareen*' (106 *d*). Her intermediary position ('Margareena she's very fond of Burrus but, alick and alack! She velly fond of chee'; 106 *e*) is appropriately presented as an intermezzo in the 'antomime art of being rude' (106 *e-f*). In *The Art of Being Ruled*, Lewis had made a link between Joyce's literary project and the 'exploitation of madness, of tics, *blephorospasms*, and eccentricities of the mechanism of the brain' (347; emphasis added), which Joyce alludes to on page 106 *f* ('a boosted blasted bleating blatant bloaten blasphorus blesporous idiot'), before finishing the wordy answer to question 11 and concluding the questionnaire with the brief answer to question 12: '*Semus sumus!*' So, the next author in *transition* 6, Robert Desnos, could not take the floor on page 107 ('Liberty or Love', *t6* 107) until after these six extra pages (106 *a-f*) and the very last words of 106 *f*: '*(to be continued)*'.

Immediate Reception: Press Clippings

'Somewhat belatedly the September number of *Transition* reaches us', the Paris *Times* ('In the Quarter') reported on 29 August 1927 (UBC 69: 244). Two weeks later it was only 'just out' according to the St Louis *Post Dispatch* (10 September 1927), in which *transition* was described as a magazine 'for the obstreperously modern and the unintelligibly futuristic'. That the magazine's name was not capitalized was still an issue; this time the explanation was that 'Only the bourgeois-minded, the hopelessly unoriginal philistines submit to rules these days'. More than 30 lines were quoted from the instalment of Joyce's 'latest masterpiece', for that was 'Perhaps the most distinguished contribution to the September issue' (UBC 68: 2157). The Chicago *Tribune* (24 September 1927), however, was more interested in the fact that 'Two Chicagoans' were represented, Ernest Hemingway and Blanche Matthias (UBC 69: 2170). In the 'Magazines' section of the *Irish Statesman* (10 September 1927), the September issue of *transition* – 'Here we have the ultra-moderns' – was compared to other magazines: '*The Criterion* appears mediæval, almost classical in its remoteness from the world revealed in Transition. Here Gertrude Stein prattles on like a child singsonging in the nursery some phrases it has heard [. . .] while James Joyce burrows deeper into the mysteries of language'. The metaphors describing Joyce's work are strikingly animalistic: 'He is like a terrier who burrows energetically into a hole so that at last one only sees an agitated ceaseless waving of the tip of its tail: a great literary talent wasting itself on obscurities which it will never be worth anyone's while to unravel [. . .] All there is here is an immense virtuosity in the use of words, and an energy in the writing as tireless as the wriggling of eels' (UBC 33: 589).

transition 7

'Continuation of a Work in Progress', *transition* 7 (October 1927), 34–56 [FW 169–95] (Slocum and Cahoon 1971 [1953], 101, C.70)

In *This Quarter*, Shem's 'improperia' had already been presented as 'shemeries': 'Shem Macadamson, you know me and I know you and all your shemeries' (*TQ* 119; cf. *FW* 187.35–36). This is one of the coinages based on the negative reviews of *Ulysses*, notably James Douglas' 'Beauty – and the Beast' (*Sunday Express*, 28 May 1922), on which Joyce made a few notes in notebook VI.B.06, page 117. The original word was 'Joyceries', mentioned in a particularly negative context: 'if Ireland were to accept the paternity of Joyce and his Dublin Joyceries, which outrosse the rosseries of the Parisian stews, Ireland would indeed [. . .] degenerate into a latrine and a sewer' (Douglas 1922, 5; cf. Van Hulle 2008, 86). After the description of Shem's home-made ink in a Latin latrine of verbal faeces – '*in manum suam evacuavit* (highly prosy, crap in his hand, sorry!)' (*TQ* 118; cf. *FW* 185) – the discussion of his shemeries contains some excellent examples of the performative quality of Joyce's language.

One of these examples is the one Samuel Beckett picked out to argue that the English language was 'abstracted to death' (Beckett 1972 [1929], 15) and to illustrate how Joyce 'desophisticated' (15) it by enacting what it is about (see also Introduction). The example is the phrase 'in twosome twiminds' (*FW* 188.14), which, in the first draft, read: 'you have become a **doubter** of all known gods and [. . .] you have reared your kingdom upon the void of your ~~very~~ more than doubtful soul' (*FDV* 120). The manuscripts show the process of Joyce's 'de-abstraction'. In the second draft, the '**doubter**' became a '**rawdoubter** in all known & unknown gods' and the soul not just 'more than doubtful' but 'far more than dubious' (*JJA* 47: 382; 47471b, 69r). The fair copy speaks of a '**raw doubter** in gods known and unknown' (*JJA* 47: 392; BL MS 47474, 16). In the second typescript of chapter I.7, sections 1+2, Shem has 'become a ~~raw doubter in~~ of **twosome twiminds** fornenst gods ~~known and unknown~~ hidden and discovered' and the 'far more than dubious' soul has become 'most intensely doubtful' (*JJA* 47: 444; BL MS 47474, 66). This is how Shem was presented in *This Quarter*: 'you have become **of twosome twiminds** fornenst gods, hidden and discovered [. . .] you have reared your disunited kingdom on the vacuum of your own most intensely doubtful soul' (119; cf. *FW* 188) – which is also how it appeared in *transition* 7 (51).

The marked pages of *transition* served as a starting point for the printer of *Finnegans Wake* in the mid-1930s (*JJA* 47: 503). To these marked *transition* pages, Joyce added an extra fragment, which however never made it into *Finnegans Wake*. The text in *transition* 7 (page 35; cf. *FW* 169.20) describes 'Shem's bodily getup' which consists of a long list of malformations, 'an adze of a skull, an eight of a larkseye, the wheol of a nose, one numb arm up a sleeve' etcetera ending with 'a bladder Tristended' (*t7* 34–5). After 'Tristended', Joyce wanted the printers to insert a full stop and the following explanation:

To enjoy to the full best the absent vignette on the opset page (perhaps **the madest ting that was ever here done**) one has merely to moor in mind that the skull of Shemus, the ~~bard~~ ˢⁱᵐᵖ, suffering is the skull of [blank space], that the eye of S. the b. s. is the eye of Tiresias Furlong, that the nose of S. the b. s. is the nose of Artlove Coogan, that the arm of S. the b. s. is the arm of Emitharmon MacNeill [. . .]

(*JJA* 47: 553; BL MS 47475, 278v; cf. Joyce 2002, 638)

The title of one of the three *Tales Told of Shem and Shaun* ('The Muddest Thick That Was Ever Heard Dump'; see Chapter 5) reverberates in the highlighted passage, 'the madest ting that was ever here done'. The 'bard' was substituted with the 'simp' and this change was made with the same writing tool as the one used for the second half of this two-page addition. This second half continues the enumeration, explaining 'that the shoulder of Shem, the serf, militant, is the shoulder of George Gordons Natans' (*JJA* 47: 553; BL MS 47475, 278v). The list ends with the explanation 'that the liver of Shem, the scribe, triumphant is the liver of which Dr Jecus divides with Mr Hoyt' (*JJA* 47: 554; BL MS 47475, 279r). The evolution from a 'simp, suffering' to a 'serf, militant' and finally 'the scribe, triumphant' indicates why the original 'bard' had to be changed to a 'simp'. The 'simp' recalls Wyndham Lewis's 'The Revolutionary Simpleton', suggesting that with this late addition Joyce tried to paint a portrait of Shem the Penman as the criticized and misunderstood bard who triumphantly managed to write himself out of this period of suffering. Whatever may have been the motivation for Joyce to write this addition, it certainly did not fit in with the negative picture of Shem by his brother Shaun in chapter I.7 and it was not incorporated in the text. After the enumeration of all the 'shemeries', the floor is given to 'the sloothering slide of her, giddygaddy, grannyma, gossipaceous Anna Livia' (*t7* 56).

Immediate Reception: Press Clippings

After the long quotation from Joyce's contribution to *transition* 6 in the St Louis *Post Dispatch* of 10 September, the newspaper (11 October 1927) was convinced that 'no doubt those who read it [were] eager for more'. It therefore published yet another 'masterly passage' from 'A further installment of the new masterpiece by James Joyce, author of the immortal "Ulysses"' – a quotation of more than 20 lines from the portrait of Shem the penman, producing 'from his unheavenly body a no uncertain quantity of obscene matter not protected by copiright in the United Stars of Urania'. By alluding to the Roth affair, Joyce again incorporated his immediate '*Umwelt*' – his perception of his cultural and material circumstances – in his 'Work in Progress', and the reference was clearly picked up by his contemporary readers, as the selection of this particular reference to the United States in the US press shows. The comments in the newpapers were, in their turn, (re-)recycled in Joyce's autographic system of writing 'over every square inch of the only foolscap available, his own body, till by its corrosive sublimation one continuous present tense integument slowly unfolded all marryvoising moodmoulded cyclewheeling history' (UBC 68: 978).

transition 8

'Continuation of a Work in Progress', *transition* 8 (November 1927), 17–35 [*FW* 196–216] (Slocum and Cahoon 1971 [1953], 101, C.70)

In *Le Navire d'Argent*, the title 'From Work in Progress' had been followed by an explanatory note, emphasizing that the English printers of *The Calendar* had 'once again' ('une fois de plus') refused to print the text of the fragment in its entirety ('intégralement'):

> *Une revue londonienne 'The Calendar' devait publier en Octobre un fragment d'une œuvre inédite de James Joyce. – Les imprimeurs anglais, une fois de plus, refusèrent d'imprimer* intégralement *le texte. La Rédaction du 'Calendar' pria l'auteur de faire des modifications. M. Joyce refusa de discuter la question et retira son manuscrit. – Nous pensons être agréables à ceux de nos lecteurs qui aiment la littérature anglaise en leur offrant dans ce numéro le texte incriminé.*
>
> (*Nd'A* 59)

For the publication in *transition* 8, an English version of this note was typed to be included as a footnote on the opening page of the fragment:

> A London magazine <u>The Calendar</u> was to have printed in October (1925) a fragment of the unpublished work by James Joyce. The English printers – once again – refused to set up the text as it stood. The editors of The Calendar requested the author to make certain modification. Mr. Joyce refused to discuss the question and recalled the manuscript. For the benefit of our readers who are interested in English literature, we are submitting the incriminating text in this number.
>
> (From *Le Navire d'Argent*, September 1925)
>
> This extract is reprinted (in its revised form) by kind permission of Mlle Adrienne Monnier.
>
> (*t8* 17; cf. *JJA* 48: 173; Yale 6.1–1)

Another footnote appeared on the instalment's last page, after the 'hitheranthithering waters of. Night! (1.)': '(1) This piece concludes Part I. of James Joyce's new work. The opening pages of Part III. will appear in the next number of *transition*' (*t8* 35). But the note was a bit too optimistic. The first chapter of Book III would not appear until March 1928. In the meantime, Joyce changed his mind and decided to publish a piece from Book II first.

transition's campaign to defend its champion was in full swing. William Carlos Williams addressed the pressing question whether Joyce's 'Work in Progress'

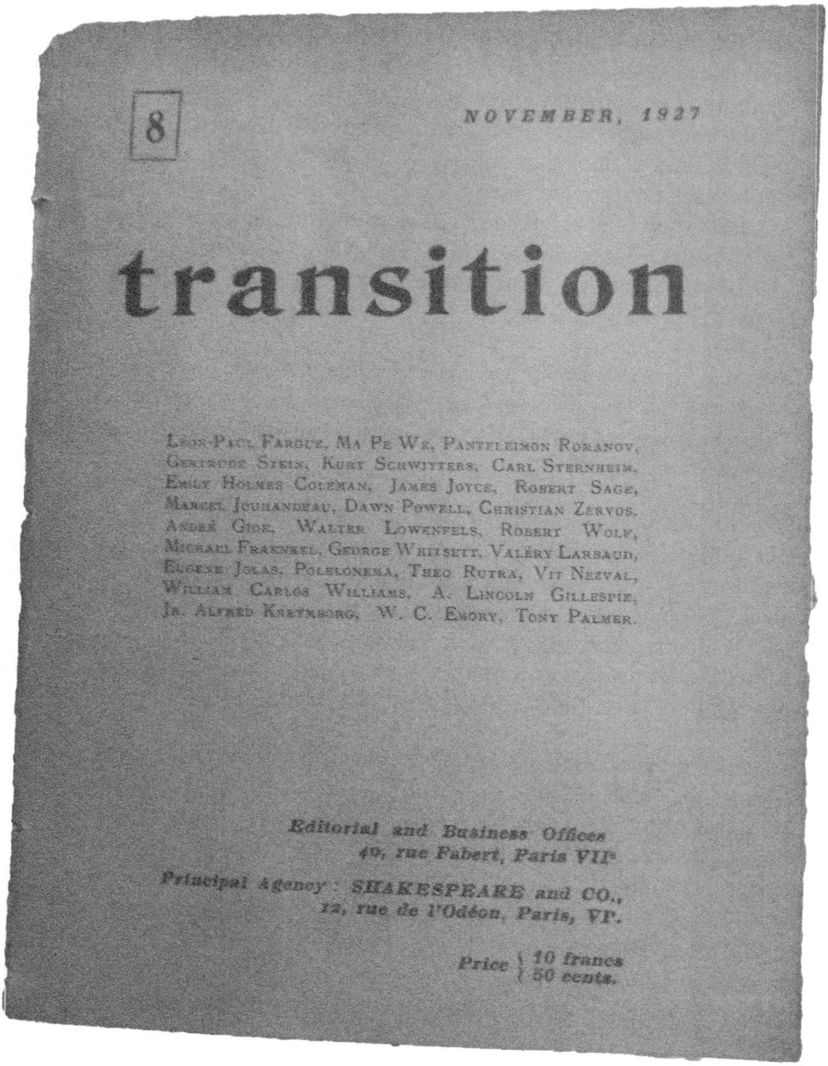

8

NOVEMBER, 1927

transition

Léon-Paul Fargue, Ma Pe We, Panteleimon Romanov, Gertrude Stein, Kurt Schwitters, Carl Sternheim, Emily Holmes Coleman, James Joyce, Robert Sage, Marcel Jouhandeau, Dawn Powell, Christian Zervos, André Gide, Walter Lowenfels, Robert Wolf, Michael Fraenkel, George Whitsett, Valéry Larbaud, Eugene Jolas, Polelonema, Theo Rutra, Vit Nezval, William Carlos Williams, A. Lincoln Gillespie, Jr. Alfred Kreymborg, W. C. Emory, Tony Palmer.

Editorial and Business Offices
40, rue Fabert, Paris VIIe

Principal Agency: SHAKESPEARE and CO.,
12, rue de l'Odéon, Paris, VIe.

Price { 10 francs
{ 50 cents.

Figure 3.4 Cover of *transition* 8

wasn't actually a form of regress: 'Has he gone backward since *Ulysses*?' Williams is quick to deny the suggestion of his rhetorical question. Starting from Keats's 'Beauty is truth, truth beauty', he claims: 'we have discarded beauty; at its best it seems truth incompletely realized' and he suggests 'it would not be stretching the point to describe all modern styles [. . .] as ways through a staleness of beauty to tell the truth anew': 'If to achieve truth we work with words purely, as a writer must, and all the words are dead or beautiful, how then shall we succeed any better than might a philosopher with *dead abstractions*? or their configurations?' (emphasis added).[14] To counter these dead abstractions, Williams argues that 'There must be something new done with the words. Leave beauty out or, conceivably, one might begin again, one might break them up to let the staleness out of them as Joyce, I think, has done' (*t8* 149–50). According to Williams, 'Joyce has not gone back but forward since *Ulysses*'. He finds 'his style richer, more able in its function of an unabridged commentary upon the human soul, the function surely of all styles'. Interestingly, Williams – who tries to stress the Catholicism of Joyce's work – refers to an 'old master' to explain Joyce's modernist approach to style: not Dante, but Rabelais:

> Every day Joyce's style more and more resembles that of the old master, the old catholic and the old priest. It would be rash to accuse Joyce of copying Rabelais. Much more likely is it that the styles are similar because they have been similarly fathered.

Rabelais 'was not all the fatheaded debauchee we used to think him, gross, guffawing vulgarly, but a priest "sensitized" to all such grossness'. Similarly, the 'catholic' aspect of Joyce's style, according to Williams, is its sensitivity to what he calls 'humanity', as opposed to 'the inhumanity of the scientific or protestant or pagan essayist' (Williams 1927, 152–3; rpt in Fargnoli 2003, 297).

At the back of *transition* 8, the volume contains an advertisement for 'The Surrealist Gallery – 16, rue Jacques-Callot, Paris (6°)':

> You will find there books, manuscript [sic], paintings and drawings by Hans ARP, Georges BRAQUE, Giorgio de CHIRICO, Marcel DUCHAMP, André MASSON, Joan MIRO, PICABIA, Pablo PICASSO, Man RAY, Kurt SCHWITTERS, Yves TANGUY and others. (see Figure 3.5)

Facing this advertisement, the number's last paragraph is devoted to Wyndham Lewis: 'We received the second number of *The Enemy* too late to answer the attacks Wyndham Lewis attempts to make on "the radical institutions" in the modern arts. We propose to state our opinions about his ideological confusions in due time' (see Figure 3.5). Lewis had clearly infuriated the editors of *transition*, and thus managed to force them into the role of *The Enemy*'s enemy:

> We wish merely to say now that the general unreliability of his white man's intellect he rates so highly is shown by his complete misconception of *transition*'s trends. *The Enemy*'s blunder stems from a characteristic Anglo-Saxon prejudice that no venture in the arts can be undertaken for its own sake, for the pleasure it may give

---

[14]   A few numbers of *transition* later (the double issue 16/17), Samuel Beckett would elaborate on what Williams called dead abstractions, arguing that the English language was 'abstracted to death' (see above; Beckett 1972 [1929], 15).

a few readers, for the charm which the element of research has. In the meantime we shall leave Mr. Lewis to the pleasure he craves of receiving the plaudits of that most despicable of vermin: the American and English literary hack.

(t8 184)

The closing pages of this issue contained advertisements for *La Nouvelle revue française* (*NRF*), the French translation of Italo Svevo's Zeno, and for Adrienne Monnier's 'La Maison des amis des livres' and Sylvia Beach's 'Shakespeare and Company' side by side on one page (see Figure 3.6), as on the back cover of *Le Navire d'Argent* (October 1925; see Plate 1).

The next two issues of *transition* (nrs 9 and 10) did not contain any piece by Joyce, but the defence of his 'Work in Progress' continued. Elliot Paul's essay 'Mr. Joyce's Treatment of Plot' came out in *transition* 9, and the defence continued in subsequent issues, with Eugene Jolas's 'The Revolution of Language and James Joyce' (*transition* 11); Marcel Brion's 'The Idea of Time in the Work of James Joyce' (*transition* 12); Frank Budgen's 'The Work in Progress of James Joyce and Old Norse Poetry' and Stuart Gilbert's 'Prolegomena to Work in Progress' (*transition* 13); Thomas MacGreevy's 'Note on Work in Progress' and John Rodker's 'The Word Structure of Work in Progress' (*transition* 14); Eugene Jolas's 'Construction of the Enigma' and Robert McAlmon's 'Mr. Joyce directs an Irish Prose Ballet' (*transition* 15); Stuart Gilbert's 'Joyce Thesaurus Minusculus' and Samuel Beckett's 'Dante . . . Bruno.Vico.Joyce' (*transition* 16/17).

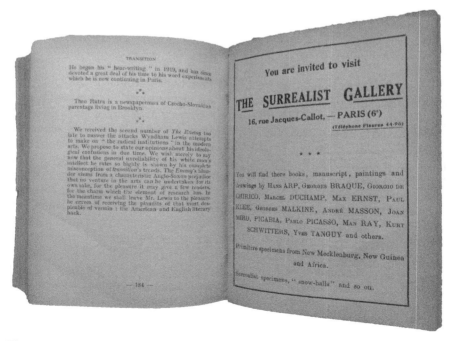

Figure 3.5   Closing pages of *transition* 8

Figure 3.6   Inside back cover of *transition* 8

Immediate Reception: Press Clippings

The 'Magazines' section of the *Irish Statesman* (26 November 1927) called the new 'Continuation of a Work in Progress' the 'chief feature' of *transition* 8, and Joyce 'a man of very great literary ability, a virtuoso in the art of language', but continued the tendency in several contemporary reviews to complain about the unsound 'exercise of his power', which was simply 'a mistake' (UBC 68: 587). By contrast, the jolly report on 'The Very Latest Things' in *Punch* ('Evoe', 16 November 1927) is a welcome diversion from the painfully serious common-sense reactions in the general press. No comments on the lower-case *t* in *transition* here, but joyous mimicry: '*transition* lies before me as i write. i have read a complaint somewhere recently that mr. punch is not sufficiently ruthless, not sufficiently wide and rude in his grasp of british existence. But it shall never be said that so far as the english language and english literature is concerned he does not try to keep abreast of the roaring stream, no, no'. The magazine is presented as 'the organ of the surrealists' and the opening of the 'Anna Livia' chapter (*transition* 8) is quoted as if it were last year's fashion: 'This is disappointing. This is not at all like Mr. James Joyce in the latest phases of his style'. But 'he improves as he goes on' and the latest Joyce – 'Don Dom Domb domb and his wee follyo!' – is cheered:

'That is good, and there is much more of it, free from the tiresome shackles of the Oxford Dictionary'.

The piece in *Punch* ends with an interesting short survey of *transition*'s reception so far:

> *transition* has had a poor reception, I understand, in the United States of America [. . .] The third number was found by Mr. Fuller, manager of the Old Corner Book Store at Boston, 'to contain material in violation of the Massachusetts law'. The fourth was turned back by the Philadelphia Customs officials on the ground that it was copyrighted material. The fifth was held up needlessly for weeks by the post authorities of New York. The sixth was confiscated because it was improper. This is the eighth. It has not done me much harm, and I hope its producers will admit that mr. punch is always ready to give a frank hearing to the latest emanations of modern thought in the mother tongue.

(UBC 68: 1149)

In the subsequent months, no continuations of 'Work in Progress' were published, which was noticed by some reviewers. Harry Hansen ('The First Reader') in the New York *World* (17 December 1927) remarked that 'Transition is getting more coherent every day. In the present issue both Gertrude Stein and James Joyce are missing and the only writer speaking the new tongue is Djuna Barnes'. Hansen also noted that 'poor old Wyndham Lewis, who had the temerity to attack Transition in "The Enemy", gets nicely scalped' (UBC 68: 2165).

Joyce's temporary absence soon became 'a new and absorbing topic' for gossipmongers in Paris *Times* ('In the Quarter', 14 December 1927): 'The rumor is that one of the high priests of modernism is weakening in his faith – that he may even recant. A short time ago he had a vision that perhaps, after all, the literary style which he evolved and which has given rise to a whole new school of writers, may not be art. A friend in whose literary judgment he has confidence frankly confirmed his suspicion. The blow was a hard one. What he is going to do about it the Left Bank does not know. It may be significant, or it may be coincidence, but the December number of *transition* does not contain a further instalment of his work' (UBC 69: 2053). The editors of *transition*, Eugene Jolas and Elliot Paul, immediately reacted with a letter to the editor of the Paris *Times* (Friday evening, 16 December 1927), objecting to 'the baseless gossip about Mr. James Joyce', stating unambiguously that the insinuation that Joyce would have come to the conclusion that he was in error was 'cowardly and false': 'There is no question, and never has been any, of this work being discontinued in *transition*, and publication will be resumed in the February issue' (UBC 69: 2053[2]).

transition 11

'Continuation of a Work in Progress', *transition* 11 (February 1928), 7–18 [FW 282–304] (Slocum and Cahoon 1971 [1953], 101, C.70)

The February issue did contain the continuation of Joyce's 'Work in Progress'. The passage on 'Shemus the simp, suffering', which Joyce had intended to incorporate in the text of *transition* 7 but eventually omitted (see above), suggested that 'the absent vignette on the opset page' was perhaps '**the madest ting that was ever here done**' (*JJA* 47: 553; BL MS 47475, 278v). 'The Muddest Thick That Was Ever Heard Dump', the fragment or 'vignette' that was absent from the first issue of the *Enemy*, was published in *transition* 11. The fragment (also known as the 'Triangle'; see Chapter 2) is about the mathematics lesson on Euclid, during which the nuclear family's two sons, curious about their origins, study the geometry of ALP's genitalia (see Chapter 5). At this stage in the fragment's genesis, the footnotes and marginalia had not been added yet.

Immediate Reception: Press Clippings

In the press, Joyce was increasingly being presented as the founder of a new school of writing. The New York *Telegraph* (26 February 1928) painted an impressionistic picture of the 'Joyce School' in Paris: 'His latest writings now are read aloud evenings in the cafés of the Latin quarter where the young intellectuals gather' (UBC 68: 2020a). *El Diario* in Buenos-Aires also spoke of 'la nueva bandera de Joyce, cuyos discípulos dicen que promete revolucionar no solamente la literatura sino también el idioma'['Joyce's new banner, whose followers say it promises to revolutionize not only literature but language itself'] (UBC 68: 568). The New York *Telegram* (1 March 1928), the Portland *News* (5 March 1928) and the San Francisco *News* (6 March 1928) introduced Joyce as the author of 'that monumental volume of gibberish, "Ulysses"', and concluded that his new project was 'quite useless': 'Language isn't manufactured. It grows' (UBC 68: 2029). In the same vein, the Bethlehem *Globe Times* noted that 'if all the other moderns in the field of literature take to inventing their own languages, a lot of us are going to have plenty of time to go back and read those old classics we've been meaning to get at for so many years' (UBC 68: 2175).

transition 12

'Continuation of a Work in Progress', *transition* 12 (March 1928), 7–27 [FW 403–28] (Slocum and Cahoon 1971 [1953], 101, C.70)

The instalment corresponding to Book III, chapter 1 of *Finnegans Wake* is the elaboration of what Joyce once described in a famous letter to Harriet Shaw Weaver as 'a description of a postman travelling backwards in the night through the events already narrated [. . .] written in the form of a via crucis of 14 stations' (24 May 1924; *LI* 214). At that point, chapters III.1 and III.2 were still conceived of as a single unit: the questioning of Shaun, followed by his 'long absurd and rather incestuous Lenten lecture to Izzy, his sister' – as Joyce described it a month later to Weaver (27 June 1924; *LI* 216) – after which he takes leave of her. Even the first proofs for *transition* were still a composite set. Wim Van Mierlo suggests that the separation may have been prompted by material circumstances and pragmatic considerations: III.1–2 may simply have been too long for one instalment, 'for the chapters combined would have comprised forty-seven pages, about double the size of most other chapters from "Work in Progress" that were published in *transition*' (Van Mierlo 2007, 381 note 62). This quantitative expansion was due to the addition in separate phases of several episodes, such as 'Dave the Dancekerl' and the fable of 'The Ondt and the Gracehoper'. The addition of this fable was one of the later phases in the genesis (for a more detailed discussion of 'The Ondt and the Gracehoper', see Chapter 5). It was drafted in February 1928, while Joyce was already revising the proofs for *transition* 12 and 13 (Van Mierlo 2007, 382 note 68). By the time of these publications in *transition*, the character of Shaun – originally a drunken postman zigzagging along the road – had evolved into an elaborate metaphor of movement through space, his brother Shem representing time.

Immediate Reception: Press Clippings

Joyce's idea of presenting world history in terms of rumour-mongering continued to be reinforced by the press's reception of his work in progress, for instance in the 'Bookstall Gossip' by Dorothy Foster Gilman (the Boston *Transcript*, 26 April 1928), who appropriately chose to quote a fragment that opens with the word 'Hark!' (UBC 68: 2178). Although many reviewers preferred to ignore 'the latest dribble by Joyce' (Boston *Transcript*, 19 May 1928; UBC 68: 1157), some were prepared to 'hark' and listen to the 'rich tones in word formation', as the New York *Telegraph* called them (17 June 1928; UBC 68: 2030), but the illustration of this word formation ('he combines "blood" and "battlefield" to make "bluddleflith"[sic]') was an echo of the *Telegraph*'s earlier article of 26 February 1928 ('"Blood" and "battlefield" he combines to make "bluddleflith"'; UBC 68: 2030a). With the transmissional departure 'bluddleflith > bluddleflith' the press thus inadvertently confirmed and illustrated the inevitable distortion characterizing Joyce's Chinese-whispers model of history.

transition 13

'Continuation of a Work in Progress', *transition* 13 (Summer 1928), 5–32 [*FW* 429–73] (Slocum and Cahoon 1971 [1953], 101, C.70)

One of the reasons for the separation of the originally integrated chapters III.1 and III.2 was the elaboration of the so-called 'Dave the Dancekerl' episode (*FW*

461.33–468.19). As Wim Van Mierlo has shown, Shaun's description of Dave
as his 'innerman' (*FW* 462.16) is based on a jotting in notebook VI.B.9
(page 12), where Shem is called Shaun's 'inner man', possibly a surrogate of
Shem created by Shaun (Begnal and Eckley 1975, 50). In the first draft, Shaun
told his sister Issy: 'I'm leaving my proxy behind for you. Dave the Dancer. [. . .]
He's like nobody else with that potful of ~~brains~~ ᵇʳᵉᵉⁿˢ on him' (*FDV* 226). The
section was written in reaction to Wyndham Lewis's *The Art of Being Ruled*,
which Joyce had been reading toward the end of March 1926. On the 30th of
that month, Joyce told Harriet Shaw Weaver that he was replying to Lewis in
'a most grotesque addition to /\b' (BL Add. 57348–129). By the time the piece
was published in *transition*, the 'innerman' had grown. The episode opens with
the capitalized exclamation: 'MEN!' – possibly in response to Wyndham Lewis's long exposition of his ideas on the rise of feminism, 'The Matriarchate and
Feminine Ascendency' (Part VII, Chapter X) and the 'sex war', which according to Lewis 'does not end in a stabilization in which the man and the woman
exist on equal terms', but 'in a situation in which feminine values are predominant' (199). Lewis mentions *The Dominant Sex* by Matilda and Mathias Vaert-
ing (199; Joyce jotted down the title in his notebook VI.B.20, page 49).
Feminism, according to Lewis, was 'recognized by the average man as a conflict in which it was impossible for a man, as a chivalrous *gentleman*, as a
respecter of the rights of little nations (like little Belgium), as a highly evolved
citizen of a highly civilized community, to refuse the claim of this better-half
to self-determination' (194).

But eventually, the 'gentleman' was the dupe of his gentility: 'He suffers
from the accident that he symbolizes "authority" in an era of change and militant revolutionary revaluation' and 'in the sex department [. . .] the revolutionary attack would [. . .] have the character of an attack on *man* and on masculinity'
(194). In the chapter '"Call Yourself a Man!"' (Part IX, Chapter III),
Lewis capitalized 'MAN' (247) and italicized '*erectness*' (248) to stress his
point that 'the male is not naturally "a man" any more than the woman'; that
he has to be 'propped up into that position'; that he 'has been persuaded to
assume a certain onerous and disagreeable rôle'; and that 'Women may in the
first place have put it into his head' (250): 'Be a *man*! may have been, meta-
phorically what Eve uttered at the critical moment in the garden of Eden'
(250). With a typographical nod to Lewis's capitalizations, Joyce made Shaun
address both men and women – 'ladies upon gentlermen' – with the opening
word 'MEN!'

But the main reason for this response to Lewis was the latter's criticism of
Joyce's work. In his notebook VI.B.20, Joyce took several notes,[15] some of which

---

[15]   For a genetic analysis of this cluster of notes, see Van Hulle 2008, 77–82.

clearly refer to the deliberately antagonistic position of Wyndham Lewis, such as 'regard me / as an / enemy' and 'regard me / as enemy' (on pages 76 and 77 of notebook VI.B.20). A few of these notes were used to write the episode about 'Dave the Dancekerl', who is invoked by Shaun, but never actually appears. When Joyce mentioned *The Art of Being Ruled* to Harriet Shaw Weaver (23 March 1926), referring to the epithets 'demented', 'stuttering' and 'squinting' (see above), he told her he was trying 'to get at his use of these terms' (BL Add. 57348–127). Lewis's description of Gertrude Stein and her stammering followers (Lewis 1989 [1926], 344) is recognizable in 'the stammer out of his bladder' – added to the first fair copy (*JJA* 57: 200; BL MS 47483–127), to which Joyce later added 'his diarrhio', possibly after reading Lewis's characterisation of *Ulysses* as a 'record diarrhoea' (in his 'Analysis of the Mind of James Joyce'; Lewis 1993 [1927], 90): 'I see by his diarrhio he's dropping the stammer out of his silenced bladder'.[16]

Immediate Reception: Press Clippings

When the March number of *transition* came out, the Paris *Times* ('On the Left Bank', 27 March 1928) reported that hereafter it was to appear quarterly instead of monthly: 'No. 13 is to be published in June. As a quarterly, *transition* will be much larger in format'. Looking forward, the continuation of part III of Joyce's new work in *transition* 13 was already announced; and looking back, the Paris *Times* noted that *transition* was now one year old. In that single year, it had published 12 numbers 'with a regularity that is almost unique among such publications' (UBC 69: 2192). The European edition of the Chicago *Tribune* (15 July 1928) announced that 'An unusually generous portion of James Joyce's amazing new work opens up the summer number' of *transition* in its 'new format': from now on 'Transition [would] appear every three months under the editorship of Eugene Jolas, with Robert Sage as associate editor' (UBC 69: 2166). The London *Times* (16 August 1928) also noted that *transition* had become a quarterly ('An International Quarterly for Creative Experiment') and drew attention to the 'diversity and violence' in the more than 20 continental opinions of America's influence on Europe. This 'American Number' largely consisted of answers by European writers to a questionnaire about the United States sent out by Jolas. Joyce's contribution was not part of this questionnaire, but a further instalment of 'Work in Progress'. The *Irish Statesman* (25 August 1928) was quite positive about Joyce, calling him 'The one really original mind' among a generation of writers who are trying each to evolve a language of their own' (UBC 33: 585).

---

[16] The 'diarrhio' was not added until the fifth proofs for *transition* 13, dated by the printer 13 and 15 June 1928 (*JJA* 57: 423; BL MS 47483–229).

Joyce's 'language' was even used as a contrastive background in a review of Otto Jespersen's *An International Language* in the *New Statesman* (1 September 1928). Jespersen's was 'a good deal easier' (UBC 68: 2202). Joyce's 'new language', which in a later issue of the *New Statesman* (10 November 1928) was characterized as 'a typical stew of allusions, parodies and of words pulled to pieces and ridiculously put together' (UBC 69: 1816). Across the Atlantic, Joyce was again being vilified by Wyndham Lewis, who was on tour in New York. The Montreal *Daily Star* reported from New York on 11 September 1928: 'Lewis, who speaks in staccato as the result of being twice shell-shocked during the world war, emits opinions with a lively violence that has already attracted the attention of New York wits and promises him an active month's visit'. What he had to say about Joyce was that he was 'turning out the "most awful stuff now"' (UBC 68: 2179; see Figure 3.7).

But Joyce's defence was also on tour. The Cincinnati *Times Star* (3 November 1928) reported that, 'During a brief visit to Cincinnati a few days ago',

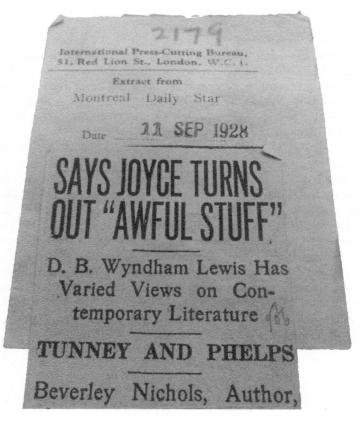

Figure 3.7   Report on Wyndham Lewis's tour in New York in the Montreal *Daily Star* (11 September 1928) (The Poetry Collection, Buffalo)

Padraic Colum had commented on Joyce's new work in *transition*, which he had described as 'an encyclopedic study of the night life of the human consciousness' (UBC 68: 39).

In the Meantime

Anna Livia Plurabelle was published by Crosby Gaige on 20 October 1928 (see Chapter 4).

transition stories

'A Muster from Work in Progress', in *transition stories: Twenty-three stories from 'transition', selected and edited by Eugene Jolas and Robert Sage* (New York: Walter V. McKee, 1929), 177–91 [seven excerpts, corresponding to *FW* 30–34.29; 76.33–78.6; 65.5–33; 454.26–455.29; 413.3–24; 23.16–26; 74.13–19] (Slocum and Cahoon 1971 [1953], 78, B.11)

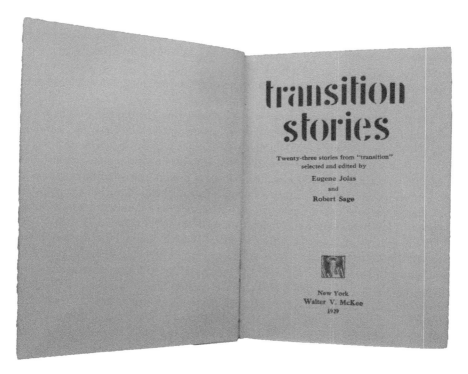

Figure 3.8　　Title page of *transition stories*

In January 1929, Eugene Jolas and Robert Sage collected 23 pieces that originally appeared in *transition*. The collection was coloured by the manifesto style of Jolas's preface, in which he vociferated on behalf of the contributors that they were 'no longer interested in the bourgeois forms of literature':

> We demand a sense of adventure that leads the individual toward a collective beauty, that is for every movement tending to demolish the current ideology, that seeks again the root of life in an impulse toward simplicity. [. . .] It is necessary to break up the word, to construct an organic world of the imagination and to give life a changed and spontaneous reality.

This rhetoric largely determined the response in the press, which was often one of ridicule.

Immediate Reception: Press Clippings

In 'Self-Determination for Words' (St Louis *Post Dispatch*, 21 January 1929), John G. Neihardt mocks Jolas's suggestion that, for too long, words have been 'subject to the bourgeois tyranny of lexicographers and grammarians' (UBC 69: 823). The 'Muster from Work in Progress' is ironically derided as 'Joyce's new masterpiece' and the volume is said to close with an equally 'masterly piece by Gertrude Stein', which was placed last 'for the obvious reason that a considerable previous exposure to nuttiness is essential to a proper appreciation'. Neihardt's own piece closes with the ironic sneer that 'This is a book of genuine value' as it serves 'to show what happens when little self-isolated groups get to jabbering among themselves about any "art"' (UBC 69: 823).

The main problem with *transition*'s endeavour was 'the process of seeking an audience for this individual art', as William Soskin noted in the New York *Evening Post* (24 January 1929, section 'Books on Our Table'). The question came down to an old dilemma: 'Is it the purpose of the artist to translate his impulses and instincts into a form significant to a "normal" audience, or does the artist's fulfillment lie in the simple act of creation for his own conscious satisfaction'. Soskin's conclusion was that in the case of *transition stories* the search for an audience was a 'futile business': 'It is best to leave such talents for restless misery alone' (UBC 34: 2173).

Many reviews pick up *transition*'s creed: 'We are no longer interested in the bourgeois forms of literature' – with which Norman MacDonald opens his review in the *Evening Union* (Springfield, Mass., 25 January 1928). His reaction is strategically interesting, for he realizes that there is no use wasting time in criticism of 'this new movement' and of *transition stories*, 'for the inevitable answer comes "bourgeoise"'. So instead, he confesses to his 'abiding curiosity' as to the reverence in which Gertrude Stein is held – 'that high priestess of the new literature' – together with 'that most fey of all Dubliners, James Joyce', both of whom encourage their 'disciples on the Left Bank' to follow their example, 'delving into their subconscious to turn out what may be lurking there'. In spite of this 'esoteric mental machinery' and in spite of the 'post-*Ulysses* anguish of mind', their literary experiment is recognized as interesting and 'even important' because of its 'striking realism': 'it is a realism that is so undiluted that it seems wholly artificial on first reading' (UBC 68: 826).

The *Milwaukee Journal* (26 January 1929) focused on the authors and editors of *transition*, 'playboys at literature' and 'Young Moderns with Chips on Shoulders', calling the stories 'ultra modern with a vengeance', some of them simply 'unintelligible gibberish' (UBC 68: 227). The Hartford *Courant* (27 January 1929) played down the importance of the *transition stories* by labelling them 'All Very Ordinary' – apart from 'the arrogant and pitiful extravagances of Miss Stein and Mr. Joyce' (UBC 68: 415). The Boston *Herald* (2 February 1929) noted that all the stories were 'highly unconventional', many of them 'weird and eccentric in both material and manner to the point of absurdity' (UBC 69: 772).

N.L. Rothman in the New York *Evening Sun* ('Transition – to What?', 26 January 1929) tried to be more open-minded, not deciding whether the contributions were 'vestiges of a new prose' or 'abominable affectations'. But his prevailing impressions were 'chaos and bitterness': 'It is paradoxical, indeed, that there is nothing fresh or young here, but a method. Their spirits are prematurely desiccated with bitterness and cynicism'. According to Rothman, the volume's problem was that it fails to make its point and to carry out its manifesto: 'If there is any new view in this book it is totally obscured by the inability to tell of it' (UBC 69: 825).

To assess the immediate effect on a conservative audience, 'The Weekly Book Review' of the Brooklyn *Eagle* of 27 January 1929 ('Transition Offers a Great Cause') can serve as a representative sample. Bearing his audience in mind, George Currie believes 'it is to be doubted that many readers of this fine old family newspaper will greatly enjoy "Transition Stories", published by Walter V. McKee'. He does not fail to remind his readership of familymen and -women that Joyce is a censored author: 'James Joyce, you will recall wrote "Ulysses", a book which the censors on this side of the water lost little time in putting behind locks and bars'. Currie calls *transition* a 'sturdy little rebel of a magazine', which, admittedly, published some 'stuff' that has been 'uncannily prophetic', but 'Most of it, you will probably decide, is lamentably idiotic'. To characterize Gertrude Stein ('a lady whom few are willing to accept seriously'), Currie quotes the editors' foreword to 'As a Wife Has a Cow a Love Story':

> Her early book, 'Tender Buttons' (a work which was unobtainable for years until it was reprinted in *transition* No. 14), first brought her to the attention of the critics, who unanimously found this work to be utterly nonsensical. [. . .] Today she has a large number of readers who enjoy and appreciate her writing. [. . .] What few of the general public realize is that her manner continually changes and develops.
>
> (UBC 33: 872)

Basically, the whole passage is quoted to show that the changes and developments have not resulted in a less nonsensical result. 'Unreason' is the only alternative the 'reformers' can come up with: 'M. Jolas is like all other reformers. He can tear the old down, but he has nothing from which to build anew' (UBC 33: 872). In the context of this constructive metaphor, it is interesting that Joyce's next instalment in *transition* 15 (February 1929) would be the fragment that contains the 'Haveth Childers Everywhere' episode, presenting HCE as the boasting bourgeois and 'builder'*par excellence.*

The term 'bourgeois' in Eugene Jolas's preface triggered various reactions – including the laconic parenthesis in the anonymous announcement in the San Francisco *Chronicle*: 'The editors print the name of their magazine with a small t, but perhaps they won't mind if we use a capital T; it is easier on our as yet unemancipated eyes'. Instead of discussing the content, the *Chronicle* just shows how 'extensively' Jolas explains 'What it is all about' by printing a long quote from his worked-up prose that takes up three-quarters of the announcement (UBC 69: 671).

One of the few relatively neutral reviews was Clifton P. Fadiman's 'Experiments in Futurism' (*The Nation*, 27 Feb. 1929, 259; UBC 33: 1007). Fadiman characterizes the work published in *transition* as 'experimental, almost in a laboratory sense', which implies that 'it is both useless and unintelligent to apply to it the current formulae of aesthetic appreciation'. Still, *transition* has met with 'contempt and misunderstanding', which is partly ascribable – according to Fadiman – to 'that facile snobbery peculiar to democratic communities', and 'to the influence which nineteenth-century fiction continues to exert':

> The propaganda-naturalist novel and the religious aesthetic of Tolstoy combined
> to influence the reader so as to make him demand from his fiction, above all other
> qualities, that of immediate comprehensibility. Nothing is to be presented to the
> reader to which his best mental powers are not absolutely equal.
>
> (259)

Fadiman recognized an interesting quality of this 'ultra-modern work', which is its dependence on the effort the reader is willing to invest in it: 'the reader must be willing to cooperate, to insinuate himself into a strange mood' (259). Fadiman thus prefigured recent developments in cognitive narratology that consider readers' cognitive processes in terms of enactive cognition and regard the process of sensemaking as part of the reader's extended mind. Fadiman predicted that it was 'more than probable' that nothing would result from these experiments, but he did not exclude the possibility that 'within a hundred years our apparatus for the reception of literary art' would be 'materially modified and enriched by the sincere efforts of the Paris group' (259).

But Fadiman's perceptive suggestion that sense is something to be made by readers as much as by any other agent in the literary enterprise remained an exception. The predominant view was that of the reader, not as an intelligent agent with an extended mind, but as a passive consumer, who expected the *text* to make sense. Making sense was the criterion by which the Syracuse *Post-Standard* (13 February 1929, signed by 'A.M.G.') measured *transition stories*, characterizing them as 'A New Literature's Birthpangs' and admitting that some of them 'at least make sense'. Even in Joyce's contribution, 'there seem to be a few passages that make sense' (UBC 68: 371). According to the New York *Times* (24 February 1929) Joyce showed, more than any contemporary writer, 'to what useless ends literature may proceed when it drops logic out of consideration' (UBC 33: 390). The Pittsburgh *Sun Telegraph* (10 March 1929) was of the opinion that the book 'reeks with insane inanities', and Joyce was just 'another of the bedlamite bunch' producing 'gibberish'. Referring to Eugene Jolas's preface or 'manifesto' – 'The domination of pure reason was abolished in the twinkling of an eye' – the reviewer's comment is the brief endorsement 'Very true!' The only sane conclusion being:

> If going to Paris affects people in this way, let us all stay home! It is cheaper to listen to the static over your radio than to go zigzagging with intoxicated cows along the sclerotic boulevards.

> (UBC 68: 661)

The pages of the volume almost came to stand for these 'sclerotic boulevards' in another review of the same day (10 March 1929): 'Dirt leaps from the page, distorted abnormal phrasing runs the gamut of red light language which is carefully disguised as coined words to foil the shears of the censor', according to Edward Straus in the Minneapolis *Tribune*. He even suggests hanging the contributors and concludes: 'We recommend this book as a most worthy contribution to your wastebasket' (UBC 69: 673).

The publication of *transition stories* was an opportunity for a retrospective evaluation of the journal by other reviewers. 'Mad or not, it's their Magazine' was the title of Lee McCardell's review in the Baltimore *Sun* (14 April 1929), which concludes in financial terms: 'after all, the thirty francs which *transition* pays its contributors per printed page are not offered with a view to encouraging popular manuscripts. Its editors announce that they "welcome new work, but not the kind that would be accepted elsewhere". They are in the market for original stuff' (UBC 69: 417). Belated reviews included mainly lukewarm reactions such as the Paris *Times*'s remark that Joyce's prose was actually 'at times understandable' (15 April 1929; UBC 68: 2190). An anonymous review (Newark, N.J., 11 May 1929) dubbed the contributors 'Geniuses – Perhaps': 'Most of the writers appear to go on the assumption that because the workings of the mind are frequently inconsequential and incoherent, the more casually and illogically they write, the nearer they come to reality' (UBC 33: 1081). As usual, Gertrude Stein and James Joyce were taken together as two writers who had 'realized that our words by this time have fallen into conventional patterns of phrase and sentence, that the rhythm and the harmony of our language have become stereotyped and shopworn' – but their 'laudable enough task' is played down as harmless pastime: 'At any rate, one can always place selected passages from both these writers in nonsense anthologies, and find them as such most pleasurable' (UBC 33: 1081).

transition 15

'Continuation of a Work in Progress', *transition* 15 (February 1929), 195–238 [*FW* 474–554] (Slocum and Cahoon 1971 [1953], 101, C.70)

The publication of *transition stories* marked a moment of evaluation. Evidently, the incomprehension in the general press did not stop either the editors or Joyce from publishing another 'Continuation of a Work in Progress' in February 1929. *transition* 15 contained the third part of Book III (*FW* 474–554), in which the four old men find Yawn on a midden heap and cross-examine him: about his place of origin, his language, the letter, his family. Several voices of other characters speak through Yawn, such as Treacle Tom (introduced in Book I, chapter 2), who gives his version of the encounter in the park. Other witnesses (Kate, Sigurdsen) are called to testify, and Issy talks to her mirror image. Finally, HCE delivers his self-defence, boasting of the magnificent city he founded. This latter part corresponds with the fragment that would be published separately as *Haveth Childers Everywhere* (see Chapter 6).

Immediate Reception: Press Clippings

On 24 February 1929, the Cuban *Diario de la Marina* (Havana) announced the birth of a new vocabulary: 'Febrero 24. En París ha nacido un nuevo vocabulario, obra de James Joyce', who was being presented as an American author ('el norteamericano autor de "Ulysses"') (UBC 68: 2055). On the same day, Richard Aldington ('All Art is Tending to the Condition of Journalism', in the London *Referee*) contrasted the lack of vitality in literature published in England with what was happening on the continent: 'The modern world [. . .] rushes like a motor-car. [. . .] The poets bathe in a stream of consciousness, and your mind has to work like lightning to follow and understand them'. Like Clifton P. Fadiman's review of *transition stories*, Richard Aldington implicitly foreshadows much of what cognitive narratology is increasingly aware of: that literary works do not just make sense, that it is 'your mind' that 'has to work' in order to make sense of the text. Aldington makes a direct link between this cognitive aspect of the reception and the genesis: 'Mr. Joyce is splitting up the English language with a giant hand, and gumming it together again with infinite patience and dexterity' (UBC 33: 263).

'Y.O.'[17] in the *Irish Statesman* (16 March 1929) was less enthusiastic: 'as the world underappreciates him [Joyce], his friends overappreciate him'. His followers were 'all a little too self-conscious', on the whole, 'Transition is worth buying and keeping': 'It will be valuable either as one of the curiosities of literature or as a fountain from which a new literature has sprung' (UBC 33: 591). The London *Daily*

---

[17]   A.E., George Russell (Deming 1977 [1970], vol. II, 395).

Express (16 March 1929) announced the new number of *transition* as a 'quarterly delight' and 'the best thing in the number is, of course, forty solid pages of Mr. James Joyce, who is still hard at it' (UBC 68: 572). The meta-texts, such as Robert McAlmon's 'Mr. Joyce Directs an Irish Prose Ballet', also attracted attention. According to the *New York Times* (24 March 1929) it was 'eminently fitting' that the journal that published so many fragments of 'Work in Progress' should offer an explanation of it as well. But no matter how 'satisfactory' McAlmon's explanation was, it did not seem likely that there would ever be many readers who would really enjoy and appreciate this 'Irish prose ballet' (UBC 69: 2189).

The New York *Herald* ('Looking Over the Magazines', signed 'W.C.B.', 8 April 1929) characterized *transition* as 'a magazine that attempts to express itself in a speech above the level of Wall Street, which, of course, the average American magazine does not' and which was said to 'deserve praise for what it is doing to the English and American vocabulary and syntax'. What *transition* did, in particular, was misconstrued in a strange combination of late Enlightenment striving and Victorian 'onwardness'. The author claimed that *transition* 'moves *forward* toward a newer and richer vocabulary and a more subtle and more *manly* syntax' (emphasis added). The review mentions the small print run ('After fifteen issues its circulation is about 1,000 copies a number'), presenting it as a David against the Goliaths of critics and 'nickel-grabbers of literature' who generally 'adopt the attitude that it is bawdy, pathologic, morbid': 'They say they cannot understand Mr. Joyce. Does it matter? As Robert McAlmon and Eugene Jolas ask in the current "transition". Is it not sufficient that a writer should evoke pictures and feelings and rhythms by an amazing vocabulary, by a complete disregard of ordinary sentence-structure?' Although, according to the reviewer, the current number was 'not so good as earlier numbers', the bibliography of Gertrude Stein's works was appreciated and 'William Carlos Williams rebukes Miss Rebecca West as she has needed it for months' (UBC 33: 1095).

The reception of Joyce's work was often second-hand. *New Age* (18 April 1929), reporting on the first number of a new monthly magazine called *The Realist*, referred to Arnold Bennett's contribution, which characterized 'Work in Progress' as 'a travail to the spirit of his best friends and admirers' – interesting only 'until one sees the trick' and 'more related to what the incendiaries of the Great Library of Alexandria did than to the creation of new form'. Nonetheless, of all the authors Bennett discussed – including Marcel Proust, D.H. Lawrence and Virginia Woolf – he considered that 'only Joyce is of the dynasty of precursors and sure of a place in the history of the development of the novel' (UBC 68: 2206). The *New York World* (4 May 1929) reported on Wyndham Lewis, who had 'published another issue of the Enemy' and had 'particularly aimed his shots at the "transition" group in Paris', which he called '"professional false-revolutionaries"'. Joyce's 'polygluttonous volume' struck Lewis as 'uproariously funny' and he advised Gertrude Stein to 'get out of English' in a similar way; for if she did, she '"would get out of English more thoroughly than Joyce (who is half in and half out)"', and whom Lewis calls '"that able Dublin executant"' (UBC 69: 699).

Our Exagmination

Our Exagmination Round His Factification for Incamination of Work in Progress
(Paris: Shakespeare and Company, 1929)

In response to the general press's rather hostile reception of '*Work in Progress*',
Joyce chose an interesting strategy. Instead of writing letters to the editors or giving

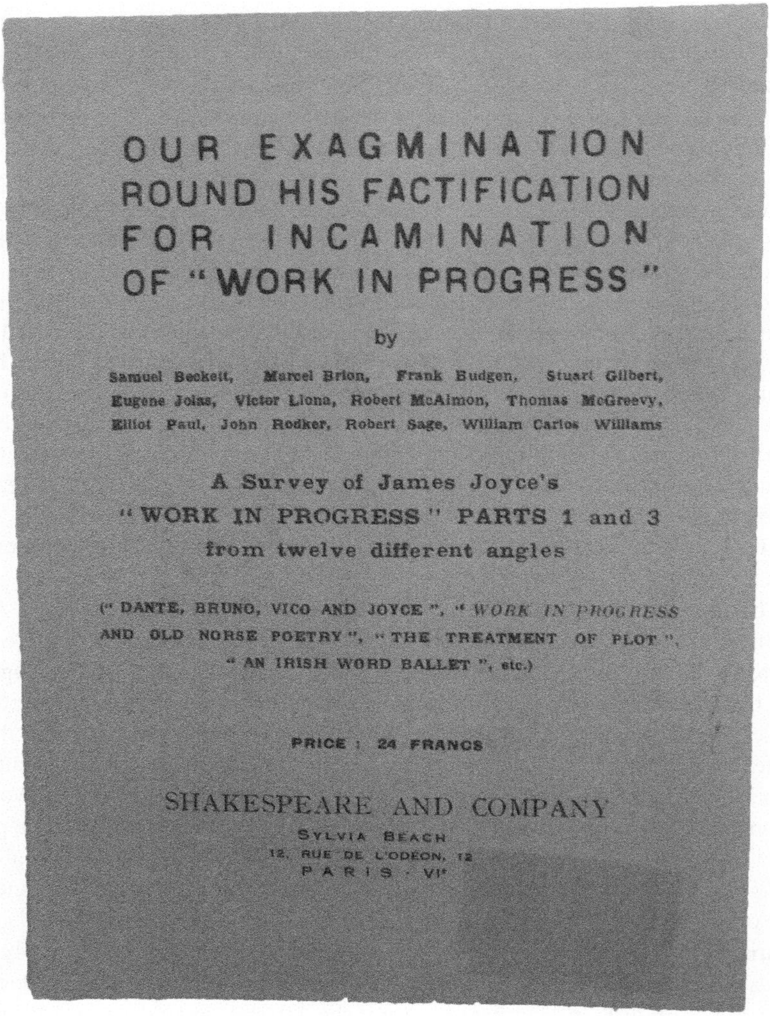

Figure 3.9   Flyer advertising *Our Exagmination round His Factification for Incamina-tion of 'Work in Progress'* (The Poetry Collection, Buffalo)

interviews, he made others do the talking for him, as Tim Conley notes: 'He outsourced. The "Joyce industry" starts here, and "incamination" can be understood as a multifarious process in public relations, literary analysis, and canonisation – or its opposite, "incrimination", which is likewise best left to others' (Conley 2010, xvi). The others were Samuel Beckett, Marcel Brion, Frank Budgen, Stuart Gilbert, Eugene Jolas, Victor Llona, Robert McAlmon, Thomas McGreevy, Elliot Paul, John Rodker, Robert Sage, William Carlos Williams, G.V.L. Slingsby and Vladimir Dixon. The volume was published on 27 May 1929 (*LI* 279). Many of their essays had already appeared in *transition*.

Immediate Reception: Press Clippings

Arnold Bennett regarded it as 'a bad sign that an unfinished work should be the subject of an exegetical volume (200 pages) by twelve disciples'.[18] He acknowledged that 'None but a man of very remarkable gifts of imagination and pure brain' could have come up with a project like Joyce's, which 'does immense credit to his brain and his imagination. But little to his commonsense'. The common-sense approach and appeal to 'normality' run through the entire review, which claims that, apart from Joyce himself and 'a dozen other bizarre human beings', the work 'will not be read, because it cannot be read by any individual normally constituted'. Joyce was not just wasting his and other people's time, he was 'culpably wasting [. . .] his genius' (495).

The *Manchester Guardian* ('Books of the Day', 3 September 1929, signed 'H. I'A. F.') objected against the 'reversal of the consecrated order of things' – the publication of critical analyses in advance of the text under consideration. But on the other hand, it also acknowledged that, 'since it is so revolutionary as to be at first almost unintelligible', it was perhaps not a bad idea to let a few scouts explore the field before the book was published 'to challenge alike our wits, our learning, and our most tenacious preconceptions'. The way they prepared 'the ground for understanding' was characterized as 'combative appreciation' (UBC 34: 2051). In 'The Assault on Time' (the *Yorkshire Post*; 3 August 1929), Winifred Holtby reacted to Marcel Brion's essay on 'The Idea of Time in the Work of James Joyce' in *Our Exag*, in which he claims that 'Space is nothing', because even two men seated side by side 'do not live in the same time' (UBC 34: 2171).

The *Library Review* (Autumn 1929) argued that Joyce's new, 'exceedingly turgid' work was as extraordinary as the 'composite study in which his disciples advocate his claims'. Joyce had in fact confessed to Harriet Shaw Weaver that 'Up till the last day I had to supervise it and check the references etc. made by the 12' (*LI* 279), and the presence of the author behind the publicity stunt was too transparent according to the *Library Review*: 'Doubtless they have been duly instructed that Joyce [. . .] has exploited the ideas of Vico, Bruno, and Dante in curious ways'.

---

[18] Arnold Bennett, 'Books and Persons: The Oddest Novel Ever Written', *Evening Standard* (8 August 1929), 7. See also Deming 1977 [1970], vol. II, 493–5.

Given that Joyce's new work was a 'dreadful philological creation', the disciples 'made the best of a bad job' (UBC 34: 2069). The *Irish Statesman* (12 April 1930, 114–5) thought especially the essays by Beckett, Jolas and McGreevy would have been first rate criticism if they had shown 'a little more detachment'; the others were merely dull, but that did not matter because, 'good or bad, the ideas are Joyce's, and as such to be treated with respect' (UBC 34: 2076).

The summer issue of *transition* did not contain a new instalment of 'Work in Progress', but as the *New York Herald* (17 June 1929) reported, it did contain three essays that discussed it – by Samuel Beckett, Stuart Gilbert and Ernst Robert Curtius (UBC 69: 822). Joyce did not write so much as he was being written about. And the gossip continued. In 'Gossip About Books', for instance, the *Montreal Daily Star* (15 June 1929; see Figure 3.10) neither read nor reviewed Joyce's 'latest word-puzzle', but was glad it had so far been spared his 'incomprehensible eccentricities' (UBC 68: 2191).

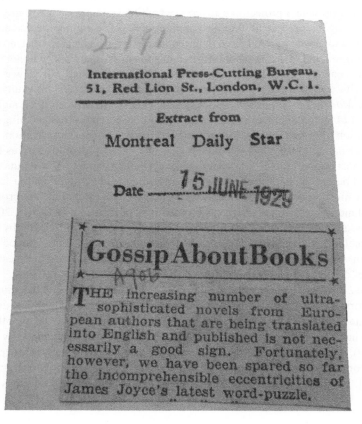

Figure 3.10   'Gossip About Books' in the *Montreal Daily Star* (The Poetry Collection, Buffalo)

The *Toronto Star* (11 October 1929) did not review 'Work in Progress' either, but reported on 'a publisher who was talking about Joyce', referring to him as 'the eccentric Irish writer': 'There's not a paragraph in his new book without 20 or 30 Joyce-coined words in it' (UBC 69: 874). A reader of the *Irish Statesman* ('Wilhelm O Rinn') wrote a letter to the editor in a 'new language', suggesting that Joyce was pulling the 'monde western' a leg: 'In andere verby measaim dass ille est pulling la jambe' (UBC 68: 582).

In the Meantime

Tales Told of Shem and Shaun was published by the Black Sun Press on 9 August 1929 (see Chapter 5).

transition **18**

'Continuation of a Work in Progress', *transition* 18 (November 1929), 211–36 [*FW* 555–90] (Slocum and Cahoon 1971 [1953], 101, C.70)

The thirteenth instalment of 'Work in Progress' corresponds with the last chapter of Book III in *Finnegans Wake* (*FW* 555–90): it is night in the house, and Matt, Mark, Luke and John, located at the four bedposts, give their views of the parents' sexual intercourse after they have been woken up by their son's nightmare about a terrifying father figure. As Daniel Ferrer has shown, the scene is inspired by Joyce's reading of (the third volume of) Sigmund Freud's *Collected Papers* (Ferrer 2007, 413), notably a footnote in 'The Wolfman': 'These dreams represented the coitus scene as an event taking place between heavenly bodies' – from which Joyce excerpted the words 'coitus between / heavenly bodies' (notebook VI.B 19, page 90). As Ferrer notes, 'This is clearly the origin of the passage [. . .] where the parental coitus is projected first on the window blind, to the view of the passersby, and then assumes cosmic dimensions' (Ferrer 2007, 415). In Joyce's text, this was applied to 'the first payrents' (*FDV* 259), Adam and Eve, who soon became 'the ~~first~~ ᶠᵒʳᶜᵉᵈ payrents' (*FDV* 259), building on Freud's suggestion that the parental coitus was 'a point of universal origin, not only biological but psychological' (415). The colourful, graphic descriptions of the lovemaking couple from four different angles were developed relatively late in the genesis of the chapter (424).

The most important aspect of this primal scene, both from a psychological and from a narratological perspective, was not the sex itself but the act of watching it. This time, the theme of voyeurism was connected to Freud's effort to explain the Wolfman's identification with both his father and his mother as sexual models by linking it to the child's observation of its parents' lovemaking in a particular position, the coitus *a tergo* (from behind), as it would afford the child the most complete view. This view was presented as the fourth position. In the first two positions –

CEH and EHC ('Domicy' and 'Meseedo', or mi-si-do in musical notation) – the male is partly masking the female; in the third position, HCE ('Sidomy') is partly masked by ALP; whereas in the fourth position – CEH ('Twomesee') – 'male and female unmask we them' (*JJA* 60: 115; BL 47482a, 59). The link with the three soldiers watching in Phoenix Park is suggested in the first draft ('O. ~~Why were~~ ^{Were} you in ~~the~~ ^{your} prickly hedges, redcoat ~~robin~~ ^{robins}[. . .] Answer by your numbers. ^{1 to 3}'), suggesting the primal scene as the 'woid' around which the whole gossipmongering is whirling. By the time the text appeared in *transition*, this link may have been less evident, but it remains remarkable that, while the voyeurism and masturbation in the 'Nausicaa' episode had been the occasion for *Ulysses* to be banned as an obscene work, none of the readers of the instalment in *transition* 18 seemed to mind watching the mother and father figure, 'f***ing' in fourfold focus.

Immediate Reception: Press Clippings

On the day *transition* 18 came out, the *Chicago Tribune* (European Edition, Paris, 11 November 1929) reported that 'the *synthetist* number of *transtion*' had just appeared and announced that Joyce –'in spite of difficulties due to the condition of his eyesight'– had concluded Part III of his 'epochal' work in progress. Joyce's bad eyesight was unwittingly connected to the fragment full of voyeurism, but the irony was that the *Chicago Tribune* itself was totally blind to what was going on in the instalment, which it described as 'a fragment representing a picaresque dialogue between hill and tree' (UBC 69).

While Sylvia Beach kept track of the people to whom a copy of *transition* 18 had been 'sent for JJ',[19] the press continued to overlook the naked narrative of the instalment and to concentrate instead on the circumstantiating language. In 'Le Règne des Mots' (*Candide*, 14 November 1929), Benjamin Crémieux wondered how one should react to *transition*'s proclamation of total and absolute lexical freedom. He acknowledged that the distortion of words did force the reader to recognize that words are not a transparent medium, that they have a life of their own.[20] But Joyce's enterprise was of a different order, according to Crémieux. The

---

[19] 'transition No 18 sent for JJ:

    Nov 8 Sinclair / Sainsbury/ Magee / Moore / Hughes / Ogden / Goyert / Steyn / Weaver / Griffith
    Nov 9 Healy / Sykes' (BU XVIII.G: Miscelaneous material related to 'Work in Progress'/*Finnegans Wake*).

[20] 'Une revue anglo-américaine, mais qui paraît à Paris, *Transition*, vient de proclamer la liberté totale et absolue du vocabulaire. [. . .] Comment juger l'initiative des collaborateurs de *Transition*? Faut-il se mettre en colère, éclater de rire ou prendre ces déclarations au sérieux, les discuter? [. . .] cet emploi de mots déformés ou inventés oblige à reprendre pleine conscience que la littérature est faite avec des mots, qu'elle est une matière verbale et que les mots ont une existence, ne sont pas une simple vitre incolore à travers laquelle on peut voir la pensée' (UBC 33: 1018).

purpose of distorting words was to escape from the abstract symbols they represented and to bring them closer to cognition. From a cognitive perspective, this
moment in the work's reception is quite interesting because it presages one of the
key metaphors in late 20th- and early 21st-century cognitive philosophy, namely
Daniel C. Dennett's 'multiple drafts model' (see Introduction). Crémieux had
clearly read Beckett's article 'Dante... Bruno.Vico... Joyce' in *Our Exagmination*,
but he also made the link with cognition more explicit. What Joyce was searching
for and aiming at, according to Crémieux, was to allow the words 'to reproduce the
hesitations, the errors, the drafts of cognition' ('les ébauches de la pensée').[21] Crémieux's idea that conciousness does not simply 'happen', but that it is a process of
continuous revision was inspired by Joyce's 'Work in Progress'. And Joyce's own
cognitive process, in its turn, was inspired again by this kind of critical engagement
with his work, and this feedback loop accorded with an enactive model of the mind.
Crémieux concluded with the rhetorical question 'why would one allow grocers,
pharmacists and scholars to create words and keep only poets from doing so?'[22]

Crémieux's notion of the 'drafts of the mind' was translated quite literally to the
drafts and proofs of 'Work in Progress' in an article in *La Nacion* by Ramón Gómez
de la Serna (Santiago de Chile, 23 November 1930, p. 10ff.), called 'El escritor y
las pruebas' (UBC 33: 381). The article discusses various authors' proofs, and also
uses one of the 'Pruebas de Work in Progress de James Joyce' as an illustration.[23]

As opposed to Crémieux's notion of the 'ébauches de la pensée', Rebecca
West (in the *New York Herald Tribune*, 12 January 1930)[24] insisted upon a representational model of the mind: 'The first point on which one would like to be
satisfied is whether the main function he [Joyce] is trying to make the word
perform is not one which is properly performed by *the image in the mind* for
which the word is only a counter' (emphasis added). This was one of West's main
objections, which 'rise up [. . .] in the mind of any reader outside the cult'. Evidently, the 'cult' implicitly included William Carlos Williams, who had criticized
West in his contribution to *Our Exagmination*. Another objection related to the
'unmaking' of Joyce's portmanteau words ('such as Lewis Carroll invented when
he wrote "Jabberwocky"'): 'even Mr. Joyce's most devoted followers do regard

---

[21] 'Ce que recherche l'auteur d'*Ulysses*, en créant ou en déformant les mots, c'est
d'échapper au symbole abstrait qu'ils représentent, c'est de les rapprocher de la pensée, de
leur permettre de reproduire les hésitations, les erreurs, les ébauches de la pensée, de
reproduire le courant interrompu de la pensée' (UBC 33: 1018).
[22] 'Pourquoi autoriserait-on seuls les épiciers, les pharmaciens et les savants à créer des
mots et l'interdirait-on uniquement aux poètes?' (UBC 33: 1018).
[23] The facsimile illustrating the article is of poor quality, but it seems to be the missing
part of the Galley proofs for the 'Triangle' episode (the Euclid lesson) in *transition* 11 (*JJA*
53: 57; MS 47478, [25r]); it corresponds with the facsimile in Jean-Jacques Mayoux's *Joyce*
(in the series 'La Bibliothèque idéale', facing page 192), where it is said to be part of the
'Collection Maria Jolas'.
[24] Rebecca West, 'James Joyce and His Followers', in the *New York Herald Tribune* –
'Books' section, Sunday, 12 January 1930, pp. 1, 6.

it as essential that they should unmake his words into the constituents of which he made them'. Yet, the reader's investment to unpack the portmanteau words was not seen as a quality:

> It would seem that the intellectual effort required to unmake James Joyce's words into their constituent parts would perpetually be splitting up the attention and breaking up the state of unity in which the mind must be to accept, say, his personification of the life of a river, the stream of creation.

According to West, Joyce was 'misapplying his genius', but she also acknowledged that her objections themselves proved that 'Work in Progress' was fascinating: 'Can one think of any other writer concerning whose work such interesting considerations arise? Do they not make the ordinary naturalist novel by Arnold Bennett or John Galsworthy seem like the very body of death?' (UBC 33: 2003).

More and more announcements appeared, mentioning Joyce's deteriorating eyesight. The Lancaster *Intelligencer* (7 May 1930) reported that Joyce was hunting for a doctor who could save him from blindness. Joyce is described, not only as 'banned in both England and the United States', but also as a hard working craftsman, 'probably the hardest working writing man who lives in the Latin quarter': 'He does a piece of work over and over. His final draft often is more than double the original' (UBC 69: 1572). The Glasgow *Daily Record* (13 April 1931) also emphasized the heroic efforts of this honest craftsman in spite of his bad eyesight: 'Though handicapped by very defective eyes [. . .] he writes every word with his own hand and himself revises all his manuscripts and proofs – generally with the aid of a powerful magnifying-glass and a big red pencil' (UBC 68: 2104). The emphasis on the 'métier' and the craftsman's tools highlights the material aspect of writing that is so central in Lambros Malafouris's theory of 'material agency' (see above).

In the Meantime

Haveth Childers Everywhere was published by Babou and Kahane and the Fountain Press in June 1930.

Anna Livia Plurabelle was published by Faber and Faber on 12 June 1930.

'From "Tales Told of Shem and Shaun: Three Fragments from Work in Progress" by James Joyce' appeared in *Imagist Anthology* (London: Chatto & Windus: 1930), 121–2 [FW 417.24–419.10] (B.12)

Some of the very early reviews of *transition* 1[25] had compared Joyce's compound words to Lewis Carroll's portmanteau words in 'Jabberwocky'. On 28 August 1930,

---

[25] For instance, 'Gyring and Gimblin (Or Lewis Carroll in Paris)', New York *Saturday Review of Literature* (30 April 1927) (UBC 33: 986).

Philip Henderson ('James Joyce and Lewis Carroll: An Unsuspected Comparison', *Everyman*, 142) rediscovered the comparison: 'Although it is not my intention to disparage Mr. James Joyce's brilliant experiments, [. . .] I do not think it has ever been pointed out that Lewis Carroll was doing very much the same sort of thing sixty years ago. The difference is that Carroll did it more or less as a joke and Mr. Joyce does it in all seriousness and at enormous length'. Just like the review of *transition* 1 in *Truth* (20 April 1927; 775–6; see above), Henderson also quoted Alice's reaction to Humpty Dumpty, expressing the reader's bafflement without knowing whether the author or the reader is to blame: 'Somehow it seems to fill my head with ideas – only I don't exactly know what they are!' (UBC 33: 1683). It also seemed to fill other people's heads with ideas, leading to bizarre comments and notes such as the questionable pastiche of 'Work in Progress' by R.H. Pitney in *Argo: An Individual Review* (December 1930, 45–9), called 'Pillgrimm's Work Not in Progress' (UBC 34: 2064).

The *Times Literary Supplement* (28 August 1930) reported that in the new number of *transition* (nr. 19/20), Eugene Jolas announced that he was 'suspending the magazine indefinitely' as he could 'no longer afford the expenditure of time and labour necessary to its preparation' (UBC 69: 881). One of the essays in this double issue was an English translation of Carola Giedion-Welcker's German article on 'Work in Progress', called 'A Linguistic Experiment'[26] (*transition* 19/20, June 1930, 174; see Chapter 5).

In the Meantime

Haveth Childers Everywhere was published by Faber and Faber on 2 April 1931 (see Chapter 6).

'From Work in Progress' appeared in *New Experiment* 7 (Spring 1931), 27–9 [FW 3–29] (Slocum and Cahoon 1971, 102, C.79)

The Paris newspaper *Je suis partout* announced the death of *transition*: 'La mort d'une revue américaine'. Eugene Jolas had written a short history of *transition* in the *American Mercury*, which ends with the conclusion that *transition* was above all a laboratory and that it had managed to abolish the barrier between prose and poetry. 'And to realize that all of this has taken place in front of our eyes, in Paris, for three and a half years', the article concluded: 'Apparently it was the great revolution of American literature. And we hardly noticed it!'[27]

---

[26] Carola Giedion-Welcker, 'Work in Progress: Ein sprachliches Experiment von James Joyce', *Neue Schweizerische Rundschau* (September 1929), 658–71.

[27] 'Dire que tout cela s'est déroulé sous nos yeux, à Paris, Durant trois années et demie! Il paraît que c'était la grande révolution de la littérature américaine. Et nous nous en sommes à peine aperçus!' (4 July 1931; UBC 69: 880).

Once in a while, other magazines such as *New Experiment* (Cambridge, UK) republished a fragment of 'Work in Progress' or published new interpretations that triggered further reactions in the press. A short note in *Intransigeant* (14 August 1931; UBC 33: 908) summarizes Joyce's '*Livre en train*', characterizing it not as a novel, but as a *Divine Comedy* or a new *Paradise Lost*.[28] Joyce is recognized as one of the greatest stylists of the twentieth century, but his latest work is presented as an illness.[29] The occasion for this article seems to have been Louis Gillet's praise of *Anna Livia Plurabelle* and his defence of Joyce's enterprise in *Revue des Deux Mondes*, which was also referred to in *L'Intransigeant* four days later (18 August 1931) (UBC 33: 909). The Liverpool *Post* ('On the Table', 8 April 1932) quoted Gillet to show how Joyce 'indulges in praise': '"Mr. Joyce is beyond doubt the most amazingly gifted of living writers [. . .]; he is at the same time the most thoughtful artist, the greatest imaginable master of his medium and of his effects"'. The review concludes that writers on Joyce would be doing him a service if they told him frankly that he was 'merely playing with his gifts' (UBC 33: 894).

After the announcement of *transition*'s death, the magazine resurrected in early 1932. In a later issue, the history of the journal was summarized as follows: 'Started: April 1927. Temporary suspension: June 1930. Resumption: March 1932' (*t22* 182). After having appeared as a monthly magazine (from April 1927 to March 1928), it had become 'An International Quarterly for Creative Experiment', and now it changed into an annual with the subtitle 'An International Workshop of Orphic Creation' (see also Figure 3.11). Jolas, who was busy thinking up his theory of a 'metaphysical language', had not been able to cover the magazine's losses any longer. But a new publisher came to the rescue. 'Late in 1931 a Dutchman called Carolus Verhulst, who happened to be in Paris, approached him', as Peter de Voogd recounts: 'Not only was Verhulst prepared to publish Jolas' pamphlet *The Language of the Night* (containing his theory), but he also wanted to breathe new life into *transition*' (de Voogd 2013, 238). In February 1932, Verhulst suggested that Shakespeare and Company act as the sole distributor of *transition* for Paris; Sylvia Beach wrote to him on 13 February, regretting that this was not possible,[30] but the

---

[28] 'Il s'agirait bien plutôt d'une Divine comédie, d'un nouveau Paradis perdu, en dépit de la condition très humble des personnages: la prétention de l'auteur est de faire tenir le monde dans une guinguette, à peu près comme il tient dans les marionnettes de Guignol. Vue très philosophique. Une famille est un microcosme [. . .] Il suit de là que les caractères ne peuvent être que des figures extrêmement généralisées, des types réduits aux traits communs de l'humanité'(UBC 33: 908).

[29] 'Nul doute que M. Joyce ne soit un des plus grands stylistes connus. Mais le génie de la langue, l'espèce de démon des mots dont il est possédé arrive dans le cas présent à un développement monstrueux, à une sorte de maladie' (UBC 33: 908).

[30] In February, a contract was drafted between the new publisher, The Servire Press (Rietzangerlaan 15, The Hague, represented by Carolus Verhulst), and Shakespeare and Company, Paris (Sylvia Beach) for the French distribution rights of *transition*. In this

next month, *transition* 21 could appear nonetheless: 'In March 1932 Volume 21 duly appeared under the imprint of Verhulst's Servire Press, and was to come out annually until Volume 27 in the spring of 1938' (de Voogd 2013, 238).

Immediate Reception: Press Clippings

The *New York Times* (25 March 1932) reported that Joyce had already been working for 10 years on his new work, which was 'said to be several times more "Joycian" than "Ulysses"' (see Plate 3). The new volume of *transition*, 'a thick quarterly magazine published in Holland and edited by Eugene Jolas' had just reached the US and contained 'many pages of "appreciation" of James Joyce' (UBC 69: 892).

Indeed, although *transition* 21 (March 1932) did not contain a new fragment of 'Work in Progress', it had organized its own reception of the work so far. It featured a special section called 'Homage to James Joyce', with contributions by Padraic Colum, Stuart Gilbert, Eugene Jolas, Thomas McGreevy, Philippe Soupault ('James Joyce at the Half Century'), a caricature by César Abin, an appendix with proofs of 'Work in Progress', Louis Gillet's 'James Joyce and His New Novel' and an interesting contribution by Joyce and C.K. Ogden, 'Anna Livia Plurabelle in Basic English'.

In the introduction to the Basic English version in *transition* 21, Ogden explained that the purpose was 'to give the simple sense of the Gramophone Record made by Mr. Joyce' and he concluded that by making this translation, 'the simplest and most complex languages of man are placed side by side' (*t21* 259). The gramophone record opened with the lines:

Well, you know or don't you kennet or haven't I told you every telling has a taling and that's the he and the she of it. Look, look, the dusk is growing.

---

agreement The Servire Press appointed Shakespeare and Company 'to be the sole distributors of TRANSITION for Paris (France)', which was also to be mentioned explicitly in each copy. Shakespeare & Co guaranteed 'to dispose of not less than 300 copies of each issue of TRANSITION, the price per copy to be francs 30,- and the Shakespeare & Co to have a discount of 50%' ('The consignment of three hundred copies is to be sent to Shakespeare & Co free of charge, duties etc. to be paid by Shakespeare & Co; The Servire Press to make up their invoices in Dutch guilders and their bills to be paid according to the following scale: 1/3 one month after date of the bill; 1/3 three months after date of the bill; 1/3 five months after date of the bill'.). The agreement was to 'remain in force for twelve months' initially 'and to be subject to renewal or cancellation then' (UB JJC XX. Miscellaneous Sylvia Beach and Shakespeare & Company Material, folder 40). On 13 February 1932, Sylvia Beach wrote to Carolus Verhulst: 'You proposed that Shakespeare and Company act as agents for the new Transition. I regret that it is not possible' (UB JJC XII. Beach to Verhulst, folder 1).

In Basic English they read:

> Well are you conscious, or haven't you knowledge, or haven't I said it, that every story
> has an ending and that's the he and the she of it. Look, look, the dark is coming.
>
> (*t21* 259)

In 1931, Ogden's *Debabelization: With a Survey of Contemporary Opinion on the Problem of a Universal Language* had been published by Kegan Paul, Trench, Trubner (London). It opens with an introduction '(*in Basic English*)', starting with a definition: 'Basic English is an attempt to give to everyone a second, or international, language, which will take as little of the learner's time as possible. It is a system in which everything may be said for all the purposes of everyday existence' (Ogden 1994 [1931], 227). The grammar was simple: 'Whatever is doing the act comes first; then the time word, such as *will*; then the act or operation *put*, *take*, or *get*; then the thing to which something is done, and so on' (227–8). And the vocabulary was limited to less than 1,000 words: 'It is an English in which 850 words do all the work of 20,000, and has been formed by taking out everything which is not necessary to the sense' (228) World peace was the ultimate aim, for the absence of a common language was seen as the main obstacle to international understanding and therefore the chief cause of war. The conclusion was obvious to Ogden: 'What the World needs most is about 1,000 more dead languages – and one more alive' (229).

An interesting section in *Debabelization* is called 'Science Versus Sophistication', arguing against the interlinguists: 'The confusion of adequacy with literary adequacy has been a chief cause of their failure to carry conviction'. To some extent, Ogden here prefigures C.P. Snow's 'Two Cultures' from a linguistic perspective. He does acknowledge the value of 'literary adequacy', but it can only lead to great confusion when the issue is 'adequacy'*tout court*. So, if it were up to him, the twain could meet, but never be mixed. The translation of the fragment from *Anna Livia Plurabelle* was his case in point. Joyce's 'Work in Progress' was by now almost universally recognized as the nadir of international unintelligibility, a 'bluddlefilth' of languages; what better way for Ogden to prove his point than to translate a sample from this 'obstacle to international understanding' into Basic English, and show the way to world peace.

transition 22

'Continuation of a Work in Progress', *transition* 22 (February 1933), 49–76 [*FW* 219–59] (Slocum and Cahoon 1971 [1953], 101, C.70)

More than three years after the previous instalment in *transition* 18 (November 1929), the first part of Book II (*FW* 219–59) was published in February 1933. The episode of the children's games was conceived as a play and opened with a presentation of the programme and *dramatis personae* of 'The Mime of Mick, Nick and the Maggies', which was also the title of the excerpt reprinted

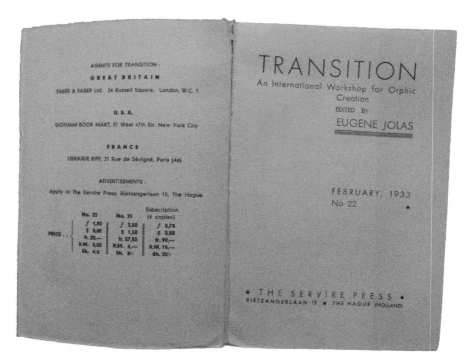

Figure 3.11   Title page of *transition* 22

in *Les Amis de 1914* and of the book, published by the Servire Press in June 1934 (see Chapter 7).

In the Meantime

'The Mime of Mick, Nick and the Maggies' appeared in *Les Amis de 1914* 2.40 (23 February 1934), 1. [FW 258.25–259.10, excerpt reprinted from *transition* 22] (Crispi and Slote 2007, 492)]

The Mime of Mick, Nick and the Maggies was published by the Servire Press in June 1934 (see Chapter 7)

transition 23

'Work in Progress: Opening and Closing Pages Part II: Section II', *transition* 23 (July 1935), 109–29 [FW 260–75; 304–8] (Slocum and Cahoon 1971 [1953], 101, C.70)

After *transition* 22 (February 1933) it took more than two years for the next number of *transition* (July 1935) to appear, this time with yet another subtitle: 'An Intercontinental Workshop for Vertigralist Transmutation' (see Figure 3.12).

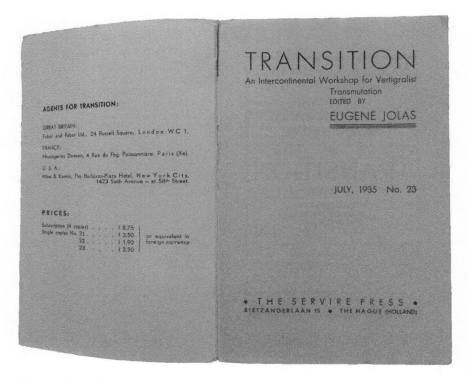

Figure 3.12   Title page of *transition* 23

The volume contained a new instalment of 'Work in Progress', corresponding with Book II, chapter 2, but without section 8 ('The Triangle', aka 'The Muddest Thick That Was Ever Heard Dump', which had been published in *transition* 11). The subtitle made explicit that this was not just a 'continuation' of 'Work in Progress', but that these were the 'Opening and Closing Pages' of the chapter. The fragment opened with a description of the tavern's location in Chapelizod and environs, followed by the children's pensums, including grammar and history, with 'Jellyous Seizer' (*FDV* 143) as one of the topics. Issy is reminded of her 'gramma's' advice that she should 'take the dative with his oblative', but mind she's 'genderous' (*FDV* 146). David Hayman (1966) and Luca Crispi (2007) have analysed the complex genesis of this part of 'Work in Progess', which was published as *Storiella as She Was Syung* in October 1937 by Corvinus Press, London (see Chapter 8).

In the Meantime

Storiella as She Was Syung was published by Corvinus Press in October 1937 (see Chapter 8)

transition 26

'Work in Progress: Opening Pages of Part Two, Section Three', *transition* 26 (February 1937), 35–52 [*FW* 309–31] (Slocum and Cahoon 1971 [1953], 101, C.70)

In *transition* 26 (February 1937) and 27 (April–May 1938) Joyce chose to publish only the two clearly isolatable tales told in chapter II.3. The one in *transition* 26 (preceding Kafka's 'Metamorphosis' in the same volume; see Figure 3.13) is the tale of Kersse the tailor and the Norwegian captain who orders a suit. The finished suit does not fit, and the captain reproaches Kersse for being unable to sew. The tailor in his turn blames the captain for being impossible to fit. The suggested link between tailoring and taletelling was already present in the first draft, where the tailor is called the 'talerman' (*FDV* 176), suggesting taletelling as a similarly central function of human nature as Jonathan Gottschall's suggestion in *The Storytelling Animal* that the 'hunger for meaningful patterns translates into a hunger for story' (104) – but not without the Joycean ironic distance, which seems to be missing in Gottschall's analysis.[31] The fragment in *transition* 26 ended – on the page opposite the opening of Kafka's story 'Metamorphosis' – with a reference to *Our*

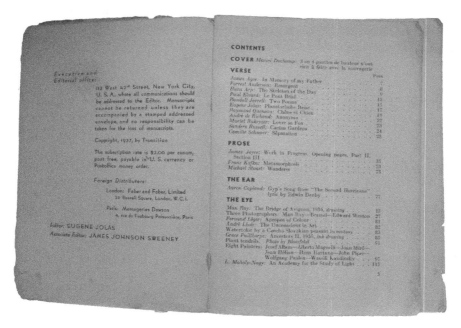

Figure 3.13   Table of Contents of *transition* 26

---

[31] 'The storytelling mind is a crucial evolutionary adaptation. It allows us to experience our lives as coherent, orderly, and meaningful' (Gottschall 2012, 102).

Exagmination: 'To the laetification of disgeneration by neuhumorisation of our kristianisation. For the joy of the dew on the flower of the fleets on the fields of the foam of the waves of the seas of the wild main from Broneholm has jest come to crown' (*t26* 52).

transition 27

'Fragment from Work in Progress', *transition* 27 (April-May 1938), 59–78 [FW 338–55] (Slocum and Cahoon 1971 [1953], 101, C.70)

While the first 'pub tale' (in *transition* 26) was presented as though it was broadcast over the radio, the second 'comes as though on a futuristic television screen' (Hayman 2007, 256). It is the story of 'How Buckley Shot the Russian General', told by Butt and Taff. Buckley, an Irish soldier, is about to shoot a Russian general, hesitates when he sees him defecating, but kills him when the general wipes himself with a clod of turf. Even though these two tales were not published in separate booklets, their pre-book publication in *transition* confirms a pattern of interlinked but isolatable tales that shaped 'Work in Progress'. Joyce always made clear that they were part of a bigger picture, but he also played an active role in the publication of the tales and fragments in separate books or booklets, often by fine arts presses. This 'Work in Press' is the subject of Part II.

PART II
Work in Press

Chapter 4
Anna Livia Plurabelle

During the first five years of Joyce's work in progress, the pre-book publications had appeared in magazines and collections. The first separate publication was *Anna Livia Plurabelle* (Crosby Gaige, October 1928). Two years later, it was published in a cheaper edition by Faber and Faber (1930). The first two versions of this section had been drafted in the 'Guiltless' copybook (the red-backed notebook that opens with the word 'Guiltless'; BL MS 47471b; see Introduction), the first draft stretching from page 74r to 78r; the second from 79r to 90r. In these versions, the piece starts with 'O tell me all now about Anna Livia', very close to its final version, but without the triangular typography of the opening lines. On 26 September 1926, Joyce sent a revised version of ALP to Harriet Shaw Weaver: 'Here is Δ2 MS and typescript. Please let me know what you think of it, when read? [. . .] "And I have done with you too, Mrs Delta" – for the moment. She will babble anon' (*LIII* 142).

'Anna Livia Plurabelle' had already appeared in *Le Navire d'Argent* and in *Two Worlds*, but this did not prevent Joyce from making changes and adding passages. One of these passages was the italicized part (below), after the following account:

> It was ages behind that when nullahs were nowhere, in county Wickenlow, garden of Erin, before she ever dreamt she'd lave Kilbride and go foaming [. . .] to wend her ways [. . .] in the barleyfields and pennylotts of Humphrey's fordofhurdlestown.

The account is then questioned: 'Wasut? Izod? Are you sarthin suir? *Not where the Finn fits into the Mourne, not where the Nore takes lieve of Blœm, not where the Bray diverts the Farer, not where the Moy changes her minds between Cullin and Conn and Conn and Cullin?*' But this suggestion is immediately denied: 'Neya, narev, naux and no!' (*ALP* 23) The passage in italics was based on a note, which Joyce made on the back of a loose sheet of stationery of his eye clinic.[1] The original affirmative description of the location is subsequently repeated in the form of a question:

> Where the Moy ~~changes~~ ^changez^ her ~~mind~~ ^minds moynds^ myonds
> ~~between~~ ^tween^ Cullin and Conn ~~and~~ ^and twixt^
> ~~Conn~~ Cunn and ~~and twixt~~ ^and^ ~~Cullin~~ ^Collin^
> Not where the Moy changez her
> myonds twixt Cullin and Conn
> and tween Cunn and Collin?

---

[1] 'Clinique Ophtalmique | Traitement des Maladies des Yeux | 39 RUE DU CHERCHE-MIDI [Paris]' (document preserved at Buffalo University, UB JJC VI.I.23).

If Daniel C. Dennett's metaphor for the workings of consciousness in terms of 'multiple drafts' (see Introduction) can be applied to the extended mind at work, this microdraft not only illustrates the process of 'thinking on paper', but simultaneously thematizes this process. The multiple drafts of the conscious self ('Moy') first 'changes', then 'changes', then ᶜʰᵃⁿᵍᵉᶻ, then (in the second draft) definitely 'changez' her singular 'mind', her plural 'minds', her 'moynds', her 'myonds', emulating and enacting the continuous mental revisions that make her change her mind. And when the fragment was inserted as a marginal addition to the marked pages of *Le Navire d'Argent* (*JJA* 48: 178; Yale 6.1–65), 'changez' changed into 'changes' again and 'myonds' into 'mind'. On the Galley proofs of *transition* 8, 'mind' became plural again: 'Moy changes her mind^ds' (*JJA* 48: 195; BL MS 47474, 215). And on the page proofs 'changes' is crossed out and replaced by 'changez' (*JJA* 48: 209; BL MS 47474, 233); that, however, is not how it appears in the published version of *transition* 8, 'where the Moy changes her minds' (*t8* 23). And 'changes' was changed again into 'changez' (*JJA* 48: 221; Yale 7.7–23) on the marked pages of *transition* for the Crosby Gaige edition of *Anna Livia Plurabelle*. These bibliographical and textual variants can easily be disparaged as mere cosmetics, but this textual make-up does reflect the making up of a mind – or minds – both on the level of the genesis and on the level of the text, that is, not just the writer's mind (level [1]) but also the evocation of the fictional mind (level [2]) at work.

'The pleasure of watching the mind at work' – that is how Fred Higginson described 'what is enjoyable about F[innegans] W[ake]' (Higginson 1960, 14). In this respect, Higginson compares Joyce's work to 'Euclid, Mendelejeff, or Beethoven's notebooks, FW being a Work in Progress, being no more totally complete than geometry, or the atomic table, or a late quartet' (14). There is something to say for Higginson's equation of *Finnegans Wake* with 'Work in Progress', since the work's circular structure is an invitation to keep rereading the text and each reading will definitely be different from the previous one. But this interpretation of the equation shifts the emphasis from the mind of the author (level [1], which is Higginson's main interest) to the mind(s) of the reader(s) (level [3]). Between these two levels, there is the level of the text (level [2]). In a novel, the object of cognitive narratology on level [2] is the evocation of the characters' minds. *Finnegans Wake* / 'Work in Progress', however, is not a novel, according to Higginson, because in order to be a novel, it would need more 'story'. 'And in the Wake there is a constant movement away from the story in total effect' (Higginson 1960, 5). Higginson's suggestion is to label it 'a work of the fictive imagination' (5). The adjective 'fictive' implies that the noun it refers to is created by the imagination. In other words, 'Work in Progress' is here defined as a work of the imagination created by the imagination. The work's fictive universe is 'imagination' itself. Higginson seems to interpret this in a rather biographical way, applying the topic of 'imagination' to James Joyce: 'What makes FW a great book is that there is in it as much of these pleasurable workings of *one man's mind* – the whole of it, shoddy and magnificent both – as has ever been put between covers' (14; emphasis added). It is hard to separate the 'one man' from the historical person James Joyce; but Higginson does not make a clear distinction between levels [1] and [2]. There is a difference between the workings of Joyce's mind and the text's evocation of a fictive mind ('fictive imagination'). The text is not merely a result of Joyce's imagination; it *performs*'imagination', it enacts the workings of a mind. This performative rendition of the notion of 'stream of consciousness' adds a cognitive dimension to what A. Walton Litz called Joyce's '*rendering* of the river' (Litz 1964, 113). From this perspective, it does not seem to be a coincidence that this work is both *Finnegans Wake* and a 'Work in Progress'. The text one happens to be reading, say a 1975 Faber and Faber paperback edition, is only one instantiation of the work in progress, or – to employ Daniel C. Dennett's metaphor – one draft in the 'multiple drafts model' that characterizes human consciousness. This would imply, however, that 'Work in Progress' is more than 'just a dream', in which the subconscious runs riot. The 'dream' explanation of *Finnegans Wake* invites the well-known criticism that the book would be a gratuitous, arbitrary compilation of dream images. Even if *Finnegans Wake* is the 'nightpiece' (Beach 1980, 185), following after *Ulysses* as the book of one day, the text is more complex than an evocation of the mind in a somnolent state.[2] It imaginatively asks the question how imagination works and where 'thoughts' come from: 'Where did thots come from?' (*FW* 597).

Until recently neuroscientists assumed that the neural activity when at rest could be compared to a somnolent state. The standard image was that of white noise on a TV screen when a station was not broadcasting. Recent developments in cognitive neuroscience and neuro-imaging have revealed that even when a human being is doing nothing at all, a substantial amount of meaningful activity – referred to as the brain's default mode – takes place in a network of brain regions that are at work when the person is not focused on the outside world. As opposed to the task-positive network of regions that are active when the individual does focus on the outside world, the default mode network[3] of task-independent introspection is

---

[2]   Georg Christoph Lichtenberg spoke of the mind as a 'sleeping system' that had to be woken up; and the act of writing was an excellent tool to accomplish such an awakening: 'Zur Aufweckung des in jedem Menschen schlafenden Systems ist das Schreiben vortrefflich, und jeder der je geschrieben hat, wird gefunden haben, dass schreiben immer etwas erweckt, was man vorher nicht deutlich erkannte, ob es gleich in uns lag' (qtd in Ortner 2000, 74). With his metaphor of a sleeping system inside every human being, which can be woken by means of writing, Lichtenberg expressed the standard view of the last few centuries.

[3]   'The concept of a default mode of brain function arose out of a focused need to explain how the appearance of activity decreases in functional neuroimaging data when the control state was passive visual fixation or eyes closed resting. The problem was particularly compelling because these activity decreases were remarkably consistent across a wide variety of task conditions. Using PET, we determined that these activity decreases did not arise from activations in the resting state. Hence, their presence implied the existence of a default mode. While the unique constellation of brain areas provoking this analysis has come to be known as the default system, all areas of the brain have a high level of organized default

believed to generate spontaneous thoughts and to be an essential component of creativity.

From a cognitive philosophical point of view this metaphor of the network accords with David Lodge's metaphor of the 'web of discourses' as interpreted by Daniel C. Dennett (1991, 416), that is, as just as much a biological product as for instance the spider's web. Telling tales is a 'fundamental tactic of self-protection, self-control, and self-definition' (417). The difference with the spider's web, however, is that human beings do not just exude their narratives; 'we don't spin them; they spin us. Our human consciousness, and our narrative selfhood, is their product, not their source' (1991, 418).[4]

With the word 'source', Dennett suggests another metaphor, which is eminently applicable to *Anna Livia Plurabelle*:

> These streams of narrative issue forth *as if* from a single source – not just in the obvious physical sense of flowing from just one mouth, or one pencil or pen, but in a more subtle sense: their effect on any audience is to encourage them to (try to) posit a unified agent whose words they are, about whom they are: in short, to posit a *center of narrative gravity*.
>
> (418; original emphasis)

Joyce's metaphor of the parlour game Chinese whispers, described by Sylvia Beach, is an equally apt metaphor for the workings of consciousness, following Dennett's suggestion of the 'centre of narrative gravity'. The 'streams of narrative' constitute a narrative self, thanks to a process from what Antonio Damasio calls a 'protoself' to 'a self in the proper sense': 'Within the narrative of the moment, it must *protagonize*' (Damasio 2012 [2010], 202; original emphasis).

This may be an apt description of what happens in *Anna Livia Plurabelle*, or *Anna Livia Plurabelle* can be seen as an excellent description and prefiguration of what Dennett and Damasio discovered only in the past few decades. ALP as a narrative self is the *product* of the 'streams of narrative' ('Tell me all'), not their *source* – to paraphrase Dennett. The streams of narrative issue forth only *as if* from a single source, or applied to *Anna Livia Plurabelle*, the opening 'O' is the effect of the streams of narrative on any audience ('I want to hear all about Anna Livia'), trying to posit a unified agent ('Well, you know Anna Livia? Yes, of course, we all know Anna Livia. Tell me all'), a centre of narrative gravity: 'O'.

Against this background, we should nuance Higginson's statement about *Finnegans Wake* not being a novel because of its 'movement away from story'. It is

---

functional activity'. Marcus E. Raichle and Abraham Z. Snyder, 'A Default Mode of Brain Function: A Brief History of an Evolving Idea', *Neuroimage* 37.4 (2007): 1083–90.

⁴ In *Intuition Pumps and Other Tools for Thinking* Dennett revisits his concept of 'narrative selfhood' as a centre of gravity, noting that, in spite of its abstractness, this centre of gravity is 'tightly coupled to the physical world' (2014, 334).

true that the notion of a single, straight story is hardly applicable to *Finnegans Wake*, but the movement is not necessarily 'away from story'. The movement that is at play, both in *Finnegans Wake* and 'Work in Progress', is comparable to the storytelling process of our consciousness, as described by Dennett and more recently by Jonathan Gottschall, who argues that the human mind is 'tuned to detect patterns' (Gottschall 2012, 103). Its 'hunger for meaningful patterns translates into a hunger for story' (104), and if it cannot find meaningful patterns in the world, 'it will try to impose them' (103). The difference between Gottschall and Joyce, however, is that the latter parodies and questions this urge to find meaningful patterns as the engine that drives his version of a history of the world (for instance the patterns that are imposed by the gossip-mongerers on the lack of evidence regarding what happened in Phoenix Park).

From the perspective of Dennett's 'multiple drafts model', there is a cognitive dimension to the study of Anna Livia's multiple drafts and publication history, even to typographical changes such as the variants in the opening lines between the publication of *Anna Livia Plurabelle* in *Le Navire d'Argent* (see Chapter 1) and *transition* 8, the 1928 Crosby Gaige edition, the 1930 Faber and Faber edition and the opening of chapter 8 in *Finnegans Wake*. Whereas the journal publications did not open with any special typography, the pre-book publication by Crosby Gaige introduced the typographical Δ suggesting a river mouth (see Figure 4.1). But this triangle was limited to only two lines:

O

tell me all about

The version of the text as published by Faber and Faber has three centred lines (see Figure 4.2; as in *Finnegans Wake*) before the rest of the text continues with the left and right margins justified:

O

tell me all about

Anna Livia! I want to hear all

Every textual or even typographical change alters the way Anna Livia 'protagonizes'. And what applies to the 'protagonists' or the protagonizing character amalgams on the level of the text (level [2]), also applies to the agents in the publication history, on the level of the text's production process (level [1]), and to the readers, on the level of the text's (early) reception (level [3]), no matter how dry the historical facts may seem at first. I propose to retrace this history with a multiple drafts model of narrative selfhood in mind, taking into account Joyce's direct cultural and material circumstances, including textual agents (and publishing angels) such as Sylvia Beach, technological and typographical concerns such as those of the printer of the Black Sun press (see Chapter 5), and the immediate reception in reviews, which formed the 'web of discourses' and 'streams of narrative' that constantly shaped and reshaped the image of both Joyce and his 'Work in Progress'.

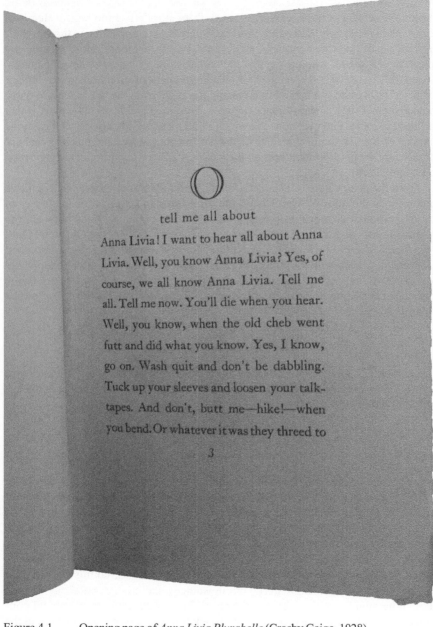

O

tell me all about

Anna Livia! I want to hear all about Anna
Livia. Well, you know Anna Livia? Yes, of
course, we all know Anna Livia. Tell me
all. Tell me now. You'll die when you hear.
Well, you know, when the old cheb went
futt and did what you know. Yes, I know,
go on. Wash quit and don't be dabbling.
Tuck up your sleeves and loosen your talktapes. And don't, butt me—hike!—when
you bend. Or whatever it was they threed to

3

Figure 4.1   Opening page of *Anna Livia Plurabelle* (Crosby Gaige, 1928)

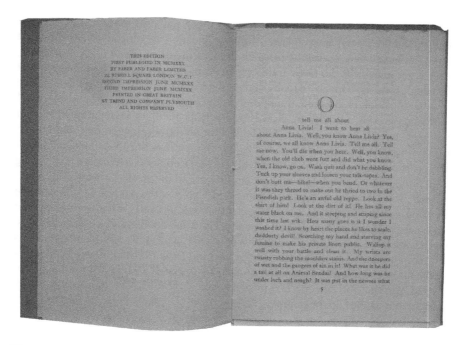

Figure 4.2   Opening page of *Anna Livia Plurabelle* (Faber and Faber, 1930)

Crosby Gaige

When the ALP instalment appeared in *transition* 8 (November 1927), Joyce received a letter from James R. Wells (15 November 1927) on stationery of 'William Edwin Rudge, Publisher' (475, 5th Avenue, New York City), of which Wells was the president. Wells was quite straightforward, requesting 'something for publication':

> I am writing you again to recall to you our conversation of some two months' ago while I was in Paris. I wish you would consider giving me something for publication. If it were a small book of poems, or a small prose work running from 32 to 72 pages, I would plan to make an edition of 500 or 600 copies, to be published at approximately $10.00 per copy. You would receive a royalty of 15% on the retail price, one-half to be paid upon the signing of the contract, and the balance thirty days after date of publication. From this you will see that the income to you would be sure regardless of sales. I shall hope to hear from you.
>
> (UB JJC XI: James Wells to Joyce, 1)

Perhaps it is also part of Joyce's 'shoppy' nature (according to Lewis 1993 [1927], 88) that he thought 10 dollars a copy was too inexpensive. On 28 November 1928, Joyce wrote to Ralph Pinker that he had declined an offer by the Viking Press, made to him by Harold K. Guinzburg in July ('Fifteen per cent royalties, of which a thousand dollars in advance, on a ten dollar publication'): 'I am advised that I ought not to undersell in America the privately printed fragment (*Anna Livia Plurabelle*, fifty eight pages) of the book I am engaged on, issued, signed to subscribers at fifteen dollars the copy, by Crosby Gaige of New York. If the Viking Press decide to issue the book at the same figure or a higher figure and renew the same terms, I will sign the copy' (*LI* 275–6). However, the 'fifteen dollars' he mentioned had not yet been agreed upon with Crosby Gaige. Not until a week later, on 5 December, did Sylvia Beach send a reply to Wells, which mentions the 15 dollars and was at least partially drafted by Joyce.[5] She had sent him a copy of *transition* 8, explaining that, although it was a fragment of a larger work in progress, it was also a 'book' in and of itself: 'The extract in "Transition" No.8 is the ANNA LIVIA episode forming the end of Part I; it is really a little book in itself'. This is an important statement in that it makes explicit how Joyce saw the double status of his episodes: on the one hand as preliminary sections of a work in progress, on the other hand as autonomous books. In the particular case of *Anna Livia Plurabelle*, Joyce's reading of the newest version of this piece around 17 November 1927[6] seems to have convinced him that the episode had now reached a form of completion, and Beach presented it as the 'final version':

> Besides the first version, ANNA, which appeared in 'Le Navire d'Argent' (October 1925), and the second, ANNA LIVIA, which appeared in No.8 of 'Transition', there is a third and final version, ANNA LIVIA PLURABELLE, unpublished and known only to a few of Mr Joyce's friends who heard him read it at his house a fortnight ago. He had made at least three hundred alterations and additions to the text that appeared in 'Transition' No.8.
>
> (UB JJC XII: Beach to James Wells, Folder 1)

To Claud W. Sykes, Joyce had written a postcard on 19 November 1927, thanking him for his 'kind references' to his new work and boasting that he had 'spent 1200 hours writing the piece' (*LIII* 167), again unwittingly (or seemingly) confirming Wyndham Lewis's description of Joyce as a 'craftsman' – 'not so much an inventive intelligence as an executant' (Lewis 1993 1927], 88). Sylvia Beach mentioned the same effort, expressed in quantitative terms: 'Mr. Joyce attaches more importance to this piece than to anything else in his new work, or perhaps to anything that he has done. Indeed it is the opinion of many that in boldness of conception, in skill with which the pattern is woven and in richness of harmony it surpasses

---

[5]   BU JJC XII: Beach to James R. Wells, folder 1. A pencil sketch of the last paragraph in Joyce's hand is enclosed with the letter, kept at Buffalo University.

[6]   See report in the Paris *Times* of 19 November 1927: 'A night or two ago James Joyce entertained at his home a few of his friends with a reading from his "work in progress"' (UBC 68: 2028).

even his own preceding work. He has spent twelve hundred hours writing it (though it can be read in a half hour) and taken an infinite amount of trouble with it'.

Sylvia Beach elaborates on the double status of the text as both fragment and self-contained work: 'It will be some time before the entire book is finished and meanwhile Mr. Joyce would be glad to see ANNA LIVIA PLURABELLE appear separately in book form in an edition such as you propose, for which it seems admirably suited. He has no other unpublished work, either poetry or prose to give you, nor does he contemplate writing anything besides this book upon which he is now engaged exclusively'.

After having mentioned the craftsman's working hours, Sylvia Beach raises the matter of the book's price: 'Mr. Joyce agrees with me that you should make the price of the copies $15 instead of $10 which you mentioned. I am sure that the demand for a book with the name of James Joyce on it would be large enough to sell the edition many times over'. Apparently to justify this price, she enclosed two French critics' opinions, including Louis Gillet's essay in *Les Nouvelles littéraires*.

Joyce seems to have been quite keen on the publication of *Anna Livia Plurabelle* as a separate book. The letter ends with a paragraph assuring Wells that all the copyright matters have been taken care of: 'The A.L.P. piece (as well as the rest of the new work appearing in "Transition") is copyright in the U.S.A. having been specially set up by American printers in three copies, two deposited in the Library at Washington and one for the writer, by arrangement of the American lawyers of Messrs. Jolas and Paul, editors of "Transition"'. This paragraph is drafted in pencil in Joyce's hand, which is an interesting detail, given that the last few sentences concern Sylvia Beach and are written from her perspective:

> As publisher of ULYSSES and by term of my contract with Mr. Joyce I hold the right of refusal of his new book, but I would agree to such publication in the form you suggest, which would not in any way invalidate that right, and even forge my claim to the very interesting and picturesque corrected printed pages of 'Transition' No.8 in deference to Mr. Joyce's interest and out of admiration for the piece itself.[7]

Wells replied on 16 December and Beach sent him another letter on or before 3 January 1928: 'There are about 7120 words in "Anna Livia Plurabelle". In your letter of November 15th you spoke of bringing out an edition of 500 or 600 copies, but in that of December 16th you mentioned only 400 copies. The size of the edition is a matter which of course you must decide yourself, but I do not think that Mr. Joyce would consider giving you "Anna Livia Plurabelle" unless it were worth at least thirteen hundred dollars to him' – that is, at least one dollar per working hour for the craftsman who had worked 1,200 hours on it. And to guarantee that salary, Sylvia Beach

---

[7]   UB JJC XII: Beach to James R. Wells, folder 1.

continued to devote the best of her business talents to this correspondence with Wells: 'I sent you a cable he had ᵃᵈ from Messrs. Boni & Liveright. Since then he has received a good offer from an English Publishing House. Were there no other offers however, I am afraid that the arrangement that you propose in your last letter, that is, 400 copies with 15% royalties would scarcely interest him'.[8] And four days later, on 7 January, the manuscript was sent to Wells, together with a telegram, specifying the details of the agreement – notably the print run of 600 instead of 400 copies:

> MANUSCRIPT SENT WITH LETTER JANUARY 4 AGREE YOUR SEPA-
> RATE PUBLICATION ANNA LIVIA PLURABELLE FOR 600 NOT 400 COP-
> IES ON TERMS AND CONDITIONS OF PAYMENT AS PER YOUR LETTER
> DECEMBER 16 NAMELY 1350 DOLLARS INSTEAD OF 900.
>   SYLVIA BEACH

While all the correspondence so far had been sent to Rudge publishers (475, 5th Avenue, New York City), the contract was sent from a new address, and another company, Crosby Gaige Publisher (229 West 42nd Street, New York, New York; directors: Crosby Gaige and James R. Wells), on 13 January:

> Dear Mr. Joyce:
> This will serve as an agreement between us for the publication of a portion of your work in progress, entitled ANNA LIVIA PLURABELLE.
> I will print and publish Six Hundred (600) copies of this work, each copy to be signed by you, for the sum of One Thousand Three Hundred and Fifty ($1350.00) Dollars – one-half of the amount to be paid to you upon the signing of this contract, the balance forty-five days after the date of publication, or not later than June 1, 1928.
> Miss Sylvia Beach has agreed that for this consideration you are also willing to give me your manuscript with corrections in your hand.
> It is further understood and agreed that you are not to permit any other edition of this work to appear in English for a period of six months from the date of my publication of this work. It is understood that each copy is to be signed by you.
>   Very truly yours,
>   [signed by Crosby Gaige]

> Dear Mr. Gaige:
> I accept the above conditions and hereby acknowledge receipt of the sum of Six Hundred and Seventy-five ($675.00) Dollars.
>   [signed by James Joyce]

In the accompanying letter (dated 13 January 1928), Wells also suggested the possibility of more book publications and he tried to obtain a few extra perks, such as

---

8   UB JJC XII: Beach to James R. Wells, folder 4.

a copy of *Pomes Penyeach* and the manuscript of *Anna Livia Plurabelle*.[9] Three days later, Sylvia Beach sent Joyce's idea for the 'turf-brown' cover: 'If Mr. Joyce may give a suggestion, he would be very glad if the binding might be a turf-brown and the title in red letters inside a gilt delta. Also, could there be red edges, at least at the top?' Here, Sylvia Beach drew a sketch of what Joyce had in mind, probably based on the draft Joyce had made on a sheet of graph paper, cut (in the shape of a triangle) from notebook VI.B.9, showing a triangle in pencil enclosing the title of the book, written in capitals:

ANNA

L I V I A

PLURABELLE

Sylvia Beach copied this design in her letter, specifying that Joyce was thinking of 'red lettering' inside a 'gilt triangle'. Joyce was clearly directing the whole enterprise, taking the liberty to include an introduction and even approaching someone to write it: 'Mr. Joyce has arranged for Mr. Padraic Colum to contribute a 500 word introduction to the work, as otherwise the intention and position of this piece in the entire work will be open to misinterpretation. This note is now written and a copy can be sent to you. If you agree, it would appear first in the *Dial* or some such review, calling attention to your publication. A full page announcement will also appear in the next number of *transition*'.[10]

Joyce not only attempted to control the cover design by letting Sylvia Beach send a 'suggestion' to Wells, he also tried to adjust the content of the Preface, by making 'suggested additions' to Padraic Colum's text – supervising it the way he would supervise 'the 12' for *Our Exagmination* (*LI* 279). When Colum mentions the 'evening sun', Joyce notes: 'Perhaps you could slip in a phrase somewhere to let readers know that it – the whole book – deals with night, takes place during a night, etc. etc.'. He also suggests that the publication in *Le Navire d'Argent* be mentioned and wonders: 'Is it useful to point out that in most languages the river is masculine or neuter and a rivergod is worshipped as Father Thames, Tiber etc. cf., fluvius, flumen, potamos, elven, fleuve, fluss, flod. In Irish it is feminine. And all

---

[9] 'I believe we could publish portions of your work "in progress" from time to time, to our mutual advantage, on the same terms as called for in this initial contract.

Miss Beach has indicated her willingness to give me, as part of the agreement, your manuscript with correction in your hand. I wonder if you would not be willing to make this a presentation of some sort to me. I would appreciate it very much.

I would like to hear from you in regard to the publication of any material you may have in future and will look forward to meeting you sometime this Spring in Paris. I have tried to obtain, without success, one of the thirteen copies of "Pomes Pennyeach". Is it possible you could help me to obtain it?' (UB JJC XI: Crosby Gaige to Joyce).

[10] UB JJC XII: Beach to James R. Wells, folder 7.

the heads representing the rivers of Ireland around the Customhouse, Dublin, are male heads except that of "we all love little Annie Ruiny, or we mean to say, lovelittle Anna Rainy when unda her brella" etc. etc. and etcetera et in fluvio fluviorum. E cosi sia' (UB JJC VI.J.7.b.i).

Through Sylvia Beach, Joyce kept putting pressure on the publishing schedule with urgent requests. Thus, on 6 February, Beach sent a telegram regarding the proofs:

> JOYCE URGENTLY REQUESTS IMMEDIATE SENDING OF PROOFS OF TEXT AS EXACT POSITIONS OF MARGINAL ADDITIONS AND CHANGES ARE NOT INDICATED ON TEXT IN YOUR POSSESSION PROOF WILL BE RETURNED ONE DAY AFTER RECEIPT
>
> SYLVIA BEACH

And another on 12 April:

> JOYCE REQUESTS SHEETS FOR SIGNATURE AND PROOFS

But on 7 June, Joyce was still making revisions to the text.[11] On the same day, the corrected galley sheets were received in New York and forwarded to Princeton University Press.[12] In the meantime, the marketing was already in full swing. On 1 February 1928, the magazine *Variety* had announced the imminent publication of 'a novel by James Joyce called "Anna Livia Plurabelle"' (UBC 36: 2145). The announcement (under the heading 'Gaige, Book Publisher')[13] also mentioned that Bennett Cerf and Donald Klopfer, publishers of the Modern Library and the Random House books would 'handle the distribution for Gaige'. The Spring 1928 Random House catalogue[14] featured a listing for Crosby Gaige's *Anna Livia Plurabelle*, announcing it, not as a work in progress, but as the 'new work' by James Joyce:

---

[11] See for instance the following emendations: 'Mr. Joyce asked me to send you the following additional corrections in "Anna Livia Plurabelle": / Page 1 line 27 for "lough" read "loch" / Page 5 line 13 for "alas alacs" read "aleffe, the leaks"'. (UB JJC VI.I.26: 'Emendations for the Second set of Galleys of *Anna Livia Plurabelle* (Crosby Gaige)').

[12] *JJA* 48: 299–311 and 285–97; Yale 7.1 and 7.2.

[13] Apparently, the news of the change from Rudge publishers to Crosby Gaige had not yet reached Paris, for on 16 February 1928, the *Paris Times* announced: 'Joyce's new book [. . .] will be published very soon by William Edwin Rudge, the New York publisher', who had 'gained an enviable reputation for his finely-printed tastefully-bound books' (UBC 69: 2160).

[14] UB JJC XVIII: Miscellaneous Material Related to Joyce's Works, G: 'Work in Progress'/ *Finnegans Wake*, folder 6.

RANDOM HOUSE NEW YORK
20 EAST 57 STREET
ANNOUNCEMENT FOR SPRING NINETEEN TWENTY-EIGHT
[. . .]
CROSBY GAIGE IMPRINTS

Crosby Gaige, identified with the play 'Broadway' and scores of other successful theatrical ventures, and a recognized collector of manuscripts and first editions,
is entering the publishing field with a first list that is astonishing in its variety and
richness. Random House has undertaken the distribution of Mr. Gaige's books for
two reasons: each is a first edition of a prominent author, and each is a collector's
item for typographic interest. There will be no separate English edition of any book
on this list; the English market will be supplied from the American printings.
  The eight books on Mr. Gaige's list are:
  The Heart's Journey by Siegfried Sassoon [. . .] / *Reminiscences of Andreyev*
by Maxim Gorki [. . .] / *Mid-Summer Eve by A.E.* [. . .] / *Letters of Joseph Conrad
to Richard Curle* [. . .] / *Fifty Romance Poems. Translated by Richard Aldington*
[. . .] / *Red Barbara and Other Stories* by Liam O'Flaherty [. . .] / *The Craft of
Verse*. The Oxford Poetry Essay by Humbert Wolfe [. . .] /
  Anna Livia Plurabelle. James Joyce's eagerly awaited new work. 600 copies,
signed by the author and designed by Frederic Warde. Ready in May. $15.

But the book was not 'Ready in May'. The *Enquirer* (Cincinnati, Ohio) did mention
on 5 May 1928 that 'Crosby Gaige, theatrical producer and book collector, ha[d]
entered the publishing field with an organization which will devote itself exclusively to the publication of new works by noted contemporary writers in fine limited editions', listing Joyce first (UBC 36: 2143). But it would take another summer
for *Anna Livia Plurabelle* to appear in this deluxe outfit, with 'Eight hundred copies
printed' in the issue with the 'turf-brown' cover, 'Each copy signed by Joyce', and
a special issue of 50 copies with a binding in black cloth (see Plate 4) instead of
brown, printed on pale green-tinted paper, watermarked 'Alexandra Japan' (Slocum
and Cahoon 1971 [1953], 44–5). The book was published on 20 October 1928.
    Less than two months later, Gaige sold his publishing house. On 11 December
1928, he sent a typed letter to Joyce, notifying him that he had handed over his firm
to his business partner, James R. Wells,[15] whereupon Wells changed the firm's name
from Crosby Gaige to Fountain Press (Banta and Silverman 1987, 159).
    Meanwhile, in Europe, there was still some confusion regarding this new work.
On 4 December 1928, *L'Intransigeant* did not know yet that *Anna Livia Plurabelle*

---

  [15] 'This is to inform you that I have disposed of my publishing business to Mr. James R.
Wells and associates of 522 Fifth Avenue, New York City. In the future I expect that my only
connection with publishing will be by way of my hand press. Frederic Warde and I plan to
produce some modern books by old time methods' (UBC JJC XI: Gaige to Joyce, folder 2).

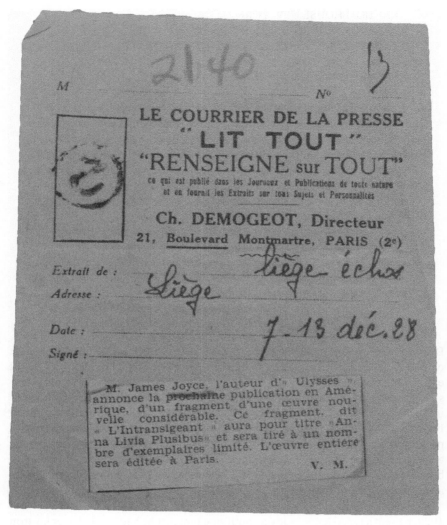

Figure 4.3   Announcement of 'Anna Livia Plusibus' [sic] in *Liège échos* (The Poetry
                Collection, Buffalo)

had already been published in New York; it was announced as an imminent publication, called '*Anna Livia Pluribus*' (UBC 36: 2138).[16] *Liège échos* (7–13 December
1928) echoed the misunderstood title adding an extra distortion: 'Anna Livia Plusibus' (UBC 36: 2140; see Figure 4.3). In the context of Joyce's literary project,

[16] By 11 January 1929, *Die Literarische Welt* in Berlin was still announcing it as 'Anna
Livia Pluribus' (UBC 36: 2137).

these are more than just instances of incompetence. Again, the 'Chinese whispers' logic of communication feeds into Joyce's view on history, and this feedback loop illustrates the enactive cognition at work during the publication history and simultaneous writing process of 'Work in Progress'.

Immediate Reception: Press Clippings

One of the aspects that was immediately commented upon in the early reviews was the book's 'expensive format', as it was described in an unsigned review in the Glasgow *Herald* (Thursday, 19 April 1928; UBC 1: 2042). More than the later pre-book publications, *Anna Livia Plurabelle* was mostly received in the press as Joyce's 'new work', that is, the way it was announced in the Random House catalogue. Nonetheless, it was presented as an 'episode' in Padraic Colum's Preface, which was indeed first printed separately in *The Dial* (April 1928; see above), with a footnote indicating: 'To Anna Livia Plurabelle, by James Joyce (12mo; 72 pages; Crosby Gaige, Publisher; limited edition; fifteen dollars) this essay constitutes the preface' (318; UBC 1: 1998).[17] The essay immediately opens with a crucial point by juxtaposing *A Portrait* with *Anna Livia* and implicitly drawing attention to the performative qualities of the latter: whereas Stephen Dedalus 'looked *upon*' the river ('In the distance along the course of the slowflowing Liffey slender masts flecked the sky'), the new work is different in that 'at once we are *in* the water' (318; emphasis added).

This form of enactment is already quite special in and of itself, but it becomes especially fascinating from a cognitive perspective when the water also operates as a metaphor of the 'stream of consciousness'. The notion of enactment – which was so important to F.R. Leavis (1952)[18] and liberal humanism, and which Peter Barry criticized in 'The Enactment Fallacy' (1980) – here applies to both a river and a stream of consciousness, that is, the evocation of a cognitive process. This suggests an interesting connection between 'enactment' in literature and 'enactivism' in cognitive philosophy. Whereas Stephen Dedalus was looking 'upon' the stream, the reader of 'Work in Progress' is 'in' it, in Colum's words; or to paraphrase Samuel Beckett: the text is not *about* a cognitive process, it *is* that process itself. In this sense, 'this puzzling, discontinuous, and counterintuitive book affords greater insights into the workings of the human mind than is usually credited', as

---

[17] In 'Footnotes' (in the Chicago *Tribune*, European Edition, 5), Robert Sage made extra publicity by calling Colum's essay 'The first article to appear in New York treating James Joyce's new work as anything more than, at the best, an unintelligible error of judgement or, at the worst, a deplorable sample of insanity' (UBC 35: 2047).

[18] In 'Tragedy and the Medium', for instance, Leavis notes: 'We don't, when we are responding properly, say that "Shakespeare gives us Macbeth's speech": it comes to us, not from the author, but from the play, emerging dramatically from a dramatic context. It offers no parallel to Seneca's "high maxims". And the "philosophy", moral significance, or total upshot, of the play isn't stated but *enacted*' (Leavis 1952, 123; emphasis added).

Tim Conley notes (2014, 35), not because it presents an explicit, philosophical model of the mind, but because it enacts the 'continuing incompletion' (Abbott 1996, 20) of an enactive thought process. A similar implicit suggestion of these performative qualities of the text was made by Norah Meade in the 'Books' section of the *New York Herald Tribune* (Sunday, 13 September 1931, pp. 1, 6): 'Joyce's matter is hardly distinguishable from his form' (UBC 34: 2024).

In addition to pointing out the performative quality of the text, Padraic Colum's essay in *The Dial* situates the new work, not only in Joyce's œuvre so far, but also in the genesis of 'Work in Progress': 'although it is epical it is an episode, a part and not a whole. It makes the conclusion of the first part of a work that has not yet been completed'. The pre-history of its publication is also explicitly mentioned on the opening page: 'The episode was first published in *Le Navire d'Argent* in September 1925. It was expanded and published in *Transition* in November 1927. Again expanded, a title has been given it: Anna Livia Plurabelle' (318).

One of the first reviewers who took this publication history as an invitation to perform 'A careful comparison of the first and last versions' was J. Leon Edel.[19] Interested not so much in Joyce's 'aims', but especially in 'his method' (330), Edel tries to discover how 'Joyce begins to combine words, to deform them', which 'gives it a peculiar richness':

> 'I know by heart the places he likes to soil' remarks one of the washerwomen as she throws a garment into the water. In the second version this becomes 'I know by heart the places he likes to saale, duddurty devil!' The proximity of the deformed 'saale' to the English 'soil' and the French 'sale' is to be remarked. The same is true when Mr. Joyce expands this changing of the language from the simplicity of 'Wait till the rising of the moon' in the first, to 'Wait till the honeying of the lune, love!' Here he substitutes the French word for the English and gives the whole phrase an additional two-fold association, on the one hand with the English 'honeymoon' and on the other with the French equivalent 'lune de miel'.
>
> (330; UBC 1: 1987)

Edel draws attention to the increasing complexity ('More complex perhaps is the sentence inserted in the second version "Reeve Gootch was right and Reeve Drughad was sinistrous"'), but he is careful in his appreciation: 'Mr. Joyce is giving us an important experiment; what will be its later value we cannot now estimate. But that it is worthy of consideration I am certain'(330). Edel suggests it is quite possible that Joyce is 'trying to do too much' and that there is a 'limit to the suggestive power of literature', but that is a matter of 'aesthetics', whereas he is interested in 'poetics' in the etymological sense of 'making' (Gr.: 'poiein'): 'What concerns us at the moment is method in *Work in Progress*; there is sufficient in it, I feel, to warrant a close scrutiny rather than a careless dismissal' (330).

---

[19]   J. Leon Edel, 'The New Writers', *Canadian Forum* X (June 1930), 329–30.

The emphasis on 'method' makes sense against the contrastive background of the early critics' focus on 'madness'. 'The only water it all suggests to me is water on the brain', Gerald Gould commented in *The Observer* (Sunday, 9 December 1928) under the heading 'New Novels' (UBC 1: 2144).

The *Times Literary Supplement* published an unsigned review that called *ALP* an 'experiment' (20 December 1928), which seems to suggest that no matter how crazy the experiment is, it is pretty harmless as long as it stays within the covers of Joyce's own work: 'We may be fairly sure that such an effort will not change the literary language outside Mr. Joyce's books, but inside them there is little harm and great interest in the change' (UBC 1: 2049). *Vogue* (May 1929) reviewed *Anna Livia Plurabelle* ('a little book of experimental nonsense') together with *The Enemy* – 'full of fascinating observations (on Joyce and Stein and the contributors to *Transition*)' – agreeing with Wyndham Lewis's suggestion that Joyce's work is 'a good example of the "Back to Infancy" movement' and a 'pendant to Gertrude Stein's *Tender Buttons*'. But then again, 'Mr. Wyndham Lewis deals out birchrods and codliver oil, thumbscrews and racks, Louis XI-like cages all round for anyone and everyone upon whatever errand caught' (UBC 1: 511). Anyhow, whatever Joyce was trying to do, it was all too vague for *Vogue*: 'What is it about?', that was the question.

Arnold Bennett played the role attributed to him by Virginia Woolf (in her essay 'Modern Fiction') as a representative of the previous generation against which her own (including Joyce) was rebelling: 'The last of my rebels is James Joyce', he wrote in the London *Evening Standard* ('Three Modern Rebels', 19 September 1929, p. 7), praising the material appearance of the Crosby Gaige edition ('I am charmed to have it') rather than the content ('I cannot comprehend a page of it'). He only needed two short paragraphs to apodictically pronounce his verdict: '*Anna Livia Plurabelle* will never be anything but the wild caprice of a wonderful creative artist who has lost his way' (UBC 1: 931).

The *New York Herald* ('In the World of Books', 1 October 1928) had already chosen the same approach, focusing on the material aspects of the book ('printed most artistically by Crosby Gaige'; UBC 35: 2046). And in the *Irish Statesman* (29 December 1928), 'Y.O.' – pseudonym of George Russell, A.E. (Deming 1977 [1970], vol. II, 395) – similarly opened his review with a paragraph praising the outside, implicitly downplaying the inside ('if one could understand it'): 'This is a book for collectors [. . .] this book is the really extraordinary part of the work which is in progress and which is appearing in *transition*' (*Irish Statesman* xi, 339).[20] Sean O'Faolain reacted on 5 January, arguing that 'Joyce's technique ceases to serve any useful purpose. That the mind should be in chaos is not at any

---

[20] On the same day, 29 December 1928, the Newcastle *Chronicle* published a relatively open-minded, unsigned review, which concisely summarizes the immediate reception of 'Work in Progress': 'It is easy to make fun of Mr. Joyce, although he is one of the most considerable writers of our time, and it is perhaps even more easy, and more ridiculous, to treat him as though he were a god above criticism' (UBC 35: 2040).

time desirable'.[21] O'Faolain had no doubt that Joyce's work would have its influence on literature, but it was 'not sane enough' to be literature in and of itself (355). In April 1928, O'Faolain had already spoken of Joyce's 'maltreatment of language'.[22] Eugene Jolas reacted in his turn to O'Faolain, first in the *Irish Statesman* (26 January 1929, 414, 416) and then in *transition* 15 ('The New Vocabulary', February 1929), referring directly to O'Faolain's earlier essay as it appeared in *The Criterion* ('Style and the Limitations of Speech'): 'Mr O'Faolain attempts to dispose of the Joycian onslaught on traditional language by insisting on the "immobility of speech"', arguing that 'The most cursory glance at the evolution of English, or other languages, shows that speech is not static' (414; UBC 1: 2057).[23]

The polemic continued on 2 March 1929, when O'Faolain assured Jolas in a letter to the editor of the *Irish Statesman* (513–4) that that was not what he attempted at all. Instead, he proposed that 'precision is the cardinal virtue of good English prose', whereas Joyce's 'new manner' works with 'implication and suggestion – as vague and unprecise as possible' (514): 'Our vocabulary is limited, certainly. If it were not it would be unintelligible, frustrating itself by its own endlessness, its innumerable meanings. [. . .] I know but one set of men who succeeded in re-arranging English with success, and these were the nonsense writers' (514; UBC 1: 2058). Against this statement, Walter Lowenfels replied in yet another letter to the editor of the *Irish Statesman* (16 March 1929), noting that 'every great English poet has rearranged English; that the use of language expands to follow the usages of poetry; that the introduction of "new

---

[21]   *Irish Statesman*, xi (5 January 1929), 354–5 (UBC 1: 2057; Deming 1977 [1970], vol. II, 397).

[22]   Sean O'Faolain, 'The Cruelty and Beauty of Words', *Virginia Quarterly Review* 4.2 (April 1928), 211, 22, 225. Republished as 'Style and the Limitations of Speech' in *The Criterion* 8.30 (September 1928), 71, 83–4, 86–7. See also Deming 1977 [1970], vol. II, 391.

[23]   Other readers joined in, with letters to the editor ('Dear Sir, I have been reading the articles by yourself, Sean O Faolain'), such as this mock analysis of the word 'Balderdash' by '"Shakespere"' (*Irish Statesman*, 2 February 1929), a parody of the analyses of 'Work in Progress' by Padraic Colum and Eugene Jolas:

'BALDERDASH. – This contains more than four references. First let us divide the word into 'Balder' and 'dash'. As educated people are aware, Balder is the Scandinavian God of Spring. The moving pleonasm: 'Balder the Beautiful is dead, is dad', is a well-known line of the old-fashioned poetry. 'Dash' suggests at least a sudden self-removal or even death. But that is only a part of my meaning. Let us get about cutting out unnecessary letters: take the B from 'Balder' and the D from 'dash', and what remains? Here the thing assumes necromantic proportions. We have 'alder' and 'ash': two magical trees. Ygdrasil was the giant ash . . . I am called back to join my colleagues. Forgive me! – Yours faithfully.
'SHAKESPERE" (UBC 35: 2042)

words" is perhaps secondary to the way old words are reborn in the pens of poets; that people do not create a vocabulary so much as poets extend one, keeping it lively by using it in a new way to show the "before unapprehended relation to things"; that those who accept a vocabulary from the ages die with the ages; that though the poet is not the creator of all the meaning in his use of words, as he is a poet he develops the infinite meaning inherent in any word' (31). He therefore proposed 'an armed truce about Mr. Joyce until an agreement is reached about the general principles that underlie language and its development' (31; UBC 1: 2061).

During this 'armed truce', Cyril Connolly wrote a long review essay (*Life and Letters* 2 April 1929], 273–90), presenting 'Work in Progress' as an experiment: 'it may be a failure, but it is surely an absorbing one, and more important than any contemporary successes'. Perhaps 'Work in Progress' was indeed an 'important failure', to borrow Auden's phrase, and as such it also drew attention to the importance of failure as a crucial element of cognitive processes, as scientists increasingly come to appreciate.[24] Quoting the end of *Anna Livia Plurabelle*, he added between brackets: 'All this has to be read as carefully as it has been written'. No matter how reserved Connolly remains, he does show his respect and admiration: 'the new work of Joyce is respect-worthy and readable. There is nothing insane in its conception nor bogus in its execution'. And as for the linguistic distortions, he approached the issue from an Irish perspective: as an Irishman, Joyce was 'under no obligation whatever to rest content with the English language' (Connolly, qtd in Fargnoli 2003, 313).

Faber and Faber

While the press was making up its mind about what to think of Joyce's new work, T.S. Eliot suggested Faber and Faber might re-issue *Anna Livia Plurabelle*. He wrote to Joyce on 30 July 1929: 'A.L.P. has arrived from Paris and I have read it with real enjoyment. Personally I should very much like to carry out the project I suggested to you but I shall have to wait a week or so until I can even take the

---

[24] See for instance the exhibition 'Fail Better' at the Science Gallery at Trinity College, Dublin (7 February 2014–27 April 2014), whose aim was formulated as follows: 'The goal of "Fail Better" is to open up a public conversation about failure, particularly the instructive role of failure, as it relates to very different areas of human endeavour. Rather than simply celebrating failure, which can come at great human, environmental and economic cost, we want to open up a debate on the role of failure in stimulating creativity: in learning, in science, engineering and design' (dublin.sciencegallery.com/failbetter).

matter up as two out of the five Directors are away on holiday'.[25] On 22 August, Eliot sent the contract to Joyce:

> Dear Joyce,
>
> I am enclosing an agreement for you about ANNA LIVIA PLURABELLE. Not being sure that I have your present Paris address I have left it to you to fill in. If this is all right will you complete it and let me have it back. I also enclose a specimen page in a type which would allow the whole thing to be printed in 32 pages. 32 pages is a convenient form and would certainly allow us to publish the book at a shilling. *We quite agree with you on the question of price and are anxious to keep it down to a shilling if possible* but I do not know whether you will think this page too closely crowded. I shall get the opinion of the other directors on that point anyway but if you have any doubt yourself about this page I should suggest that you look in on Monday about noon and we will talk it over with de la Mare who is the Manager responsible for the printing.
>
> (UB JJC XI: Eliot to Joyce, folder 8; emphasis added)

It is remarkable that Joyce, who had urged Wells to increase the price of the Crosby Gaige edition to $15, now apparently insisted on a cheap edition. In autumn, the news started spreading that Anna Livia was to be 'published next spring by Faber and Faber in the "Criterion Miscellany"' (T.P. & Cassell's Weekly, 12 October 1929; UBC 36: 1009), and its price did not go unnoticed.

By February 1930, 'Brother Savage' in the Liverpool *Post* announced the news that Faber and Faber was going to offer 'James Joyce at a Shilling' (UBC 36: 1023; see Figure 4.4). On Thursday 3 April 1930, the *TLS* announced its publication for 'Early in May' (289) (UBC 36: 592).

Anna Livia Plurabelle was published by Faber and Faber as number 15 in the Criterion Miscellany series on 12 June 1930 (Norburn 2004, 143).[26] On that day, the *Daily Herald* announced the publication 'in booklet form' ('Anna Livia Enters'): '"Anna Livia Plurabelle" [. . .] is published by Faber and Faber. Despite the employment of what is virtually a new language, there are rhythm and lilt in the writing that make fascinating reading' (UBC 35: 883).

The Aberdeen *Press* announced the booklet as 'Joyce's Outpouring', 'bound in a dun colour, as near as the publishers can get to the colour of the Liffey' (12 June 1930; UBC 35: 904; see Plate 5); according to the Cardiff *Western Mail* ('Published To-day') Joyce possessed 'a genius of such tropical luxuriance that it has become rank

---

[25] UB JJC XI: Eliot to Joyce, folder 6. In addition to G.C. Faber, C.W. Stewart, R.H.I. De la Mare and F.V. Morley, Eliot was one of the Directors himself.

[26] The information in *A James Joyce Chronology* is ambiguous: the entry for 1 May 1930 reads: '*ALP* is published by Faber and Faber' (Norburn 2004, 142); the entry for 12 June 1930 reads '*Anna Livia Plurabelle* (now *FW* 196–216) is published by Faber and Faber' (143).

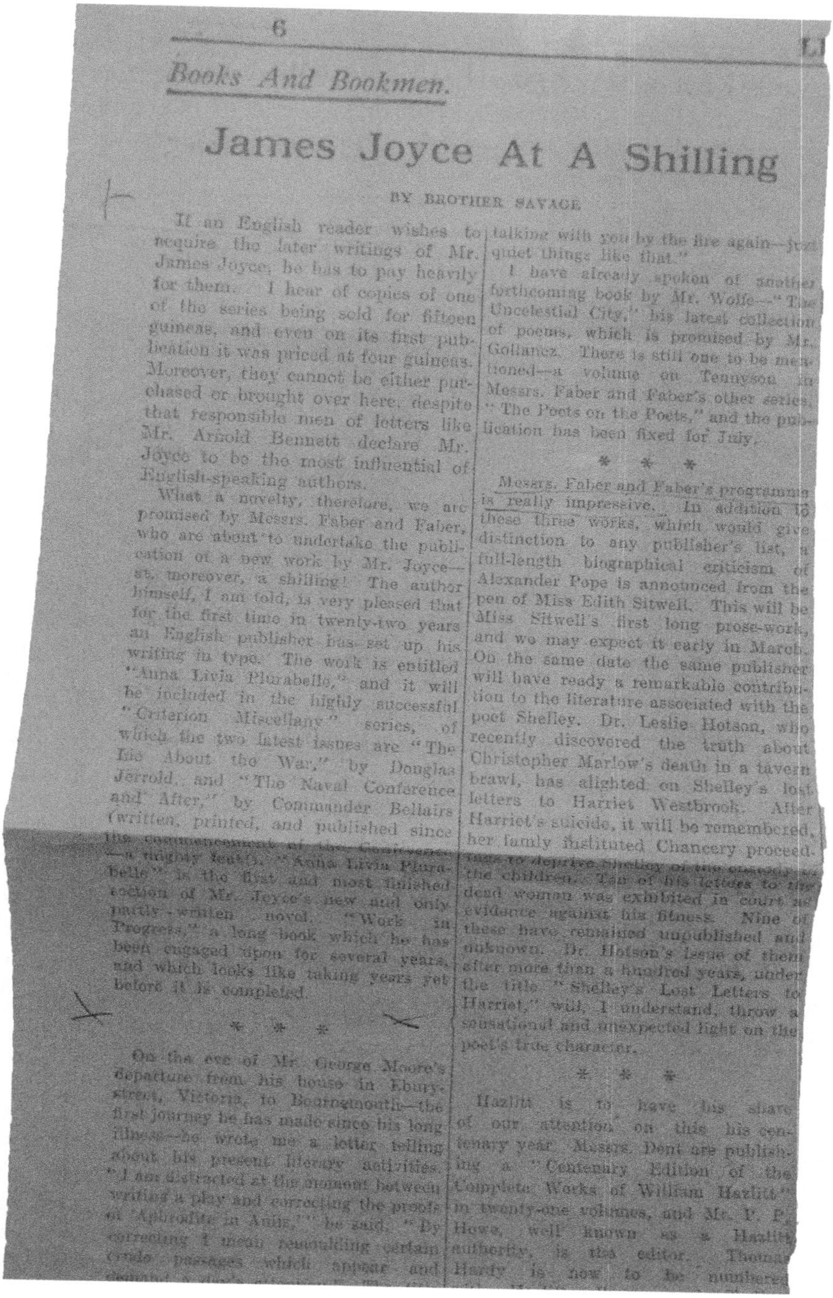

Books And Bookmen.

James Joyce At A Shilling

BY BROTHER SAVAGE

If an English reader wishes to acquire the later writings of Mr. James Joyce, he has to pay heavily for them. I hear of copies of one of the series being sold for fifteen guineas, and even on its first publication it was priced at four guineas. Moreover, they cannot be either purchased or brought over here, despite that responsible men of letters like Mr. Arnold Bennett declare Mr. Joyce to be the most influential of English-speaking authors.

What a novelty, therefore, we are promised by Messrs. Faber and Faber, who are about to undertake the publication of a new work by Mr. Joyce—at, moreover, a shilling! The author himself, I am told, is very pleased that for the first time in twenty-two years an English publisher has set up his writing in type. The work is entitled "Anna Livia Plurabelle," and it will be included in the highly successful "Criterion Miscellany" series, of which the two latest issues are "The Lie About the War," by Douglas Jerrold, and "The Naval Conference and After," by Commander Bellairs (written, printed, and published since the commencement of the conference —a mighty feat!). "Anna Livia Plurabelle" is the first and most finished section of Mr. Joyce's new and only partly written novel, "Work in Progress," a long book which he has been engaged upon for several years, and which looks like taking years yet before it is completed.

* * *

On the eve of Mr. George Moore's departure from his house in Ebury-street, Victoria, to Bournemouth—the first journey he has made since his long illness—he wrote me a letter telling me about his present literary activities. "I am distracted at the moment between writing a play and correcting the proofs of 'Aphrodite in Aulis,'" he said. "By correcting I mean remodelling certain crude passages which appear—and

talking with you by the fire again—just quiet things like that."

I have already spoken of another forthcoming book by Mr. Wolfe—"The Uncelestial City," his latest collection of poems, which is promised by Mr. Gollancz. There is still one to be mentioned—a volume on Tennyson in Messrs. Faber and Faber's other series, "The Poets on the Poets," and the publication has been fixed for July.

* * *

Messrs. Faber and Faber's programme is really impressive. In addition to these three works, which would give distinction to any publisher's list, a full-length biographical criticism of Alexander Pope is announced from the pen of Miss Edith Sitwell. This will be Miss Sitwell's first long prose-work, and we may expect it early in March. On the same date the same publisher will have ready a remarkable contribution to the literature associated with the poet Shelley. Dr. Leslie Hotson, who recently discovered the truth about Christopher Marlow's death in a tavern brawl, has alighted on Shelley's lost letters to Harriet Westbrook. After Harriet's suicide, it will be remembered, her family instituted Chancery proceedings to deprive Shelley of the custody of the children. Ten of his letters to the dead woman was exhibited in court as evidence against his fitness. Nine of these have remained unpublished and unknown. Dr. Hotson's issue of them after more than a hundred years, under the title "Shelley's Lost Letters to Harriet," will, I understand, throw a sensational and unexpected light on the poet's true character.

* * *

Hazlitt is to have his share of our attention on this his centenary year. Messrs. Dent are publishing a "Centenary Edition" of the Complete Works of William Hazlitt" in twenty-one volumes, and Mr. P. P. Howe, well known as a Hazlitt authority, is the editor. Thomas Hardy is now to be numbered

Figure 4.4   'James Joyce at a Shilling': Announcement of *Anna Livia Plurabelle* (Faber and Faber) in the *Liverpool Post* (The Poetry Collection, Buffalo)

and poisonous', producing a 'murky stream of subjective meanderings' in which 'we can detect a moral obliquity' (UBC 35: 903); the *Yorkshire Herald* (11 June 1930) treated it as the 'croonings of an old Irishman', 'a torrent of verbiage', 'the subdued soliloquy of a madman [. . .] who loses control over a cascade of ideas, memories and impressions which surges into articulation' – concluding condescendingly:

> You feel inclined to say: 'There! there! steady now!' in soothing encouragement,
> but in your own *mind* you think: 'What a pity! And with such a grand *brain*, too'.
>
> (UBC 35: 900; emphasis added)

The use of the words 'mind' and 'brain' in this short article nicely illustrates the then predominant, Cartesian, dualistic view of the mind as something that does not go beyond the brain and clearly separates an inside from an outside.[27] The announcement in the Glasgow *Evening News* (13 June 1930) opened with a poor imitation of Joyce's language, wondering 'Is it a cod he is amaking of us orl? Or a whale?': 'It is no use. One cannot beat Mr Joyce at his own game or come anywhere near either his prolixity or his obscurity. [. . .] It might be for all one can make of it the nightmare of a compositor who has been setting an argument between a drunken lunatic and an ill-informed disciple of Einstein' (UBC 35: 907).

A fortnight later, the *Daily Sketch* noted that 'James Joyce is scarcely accessible to English readers', blaming it on the episode's 'freak spelling and still more freakish grammatical structure' (26 June 1930; UBC 35: 898). The Yorkshire *Evening Post*'s reviewer, despite the 'expenditure of time' and effort 'deciphering [. . .] the new opus', was 'no wiser as to the significance of it all' (27 June 1930; UBC 35: 902). The next day, a mere six-line impression in *Newsagent* also admitted defeat (28 June 1930): 'I have tried to read "Anna Livia Plurabelle" [. . .] but I am beaten. What extraordinary stuff, but how some people like it or pretend to, for it is selling like hot cakes' (UBC 35: 483).

By 29 October 1930, Eliot could report to Joyce that *Anna Livia Plurabelle* had 'sold up to date over 4600 copies – 57 last week' and he thought it would 'go on indefinitely, even after the publication of the complete work': 'and I think it will help the sale of the work [. . .]. We are more than satisfied' (UB JJC XI: Eliot to Joyce, folder 12). By 27 January 1931, the number of copies sold was 5167 (folder 15); by 16 December 1931, 6100 (folder 23); by 16 February 1932, 6546 (folder 25).

---

[27] This dualistic concept of consciousness is problematic with regard to what is often referred to as the 'hard problem of consciousness', the difficulty in explaining how consciousness and experience are related to the body (the brain), or what Joseph Levine called the 'explanatory gap' (the problem of physicalist theories of mind in explaining how the material brain generates or occasions subjective, conscious experiences or so-called qualia (Joseph Levine, 'Materialism and qualia: the explanatory gap', *Pacific Philosophical Quarterly*, 64 (1983): 354–61). As Evan Thompson notes, 'The problem with the dualistic concepts of consciousness and life in standard formulations of the hard problem is that they exclude each other by construction' (Thompson 2007, 225).

Even before the publication in the 'pamphlet series' was ready, some critics called it an abomination by the 'fallen' genius, 'sinking to a new method of verbal expression on which few normal human beings can have time or ingenuity to waste', as the 'sober' and 'normal' reviewers of the Yorkshire *Post* in Leeds reported in 5 February 1930, 'shaking their heads in sorrow over the fall of Mr. Joyce' (UBC 1: 801). Just like the reviewer in *Vogue* a year earlier, *Notts Journal*'s C.H. Hodgson called it 'sheer balderdash' and wondered 'in the name of common sense': 'Really, Mr. Joyce, what is it all about?' and 'Is it worth while?' (Nottingham, 2 July 1930; UBC 1: 901).

In its section 'The World of Books', the *Western Independent* (20 September 1930) published a few 'Reflections of a Reader', offering 'an explanation of the phenomenon of Mr. James Joyce in the last score of years [. . .] to the pathologists and the Freudians': it was simply the effect of 'Encephalitis lethargica' on Joyce's brain (UBC 1: 472). Again, the 'common-sense' view reduced the mind to the brain, explaining away the literary enactment of a mind at work as incomprehensible balderdash due to the alleged degeneration of Joyce's brain.

As in several review of *transition* (see Chapter 3), the 'unintelligible' aspect of Joyce's work was presented as a clever trick to mislead the censors. On 16 May 1930, G.W. Stonier wrote in the *New York Sun* that 'James Joyce is continually referred to in books and critical articles as perhaps the most important novelist of the age, yet it is a criminal offense to possess a copy of *Ulysses*' ('A London Letter'). But he had found a solution: 'Mr. Joyce is getting over this difficulty of censorship in his own way. His latest work, "Anna Livia Plurabelle"[. . .] is at the first glance such an unintelligible compound of languages that not even an English official will think to call it "obscene"' (UBC 35: 2125).

In October 1930, shortly after the publication of *Anna Livia Plurabelle* in the Criterion Miscellany series, the journal *The Criterion* published a letter to the Editor by Sean O'Faolain, in which he actively contributed to the 'armed truce' (cf. supra) by means of a 're-reading': 'A re-reading of *Anna Livia Plurabelle*, with much more pleasure than at any previous reading, convinces me that in an article which you kindly published in *The Criterion* of September, 1928, I did not do complete justice to Mr. Joyce's new prose' (*The Criterion*, October 1930, 147). O'Faolain now admitted that Joyce's new work could be 'tantalizingly delightful' if one did not maintain a strict distinction between prose and poetry, 'if approached as prose from which an explicit or intellectual communication was never intended' (147; qtd in Deming 1977 [1970], 413). Joyce's 'Work in Progress', indeed, was less of an 'explicit or intellectual communication' than an enactment of enactive cognition.

Gramophone Record

In autumn 1927, the Paris *Times* (19 November 1927) reported that Joyce had 'entertained at his home a few of his friends with a reading from his "work in progress". Those present felt that the new prose style of Mr Joyce gains enormously in wit and comprehensibility by being read aloud by the author' (UBC 68: 2028). Three years later, this impression led to *Anna Livia Plurabelle*'s translation into another medium, offering a more literal interpretation of the line 'I want to hear all about Anna Livia'. In July 1929, Joyce wrote to Sylvia Beach that he had seen C.K. Ogden in London, who wanted 'to do a disc of my reading last 4 pages of Alp' (*JJSB* 164). The record was produced in August 1929 at the Orthological Institute in London. Some of the reports, such as the New York *Herald*'s 'In the Latin Quarter', give a sense of the degree to which – in contrast with the growing number of negative reviews – there was also a community in Paris that idolized Joyce, watched his every move and worshipped each object he touched. The scroll from which Joyce read the text to be recorded (now held at the University at Buffalo) was treated almost as a sacred object with the aura of a religious relic: 'Only a very few persons have been permitted a glimpse of the specially printed scroll of Mr. Joyce's *Anna Livia Plurabelle*, done in large clear lettering, from which the author read this latest work while in London, for a phonographic record'. And for those who wondered how the recording session proceeded: 'The author is stated to have sat back comfortably in an easy chair, reading his own manuscript in scroll form' (24 September 1929; UBC 36: 36).

Many of the reactions in the press came with a delay of sometimes more than a year. The *Daily Express* announced on 10 September 1930 that a gramophone record had been made of Joyce's reading of the last four pages of *Anna Livia Plurabelle*: 'an organization called the Orthological Institute in London is supplying it to such of the elect as agree, with Mr. Joyce, that English ought not to be "as she is spoke" but as Mr. Joyce would have her spoke' (UBC 36: 885). A few critics wrote somewhat slightingly of the 'hitherandthithering' double 12-inch record, like Wyndham Lewis ('Mustard and Cress') in the *Sunday Referee* of 30 August 1931: 'One perceives a new form of evening entertainment for the intelligentsia' (UBC 35: 910). But on the whole, the project seems to have helped many readers and reviewers appreciate *Anna Livia Plurabelle*. In a review of the Faber and Faber edition, for instance, Geoffrey Grigson noted: 'Read as Mr. Joyce intends them to be (and Joyce himself has recorded his reading of the last four pages on a double-sided gramophone record) these lines are efficient and beautiful'. This aural quality of the texts contributed to his appreciation: 'To say [. . .] that the latest product of the mind which produced *Ulysses* is nothing but the drunken dribbling of a lunatic, seems to me prejudice and lazy self-satisfaction' (UBC 1: 2001). Nino Frank (in *VU* n° 105, p. 256) noted Joyce's clear and suggestive diction, accentuating the magic force ('puissance magique') of 'Work in Progress' (UBC 36: 476). Both *Les Nouvelles littéraires* (4 April 1931) and the *Paris Soir* (7 April 1931) characterized the recording as an 'incantation' (UBC 36: 293).

C.K. Ogden never tired of promoting the record and his Orthological Institute, using for instance the translation into Basic English (in *transition* 21, 1932; see Chapter 3) as an opportunity to mention 'the Gramophone Record made by Mr. Joyce', adding all the commercial details in a footnote: 'To be obtained from the Orthological Institute, 10 King's Parade, Cambridge, Price 1 Guinea or 25-post free' (*t21* 259). The record had also been played in public, during a 'Soirée James Joyce' at Adrienne Monnier's bookshop 'la Maison des Amis du Livre'. According to Leon Edel – who notes that Joyce 'has found more sympathy and understanding here [in France] than in the English-speaking countries' – the record was 'perhaps the most important event of the evening' (*The Canadian Forum*, Autumn 1929, 460; UBC 1: 2063). The main purpose of the evening, however, was the presentation of the French translation of *Anna Livia Plurabelle*, read by Monnier.

Translation into French

In the meantime, Samuel Beckett and Alfred Péron had started their attempt to translate the first part of the Anna Livia episode in July 1930 (Aubert 1985, 417). In their version,[28] 'duddurty devil' became 'le misérable' ['the wretch']. At first sight, this seems to be a rather reductive, impoverished translation, but as Patrick O'Neill points out, 'le misérable' nonetheless introduces three new rivers, the Czech Iser, the German Isar, and the French Isère (O'Neill 2013, 182). But the stutter was lost in translation. When Joyce, with the help of Yvan Goll, Eugene Jolas, Paul Léon, Adrienne Monnier and Philippe Soupault, reworked the version by Beckett and Péron, 'le misérable' became 'le mymyserable',[29] giving HCE his stutter and adding a reference to the Franco-Belgian river Yser.

Beckett and Péron seem to have been keen on emphasizing the instance in the chapter where language becomes thematic. Thus, they translated the phrase 'loosen your talktapes' (Higginson 1960, 78) as 'délie ta langue' (Joyce 1985 [1930], 418), whereas Joyce would later change this to 'délie ton battant' (Joyce 1931, 637). Beckett and Péron's linguistic awareness also shows in their emphasis on their own translation's status as a translation, changing 'Tell us' in 'Traduis':

> O, tell me all [. . .] Tell us in franca langua. And call a spate a spate. Did they never sharee you ebro at skol, you antiabecedarian?
>
> (Joyce qtd in Higginson 1960, 80)

In Beckett and Péron's translation, this reads as follows in the galley proof version that was on the verge of being published in the magazine *Bifur*:

> O dis-moi tout [. . .] Traduis en franca lingua. Et appelle une crue une crue. Est-ce qu'on t'a jamais anseigné l'ébreu à l'eskole, espèce d'analphabête?
>
> (Joyce 1985 [1930]: 419)

---

[28] The original proof pages are held in the Beinecke Rare Book and Manuscript Library, Yale University, Gen MS 112, Box 5, Folder 103. See Megan M. Quigley, 'Justice for the "Illstarred Punster": Samuel Beckett and Alfred Péron's Revisions of "Anna Lyvia Pluratself"', *JJQ*, 41 (Spring 2004), 484 n. 4.

[29] Joyce, 'Anna Livia Plurabelle', trans. Beckett, Péron, Yvan Goll, Eugène Jolas, Paul L. Léon, Adrienne Monnier and Philippe Soupault, *La Nouvelle Revue Française*, 19 (1 May 1931), 633–46. As Megan Quigley notes, '"mymyserable" [. . .] is a penciled correction on the proof pages of the manuscript' in the Beinecke Library (Quigley 2004, 484 n. 4).

Joyce's last-minute decision to withdraw the translation and to adapt it with the help of Ivan Goll, Eugene Jolas, Paul Léon, Adrienne Monnier and Philippe Soupault, resulted in a new version, published in the more prestigious *Nouvelle revue française* (May 1931):

> O dis-moi tout [. . .] Pousse le en franca lingua. Et appelle une crue une crue. Ne t'a-t-on pas instruit l'ébreu à l'escaule, espèce d'antibabébibobu?
>
> (Joyce 1931, 639–40)

By translating 'ebro at skol' as 'l'ébreu à l'escaule', the river Escaut was added to the Ebro, and the 'antiabecedarian' times before and against the invention of the alphabet became anti/ante-Babel and antediluvian, ending in the fluidity of the past participle '-bu'. Philippe Soupault reported in his introduction to the publication in the *Nouvelle revue française* that their translation method consisted in finding alternatives to whatever was 'contrary to the rhythm, the sense and the metamorphosis of the words' (Soupault 1931, 633).

Analogous to the way the Ebro flows into the Escaut in 'l'ébreu à l'escaule', Robert Sage called his review of the French translation 'The Liffey Flows Into the Seine' (the Chicago *Tribune*, 17 May 1931). He did not appear to be too impressed by the (admittedly difficult) translation, but he gave an excellent summary of the 'unique history'*Anna Livia* had been accumulating 'during its six years of existence', concisely wrapping up the fragment's publication history so far:

> Its original publication was scheduled for the October 1925 number of a London literary review called *The Calendar*, but an unforeseen obstacle arose when the English typesetters, sharing the Anglo-Saxon superstition that what one can't understand must be obscene, indignantly refused to set up the text. Following this senseless refusal, the manuscript was recalled and given to Mlle. Adrienne Monnier, who at once printed it in her magazine, *Le Navire d'Argent*. Mr. Joyce considerably expanded his original text during the next two years, and, in October 1927, the second version appeared in *transition*, which had already published the preceding instalments of Part 1. In 1929, the text having been again expanded, a third version was issued in a small and expensive edition by Crosby Gaige, New York. This version was made available to the general public a year later by Faber & Faber of London, who added it to the pamphlets in the Criterion Miscellany (the English printers having apparently recovered from their earlier misgivings). At the same time, the Orthological Institute of Cambridge issued a photograph[sic] record of the last four pages, read by Mr. Joyce.
>
> (UBC 36: 2043)

The subsequent translation into French was not always received as positively as during the 'soirée' at Monnier's bookshop. According to *La Quinzaine critique* (10–25 September 1931) the work merely imitated the divagations of an illiterate lunatic (UBC 36: 873) and *Le Monde* (Saturday 2 May 1931) denounced 'le snobisme' of intellectuals juggling with words ('Passe-temps d'intellectuels jonglant avec les mots'; UBC 1: 2207). The *Literarische Welt* (Berlin, 2 May 1931) was less negative, but did think it was symptomatic that it took seven versions to arrive at this translation, which already indicated that Joyce's new work would be even harder to read ('noch schwerer zu lesen') than *Ulysses* (UBC 68: 614). In *La République* (6 May 1931), Frédéric Lefèvre called 'Work in Progress' a mistake, in spite of the author's laudable aim ('d'exprimer la vie profonde des êtres et des choses dans son innombrable complexité'). According to Lefèvre 'L'erreur de James Joyce' was a waste of energy ('un tel gaspillage de forces'; UBC 34: 2214).

Still, he was not entirely indifferent to Joyce's work, for a few months later (16 August 1931) he returned to it in a short piece on 'Le monologue intérieur' in *La République*.[30] Lefèvre's point is that 'interior monologue' is only a means to an end and should be applied with moderation. He still saw it as a monstrous development and a sort of illness ('un développement monstrueux [. . .] une sorte de maladie').[31] In the section 'En lisant revues et journaux' in *Les Lettres* (June 1931, 575–6), J. Calvet wrote a caustic review, calling the translation a 'matagrobolisation stupide à la Rabelais' (575).[32]

It is most appropriate that this communal indignation inadvertently turned into precisely the kind of scandalmongering that is thematized in 'Work in Progress'. Thus, for instance, *Action française* (25 June 1931) did not review the translation, but simply referred to the review in *Latinité* by Henri Ghéon, who had called it a 'propos savant, concerté, constipé', and who had claimed that, for a writer, not being able to work with the linguistic tools on offer is a sign of extreme weakness ('un signe d'extrême faiblesse'; UBC 34: 2218).

A milder voice was heard in Brussels. In his column 'Plat du Jour' in the newspaper *Le Soir*, 'Casimir' mentions that many critics are of the opinion that Joyce's effort is quite useless ('que James Joyce s'est donné une peine bien inutile'), but he concludes he cannot judge, admitting that in the few pages he read he did hear the waters murmuring.[33] In contrast with Lefèvre's preconceived opinions on the

---

[30] To illustrate his point he refers to Dujardin's definition: 'Voici d'ailleurs la définition proposée par M. Edouard Dujardin: Le monologue intérieur est, dans l'ordre de la poésie, le discours sans auditeur et non prononcé, par lequel un personnage exprime sa pensée la plus intime, la plus proche de l'inconscient, antérieurement à toute organisation logique, c'est-à-dire en son état naissant, par le moyen de phrases directes réduites au minimum syntaxial, de façon à donner l'impression "tout venant"' (UBC 34: 2215).

[31] Lefèvre did conclude: 'Ce goût du risqué témoigne d'une grande noblesse . . .'; UBC 34: 2215).

[32] 'Tout cela sent le moisi; ceux qui s'obstineront dans ces turlupinades désuètes perdront l'audience de la jeunesse; ils ont déjà perdu la confiance des hommes' (576; UBC 35: 1624). *Petit [Nice]* (13 May 1931) called the translation 'un épouvantable fatras de mots incompréhensibles et biscornus', perhaps an esthetic game, but one that might be taken seriously: 'Mais on doit regretter qu'un tel jeu puisse être pris au sérieux' (UBC 35: 917).

[33] 'Casimir ne s'est pas encore fait une opinion sur ce point. Il n'a lu que quelques pages, mais il lui semble bien avoir entendu le murmure des eaux courantes'. His conclusion

interior monologue, Casimir's unprejudiced reading intuitively applies a sort of phenomenological 'bracketing' or Husserlian *epochè*, suspending judgements to examine phenomena such as the running of a river as it is originally perceived. It takes the stream of consciousness as it comes, without preconceived ideas about its workings, and is open to the possibility of using the techniques of interior monologue and 'stream of consciousness', not merely as a means to an end, but as an end in and of itself: the enactment of the human mind at work.

Translation was one of the ways in which 'Work in Progress' was most appreciated, as the early Czech translation of *Anna Livia Plurabelle* illustrates. This translation was made by 'the wife of one of the Eton staff', as the *Yorkshire Post* (Leeds, 27 February 1931) reported, wondering how one could translate words like 'arundigirond in a waveney lyne' (which – the reviewer assured – was 'not myself carried away into opium-clouded ecstacies'), concluding: 'Perhaps Czech is a meek, lamb-like adaptable language' (UBC 36: 482). Prompted by its publication (a print run of only 300 copies), a review in German signed by 'P.E.' in the *Prager Presse* ('Joyce oder die Höllenmaschine', 3 March 1932) presented Joyce's prose as a work of genius in its 'destruction' of language and linguistic principles that have been regarded as untouchable and unchangeable for far too long ('ein an der Sprache und ihren für unverrückbar gehaltenen Prinzipien vollbrachtes geniales Zerstörungswerk').

As opposed to the strategy of Dada – which only strengthened the film or skin of meaningfulness – Joyce's 'verbal homunculi' ('Wort-Homunkulusse') are seen as an organic reaction to the 'Organismus' of language, attacking its skin in a deadly way – 'ein tödliches Carcinoma linguae humanae'. People who believe in language as a mystical, sacred principle will realize – through reading Joyce's work – that their God is merely an idol of very arbitrary proportions. For that is Joyce's accomplishment: it is not a new literary trend to be followed by others; instead it is a hellish machine ('Höllenmaschine')[34] that uncovers the arbitrariness and contingency underlying the so-called canon of language itself ('den Kanon der Sprache selbst').

As if to emphasize this point, Joyce allowed C.K. Ogden in 1932 to do an experiment in the opposite direction: 're-translate'*Anna Livia Plurabelle* into that canon of language (see Chapter 3), not just 'back' into English, but into Ogden's 'Basic English'. By domesticating Joyce's prose, reducing its linguistic richness by undoing anything that did not strictly belong to its 'communication', they created the perfect contrastive background to emphasize the enormous semantic potential of the 'Höllenmaschine'.

---

is: 'Il faut savoir, de temps en temps, aimer les choses, non pour ce qu'elles sont, mais pour ce qu'elles signifient, non pour ce qu'elles paraissent, mais pour ce que les auteurs y ont mis' (8 November 1931; UBC 35: 2213).

[34] A similar reference to the 'devilish' nature of 'Work in Progress' is made in the 'Literarische Chronik' of the *Neue Zürcher Zeitung* ('Joyce in der "Revue des Deux Mondes"', 25 August 1931), calling Joyce's work 'das Laboratorium dieses Sprachdämons'.

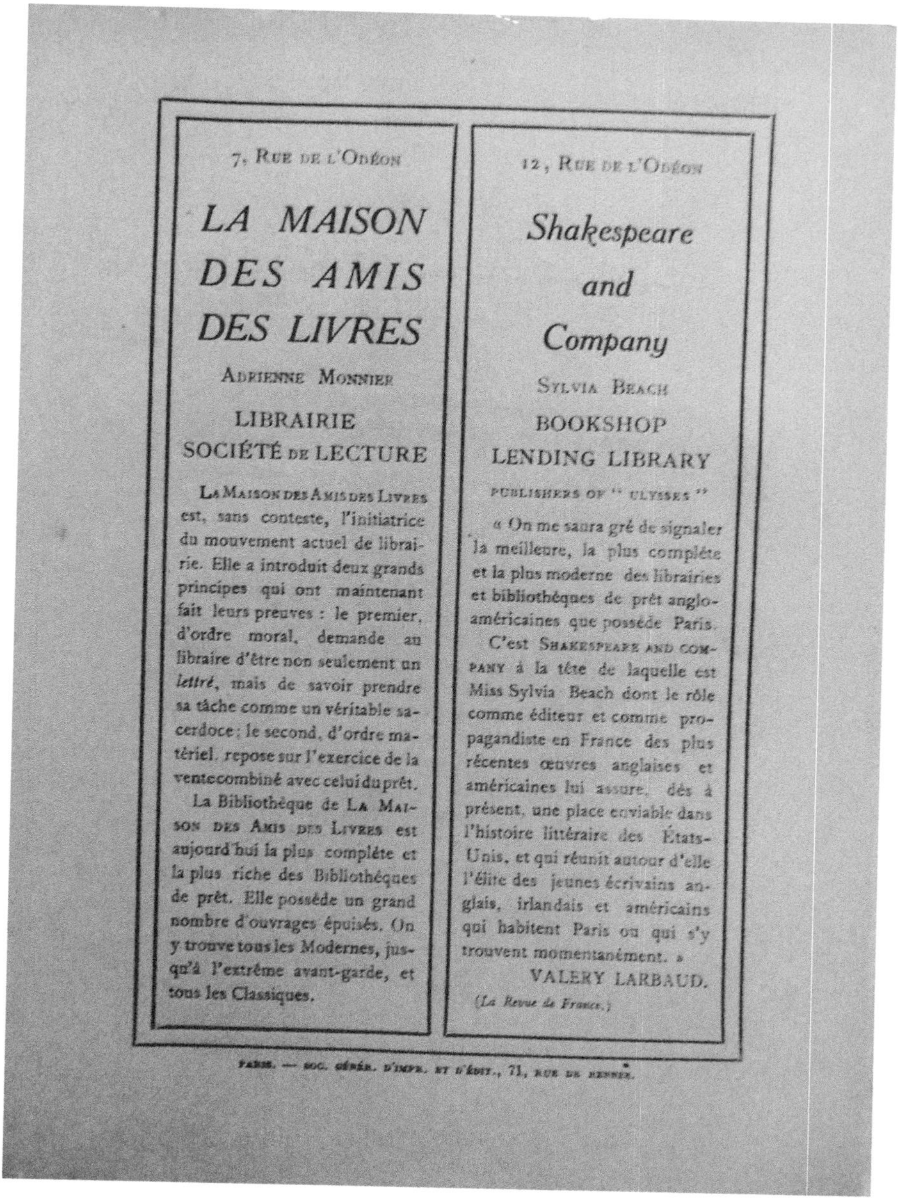
7, Rue de l'Odéon

LA MAISON DES AMIS DES LIVRES

Adrienne Monnier

LIBRAIRIE

SOCIÉTÉ de LECTURE

La Maison des Amis des Livres est, sans conteste, l'initiatrice du mouvement actuel de librairie. Elle a introduit deux grands principes qui ont maintenant fait leurs preuves : le premier, d'ordre moral, demande au libraire d'être non seulement un *lettré*, mais de savoir prendre sa tâche comme un véritable sacerdoce; le second, d'ordre matériel, repose sur l'exercice de la vente combiné avec celui du prêt.

La Bibliothèque de La Maison des Amis des Livres est aujourd'hui la plus complète et la plus riche des Bibliothèques de prêt. Elle possède un grand nombre d'ouvrages épuisés. On y trouve tous les Modernes, jusqu'à l'extrême avant-garde, et tous les Classiques.

12, Rue de l'Odéon

Shakespeare and Company

Sylvia Beach

BOOKSHOP

LENDING LIBRARY

PUBLISHERS OF "ULYSSES"

« On me saura gré de signaler la meilleure, la plus complète et la plus moderne des librairies et bibliothèques de prêt anglo-américaines que possède Paris.

C'est Shakespeare and Company à la tête de laquelle est Miss Sylvia Beach dont le rôle comme éditeur et comme propagandiste en France des plus récentes œuvres anglaises et américaines lui assure, dès à présent, une place enviable dans l'histoire littéraire des États-Unis, et qui réunit autour d'elle l'élite des jeunes écrivains anglais, irlandais et américains qui habitent Paris ou qui s'y trouvent momentanément. »

VALERY LARBAUD.

(*La Revue de France*.)

PARIS. — SOC. GÉNÉR. D'IMPR. ET D'ÉDIT., 71, RUE DE RENNES.

Plate 1 Back cover of *Le Navire d'argent* (October 1925)

THREE DOLLARS A COPY   TEN DOLLARS A YEAR

Two Worlds

A Literary Quarterly Devoted to the Increase of the Gaiety of Nations

EDITED BY SAMUEL ROTH

CONTRIBUTING EDITORS

ARTHUR SYMONS—EZRA POUND—FORD MADOX HUEFFER

SEPTEMBER, 1925

CONTENTS

PUBLISHED ONCE
EVERY THREE
MONTHS AT THE
SIGN OF THE
MOCKI - GRISBALL
500 FIFTH AVE-
NUE. SUITE 405-8.
NEW YORK CITY.
WHERE CONTRI-
BUTIONS, SUB-
SCRIPTIONS, AD-
MONITIONS, AND
INVITATIONS TO
TEA WILL BE
GRACIOUSLY RE-
CEIVED.

500 COPIES OF
THIS NUMBER
WERE PRINTED
AFTER WHICH
THE TYPE WAS
DISTRIBUTED. OF
THE 450 COPIES
SET ASIDE FOR
SUBSCRIBERS
THIS IS NUMBER

Plate 2   Cover of the first issue of *Two Worlds* (September 1925)

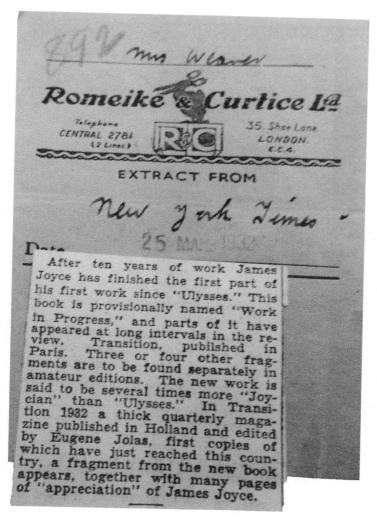

After ten years of work James Joyce has finished the first part of his first work since "Ulysses." This book is provisionally named "Work in Progress," and parts of it have appeared at long intervals in the review. Transition, publilshed in Paris. Three or four other fragments are to be found separately in amateur editions. The new work is said to be several times more "Joycian" than "Ulysses." In Transition 1932 a thick quarterly magazine published in Holland and edited by Eugene Jolas, first copies of which have just reached this country, a fragment from the new book appears, together with many pages of "appreciation" of James Joyce.

Plate 3   Announcement of *transition* 21 in the *New York Times* (25 March 1932) (The Poetry Collection, Buffalo)

Plate 4   Special edition of *Anna Livia Plurabelle* with black cover (Crosby Gaige, 1928)

Plate 5   Cover of *Anna Livia Plurabelle* in the 'dun colour' of the Liffey (Faber and Faber, 1930)

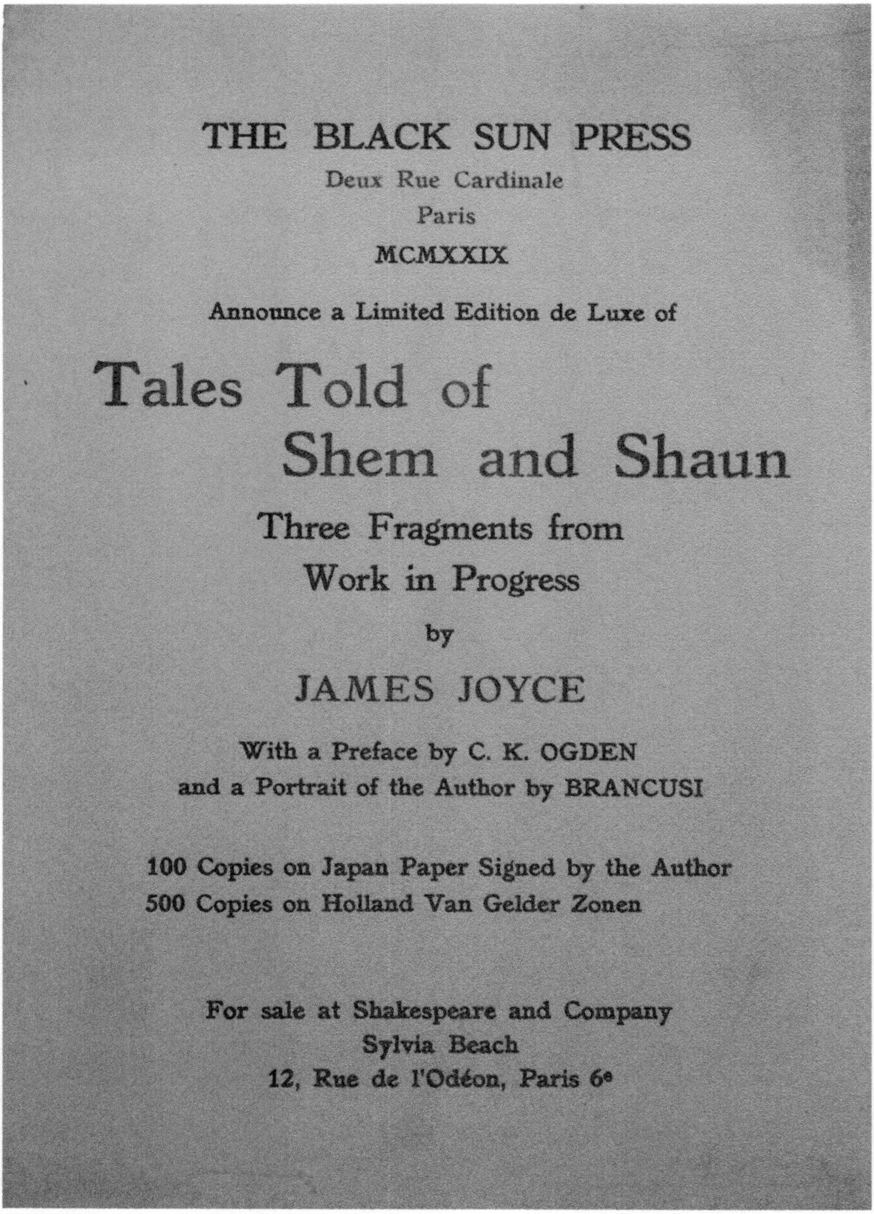

THE BLACK SUN PRESS

Deux Rue Cardinale

Paris

MCMXXIX

Announce a Limited Edition de Luxe of

Tales Told of
Shem and Shaun

Three Fragments from
Work in Progress

by

JAMES JOYCE

With a Preface by C. K. OGDEN
and a Portrait of the Author by BRANCUSI

100 Copies on Japan Paper Signed by the Author
500 Copies on Holland Van Gelder Zonen

For sale at Shakespeare and Company
Sylvia Beach
12, Rue de l'Odéon, Paris 6e

Plate 6   Flyer announcing the publication of *Tales Told of Shem and Shaun* (The Black Sun Press, 1929)

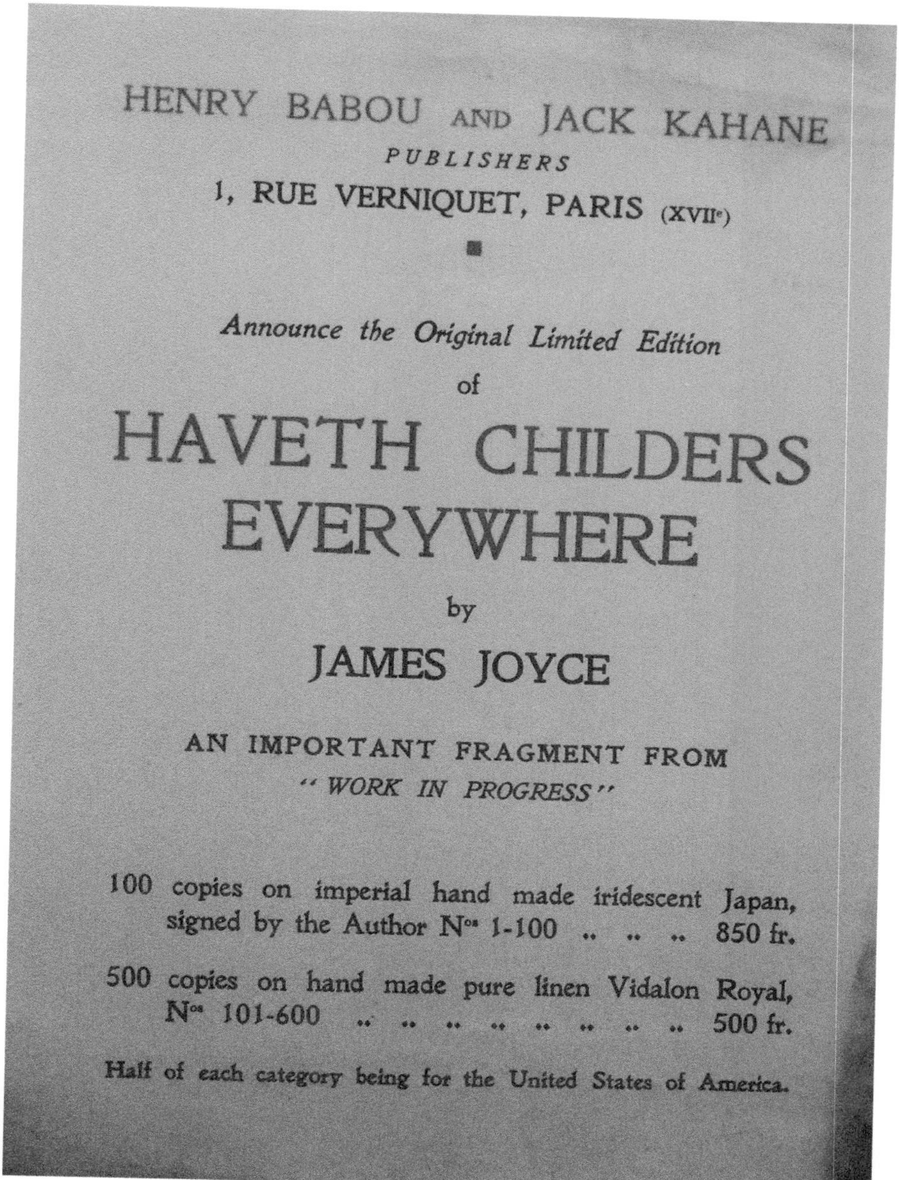

HENRY BABOU AND JACK KAHANE

PUBLISHERS

1, RUE VERNIQUET, PARIS (XVIIᵉ)

■

Announce the Original Limited Edition

of

HAVETH CHILDERS EVERYWHERE

by

JAMES JOYCE

AN IMPORTANT FRAGMENT FROM
" WORK IN PROGRESS "

100 copies on imperial hand made iridescent Japan, signed by the Author Nᵒˢ 1-100 .. .. .. 850 fr.

500 copies on hand made pure linen Vidalon Royal, Nᵒˢ 101-600 .. .. 500 fr.

Half of each category being for the United States of America.

Plate 7   Flyer announcing the publication of *Haveth Childers Everywhere*

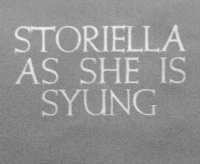

Plate 8   Cover of *Storiella as She Is Syung* (Corvinus Press, 1937)

Chapter 5

Tales Told of Shem and Shaun

The story of *Tales Told* has its origin in the genesis of 'The Triangle', the tale of Shem and Shaun trying to figure out where they come from while doing their homework on Euclid. The publication history of this search for an origin starts with an act of non-publication. Again, Wyndham Lewis plays a central role in this tale of the *Tales'* production, next to other agents such as Sylvia Beach, Harry and Caresse Crosby. In his history of the Obelisk press, Neil Pearson summarizes the life of Harry Crosby as 'the quintessentially Montparnassian biography': 'He was mad, bad, and dangerous to know. He was wealthy and handsome and sex-crazed and drug-stuffed. He died romantically, by his own hand, and left a pretty corpse. (Actually, *two* pretty corpses: Crosby and his lover, Josephine Bigelow, shot themselves in a suicide pact.)' (Pearson 2007, 3). Crosby was from a wealthy Bostonian family. He served as an ambulance driver in the First World War. When he and his wife Caresse settled in Paris after the war, they 'reinvented themselves as artists and patrons' (3). 'Caresse' was the name Harry gave his wife; they went to the *mairie* in Paris together to have it legalized (Beach 1980, 135).

In *The Passionate Years*, Caresse Crosby recalls their first meeting with Joyce, arranged through Eugene Jolas and Stuart Gilbert, and she mentions an interesting detail about the material environment in which 'Work in Progress' took shape: 'he led us after him across the hall to his bedroom where he dropped to his knees beside the iron bedstead and pulled from under it an ordinary sized but very dilapidated leather suitcase and unlocked it. [. . .] It was stuffed to over-flowing with clippings, bits of paper fully scribbled over, larger sheets of type-script like bulletins that had been five times through the machine, other miscellaneous odds and ends. "This is my desk", he said, on all fours, and smiled up at us through magnifying lenses, for the first time that afternoon. "It is all in here"' (Crosby 1953, 181–2). From the perspective of distributed cognition it is significant that what Joyce presented as his desk was not a clean slate but a chaotic collection of snippets, not a space to write on, but a space to engage with. During the Crosbys' visit, Joyce pulled out a clipping about the tenor O'Sullivan, but the suitcase also contained his own drafts. This mix of clippings and drafts in a portable 'desk' served as a kind of creative toolkit and when the Crosbys 'plucked up courage' (182) to ask Joyce if they could publish part of 'Work in Progress', he did not need to be asked twice. Caresse Crosby makes a direct connection with the suitcase: 'Evidently Joyce dumped his suitcase upside down that evening, for the very next day S.G. [Stuart Gilbert] appeared ready to do business

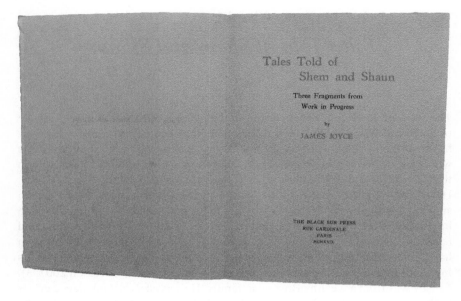

Figure 5.1   Title page of *Tales Told of Shem and Shaun* (The Black Sun Press, 1929)

for him – and so we began work on "The Mookse and the Gripes" and "The Ont and the Graicehopper"[sic]' (183).

The Caresse Crosby Collection at the Morris Library at Southern Illinois University contains a letter with Joyce's affirmative response to the Crosbys' request for permission to publish three fragments with their Black Sun Press.[1] Their dealings with Joyce usually went through Sylvia Beach: 'It was my business, of course, to arrange everything with the publishers of these pieces from "Work in Progress" and to get as much as I could for them' (Beach 1980, 135–6).

The terms of the contract for *Tales Told of Shem and Shaun* were drafted probably in early March 1929 on an undated piece of paper preserved at Buffalo. The first of nine numbered items on the list stipulated that the edition was to contain a portrait by Picasso. Apart from that, they were 'II. ready to begin to-day'; it had to be a 'III. "de luxe" edition'; 'IV. more $ [than] for Anna Livia'; with 'V. 28 copies for review'. The Crosbys were well aware that this enterprise could be a cause of stress if it was a success, but preparing the edition in Paris had 'advantages [. . .]

---

[1]   The letter with Joyce's affirmative response is preserved in the Morris Library's Crosby collection. See Melissa Hubbard, 'Raiders of the Lost Archives' (blog of the Special Collections Research Center, Morris Library, SIUC), posted on 4 November 2009 (http://scrc1.wordpress.com/2009/11/04/tales-told-of-james-joyce-and-the-black-sun-press/).

for corrections'. The last two items on the list indicated that 'VIII. Joyce can choose any format he wants' and that he would receive cash in advance: 'IX. ~~half~~ 1/3 cash paid immediately'. The amount of money the Crosbys had in mind (judging from a number written at the bottom of the list) was '$1700' for an edition of '1000 copies / of which 100 signed'.[2]

Sylvia Beach – who was by her own account 'very grasping in matters concerning Joyce' and 'reputed to be hardheaded in business' (Beach 1980, 136) – indicated that the proposal was not enough. The Crosbys had made an appointment with Joyce to meet on Friday, 8 March 1929, but they cancelled the meeting. On Wednesday, 13 March, Harry Crosby explained to him why, suggesting that it was (at least partly) because of the tough negotiation with Beach that the *Tales Told* volume would not contain a portrait by Picasso:

> The reason we did not come to see you last Friday as we had told you we would was that we did not go to see Picasso after all since Miss Beach did not think our offer for your book was enough. We both feel terribly disappointed but our Black Sun Press is small and fifty thousand francs is all we can offer. Should you ever care to have us do anything else of yours or this or any other thing we shall be very glad.

> (UB JJC XI: Harry Crosby to Joyce)

In less than a week after this letter, they did manage to find an agreement.

The Crosbys' publishing house, the Black Sun Press, produced volumes that were expensive, not only to buy but also to produce. They worked with the renowned 'Maître-Imprimeur Roger Lescaret', whose name even appeared prominently on the stationery of the Black Sun Press. In order to pre-finance the production of these sumptuous books, Harry Crosby could rely on his family, according to Neil Pearson: 'When book sales were sluggish and money for parties, drugs and racehorses ran low, Harry simply wired home for more. Daddy would heed the call, and the party would continue' (Pearson 2007, 3). The publishing enterprise, too, relied on this financial support, for Joyce always needed cash and was clearly not indifferent to the prospect of a considerable advance. Thanks to Beach's 'hardheaded' approach to business, they agreed on the original 'half', which had temporarily been substituted by '1/3' in the drafted list of terms ('IX. ~~half~~ 1/3 cash paid immediately'; see above). And on 19 March 1929, Harry Crosby paid the first half, $1,000 or 25,000 francs 'in half payment of the sum of Frs 50,000 for three fragments of *Work in Progress* by James Joyce', according to the receipt, written in Sylvia Beach's hand.[3] Instead of the '1000 copies' mentioned in the draft, the receipt mentioned a

---

[2]   UB JJC XVIII.G: Miscellaneous Material Related to Joyce's 'Work in Progress', folder 7.

[3]   UB JJC XVIII.G: Miscellaneous Material Related to Joyce's 'Work in Progress', folder 8.

print run of 600 'of which 100 to be signed'. This means that the Crosbys paid before they even had a contract, which was not drawn up until two weeks later, on 4 April 1929. In the form of a letter to Joyce, they confirmed their 'verbal arrangements in connection with the editing of three fragments' of 'Work in Progress'. The letter mentioned that the fragments had already been published:

> These fragments which have already appeared in the magazine 'Transition', to wit:
> 'The Ondt & Gracehoper',
> 'Mookes[sic]& Graipes[sic]',
> 'The Triangle',
> are to be edited by the Black Sun Press, of N°. 2, rue Cardinal, in one volume, this volume to contain also a preface. The edition will be limited to SIX HUN-DRED (600) copies, of which ONE HUNDRED (100) will be signed
>
> (UB JJC XVIII.G, folder 9).

The letter also stipulated that 'The corrected proofs of these fragments will be our property', that 'no other edition, "de luxe" or otherwise, of these fragments, whether alone or included in other works, is to be made until EIGHTEEN (18) MONTHS after the day of publication of this book' and that 'the payment [. . .] of the second half, to wit, ONE THOUSAND ($1,000.—) DOLLARS, is to be made on the day of publication'.

The same day (4 April), Joyce acknowledged receipt of 1,000 dollars, 'being the one-half payment of the sum agreed upon for the publication of the three fragments from my "WORK IN PROGRESS"' (XVIII.G, folder 10); and he confirmed that he was 'in perfect accord with the terms' of the letter that served as a contract. This perfect accord also included the preface, about which Caresse Crosby notes: 'We suggested an introduction and Joyce agreed. He weighed every suggestion we made with the greatest deliberation. Finally, he himself suggested Julian Huxley, because, he said, only a scientist could deal with the material. I wrote to Mr. Huxley, but he could not give the necessary time just then, and *we* could not be held back!' (Crosby 1953, 183). Another suggestion was the popular science writer and literary journalist John William Navin Sullivan, but Joyce later wrote to Harriet Shaw Weaver that Sullivan had declined to write a preface and that he had therefore proposed C.K. Ogden to the Crosbys (*SL* 340).[4] With the changes from Huxley to Sullivan to Ogden, the focus shifted from natural sciences to linguistics, but it was still a scientist who wrote the preface. Joyce probably asked Sylvia Beach to send Ogden the articles on 'Work in Progress' by MacGreevy, Budgen, Gilbert and McAlmon ('envoi express')

---

[4]   Dated 27 May 1929. See also letter to Weaver or 26 April 1929: 'C.K. Ogden is doing the preface' (*LIII* 189).

to help him write his preface (judging from a note in the Joyce collection at Buffalo, UB JJC XVIII.G, folder 2). Ogden's preface was ready by early May.

On 4 May he sent a typescript copy with corrections to Harry Crosby with an accompanying letter in which he wrote he was 'glad to learn that the Preface seemed suitable' and 'much obliged for the cheque' which had arrived that morning (UB JJC VI.J, folder 12). In the first writing layer of his typescript, Ogden presented the tales as 'three semi-detached satirical pieces': 'the first is from Part I, the second from Part II, and the third from Part III, of Mr. Joyce's forthcoming work' (typescript, page 2); in the overlay additions, Part II was changed into III, and III into II. In mid-April 1929, the order of the three pieces was indeed different from the original and the final I-II-III order: in the unpublished proof sheets held at McFarlin Library's special collections ('Little Magazines & Fine Arts Presses') at the University of Tulsa,[5] the fable of the Mookse and the Gripes (paginated 1–13) is followed by the Ondt and the Gracehoper (paginated 14–21); the third fragment (the text of 'The Muddest Thick That Was Ever Heard Dump', paginated 22–44) was untitled and set on larger sheets than the other two fragments. The order of the fragments in these proofs (dated 15 April 1929) corresponds with the corrections in the typescript of Ogden's preface.

One of the other corrections on the typescript of Ogden's preface is a subtle rephrasing with regard to the title of Joyce's work, 'which is not yet chosen'; this was changed into 'which is̶ ᵸᵃˢ not yet ̶c̶h̶o̶s̶e̶n̶ ᵇᵉᵉⁿ ᵈⁱˢᶜˡᵒˢᵉᵈ', suggesting that Joyce already knew the title but simply did not want to tell it to anyone yet (typescript, page 2). And on page 5, in Ogden's remark that 'at least six days may be necessary before Mr. Joyce's "word-ballet" yields its secret', the words 'six days' were crossed out and replaced by 'A DECADE' (in capitals).

In his preface, Ogden referred to the way 'Dr. Johnson triumphantly arrested the entire language' (TT xii). Unlike this 'fixation', Joyce's project was based on 'infixation', with a much more dynamic result – the opposite of Johnson's attempt to immobilize the English language. Ogden's example from an Eskimo language is the term 'Iglupakulia', whose infixes make the reference to this building so precise that he needs 30 English words to translate this one word: a 'large and capacious modern residence, built to present owner's special design and still in owner's occupation; allowance for dilapidations due to the efflux of time and normal wear and tear' (Ogden 1929, vii). Evidently, the analogy with Joyce's 'infixation' only goes so far; in 'Work in Progress' the effect of the portmanteau words is anything but a reduction of their possible meanings.

A flyer announced that *Tales Told of Shem and Shaun: Three Fragments from Work in Progress*, published by THE BLACK SUN PRESS, was 'For sale at Shakespeare and Company' (see Plate 6). It also indicated that, of the 600-copy print run, 100 copies

---

[5] McFarlin Library, Special Collection, 'Little Magazines & Fine Arts Presses', item nr. 55 (www.lib.utulsa.edu/speccoll/collections/joyce james/little_magazines.htm; see Crispi and Herbert 2003, 22–3).

were on 'Japan Paper Signed by the Author' and 500 copies on 'Holland Van Gelder Zonen' (UB JJC XVIII.G, folder 14). Apart from these 600 copies, the bibliographical note at the back of the book also mentions '50 copies Hors Commerce'.

About the 'Portrait of the Author by BRANCUSI' (also mentioned on the flyer), Joyce reported to Harriet Shaw Weaver: 'Picasso was too busy painting somebody so the next aim was Brancusi. He first did a kind of a head of me which the C[rosby]'s didn't much like' (*SL* 340); the alternative was the abstract, spiral-shaped 'Symbol of JJ' (340), on the verso page opposite the first page of C.K. Ogden's Preface, which Constantin Brancusi – according to Richard Ellmann – is said to have explained as a 'curleycue intended [. . .] to express the "sens du pousser"' (qtd in Fargnoli 2003, 315).[6] In the same letter to Weaver (dated 27 May 1929), Joyce also announced the imminent publication of the volume: 'The book is out on Saturday' (340).

But that was too optimistic. Joyce kept making additions. In the meantime, the printer would personally bring the proofs of the fragments to Joyce, giving him the opportunity to explain any changes or corrections to the printer in person.[7] The book (see Figure 5.1) would not be available until the summer.[8]

The Mookse and the Gripes

As Luca Crispi and Stacey Herbert note, the proofs of the two fables preserved at the McFarlin Library in Tulsa (not included in the *James Joyce Archive*; see above) are copies of the second setting of the text (2003, 22). Between this second set and the fourth set of proofs, the *James Joyce Archive* indicates a gap (*JJA* 47: 193). This 'missing' third set is located at Salisbury House in Iowa.[9] The document[10] is

---

[6]   This driving force was also recognized by Marcel Brion (in 'L'Actualité littéraire à l'Etranger', *Les Nouvelles littéraires*), who wrote about 'Work in Progress' that it gave the impression of a natural force ('l'impression d'une force naturelle') (UBC 33: 577).

[7]   See for instance Caresse Crosby's letter to Joyce, dated 'Vendredi [probably July 1929]' according to the UB catalogue: 'Dear Mr. Joyce / The printer will bring you the proofs of "The Ondt and the Gracehoper" to-morrow at noon. If you have any corrections to be made on the first fragment you will be very good to explain them to him – ' (UB JJC XI: Caresse Crosby to Joyce).

[8]   Published on 9 August 1929 (Slocum and Cahoon 1971 [1953], 48–9; Norburn 2004, 139; Fargnoli 2003, 313).

[9]   I wish to thank Luca Crispi and Cheryl Herr for drawing my attention to the presence of the Black Sun Press material at Salisbury House. I also owe a debt of gratitude to Eric Smith at Salisbury House for all his help, without which it would not have been possible to make the textual collation.

[10]   The proof sheets were purchased in 1930 from Harry F. Marks in New York City by Carl Weeks, who built Salisbury House. They are accompanied by a letter from C.K. Ogden, a pencilled note from Harry Crosby and an errata sheet from Joyce. The erratum relates to the Mookse and the Gripes (with a double underlined capital S in Seter: 'Hic sor a stone,

accompanied by an errata sheet made by Joyce ('J.J.'), dated [2] May 1929. The proofs are fairly heavily annotated as the following sample shows. The second set of proofs of 'The Mookse and the Gripes' reads:

My temple is my own.

(*JJA* 47: 214; Yale 9.3–5)

The subsequent versions illustrate the workings of the cognitive process in terms of constant revisions, a literal version of what Daniel Dennett described in terms of the 'multiple drafts model'. But whereas Dennett's model serves as a metaphor to describe the workings of consciousness as an internal process in the brain, the multiple drafts of 'The Mookse and the Gripes' are the actual instantiations of a constant interaction between an intelligent agent and the paper on which he thought. 'Work in Progress' thus appears as what Richard Menary calls 'writing as thinking' (Menary 2007), a process of creative revision and literary invention. The following example may illustrate this process.

A handwritten addition in the left margin indicates that ', loudy bullocker', should be inserted after 'temple', and an extra sentence is also added:

My temple, loudy bullocker, is my own. My velicity is too fit in one stockend.

(*JJA* 47: 214; Yale 9.3–5).

In the (no longer) 'missing' third set preserved at Salisbury House, the addition is incorporated in the newly set text:

My temple, loudy bullocker, is my own. My velicity is too fit in one stockend.

The handwritten corrections and marginal additions indicate that 'temple' should be replaced with 'tumble', and yet another sentence is added:

My ~~temple~~ tumble, loudy bullocker, is my own. My velicity is too fit in one stockend. And my spetial inexshellsis the belowing things above.

(Salisbury proofs, third set, page 6)

In the fourth set of proofs (*JJA* 47: 230; Texas-6) the additions are incorporated in the text, including the '**spetial**' reference to Wyndham Lewis. It is remarkable how often Joyce mentioned Lewis in letters to Harriet Shaw Weaver in April 1929 (the month after the contract for *Tales Told*). He asked her to send him a copy of *Blast* 2 (*LIII* 188; 12 April 1929) and wondered whether she had seen the latest issue of *The Enemy* – number 3, containing Lewis's essay 'The Diabolical Principle', with a reference to Joyce's 'polyglut-tonous volume (always "in progress" – Continuous Present)' (*LIII* 188).

---

singularly illud, and on hoc stone Seter satt huc sate'.) and is followed by the line 'Herewith 'O & G' with final corrections. / J.J. / [2].V.929'.

Lewis had also just published *The Childermass* (1928). The character of the Bailiff was clearly modelled after Joyce, surrounded by a 'tremulous chorus' of 'Bailiffites' (174) and '(wailing loudly above the wind) "We are factors of Time factors of Time!"' (187). The Bailiff tells the tale of how 'dear Shaun as ever was comminxed wid Shem' – which is followed by the parenthesis 'for he's a great mixer is Master Joys of Potluck, Joys of Jingles, whom men call Crossword-Joys for his apt circumsolutions but whom the gods call just Joys or Shimmy, shut and short' (174). He is 'ponderating "Neggs-in-progress" and "wirk-on-the-way" in our back office (with Vico the mechanical for guide in the musty labrinths of the latter-days to train him to circle true and make true orbit upon himself)' (175–6). Even the Roth affair seems to be evoked by means of an anagram: 'One would have said Thor in person!' (188)

So when Joyce was revising his tales and wrote to Weaver about *Blast* and the *Enemy* in April 1929, he was clearly preoccupied with 'the enemy'. What he did with this preoccupation was an impressive example of what Patrick Colm Hogan describes as simulation (see Chapter 3), that is, 'what allows us to get some idea of what it might be like to, say, ask the boss for a raise, before actually doing it' (Hogan 2013, xiii). According to Hogan there is a direct relationship between simulation and literary imagination: 'Insofar as literary particularization is a function of simulation, it is continuous with our ordinary cognitive processes of counterfactual thinking' (Hogan 2013, xiii). This mechanism is applicable in the case of *Tales Told*. Instead of reacting directly to Lewis, Joyce simulated the situation to 'get some idea of what it might be like' to be involved in such a polemic. He then particularized this antagonistic situation in different variations on this theme in his 'Work in Progress'.

The best examples of Joyce's simulation of Lewis's antagonism towards him are the three tales of Shem and Shaun. As Michael H. Begnal notes, 'each of the tales is a microcosm containing elements of the major themes and concepts which constitute the macrocosm of *Finnegans Wake*' (Begnal 1969 257), which also means that the tripartite structure of Giambattista Vico's view on the cyclic progression of history (in terms of a succession of three ages, Divine, Heroic and Civil, followed by a 'ricorso' before the same cycle begins anew) can be recognized in the tales, notably the fables. The fable of 'The Mookse and the Gripes' contains 'three dramatic sections and a conclusion' (Begnal 1969, 358) and the fable of 'The Ondt and the Gracehoper' parallels the three visits of the Prankquean to the Jarl van Hoother's castle (in the opening chapter of 'Work in Progress'/*Finnegans Wake*), as the Gracehoper 'took a round stroll and he took a stroll round and he took a round strollagain' (*FW* 416.27) resulting in 'three scenes and a concluding poem' (Begnal 1969, 358). Begnal calls the fables 'interpolations' and 'Like Vico's cycles, each interpolation is but a redescribing of the civilization of man' (358). Interestingly, the format of the fable is an invention of the first age, according to Vico himself: 'The first age invented the fables to serve as true narratives, the primary and proper meaning of the work mythos, as defined by the Greeks themselves, being "true narration". The second altered and corrupted them. The third and last, that of Homer, received them thus corrupted' (Vico 1961, 256).

But it was especially Giordano Bruno's notion of the complementing opposites that provided Joyce with a philosophical framework to incorporate the critical enmity in his work and creatively channel the animosity into a literary form, for which the fables turned out to be an excellent format, as the tale of the Mookse and the Gripes illustrates. The invocation of 'Bruno Nowlan' (*FW* 152.11) just before the beginning of the fable in *Finnegans Wake* (and the reverse, 'Nolan Browne'[*FW* 159.22], just after the end) was not part of the version in *Tales Told*, but this version did emphasize at several occasions that the two opposites complement each other: 'The Mookse had a sound eyes right but he could not all hear. The Gripes had light ears left yet he could but ill see' (*TT* 13–14; *FW* 158.12–13). They both stand for various opposite pairs: Mookse and Gripes, Shaun and Shem, stone and tree, Pope Adrian IV and Lawrence O'Toole.

In a letter to Frank Budgen, written by Lucia, Joyce explains the religious analogue in the fable of the Mookse and the Gripes, focusing on 'the Filioque clause in the creed concerning which there has been a schism between western and eastern christendom for over a thousand years, Rome saying that the Holy Ghost proceeds from the father *and the son*[*Filioque*]' (*LIII* 284–5). According to the Eastern Orthodox churches, however, 'the procession is from the father alone, ex patre, without Filioque. Of course the dogmas subsequently proclaimed by Rome after the split are not recognized by the east such as the Immaculate conception' (*LIII* 284–5).

In *A Wake Newslitter* (VIII.5, October 1971), Adaline Glasheen gave an interesting interpretation of the link between Wyndham Lewis and Pope Adrian IV. After reading Wyndham Lewis's criticism, she was amazed 'that a grown man can so unflaggingly, ingenuously, nakedly, and at such length expose his exceeding hunger for power – not just any old power, but for the particular power of imposing his urgent convictions on the minds of all men. Joyce takes hold of this glutton for infallibility' (Glasheen 1971, 74). Joyce's parody of the pontificating voice in Lewis's writings was especially clear in the introduction by Professor Jones or 'Levis' (as he was called in the first draft). But also within the fable, Lewis as pontiff is represented by the English pope Adrian IV 'who struggled, with imperfect success, for papal supremacy', as Glasheen describes him: 'Mookse-Adrian also strives for perfect supremacy and misses it because the heretic Gripes does not agree to be eaten up – i.e., acknowledge the pope's infallibility. WL had met, we may assume, with the same ungracious refusal from Joyce' (Glasheen 1971, 74).

Apart from Adrian IV, the Mookse represents other prominent Englishmen, such as Henry II, who invaded Ireland in 1171; the Gripes represents, among others, St Lawrence O'Toole, bishop of Dublin during the period of the invasion. Their dispute remains unresolved when Nuvoletta, failing to attract their attention, drops rain into the Liffey. As Joe Schork notes, 'What is going on in this passage is a solemn assembly of cardinals to elect a new pope – and Issy cannot entice her "dogmad" (*FW* 158.03) brothers to abandon the secret session to cavort with her' (Schork 2007, 136–7).[11]

Towards the end of the fable, 'shades began to glidder along the banks, greepsing, greepsing, duusk unto duusk, andit was as glooming as gloaming could be in the waste of all peacable worlds' (*TT* 14). When Nuvoletta appears 'a lass', Joyce creates a similar parallactic figure as the situation of the cloud in chapters 1 and 4 of *Ulysses*, observed from the viewpoint of, respectively, Stephen Dedalus and Leopold Bloom, thus providing – from Nuvoletta's vantage point – a bird's-eye perspective on the antagonism between the Mookse and the Gripes.

To the extent that the fable can be read as a response to Wyndham Lewis's criticism and explicit positioning as 'the enemy', Joyce's masterstroke was to take a meta-stance and to present this kind of antagonism as a recurring and continuously unresolved phenomenon, instead of letting himself be forced into the position of the enemy's enemy. This tension was the theme on which several variations were explored in the various tales. Thus, the 'hunger for power' and 'glutton for infallibility' in 'The Mookse and the Gripes' find an equivalent in the thirst for knowledge in 'The Muddest Thick That Was Ever Heard Dump'.

The Muddest Thick That Was Ever Heard Dump

Daniel Ferrer suggests that Joyce found a crucial idea for this fragment during his reading of Freud's *Collected Papers* (volume 3): 'Thirst for knowledge seems to be inseparable from sexual curiosity' (153; Ferrer 2007, 414). In narratological terms, the 'The Muddest Thick That Was Ever Heard Dump' or 'The Triangle' accords with what H. Porter Abbott (with reference to the works of Samuel Beckett) has called 'a stream of self-canceling attempts to fill a narrative gap' (Abbott 2004, 21). The same mechanism is at work (by way of a *mise en abyme*) in 'The Muddest Thick', where the boys, Shem and Shaun, are in search of the existential gap of their origin, the source of the river ALP or what Daniel Dennett calls the 'streams of narrative' that constitute the narrative self (Dennett 1991, 418; see Chapter 4). The two brothers, who are studying Euclid, use the geometrical figure of the triangle to find out where they come from and to visualize the object of their sexual curiosity. This idea is concisely formulated in a single sentence Joyce wrote

---

[11]   Schork draws attention to the addition of eastern orthodox elements in the typescript for *Tales Told of Shem and Shaun*: the Mookse is 'fore too adiaptotously farseeing' (referring to the Mookse's infallibility, from the Greek *ptotos*, 'prone to fall') and the Gripes 'much too schystimatically auricular' (from *schisma*, 'rift, split'); and Joyce added much more Orthodox vocabulary shortly before the publication of *Tales Told*, at the stage of the second set of proofs (Schork 2007, 133).

down on a small cream-coloured card[12] and used as an emendation to the second draft of the triangle episode:

Now I'm going to make you see / figuratleavely the whom of your / first geomater.

(UB JJC VI.I, folder 29)

Lifting the fig leaf, the boys figure out not only their personal origin but also what Gustave Courbet called 'L'Origine du monde', showing a fig-leafless 'whom' to represent the origin of the whole world, the 'first geomater' – thus applying Joyce's favourite method of exploring the microcosm to study the macrocosm.

When the piece was typed out, he sent it to Sylvia Beach, rather than to Wyndham Lewis directly. Before she was to forward it to Lewis's London address, Joyce advised her to send Lewis a note, 'stating simply that you now have it and asking to which address to send it. When sending it please request its prompt return if unaccepted and ask for a proof, if accepted'.[13]

Lewis did not accept the piece (see Chapter 2), but he also did not return it, as Joyce had asked. The typescript is preserved in the Wyndham Lewis collection of Cornell University's Rare Books department (described as James Joyce TM [copy, frag.] *Finnegans Wake* [n.d.] (*JJSB* 89). The antagonism between the two brothers was not as pronounced in the early drafts as in the version in *Tales Told*, and it was not until 1937 that Joyce added the footnotes and left and right marginalia, further emphasizing the opposition of viewpoints and at the same time presenting them as being interchangeable.

The Ondt and the Gracehoper

In *The Art of Being Ruled*, Lewis lashed out at the majority of modernist writers, who – in the wake of Henri Bergson – put too much emphasis on time, at the expense of space. He called them 'proustites',[14] for *A la recherche du temps perdu* served as a prototype of this preoccupation with time. Joyce was another author who belonged to the group of what Lewis called worshippers of 'the Great God

---

[12] As Luca Crispi's notes in the UB catalogue explain, the sentence on this extradraft sheet is 'a revised version of a sentence on the second draft of "The Triangle" (*FW* II.2§8; BL MS 47482a, f. 79; *JJA* 53.031). See *FW* 296.30–297.01. Joyce further revised the sentence on the fair copy (BL MS 47478, fs 10 and 11; *JJA* 53.041 and 042); therefore, the version on this manuscript does not appear on any subsequent draft or printing' (UB JJC VI.I, folder 29).

[13] UB JJC VI.I, folder 30, on a sheet of Hôtel Astoria & Claridge, Bruxelles stationery; *JJSB* 74–5.

[14] Joyce noted down this word in his notebook VI.B. 20, page 73; for a more detailed analysis of this and other excerpts from Lewis in Joyce's notebook, see Van Hulle 2004, 96–101.

Flux'. The fable of the Ondt and the Gracehoper, respectively representing space and time, can be read as a reply to Lewis's criticism of this preoccupation with time. The fable roughly follows the same narrative structure as Aesop's: the Ondt works hard during the summer, building a house and collecting supplies for the winter. Meanwhile, the Gracehoper laughs and dances, and by the time the summer is over he has to beg for the Ondt's humiliating charity. The text of the fable begins by referring to Jacko and Esaup, the fabulists Jean de la Fontaine (1621–95) and Aesop (ca. 560 B.C.). Joyce had a copy of *Aesop's Fables*, translated by V.S. Vernon Jones with an introduction by G.K. Chesterton (New York: Doubleday, Page & Co., 1919) in his personal library. In this translation the ant is replaced by a whole colony of ants (the title is 'The Grasshopper and the Ants'). When the grasshopper asks the ants if they can spare a few grains, because he's 'simply starving', the ants stop working for a moment 'though this was against their principles':

> 'May we ask', said they, 'what you were doing with yourself last summer? Why didn't you collect a store of food for the winter?'
>
> 'The fact is', replied the Grasshopper, 'I was so busy singing that I hadn't time'.
>
> 'If you spent the summer singing', replied the Ants, 'you can't do better than spend the winter dancing'.
>
> And they chuckled and went on with their work.

(125)

As Gerald Albert Michaud notes, 'Joyce's knowledge of the ant and the grasshopper is assuredly grounded in the popular circulation of the tale', rather than in a detailed study of all the adaptations of the fable. He readily and freely transformed the fable 'as no other fabulist has ever done' (Michaud 1973, 35). Not unlike the portrait of Shem in chapter 7 of 'Work in Progress' / *Finnegans Wake*, the account is biased: 'The Gracehoper was always jigging a jog' (*TT* 45), whereas 'The Ondt was a weltall fellow, raumybult and abelboobied [. . .] He was sair sair sullemn and chairmanlooking when he was not making spaces in his psyche' (*TT* 48). According to Clive Hart 'Shaun tells his fable to denigrate Shem' (1967, 14), but unlike Shaun's portrait of Shem, the narrative point of view shifts, as Michael Begnal notes (362), and this time the narrative ends with a creative product: a poem. Joyce makes his Gracehoper sing a song, hoping that he can '*sing your Ondtship song sense!*' (*TT* 55). He praises the Ondt, telling him that his '*Genus is worldwide*' and his '*spacest sublime*', but the last line ends with the crucial question: '*why can't you beat time?*' (55).

In the first draft, Joyce did not immediately conceive this final speech as a song or a poem. He continued writing the running text, as if it were still part of the body of the prose text. The crucial sentence 'I forgive you, dear Ondt' was a rather prosaic statement in the first writing layer of the first draft. The internal rhyme (**nause /** **jaws**, **count** / **Mount**) may have triggered the idea to turn this into a poem or song, and in the first overlay revisions, Joyce added an entire sentence and extra rhyming words (keeping / weeping):

He larved / & he larved & he merd / such a **nause** that the / Grachoper feared he / would [blank space] ^{swallow} his **jaws**. / ^[87v] <small>For the sake of their sakes</small> ~~who were once in my~~ <small>you are safe in whose keeping</small> I forgive you, dear Ondt, / said the Gracehoper ~~then~~ ^{weeping}. / [. . .] / As I once played the pipe / I must now pay the / **count**. So ~~it's~~ ^{saida} // [89r] to Moyhammlet and / marhaba to your **Mount**!

(FDV 223; BL MS 47483, 87v/88r-89r)

From that moment in the text onwards, Joyce started using the format of a poem:

We are Wastenot & Want, precon- / damned /
Tell Nolans ~~and~~ ^{go} volants / and Bruneyes ~~go~~ ^{come} blue, /
Your genus unbordered is [blank space], / your spaces sublime But / Holy
Saltmartin, why / can't you beat time?

To the 12-line poem Joyce immediately added six more lines on the facing verso page, so that the poem ended with the parenthesis '(May the Graces I hoped for ~~give~~ ^{sing} your Ondtship songsense)' (BL MS 47483, 88v). The poem remained rather stable in the subsequent drafts and it appeared with 18 lines in *transition* 12 (March 1928). When Joyce prepared a new version for *Tales Told*, he first added four extra lines, as well as the closing formula, 'In the name of the former and of the latter and of their holocaust. Allmen' (*TT* 55). To the proofs of *Tales Told* he added another six lines, so that the poem now had 28 lines. In *The Passionate Years*, Caresse Crosby tells the story of an 'unexpected incident'[15] relating to the master printer Roger Lescaret during the production process of *Tales Told*:

The pages were on the press and Lescaret in consternation pedaled over to the rue de Lilly to show me, to my horror, that on the final 'forme', due to a slight error in his calculations, only two lines would fall *en plaine* [sic] *page* – this from the typographer's point of view was a heinous offense to good taste. What could be done at this late date! NOTHING, the other *formes* had all been printed and the type distributed (we only had enough type for four pages at a time). Then Lescaret asked me if I wouldn't beg Mr. Joyce to add another eight lines to help us out. I laughed scornfully at the little man, what a ludicrous idea, when a great writer has composed each line of his prose as carefully as a sonnet you don't ask him to inflate a masterpiece to help out the printer! We will just have to let it go, I groaned and Lescaret turned and pedaled sadly away – but the next noon when I arrived at 2 rue Cardinale, joy seemed to ooze from the doorway of the Black Sun Press. Lescaret bounced out and handed me that final page. To my consternation eight lines *had* been added.

---

[15] According to Caresse Crosby, it 'occurred after Harry's death, for regrettably, "Tales Told of Shem and Shaun" did not appear until the spring of 1930. (Harry had died in New York in December, 1929.)' (187). Slocum and Cahoon, however, note that the New York Public Library copy has a tipped-in presentation slip from the Black Sun Press dated 9 August 1929, which they take to be the publication date (48–9).

'Where did you get these?' I accused him.

'Madame, I hope will forgive me', he beamed. 'I went to see Mr. Joyce person-ally to tell him our troubles. He was very nice – he gave me the text right away – he told me he had been wanting to add more, but was too frightened of you, Madame, to do so'.

(Crosby 1953, 187; see also Ellmann 1983, 614–5)

Since some sets of proofs are missing or incomplete, it is difficult to reconstruct the sequence of events, but to the third set of proofs for *Tales Told* (*JJA* 57: 370–371) Joyce added a few sentences in the running text and six lines to the Grace-hoper's song (Van Hulle 1999, 485), including the line 'An extense must **impull**, an elapse must elopes' – based on a draft in notebook VI.B.27 (pages 122–3)[16] where the line reads 'An extense must **expand**, an elapse must elopes'[17]– and an extra reference to the other fable in *Tales Told* ('your mocks for my gropes'). Of the incomplete, reset duplicate only one page is reproduced in the *James Joyce Archive*; it shows the first four lines of the poem, and in the bottom margin, Harry Crosby has written 'Where in hell is the last page?' The number of pages of the (incomplete) fourth set of proofs corresponds with what Caresse Crosby described as one 'forme' (having only enough type for four pages at a time). The result was a 34-line poem. It had almost tripled in one year's time, between the publication in *transition* and that in *Tales Told*.[18]

This accumulation is more than just a quantitative curiosity; it goes to the heart of the prodigal poetics behind Joyce's 'Work in Progress'. This verbal spendthrift was the subject of Wyndham Lewis's critique, which Sam Slote translates into a Marxian register: 'Joyce's works fail to produce anything of authentic literary value, because his energies as a writer are squandered on the proliferation of worthless trivia. Joyce just produces the wrong kind of surplus value, in other words nothing of authentic, *aristocratic* value. Value evaporates under the weight of valueless debris

---

[16]   One of the entries on VI.B.27, page 123, is 'grondt Ondt'. On the third set of proofs (*JJA* 57: 370; Texas-24), Joyce indicated that 'dear' in 'dear Ondt' (in the third line of the poem) had to be replaced by 'grondt'. In the fourth set the typesetter incorporated 'grondt', but failed to omit 'dear'; Joyce subsequently cancelled it when he corrected the proofs: 'I forgive you, grondt ~~dear~~ Ondt, said the Gracehoper, weeping' (*JJA* 57: 374; Yale 9.8–53).

[17]   The draft of the six lines in *Finnegans Wake* notebook VI.B.27 reads:

'Ere the**ose** gidflirts ~~that~~[now] gad [ding]~~you~~ you quit your mocks / for my gropes
An extense must expand, an elapse must elopes
Of my tuctacs takestock, [and ail's weal]
~~Hold me by your farlook, I'll hale you by~~ [As I view by the far look, / hale yourself to] my heal
Partiprise my thinwhins whiles my blin**d**k / points unbroken on
Your whole's whereabouts with / Tout's tightyright token on' (VI.B.27, page 122).

[18]   The last part of the fable of the Ondt and the Gracehoper was reprinted in the *Imagist Anthology*: 'From "Tales Told of Shem and Shaun: Three Fragments from Work in Progress" by James Joyce', in *Imagist Anthology* (London: Chatto & Windus: 1930), 121–2 [*FW* 417.24–419.10] (Slocum and Cahoon 1971 [1953], 78, B.12).

Joyce has accumulated' (Slote 2000, 52). But this accumulation was part of the performative quality of Joyce's work. As Fritz Senn already noted in his contribution to the 1966 volume of essays *Twelve and a Tilly*, 'insects are ideally suited to stand for the important aspect of perpetual changing forms in the *Wake*' (Senn 1966, 36). And in 1967, Clive Hart touched upon the core of the matter when he wrote that the fable of the Ondt and the Gracehoper 'hums, buzzes and flutters throughout' (14). As in *Anna Livia Plurabelle*, the performative quality of the language enacts enactive cognition at work. The text explores the mind as a system of construals and in that sense Joyce can be called an *Umwelt* researcher (Herman 2011, 266; see Chapter 3), presenting this cognitive complex in terms of a buzzing entomological ecology.

The performative quality of Joyce's language is arguably stronger in this fable than anywhere else in 'Work in Progress', stronger even than in Joyce's favourite *Anna Livia Plurabelle*: 'The constant flow of biological terminology serves something like the same mosaic function as do the river-names in "Anna Livia" and the roads in III.4, but Joyce makes it do much more besides' (Hart 1967, 14). He raises insects to divine status. By denigrating Shem and characterizing him as the 'dirty little blacking beetle' (*FW* 171.30) elsewhere in 'Work in Progress' / *Finnegans Wake*, Shaun unwittingly identifies him with the scarab beetle, which the Egyptians saw as an incarnation of Khepera, the creator of the Gods, described in *The Book of the Dead* as 'the god of matter which is on the point of passing from inertness into life' (qtd in Hart 1967, 14). Joyce received a copy of this book from Harry Crosby, who according to Sylvia Beach was 'a nervous chap', obsessed by death: 'He was fond of the Egyptian *Book of the Dead*, and presented Joyce with a fine copy of it' (Beach 1980, 134). Joyce's use of this book in the fable of the Ondt and the Gracehoper is paradigmatic of the way he was able to employ whatever presented itself to him as inert matter, incorporate it in his 'Work in Progress', and thus turn it into matter which is in the process of 'passing from inertness into life'.

Immediate Reception: Press Clippings

On 6 July 1929, 'Y.O.'[19] reviewed *Tales Told of Shem and Shaun* in the *Irish Statesman*, opening with the only thing he could claim to be certain of: that the book was a good investment, in financial terms (354):

> Undoubtedly this is a book for collectors if not for the general reader. The collector may pay his three or six guineas, lock his book away in the press where he keeps his most precious volumes, and wait for appreciation in price. Even if it does not come to-day, it is bound to come later on. It is one of those gilt-edged literary securities which will be gilt-edged so long as there are millionaire collectors of rare books.
>
> (354)

But when it came to the reader's, rather than the collector's, point of view, 'Y.O.' was more 'dubious': 'The mind of James Joyce is a whirlpool sucking sounds into

---

[19]   George Russell; A.E. (Deming 1977 [1970], vol. II, 395).

itself'. The reviewer concluded that he was 'overawed' on the one hand by a score of writers who 'have united to praise Joyce and explain him' and on the other hand 'by others who think it all lunacy': 'and I cannot agree with either'. But, again, the financial value seemed beyond doubt: 'The one thing of which I feel certain is that this is a sound investment for the collector' (354; UBC 23: 584).

Other reviewers confirmed Joyce's status as an author worth an investment. The *Spectator* (3 August 1929) opened its review of *Tales Told* with the telling statement: 'It will never do to leave Mr. James Joyce without a review'. Reviewers must have been well aware of what posterity was going to think about them, as the following remark *sub specie aeternitatis* indicates: 'He is one of the great revolutionary artists who are always unappreciated in their own times. When they are dead it turns out that we were all wrong about them; and posterity has the laugh on us for being so stupid. It is already well known that this is going to happen with Mr. James Joyce. Thousands of people have told us how sorry we shall be that we misjudged him; and his manuscripts, we believe, command unheard-of prices'. The *Spectator* still failed to appreciate Joyce's new work, mainly because 'he is doing something new with language'. The review refers to the preface, in which Ogden 'so neatly' distinguishes the qualities of Joyce's style ('the intensive, compressive, reverative infication; the sly, meaty, oneiric logorrhoea, polymathic, polyperverse') and 'so elegantly' compares Joyce to 'a promised liquidator where the machinery of literature has been clogged by the ministrations and minutiae of an osssified propaedeutic'. The review's response is quite defensive: 'Those of us who are stiff in mind, pedantic, irresponsive to change and dunderheaded, who, in short, are "ossified" ourselves, can hardly expect to understand the genius of Mr. Joyce'. The only aspect of Joyce's authorship that was appreciated was that he was 'a hard and conscientious worker': 'In spite of discouragement and in spite of irrelevant praise, he goes on perpetrating his laborious joke'. This joke was like the acrostics of the Latinists 'in the decadence of the Empire'. The problem was that 'New possibilities of speech can never be arrived at by running an artifice to death' and that was what Joyce was doing according to the spectator, 'with monomaniac intensity' (UBC 23: 2004). According to the *New York Times* ('Triumph of Jabberwocky', 23 August 1929), however, Joyce's project was not a joke at all: 'Mr. Joyce's purpose is not humor. His is the deep melancholy common to inveterate readers and writers. All words look shabby or sick to him. He hates them. He must have a new lot' (20; qtd in Fargnoli 2003, 314).

This also meant that a Joycean lexicon was required. The *Symposium* (October 1931) therefore published Michael Stuart's annotations to the fable of the Ondt and the Gracehoper, focusing on the way Joyce's neologisms function as insects, for instance: 'p. 49. bimblebeaks: bumble-bees and red noses. / nautonects: nocturnal insects; and also good-for-nothings'. The annotations were keyed to the page numbers of *Tales Told of Shem and Shaun*. The effort of trying to describe the creatures is undertaken in a truly entomological spirit, applying a scientific approach to art according to the advice suggested in the following passage: 'For if sciencium (what's what) can mute uns nought, 'a thought, abought the Great Sommbody within the Omniboss perhops an artsaccord (hoot's hoot) might sing ums tumtim abutt the Little Newbuddies that ring his panch' – which is annotated as follows: 'that is to say, that if science can teach us nought, we may learn perhaps from the little creatures, "Newbuddies;" an artsaccord: harpsichord; there is also the suggestion here of a conductor or creator "Great Sommbody" in his "omniboss"' (464–5). Stuart gave his annotations the title 'Mr. Joyce's Word-Creatures' (UBC 33: 1988) – an apt description also of Joyce's *Umwelt* research, following Samuel Beckett's characterisation of Joyce as a biologist in words (Beckett 1972 [1929], 19).

This *Umwelt* research (Herman 2011, 266) was eloquently analysed in one of the most perspicacious contemporary analyses of 'Work in Progress', which appeared in Switzerland in the wake of the publications of *Our Exag* and *Tales Told*. Carola Giedion-Welcker's essay 'Work in Progress: Ein sprachliches Experiment von James Joyce'[20] draws attention to Joyce's great interaction between the particular and the general, microcosm and macrocosm, suggesting the mind's numerous possibilities of experience.[21] The effect of Joyce's linguistic experiment is the creation of a tension, an 'eternally vivid interaction with the material', in which the word performs actively what it is about ('Es tritt aktiv [. . .] auf').[22] Giedion-Welcker chooses the sentence 'How mielodorous is thy bel chant' to indicate the synesthetic effect of the portmanteau: together with the melodious, aural quality, the other senses (taste, smell) are evoked simultaneously.[23] The analysis was so good that the editors of *transition* decided to publish an English translation in the double issue (19/20) of June 1930. According to Giedion-Welcker, Joyce's text was appropriately called 'Work in Progress', for it was 'not a closed solution, but an evolutionary process', a process that was 'positively tangible', a 'productive controversy with the basic elements of the poetic material: language, today still a petrified and exhausted form':

> Through free association of word and thought, Joyce changes it from a carrier of mental content, become more or less passive, into an actively functioning mediator of the ideological.
>
> (*t*19/20 174)

---

[20] *Neue Schweizerische Rundschau*, September 1929, 658–71; UBC 33: 1184.

[21] 'Jedes Vaterland, eures, meines, ist nur eine von zahllosen Erlebensmöglichkeiten des Geistes' (659); 'Was Joyce hier hinstellt, ist eine grosse Durchdringung von Einmaligem und Allgemeinem' (665).

[22] 'Ein Spannungszustand, eine ewig-lebendige Auseinandersetzung mit dem Material' (666). 'Das Wort wird aus seiner gesicherten, festgelegten Position gerissen und in ein schwebendes Medium mit divinatorischer Aussagekraft verwandelt. Es tritt aktiv, ideenerweckend auf' (667).

[23] 'Wenn es über Shauns Reden heisst: "How mielodorous is thy bel chant", so ist an Stelle des Wortes melodious (melodiös) dieses entstellte gewählt, weil noch neue Assoziationen hineinbezogen sind: Miel-Honig, odorous-duftend, das heisst Geruchs- und Geschmacksnerven kommen noch hinzu' (668).

The metaphor Giedion-Welcker suggests is that of a skin. Language thus no longer functions as a loose, lifeless wrapper; it is a 'vibrating skin', a 'seismograph of the enclosed organism'.[24]

Faber and Faber

In 1932, 'The Muddest Thick' was omitted from the partial republication of the tales as *Two Tales of Shem and Shaun: Fragments from Work in Progress* in The Faber Library, 'A Uniform Series of Contemporary Classics'(see Figure 5.2;

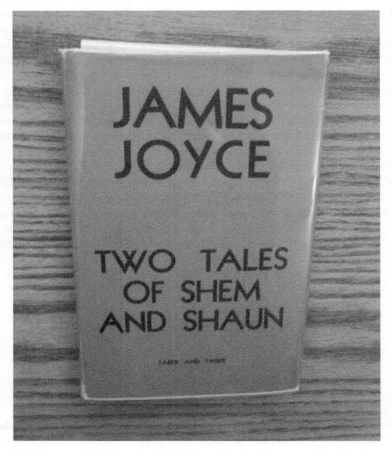

Figure 5.2   Cover of *Two Tales of Shem and Shaun* (*Faber and Faber*, 1932)

---

[24] 'Sprache, heute noch eine erstarrte und erschöpfte Form. Durch die freie Assoziation von Wort und Gedanke wandelt Joyce sie aus einer mehr oder weniger passiv gewordenen Trägerin geistiger Inhalte in eine aktiv funktionierende Vermittlerin des Gedanklichen. Aus einer schlaffen Hülle wird eine vibrierende Haut. Seigmograph des eingeschlossenen Organismus' (671).

Slocum and Cahoon 1971 [1953], 49, A.37). The back cover quoted the *Manchester Guardian* praising the series as 'A new library of compact and well-produced books to meet the demand for the best books of our time at a popular price'. The price was '3s. 6d.', more expensive than the one-shilling volumes in the *Criterion Miscellany*, but that was the extra price one paid for the better quality of the hard-cover books in the Faber Library. The inside of the orange dust jacket justified this reprinting of the 'two tales' from the limited edition of '*Tales of Shem and Shaun*'[sic] by specifying that this limited edition was 'not generally available in this country'. For those who did know the limited edition of *Tales Told*, the Faber edition was marked by the telling absence of the excluded middle:

[The Triangle]

Δ

The Mookse and the Gripes   The Ondt and the Gracehoper

By extracting the middle from *Tales Told* and allowing the two fables to be published as *Two Tales*, Joyce separated them from the story that had instigated their creation. The Triangle had been the starting point for the two fables, the origin of all the dialectic tension that constituted the narrative drive of the tales.

Chapter 6
Haveth Childers Everywhere

After Joyce's eyes had deteriorated rather suddenly in August 1928, they briefly recovered enough to allow him to revise the proofs of *Tales Told*, but by the autumn they deteriorated again. Danis Rose notes that 'By the spring of 1930 his eyes were particularly bad', which had its consequence for the text of *Haveth Childers Everywhere*: 'For this episode, not only was the base text (pages taken from the *transition* publication) already appallingly corrupt, but the auxesis – the total set of additions (once again complex and extensive) – is literally all over the place and in the handwriting of five or six different people (Stuart Gilbert, Helen Fleischmann, the Colums and a new recruit named Paul Léon), with only a small part in Joyce's blindman's scrawl' (Rose 1995, 108). These five or six collaborators played an important role in the construal of what von Uexküll would call Joyce's *Umwelt* (see Chapter 3), for they served as his eyes at that moment and thus to a large extent determined the world as perceived and experienced by the near-blind writer. The revision and publication process of *Haveth Childers Everywhere* is paradigmatic of Joyce's extended mind at work on the level of the text's production. On the narratological level of the text itself, a similar process is enacted in the extended mind of HCE, who fully identifies with the city he has built.

When chapter III.3 (parts 3A + 3B) was published in *transition* 15 (February 1929) it constituted one undivided instalment. In order 'to understand why Joyce decided to divide a compact text with a clear dramatic structure into two different entities', Jean-Michel Rabaté suggests that Babou and Kahane's offer to publish a fragment of 'Work in Progress' may have prompted Joyce to take only the second part of the already published unit (III.3) as the basis for *Haveth Childers Everywhere*. 'But' – he immediately adds – 'a deeper divisive logic seems to be at work' (Rabaté 2007, 390). Rabaté reveals this deeper logic by linking it to the way Joyce presented a universal city based on Dublin by creating a 'mimetic and performative language' (396). This language performs or enacts what *A Portrait of the Artist As a Young Man* still expressed explicitly: 'Dublin was a new and complex sensation' (Joyce 2000, 69). The language of *A Portrait* 'says'what the city does to the protagonist, whereas the language of *Haveth Childers Everywhere* 'does' the city. It performs the urban bustle, the 'network that keeps on adding layers to itself', as Rabaté puts it (396). As we have seen before, especially with reference to *Anna Livia Plurabelle* and the fable of 'The Ondt and the Gracehoper', Joyce manages to establish a link between literary 'enactment' à la Leavis and 'enaction' in terms of cognitive philosophy. Whereas other modernists such as Virginia Woolf often used tags to indicate that someone was thinking,[1] Joyce's text enacts a cognitive process that appears to be in constant interaction with elements in the environment. And as this environment is perceived by an intelligent agent, it is presented as this agent's *Umwelt* – in the case of *Haveth Childers Everywhere*: the city as HCE's construal.

Between the publication in *transition* 18 (February 1929) and the first edition of the separate book (June 1930) the *Haveth Childers Everywhere* episode became more than twice as long, from ca. 3,100 words in *transition* to ca. 7,900 in the version as published by Babou & Kahane and the Fountain Press. The most dramatic expansion occurred in early 1930 (the typescript prepared for the printer). Both Geert Lernout (in his introduction to *The* Finnegans Wake *Notebooks at Buffalo: VI.B.29*) and Jean-Michel Rabaté (in *How Joyce Wrote 'Finnegans Wake'*) refer to Stuart Gilbert's diary as a unique eyewitness account of Joyce's writing practice at the time. On 31 January 1930, Gilbert notes that Joyce – 'at last' – seems to have found a way out of the impasse that threatened to put a halt to the writing process of 'Work in Progress'. Gilbert's observation of this new dynamism is followed by two elements, whose combination served as a major help in Joyce's effort to get out of the creative crisis – prepublishing ('de luxe edition') and the *Encyclopaedia Britannica*:

> The de luxe edition by ? soon to come out – about the old lady ALP I think. Another about the city (HCE building Dublin). Five volumes of the Encyclopaedia Britannica on his sofa. He has made a list of 30 towns, New York, Vienna, Budapest, and Mrs. Fleischman has read out the articles on some of these. I 'finish' Vienna and read Christiania and Bucharest. Whenever I come to a name (of a street, suburb, park, etc.) I pause. Joyce thinks. If he can Anglicize the word, i.e. make a pun on it, Mrs. F. records the name of its deformation in the notebook.
>
> (Gilbert 1993, 20–21)

'The notebook' Gilbert referred to was probably *Finnegans Wake* notebook VI.B.24, which contains numerous notes derived from entries on cities in the *Encyclopaedia Britannica*. The other notebook used with the direct purpose of adding more cities to *Haveth Childers Everywhere* and thus making it a companion piece of the river-filled *Anna Livia Plurabelle*, was notebook VI.B.29. For instance, from the article on London in the eleventh edition of the *Encyclopaedia Britannica*, one

---

[1]   For instance in *Mrs Dalloway*, instead of letting Peter Walsh think, Woolf interrupts his thought process by explicitly stating that he is thinking with the tag 'he thought', three times in short succession: 'She's grown older, *he thought*, sitting down. I shan't tell her anything about it, *he thought*, for she's grown older. She's looking at me, *he thought*' (Woolf 1992, 44; emphasis added).

of the amanuenses read the following passage: 'LONDON, the capital of England and of the British Empire, and the greatest city in the world, lying on each side of the river Thames [. . .] The boroughs are as follows: [. . .] Hammersmith, Kensington, Paddington, Hampstead, St Pancras, Islington, Stoke Newington, Poplar, [. . .] St Marylebone (commonly Marylebone), Holborn, Finsbury, Shoreditch, Bethnal Green [. . .]' (vol. 16: 938). Several of the boroughs, such as St Pancras and St Marylebone, were jotted down on page 119 of the notebook and subsequently added to the typescript in a distorted form: 'St Pancreas' and 'the Marrolebone' (*JJA* 59: 150–1; cf. *FW* 550.10–13).

The scope of the cities on which Joyce & Co. consulted encyclopaedia entries was global. They ranged from Stockholm to Delhi and from Buenos Aires to Tokyo. The result is an urban setting that is universal and yet filled with particulars. Joyce's text thus performs a process of internalization by means of which the human mind manages to think in terms of abstract concepts, such as 'city' or 'tree' or 'leaf', even though every single leaf has a unique shape, as Nietzsche already noted in his essay 'Wahrheit und Lüge im aussermoralischen Sinn'. The text of *Haveth Childers Everywhere* enacts this phenomenon of conceptualization, applied to the notion of the 'city': in a similar way as our notion of a 'leaf' is implied by all the leaves we have seen so far and changes ever so slightly with every new leaf we see, so does HCE's construal of the 'city' consist of all the particulars that give shape to this global concept. And within this macrocosmic context, the microcosm of Dublin was recontextualized. Even though, with the publication of *Tales Told*, Joyce seemed to have written Wyndham Lewis's criticism out of his system, some aspects of it had clearly hit home, notably the comment on 'shabby-gentility' (see Introduction). When the collaborators read the entry on Dublin from the *Encyclopaedia Britannica* to Joyce, he was struck by a passage pointing out 'one of the most unfortunate and strongly marked characteristics of Dublin society', which was 'the tendency to be poor and genteel in the civil service, at the bar, in the constabulary, in the army, in professional life, rather than prosperous in business'. At that moment, Joyce asked Paul Léon to jot down 'shabby genteel' (VI.B.29, page 79). The note was never used, but the allusion to Lewis's criticism does indicate the continued importance of Joyce's critical '*Umwelt*' in the mechanics of his creative production.

To illustrate how this recycling or recombination of decomposed encyclopaedic material worked, Stuart Gilbert took the example of the word 'Slotspark' (noted down in notebook VI.B.24, page 227), which became 'Slutsgartern' in *Finnegans Wake* (*FW* 532.22–23): 'Thus "Slotspark" (I think) at Christiania becomes Sluts' park. He collects all queer names in this way and will soon have notebooks full of them' (Gilbert 1993, 20–21). In the same Paris Journal, Gilbert complains both about Joyce's attitude and about his method. His attitude in a figurative sense – playing director of a small factory of workers such as Padraic Colum, Helen Fleischman, Paul Léon, Lucia Joyce, Stuart Gilbert, making them produce a text according to a seemingly mechanical process – was embodied in a literal sense in the physical attitude or pose Joyce assumed while he instructed his collaborators, 'curled on his sofa, while I [Stuart Gilbert] struggle with Danish or Rumanian names, pondering puns'. Gilbert's reaction was that of a disgruntled factory worker: 'With foreign words it's too easy. The provincial Dubliner. Foreign equals funny' (21).

With regard to Joyce's method, Gilbert argues first of all that one cannot expect one's readers to know all these names, let alone to look them all up in an encyclopaedia; and secondly that 'The insertion of these puns is bound to lead the reader away from the basic text, to create divagations and the work is hard enough anyhow! The good method would be to write out a page of plain English and then rejuvenate dull words by injection of new (and appropriate) meanings' (21). Jean-Michel Rabaté duly points out how reductive Gilbert's attitude is, arguing that it goes against the grain of Joyce's method: 'Gilbert's position corresponds to that of the reductive reader who imagines that a first-draft version of *Finnegans Wake* would be written in "normal" English and would provide a "basic text" from which the reader might produce a continuous narrative or a "skeleton key"' (Rabaté 2007, 395).

Moreover, Rabaté tries to put the 'genetic fallacy' to rest, arguing that 'a category mistake is performed when we labor under the illusion that either genesis or source hunting is interpretation' (399). The 'criticism' part of 'genetic criticism' operates not so much on the level of the 'exogenesis' in isolation but on the level of its interplay with the 'endogenesis'. Even at the earliest stage of the writing process, the most interesting aspect seems to be the interaction between the first writing layer and the overlay additions and revisions.

Strangely enough, Gilbert's idea of the 'good method' – to write out a page of plain English and then rejuvenate dull words by injection of new meanings – does resemble the *early* stages of Joyce's work on the *Haveth Childers Everywhere* fragment. The first writing layer of the first draft (written in November–December 1924) constitutes only slightly more than a page of comparatively 'plain English':

> Sir, to you! I am known throughout the world as a cleanliving man and I think my public at large appreciates it most highly that I am cleanliving & as a matter of fact I possess that sweetest little wife on the globe. My clergyman, with the aid of my wife I mean to say, can speak to you of my private morals as clean. There is not a teaspoonful of evidence to my bad and I can humbly protest against everything to the higher personage at this moment holding down the throne. As a matter of fact I undertake to discontinue the practice. I will say that since my toils began famine has receded from the land. It were idle to inquire whether I am the product of group marriage or team work. I mean to say, had my faithful wife turned back on her ways or had she left her bed at the suggestion of some infamous fishermen there might be advantage to ask but she did ensue whatsoever pertained unto fairness and I did encompass her about with lovingkindness and with soft goods and hardware and hosiery lines and all daintiness at teatime and I did spread for her my mats of soft lawn and I gave unto my eblanite waggonways and she laughed at the cracking of the whip.
>
> Mattah markah lukah johah.

(MS BL 47482b, 105–6; *FDV* 245–6)

The first revision campaign (the overlay additions and substitutions to this first writing layer) is still in relatively plain English, as the first sentence may illustrate:

– Sir, to you! I am brought up under an old act of Edward the First, but I am known throughout the world wherever good English is spoken as a cleanliving man and I think ~~my~~ our public at large appreciates it most highly of me that I am cleanliving & as a matter of fact I possess that sweetest little wife on the globe who won the consolation prize in the dreams of fair women ~~competition~~ handicap by 2 breasts.

(*FDV* 245)

The interaction between the first writing layer ('thoughout the world') and the overlay addition ('wherever good English is spoken') already complicates the situation of the 'plain English' Gilbert wished for: the global scope of the first writing layer is reduced to an anglocentric 'wherever good English is spoken'. What for Gilbert was the starting point – a page in 'plain English', which would serve as the basic structure of the text's plot (Rabaté speaks of Gilbert's mistaken notion of the 'essence of the text's meaning', 398) – is precisely the complicating addition in Joyce's approach: 'good English' is part of HCE's boastful, imperialistic, dominant attitude. And the accretive method of Joyce's writing continuously refines his critique of 'capital' HCE. What is this 'English' language? HCE links his identity with this language: in subsequent versions 'good English' becomes 'my good Allenglisches Angleslachsen'. The identity of the speaker ('my') is complicated by the simultaneously tautological and contradictory presentation of the all-English-speaking world by means of allusions – in terms of both space and time – to a German-English ('engli*sch*') expansionism ('All'), and to this pure, 'good' English's own history as a foreign language imported by invading Angles and Saxons.

In other (and other and other) words, Joyce allows his character HCE, who stands for the capital of Dublin, to speak his 'plain English', precisely because the more he speaks, the less plain it turns out to be. In a similar way, the more HCE emphasizes that he is 'clean', the dirtier his history becomes. If Joyce can be said to show how 'the history of Dublin, like that of any "capital" city, confirms that its formation must indeed have been "dirty"', Rabaté compares this method to Walter Benjamin's attempt in his unfinished *Passagenwerk* to allegorize Paris, according to the (only seemingly) simple principle of literary montage: he only had to exhibit the trivia and the trash and put it to use ('sie verwenden'), in order to let it come into its own ('zu ihrem Rechte kommen lassen').[2] This observation is part of

---

[2]   'Methode dieser Arbeit: literarische Montage. Ich habe nichts zu sagen. Nur zu zeigen. Ich werde nichts Wertvolles entwenden und mir keine geistvollen Formulierungen aneignen. Aber die Lumpen, den Abfall: die will ich nicht inventarisieren sondern sie auf

Benjamin's notes regarding the 'Theory of Knowledge' and the 'Theory of Progress'. Against the background of these notes on the 'Theory of Progress', it becomes clearer that 'Slutsgartern' is not just a sourcehunter's delight, traceable via the note 'Slotspark' (*Finnegans Wake* notebook VI.B.24, 227) to the *Encyclopaedia Britannica*. Nor is it just a reference to the plot, a rather gratuitous pun on 'Slottsgarten in Oslo', whose function is to remind the reader of 'the gartered girls peeped on by Earwicker in the park' (Ellmann 1983, 628). Instead, it shows the garters and the underside of the Slot, of the castle, of the hurdled ford, of Baile Átha Cliath, of Dublin and, by extension, of all capitals. In a similar way, turning the 'Bronx' (VI.B.24, 205) into something 'bronxitic' (*FW* 536.13) is not just an 'easy' pun, pondered by the 'provincial Dubliner' according to the motto 'Foreign equals funny', as Gilbert suggested. Instead, it performs the allegory of progress, the ever growing city's equally growing mirror image '-itic', suggesting its highly inflammatory nature.

One of the things Joyce added at a relatively early stage (around January 1925; *JJA* 58: 103) was HCE's stammer (Eagle 2014, 90). While he was making the fair copy, he first wrote that 'our public at large appreciates it most highly from me that I am as cleanliving as could be and that my game was a fair average since I perpetually kept my wicket up' (*JJA* 58: 127; BL MS 47484a-26). He then made an instant correction (*currente calamo*), crossing out 'wicket up' and replacing it with an inline substitution turning it into a stammer: 'ouija ouija wicket up' – 'ouija' deriving from the notes Joyce took on the spirit of Oscar Wilde between December 1924 and February 1925 (see Chapter 1). Around the same time, Joyce was reading Belle Moses's book on Lewis Carroll,[3] who had a stammer. From then on, he introduced several moments of stammering, such as 'a youthful girl frifrif friend' and 'I popo possess the sweetest little wife round the globe' (*JJA* 58: 127).

The excess of allusions, which irritated Stuart Gilbert (and numerous other readers), is precisely the cunning way in which Joyce allows his vainglorious character to make a fool of himself. In that sense, exposing himself – as in his so-called crime in the park, where he is said to have exposed himself to two girls – is exactly what he does by means of the very act of denying this crime. The more he talks and boasts of his accomplishments as a captain of progress, the more he exposes himself and the way he thinks. If this performative gesture of the text can be said to accord with what Rabaté refers to as a 'deeper divisive logic' (Rabaté 2007, 390),

---

die einzig mögliche Weise zu ihrem Rechte kommen lassen: sie verwenden' (Benjamin 1991, 574).

   [3] Belle Moses, *Lewis Carroll in Wonderland and at Home* (New York and London: D. Appleton and Company, 1910, page 73: 'He stammered, not on all occasions, but quite enough to make steady speaking an effort, painful to himself and his hearers'. For a detailed description of Joyce's use of this source text, see Viviana Braslasu's PhD dissertation, '"Wordpainter and mixer": Oliver Wendell Holmes and Lewis Carroll in Joyce's *Finnegans Wake*', University of Antwerp, 2015.

it does indeed suggest an inherent reason behind Joyce's decision to separate III.3B from III.3A and publish it as a booklet in and of its own.

In his genetic analysis Jean-Michel Rabaté introduces this notion of a deeper logic with a marked '*but*', suggesting first that the idea for a separate book publication was a chance opportunity that may have played a role in the decision to divide III.3, '*but*' that this took place on a relatively superficial (that is, less deep) level (390). This remark may in turn conjure up its own 'but', for it suggests an implicit division between 'deeper' and 'shallower' logics, which to some extent accords with the inside/outside dichotomy that also marks the 'critical commonplace' of 'the inward turn' in modernism studies (see Introduction). The plural 'logics' is important here and my suggestion is that the interaction with the 'outside' (publishers, printers, amanuenses and other textual agents) may be added to the logics in Daniel Ferrer's title *Logiques du brouillon* of his book on 'modèles pour une critique génétique' (2011). The interaction with fine arts presses and the decision to publish *Haveth Childers Everywhere* separately were part of Joyce's 'extended mind', combining the interactive logics of the writer's private writing space and the public space of publishing, which seems to have had an inspiring effect in less creative periods. Joyce did not experience this public space as an intrusion on his creative privacy; on the contrary, he relied on it and was often able to 'put it to use' – in a similar way as Benjamin's '*verwenden*' – as part of the metropolitan bustle that is the topic of his text. Joyce did not passively react to 'Henry Babou and Jack Kahane's offer to do a separate book publication' (Rabaté 2007, 390). The idea for a separate publication is even presented as Joyce's own idea – at least according to a typed letter Sylvia Beach sent on 18 October 1929 to James R. Wells (the former partner of Crosby Gaige, but meanwhile associated with the Fountain Press, 522 Fifth Avenue, New York):

> With regard to Mr Joyce's new work, it was his intention, as you know, to have three or four fragments issued semi-privately with prefaces. The first two have appeared in .28 and .29 with prefaces, one by a poet and the second by a philologist. The next one deals with H C E himself and Mr Joyce wishes the preface to be written by a town planner or city historian such as the Rowntrees, Cadburys and Lord Leverhulmes in England, or the architect Le Corbusier, rather than a man of letters.
>
> A number of publishers have asked for the next part of Mr Joyce's new work to be brought out in book form, but as you published the first one he would be glad to give you the third.
>
> (UB JJC XII: Beach to James R. Wells, folder 10)

Padraic Colum also recalls an evening when Joyce suggested that the introduction 'was a job for an architect, or a mayor, or a building contractor'.[4] Colum found it

---

4   Padraic Colum, 'Work with Joyce' (*Irish Times*, 5 October 1956, 5; 6 October 1956, 7; see Deming 1977 [1970], vol. II, 487).

curious that Joyce thought of 'anybody so *externally-minded* as a builder' (487; emphasis added), but at the same time it was also 'characteristic of Joyce'. This is a remarkable statement, for it seems to confirm David Herman's suggestion (2011) that the so-called 'inward turn' of modernists such as Joyce was actually less 'inward' than the critical commonplace would have it, but in fact an intuitive prefiguration of a more 'externalist' model of cognition.

In the end, they did not find a citybuilder who was so naïve as to make a fool of himself in the preface to a satire of urban 'progress'. But they did find a publisher who was naïve enough to think that he was going to make money with it, although it took longer than expected. First, Sylvia Beach contacted James R. Wells at the Fountain Press again, on 14 November 1929:

> The part of Mr Joyce's 'Work in Progress' in question is, like A.L.P. and T.T. of S.&S., a fragment, the third of the four fragments that Mr Joyce designs to publish in this way before issuing the whole book in volume form. It is shorter than A.L.P. but he wishes it to be printed in very large type and in a big format on account of the subject matter, and with an appropriate preface of the kind I suggested. On this latter point he is very particular. The fragment itself is entrusted to the voice of the Viking father of Dublin City, and has been much amplified since it appeared in Transition No. 15, of which I am sending you a copy under separate cover. It is the last eight pages [. . .] On account of the self-gloryfying tone of old Earwicker, the format should be as gaudy and aggressive, within artistic limits, as Anna Livia Plurabelle was sober and unassuming.
>
> (UB JJC XII: Beach to Wells, folder 11; *JJSB* 160)

On 22 January 1930, Sylvia Beach reassured Wells in a telegram that the copyright in the US had already been taken care of: 'UNNECESSARY FRAGMENT ALREADY COPYRIGHTED WASHINGTON' (folder 13). But, eventually the Fountain Press preferred not to publish it. As Melissa Banta and Oscar Silverman note, 'Wells and the Fountain Press were put off by the stipulations concerning the preface and dismayed by the size of the royalty and the short length of the fragment' (*JJSB* 160). As a result, the negotiations came to a halt and Joyce eventually gave the rights to Henry Babou and Jack Kahane (160).

Sylvia Beach described Jack Kahane as 'a gassed war veteran from Manchester' whom she liked for 'his good humor and scorn of pretenses' (Beach 1980, 132). Born in Manchester in 1887 as the seventh of eight children of Roumanian Jewish immigrants (Pearson 2007, 8), Kahane had been badly wounded during the First World War as a consequence of gas attacks and shell shock. In the 1920s, he lived in France as a writer of short stories and novels, and he became a publisher in 1929 (Pearson 2007, 1). He had a family to support and used his business skills as a textile salesman in Manchester before the war to run the Obelisk Press, founded in 1929 and named after the phallic monument in the Place de la Concorde (Pearson 2007, 70). Kahane understood that publishing an avant-garde work could establish an independent publisher's reputation, even if it was not an immediate commercial success; but that it also worked the other way round: since Kahane was one of the few expatriate publishers in interwar Paris who could not rely on a wealthy family or partner, he could only publish avant-garde novels if he was able to make a profit from publishing so-called 'd.b.'s (dirty books) – several of them written by Kahane himself (Pearson 2007, 4), notably under the pseudonym of Cecil Barr. In the slip-stream of these d.b.'s he was able to publish such works as Henry Miller's *Tropic of Cancer* and *Tropic of Capricorn*. After Kahane's death in 1939, his son Maurice Girodias continued along the same lines, with a similar publishing strategy, when he founded the Olympia Press in the 1950s and managed to publish such master-pieces as Samuel Beckett's *Watt*, Vladimir Nabokov's *Lolita* and William Burroughs'*Naked Lunch*, in addition to (and thanks to) the publication of 'dirty books'.

Kahane must have been starstruck when he signed a contract with Joyce for the publication of *Haveth Childers Everywhere*. In his *Memoirs of a Booklegger*, he recalls 'the day I stood in the busy Rue de Grenelle, waiting for Miss Beach to come and lead me into the Presence' (Kahane 2010, 167). He describes Joyce as 'the Master' and the people in the drawing-room as 'his court' and 'his disciples' (168). Nonetheless, Kahane does not show himself a fan of *Finnegans Wake*, 'even if once I published a section of it with touching reverence and incomparable luxury' (Kahane 1939, 32). He called Joyce's work 'no more and no less than literary buncombe, a world for adepts at jigsaw puzzles' (32). As Neil Pearson puts it, Kahane was awed less by Joyce's work than by his reputation (Pearson 2007, 414) – not so much his fame as an avant-garde novelist, but his cult status as a banned author of an 'obscene' novel. Sylvia Beach remembers Kahane as the man who 'used to drive up in his convertible Voisin [. . .] for a chat with his colleague at Shakespeare and Company' and who admired her for her discovery of 'such an "obscene" book, as he termed it, as *Ulysses*' (Beach 1980, 133). According to Beach, Kahane never stopped trying to persuade her to 'let the Obelisk Press take it over' (133), suggest-ing that this possibility was at the back of his mind when he signed a contract with Joyce to publish a fragment of 'Work in Progress', even though he thought it was actually 'lacking in sex interest' (133).

Stuart Gilbert was present when the contract for *Haveth Childers Everywhere* was signed. He notes that Joyce came out of the room, telling him that he was now 25,000 francs richer (Gilbert 1993, 22). According to Neil Pearson, however, Joyce was telling Gilbert only half of the truth: 'Joyce, notoriously slippery on the subject of money, clearly thought better of alerting creditors to the true magnitude of his windfall. In fact, Kahane had just handed Joyce a check for *fifty* thousand francs for the right to publish a 5000-word extract from *Work in Progress*' (Pearson 2007, 415). That is indeed what Kahane claims in his *Memoirs*: after the feast, Joyce, Beach and Kahane 'repaired' to another room and 'after a short discussion I respect-fully handed to her for his account a cheque for fifty thousand francs' (Kahane 2010, 168). Whether Kahane actually paid 50,000 francs on the spot is unclear. For Joyce, it was certainly a good deal. Stuart Gilbert noted in his *Reflections*: 'Good business – for him' (8 February 1930; Gilbert 1993, 22). The contract (preserved at the University at Buffalo) mentions 50,000 francs, but it does stipulate that 25,000 francs was to be paid on signature of the agreement, and the other half in the month in which *Haveth Childers Everywhere* was published:

> MEMORANDUM OF AGREEMENT made this seventh day of February 1930 between JAMES JOYCE ESQ: c/o SHAKESPEARE & CO: 12 Rue de l'Odéon Paris, 6° hereinafter called the author of the one part and
>
> MESSRS HENRY BABOU AND JACK KAHANE of 1 Rue Verniquet Paris 17° hereinafter called the publishers of the other part whereby it is mutually agreed as follows;-

1) the publishers shall publish an edition of the third fragment from the work provisionally entitled[5] *work in progress* of which the said James Joyce is the author such edition to consist of six hundred (600) copies or fewer in the discretion of the publishers one hundred (100) copies being signed by the author and the title of the said fragment shall be:- HAVETH CHILDERS EVERYWHERE.

2) in full exchange for the world copyright of and the exclusive right to publish the said fragment which the author shall vest in the publishers the publishers shall pay the author the sum of fifty thousand French francs (Fr 50000) of which Fr 25000 on signature of this agreement and Fr 25000 in the month in which the work shall be published.

3) the possession by the publishers of the copyright of the limited edition of the said fragment shall in no way affect the author's possession of his copyright in the whole work provisionally entitled *work in progress* hereinbefore mentioned.

4) the author shall be entitled to receive on publication twenty-five (25) presentation copies of the said fragment.

Made in three copies, Paris this 7th day of February 1930.

> Lu et approuvé
> d' Henry Babou & Jack Kahane
> [signed by Kahane] [signed by James Joyce]
>
> (UB JJC XVIII.G, folder 15)

When Joyce signed the contract, the revision process of adding more cities to the piece was still in full swing. An entire notebook was filled with the help of his collaborators between early February and mid-March (Lernout 2001, 11). So, for that party, the contract was an extra incentive to finish the revision. The other

---

5   The text of *Haveth Childers Everywhere* ('Fanagan's wake', *HCE* 24) already hints at the title *Finnegans Wake*.

party must have had mixed feelings about the agreement. Kahane's business partner, Henry Babou, may have been enthusiastic initially, but they both soon realized that *Haveth Childers Everywhere* could become the company's ruin.[6] Not only was the text 'lacking in sex interest' (see above), it was perceived as being as good as unreadable and the production costs of a *de luxe* edition with such a small print run necessitated an excessively high retail price of 850 francs or $40 for the 100 signed copies on Japon nacré ('imperial hand made iridescent Japan, signed by the Author N°s 1–100') and 500 francs or $20 for the unsigned copies on handmade pure linen Vidalon royal (numbered 101 to 600) – as the flyer specified (see Plate 7).[7]

As the number of pre-orders was 'catastrophically low' (Pearson 2007, 416) and sales were 'calamitously slow' (Kahane 2010, 169), they urgently needed to find a solution – which they did: 'at the eleventh hour, when the book was on the point of going to press' Kahane happened to meet 'Elbridge Adams, who owned the Fountain Press in New York and was a fervent admirer of Joyce' (Kahane 2010, 169–70). Kahane managed to persuade the Fountain Press to buy half of the edition for distribution in the US. The title page therefore mentions both Babou & Kahane and the Fountain Press (see Figure 6.1).

On 18 March 1930, Joyce reported to Harriet Shaw Weaver that the revision of *Haveth Childers Everywhere* had been finished the night before (*LI* 289) and he informed her of the situation with the publishers: 'ALP [the Faber edition] is announced to appear on May 1st. I offered H.C.E. to the Fountain Press, successors to Crosby Gaige. They declined to pay the price asked, whereupon I gave it to Babou and Kahane of Paris, who will bring it out on the 12th April. Hearing this, the Fountain Press partner in Paris came to me and asked for a fourth fragment after having just turned down the third! I gave him an evasive answer whereupon he found out Messrs Babou and Kahane and bought up half the edition in advance' (*LI* 289). The edition did not appear on 12 April, but two months later, in June 1930 (Norburn 2004, 143). Sylvia Beach regularly ordered copies of *Haveth Childers Everywhere* for Shakespeare & Company, but only two or three copies at a time, as a dozen of receipts for Beach from Henry Babou (dated between May 1930 and April 1931) illustrate.[8]

---

[6] The company published for instance Richard Aldington's novel *Death of a Hero* in 1930, the same year Aldington edited the *Imagist Anthology*, which contained a fragment from the fable of the Ondt and the Gracehoper (see Chapter 5).

[7] The edition mentions that 'There have also been printed: 10 copies called writer's copies on imperial handmade iridescent Japan, N[os] I to X; 75 copies called writer's copies on pure linen hand-made Vidalon royal, Nos XI to LXXXV'.

[8] For instance this receipt on stationary of 'HENRY BABOU, EDITEUR / EDITIONS DE LUXE, LIVRES ANCIENS ET MODERNES / 1, RUE VERNIQUET, PARIS-XVII°': '24 Oct. 1930 / J. Joyce: Haveth Childers Everywhere / 1 ex. Japon-, signé n° 47 / 2 ex. Vidalon 443–444' (UB JJC XVIII.G, folder 18).

HAVETH CHILDERS
EVERYWHERE

FRAGMENT FROM
WORK IN PROGRESS
by
JAMES JOYCE

HENRY BABOU AND JACK KAHANE
PARIS
THE FOUNTAIN PRESS - NEW YORK
1930

Figure 6.1   Title page of *Haveth Childers Everywhere* (Babou & Kahane and The Fountain Press, 1930)

Immediate Reception: Press Clippings

On 18 February 1930, less than two weeks after the signing of the contract, the Paris branch of the *Chicago Tribune* ('On the Left Bank') reported that 'The publishing house of Babou and Kahane is busy on the third fragment of James Joyce's Work in Progress, which is due from the presses sometime within a month. The third instalment appeared in *transition*, but *as is Joyce's incurable habit*, the book printing will be somewhat different from the first publication' (emphasis added). Joyce's 'incurable habit' was explained in terms of 'expanding and completely revising' the fragment. As a result, 'A reader of Joyce who chooses the first publication of a work invariably has to buy the second one for it is likely to contain new elements and to have original ideas suppressed and to be twice as long as was the first' (UBC 69: 2195).

The edition of the 'third fragment' was announced as 'a limited edition, beautifully bound with each copy numbered' (UBC 69: 2195). On 26 February 1930, *L'Intransigeant* also announced the publication of a new fragment ('Il sera intitulé *Fragment*') and reported that Joyce feared he would not be able to finish his 'Work in Progress' because of the condition of his eyes (UBC 69: 2184).

When *Haveth Childers Everywhere* appeared, Arnold Bennett commented on it in the *Manchester Evening News* (12 June 1930). On the one hand, he appealed to his 'Anglo-Saxon' readers' chauvinism by calling 'Russian and other imaginative literature singularly lacking in fundamental originality': 'The real originators are still Anglo-Saxon. William Faulkner, in America. James Joyce, the Irishman, in Paris. And Edith Sitwell, in London'. On the other hand, however, this chauvinist sentiment seemed rather out of place, given that Bennett continued his discussion by emphasizing (twice) how incomprehensible this original work was: 'Joyce's "Anna Livia Plurabelle" has been issued at 1s. (Faber). As a curiosity it is worth possessing; but it is utterly incomprehensible to me, and will be to you. Another fragment of Joyce's "Unfinished Work" (of which "Anna Livia" is a fragment) has just been published in a limited edition, and with much luxury: namely, "Haveth Childers Everywhere" (Babou and Kahane, Paris, price unknown to me). It is utterly incomprehensible, but sounds majestic when read aloud. I wish that Joyce had not set forth to out-Ulysses "Ulysses"' (UBC 33: 979).

Apart from Bennett's rather dull, predictable and unimaginative reaction, the review does draw attention to a noteworthy phenomenon. At a time when the surrealists deliberately published their art as pamphlets and throwaways one would expect an avant-garde writer like Joyce to publish his unfinished work in a similarly 'throwaway' fashion. The tension between the 'unfinished' nature of the work and the 'luxury' with which it was published is indeed remarkable and characterizes the publication history of 'Work in Progress'. On the one hand, there is a pragmatic explanation: Joyce always needed money and although the one-shilling Faber editions proved to be a much better publication strategy it did not bring in the quick money Joyce obtained by means of the contracts with fine arts presses. On the other hand, by choosing an expensive form to publish his unfinished work, he did make a statement – or at least his pre-book publications can be read as a statement – in that he thus 'raised' the status of the draft (or multiple drafts) to that of a published work. As the review in the *Chicago Tribune* (see above) indicated, by 1930 it was already common knowledge that, no matter how 'de luxe' the editions were, Joyce's fragments were prone to change. The decision to publish these mutable versions 'with much luxury' implied a revaluation of mutability that can be read as an aesthetic statement, relating to the way Joyce chose to present what William James had dubbed the 'stream of consciousness': not just as a technique or a means to an end (like the 'interior monologue' according to Lefèvre), but as an end in and of itself. The form of the mutable pre-book publications played a role in the concept of the book's content. They were not a set of variations on a theme; variation *was* the theme.

In the *New Statesman* ('Mr. James Joyce in Progress', 28 June 1930, 372–4) G.W. Stonier reviewed both the Faber and Faber edition of *Anna Livia Plurabelle* and the Babou and Kahane edition of *Haveth Childers Everywhere*. The 'most striking fact about Work in Progress', according to Stonier, was the 'tremendous disproportion between the mass of allusions to every typical phase of contemporary life and the thin disembodied chant into which they are poured'. The effect was 'often disturbing': 'Most of the failures in Mr. Joyce's new prose come from too much distortion and the introduction of patterns and allusions which merely bewilder the reader with irrelevant deftness' (UBC 34: 2075).

The *Times Literary Supplement* (17 July 1931) also reviewed the companion pieces on ALP and HCE together. According to the *TLS*, the overall aim of Joyce's project was 'to create a composite image of human existence, regardless of time or space'. And in order to accomplish this, Joyce had altered the language where it seemed 'insufficient for his purpose': 'he has given his English a suggestiveness, a capacity for multiple associations such as his theme demands'. The *TLS* did not make explicit what this theme was, but the argument did make sense if – as argued above – one sees Joyce's enterprise, not in terms of variations on a theme, but in terms of variation *as* the theme. The narrative was 'a projection of many narratives' and it was 'part of Mr. Joyce's plan to keep his medium fluid and amorphous': 'His story is no more than the main current in a stream of associations'. Still, the intellectual investment it required was too big: 'his work asks more of our erudition and ingenuity than it is possible for us to give'. Of the two fragments under discussion, *Anna Livia Plurabelle* was the likelier to yield a sensation of understanding. *Haveth Childers Everywhere* was ignored in the rest of the review (UBC 34: 2068).

The *Manchester Guardian* ('H. I' A. F.', 7 August 1930) applied the by now familiar trick of praising the book as a collector's item, but questioning its content:

> This beautifully printed and produced edition of a fragment from Mr. Joyce's 'Work in progress' may be commended to collectors and will doubtless be treasured by those who have been devoting themselves to unravelling the meaning of so much of this new and unprecedented creation as has yet appeared in the pages of 'Transition'. To anyone else, however, it must remain almost wholly unintelligible.
>
> (UBC 14: 977)

Gerald Griffin met James Joyce and wrote 'An Explanation of His Methods', which appeared in *Everyman* (14 August 1930). Griffin mentions the Babou and Kahane edition of *Haveth Childers Everywhere* and briefly explains H.C.E.'s character:

'Aggressive, possessive, boastful about his triumphs, H.C.E., symbolized by the mountain, is the male counterpart to the Liffey, the heroine of *Anna Livia Plurabelle*'. Griffin had met Joyce on the latter's arrival in London after an eye operation. Joyce did not give an interview, but the article is laid out around a picture of Joyce, sitting in a chair with a white bandage on his left eye (UBC 34: 2011).

In the *New Republic* (17 September 1930, 131–2), Colum drew attention to the book's format as a separate publication ('"Haveth Chilers Everywhere" is the third fragment from "Work in Progress" to appear in book form') and he made the link with *Anna Livia Plurabelle*: 'The river was incarnated in a woman, Anna Livia; the city is incarnated in a man, H.C.E.'. Given the piece's linguistic complexity, Colum starts with a remarkably straightforward summary of the plot: 'Considered as a man, H.C.E. is the boss man – in every situation – he is Adam, he is Abraham, he is the Duke of Wellington, he is Daniel O'Connell. In his origin he is Norse, for Dublin was founded by Vikings and Norse merchants. It was made a municipality in the interests of Bristol merchants. And so H.C.E. has the belligerency of an intruder. As he appears before us in the present fragment, he is Everyman, for he is answering to the charge that is brought against all of us – call it Original Sin or the Fall of Man. Something has happened in a garden, in the city park, and he is protesting his detachment from it. And in the course of his defense he brags of all that he has accomplished – all that Dublin has done' (131).

Colum claims that Joyce 'has no interest in what we call history', but that he deals with the past in a special way: 'what has gone before lives. It lives [. . .] in the mind of the populace, in patterns formed in the popular mind'. And this human mind is evoked 'in our unwakeful condition' – 'the night life of humanity' (131). This 'unwakeful condition' is an interesting phrasing that prefigures recent neurological discoveries about the brain's default mode network (see Chapter 4). With regard to the evocation of this 'unwakeful condition', Padraic Colum called 'Work in Progress' a 'heroic effort', but he did want to 'counsel prudence' to Joyce: 'It is not prudent on his part to bring into his work some private piece of knowledge or to overelaborate some element of his meaning. I fancy I detect instances of both imprudences in "Haveth Childers Everywhere"'. But on the whole, his impression was positive: 'One has to work hard to get even 30 per cent of understanding of "Work in Progress". But even less than 30 per cent gives one humor, poetry, a sense of mythological character, that one cannot get in any other writing of the present day' (UBC 33: 734).

In October, Stuart Gilbert wrote a long essay in the *Fortnightly Review* on 'James Joyce's New Work' so far, suggesting that 'Work in Progress' bears out Victor Hugo's dictum '*Le mot [. . .] est un être vivant*' ('the word [. . .] is a living creature'), and that Joyce treats words as 'living things that can be grafted onto each other, fertilise and multiply' (UBC 33: 612). Again, the performative quality of the text's 'enactment' did not remain unnoticed and the reference to Hugo's 'être vivant' suggests a link between this form of 'enactment' and 'enaction' in that cognition is not seen as the representation of a pre-given world by a pre-given mind, but as a dynamic process that gives shape to the mind in the first place.

The *Spectator* (22 November 1930) reviewed the Faber edition of *Anna Livia Plurabelle* and the Babou and Kahane edition of *Haveth Childers Everywhere* together, noting that they both 'use the device of word play quite inordinately' and suggesting an almost behaviouristic explanation for it:

> Possibly to some extent this is due to the accident of Mr. Joyce's eyes, for the extravagance and distortion of his present method – as it must seem to every reader – have only reached their present gigantic dimensions with the continued failing of those organs. The sort of myopia with which Mr. Joyce is afflicted enables him to see but two or three letters at a time, and then only by the use of powerful lenses. Each syllable of each word is, so to speak, presented thus 'in vacuo', and must therefore assume for this author an altogether enhanced significance. This extra concentration would favour the intercalation of extra syllables for extra meanings with consequent distortion of the word-units. The whole sentence, having thus been thrown out of gear, extensive modifications become necessary to adjust every part of it to the author's sense of fitness.
>
> (UBC 34: 2005)

This explanation, which the review admits is 'purely mechanical', is evidently reductive and too exclusively focused on Joyce's physical condition, but it does add an interesting element to an externalist understanding of Joyce's creative production and embodied cognition. His '*Umwelt*' was inevitably changing due to his deteriorating eyesight, which may have contributed to what the *Chicago Tribune* had called his 'incurable habit' of changing his texts by means of verbal accretion. But Joyce's masterstroke was to thematize this cognitive process. His accretive method is not just the consequence of his physical condition and material circumstances; it is also his method of evoking a literary '*Umwelt*', in this particular case the '*Umwelt*' of HCE, consisting not just of the character's physical and material circumstances, but also of his cultural environment and the way he perceives it, employing it to continuously keep 'building', constructing, deconstructing and reconstructing his 'narrative selfhood' (as Dennett calls it; see Chapter 4).

The HCE fragment was regarded as 'altogether more difficult' than the companion piece on ALP. But on the whole, Joyce's work was praised as an 'outstanding contribution to the writing of this epoch', a work 'in which this age has found expression for some at least of its doubts and aspirations'. And in this context, Joyce's 'craftsmanship' was not criticized (as in Wyndham Lewis's *Time and Western Man*) but highly commended: 'In these passages the author reveals himself as one of the great landmarks of English prose. It seems unlikely that such sheer craftsmanship will, in this particular direction, ever go further' (UBC 34: 2005).

The de luxe edition was not meant for a large audience and the press understandably did not pay too much attention to it. In January 1931, the *New York Times Book Review* presented *Haveth Childers Everywhere* as a publication, not by Babou and Kahane, but by the Fountain Press ($20, and $40 for the 'Edition on vellum'). Herbert L. Matthews opened his review ('James Joyce's Linguistic Catch-all') with a comment on the progress of Joyce's new work: 'the slowness with which it is progressing is a tribute, at least, to the careful and painstaking labor with which it is being produced'. As a sort of disclaimer, Matthews had to 'admit, in advance, that Mr. Joyce's earlier books were of such high caliber as to entitle him to serious consideration in whatever he may choose to do'. But further than that he could not go, for the text remained 'absolutely incomprehensible' to him, apart from a few 'momentary flashes of recognition' (UBC 14: 773).

Instead of dealing with the content of an 'incomprehensible' text in an expensive de luxe edition, most newspapers preferred to look ahead to the cheap one-shilling Faber and Faber edition. For instance, *Everyman* (4 December 1930) announced that after *Anna Livia Plurabelle*, Faber and Faber were publishing 'Another Joyce Instalment' in Criterion Miscellany – 'so great was the success of the first' (UBC 47: 2152).

Faber and Faber

The interest in publishing 'Work in Progress' in its entirety was growing and Joyce received a few offers from various publishers, as he explained to Harriet Shaw Weaver (18 March 1930): 'Messrs Babou and Kahane *plus* Mr Adams then wrote to me via Pinker, making me an offer for an advance on the completed book and I also received a similar offer through the *Chicago Tribune* from a house in America named Selt' (*LI* 289). In this letter, Joyce also recalled the Roth case and explained to Weaver that in order to maintain his copyright in the US, he had to publish first through an American firm – which evidently upset Sylvia Beach, after all the effort she had already put into this 'Work in Progress' (*LI* 292). Less than a year later James R. Wells also wrote to Joyce: 'If your "Work in Progress" is nearly ready for publication why may I not make an offer for that?' (17 February 1931; UB JJC XI: James Wells to Joyce, folder 2).

Wells sounded quite desperate in this letter, which suggested that *Anna Livia Plurabelle* and *Haveth Childers Everywhere* had not been selling well: 'It may interest you to know that I have lost money on both "Anna L" and "Haveth Childers" and neither title is yet sold out' (folder 2). In contrast, the Faber and Faber editions for one shilling in the Criterion Miscellany were a success. The contract was made in the late summer of 1930[9] and T.S. Eliot was convinced that, since *Anna Livia Plurabelle* was selling so well, it would remain a seller. He was already making plans with Ogden for a series of records, like the recording of the *Anna Livia* fragment, adding: 'and I should certainly like to have one out of Haveth Childers' (29 October 1930; UB JJC XI: Eliot to Joyce, folder 12). On 11 December, Eliot told Joyce he was 'trying to get the British Broadcasting Corporation interested' in the gramophone record project, but another matter was preoccupying him: the contract with Babou & Kahane stipulated that they had 'the world copyright of and the exclusive right to publish *Haveth Childers Everywhere*', so they

---

[9]   On 13 September 1930, T.S. Eliot mentioned in a letter to Joyce: 'I trust that you have received my previous letter enclosing the contract for 'Haveth Childers Everywhere' (UB JJC XI: James Wells to Joyce, folder 11).

HAVETH CHILDERS EVERY- WHERE

JAMES JOYCE

ONE SHILLING NET

FABER & FABER

Figure 6.2   Cover of *Haveth Childers Everywhere* (Faber and Faber, 1931)

were protesting the planned reprint by Faber and Faber in the Criterion Miscellany, thwarting Eliot's plans: 'We had promised the H.C.E. to the booksellers in this month, and it was being well subscribed; and of course it is all ready and the sooner we can bring it out the better. A.L.P. is just on the point of reaching 5000 sale; and there is much interest in H.C.E.' (folder 13). On 27 January 1931, Eliot – who had not heard from Joyce for a while, possibly due to the death of Joyce's father – reiterated 'the misunderstanding with Babou and Kahane':

> We are very sorry about it because we had intended to bring out HAVETH CHILDERS before Christmas; however, I do not believe that the delay will inter-fere in any way with its success. According to M. Leon's advice, we have fixed publication for the beginning of May; but I asked him to let us know at any time if Babou could be persuaded to allow publication a little earlier. We are in a posi-tion to bring it out as soon as it is released.
>
> (folder 15)

In his letter of 17 February 1931, Wells told Joyce that he did not know 'at the time we decided to go ahead with it that there had been copies printed in London': 'I had had the Essay set into type, and had purchased the paper for the edition at a total cost of about $275.00. My change of plan as to the number of copies to be printed, reduction in retail price and royalty came only after Mr. Colum informed me of the London edition which would make the edition published here of little value [. . .] I am wondering if there is not some way in which I can be reimbursed' (UB JJC XI: Wells to Joyce, folder 2). Joyce felt he did not owe them anything,[10] because the Fountain Press and Babou & Kahane had broken their contracts, as he pointed out to Sylvia Beach on 5 May 1931:

> *Re* Wells. This person broke his contract with me for $375. If he now is nibbling at the book again in the usual manner of men-publishers he can have it for $500 (five hundred) on condition that Colum's fee is proportionately raised.
>
> *Re* Babou & Kahane. These people also broke their contract with me by paying what they engaged to pay 6 months late.
>
> In view of my unfortunately worded agreement with them I would like some-thing in writing 'consenting' to the publication of H.C.E. here in a trade edition. T.S.E. refuses to delay issue any longer so it comes out on 7
>
> (*JJSB* 168).

T.S. Eliot indeed published the Faber and Faber edition of *Haveth Childers Every-where* in the Criterion Miscellany, No. 26 on 7 May 1931 (see Figure 6.2).[11] By

---

[10] On 25 April 1931, Joyce wrote to Sylvia Beach: 'I have been asking Léon for the last fortnight to get a written permission from B or K which would enable T.S.E. to go ahead with H.C.E.' (*JJSB* 167).

[11] According to Norburn (148), and Banta and Silverman (*JJSB* 188) the book came out on 8 May. In any case, the bulk of the earliest reviews in the press appeared on 7 May

the end of the year (16 December 1931), Eliot reported that they had already sold 3,532 copies (UB JJC XI: Eliot to Joyce, folder 23); by 17 February, 3,655 copies (folder 25).

Immediate Reception: Press Clippings

The Yorkshire *Daily Post* (Leeds, 29 April 1931) announced that 'on May 7' *Haveth Childers Everywhere* would be joining *Anna Livia Plurabelle* in Criterion Miscellany: 'Critics may be scornful or angry about the Joycean compost of languages combined to form an extraordinary vehicle for his own outpouring, but, say what they like, there is no denying the force and skill with which he uses it' in what the announcement called 'Perhaps the greatest curiosity of literature of the twentieth century' (UBC 68: 2031). In early May, the Manchester edition of the *Daily News* already quoted some of Joyce's 'stuttering stuff' by pre-publishing the opening paragraph of *Haveth Childers Everywhere*, commenting that 'on May 7' Joyce's 'Work in Progress' would be one episode nearer completion, but it would be 'no nearer comprehension' (UBC 47: 928). The Glasgow *Daily Record* (2 May 1931) published a few lines as an *amuse bouche* ('to tickle your palate'), even though Joyce's 'latest outburst' was 'not due for publication until May 7' (UBC 47: 2181).

Clearly, Faber and Faber had been marketing the book aggressively, with advertisements such as the one in the *Observer* (Suday, 3 May 1931), where *Haveth Childers Everywhere* was publicized together with five other books, including a biography of Al Capone (see Figure 6.3; UBC 47: 2050).

On Thursday, 7 May 1931, the press reacted with a multitude of reviews and announcements. The title of the announcement in *Everyman* (7 May 1931) was telling: Faber and Faber was offering '*A James Joyce for a Shilling*' (see Figure 6.4), in other words, after all these expensive Rolls Royce editions, 'everyman' could now afford 'a' James Joyce: 'It is published to-day' (UBC 47: 2148).

Everyman (7 May 1931) also published a passage from the text under the heading '*Not What It Seems!*' (UBC 47: 2182) The *News Chronicle* discussed 'Mr. Joyce's New Language'–'(Published To-day)'– and found it 'one of the strangest curiosities of literature', although 'Something like a story occasionally becomes discernible' and 'some of the words, such as "politico-ecomedy", appear to have been worth the effort of invention' (UBC 14: 2153).

Under the sensational heading 'James Joyce's "Shocker"', the *Daily Herald* (7 May 1931) reported: 'the new James Joyce book [. . .] confronts a startled world to-day' (UBC 46: 2048). 'Mr. James Joyce stutters eloquently on', reported the *Daily Telegraph* ('L.R.', 7 May 1931), describing 'Mr. Joyce's Jargon' in sports terms: 'When Mr. Joyce wrestles with words he uses the terrible All-In methods seen at the London Sports Club recently. He jumps on them, turns them upside down, beheads them, telescopes them, and by the time he has finished the Oxford

---

(see below, 'Immediate Reception: Press Clippings').

Figure 6.3   Advertisement for *Haveth Childers Everywhere* (Faber and Faber) in the *Observer* (3 May 1931) (The Poetry Collection, Buffalo)

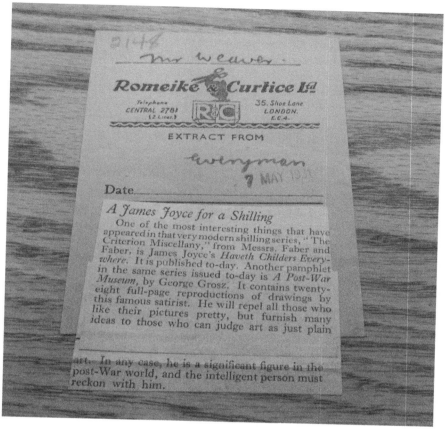

Figure 6.4   'A James Joyce for a Shilling' in *Everyman* (7 May 1931) (The Poetry Collection, Buffalo)

Dictionary cannot recognise them'. The playful treatment resembles *Punch*'s response to *transition* 8 (see Chapter 3): 'If you ask what it is all about you miss the point of the whole thing. That is Mr. Joyce's secret. It might be an exposition of the Five-Year Plan, or the truth about what Mr. Gladstone said in '86, or an explanation of the dream you had the night before last, or a primer on the Court language of Timbuctoo [. . .]. Each must search his own ego' (UBC 46: 2151). The latter sentence is especially interesting against the background of von Uexküll's definition of *Umwelt* as something that changes as the experiences change: 'As the number of an animal's performances grows, the number of objects that populate its *Umwelt* increases'. The animal's *Umwelt* is 'only a section carved out of the environment [*Umgebung*]' (von Uexküll 1957 [1934], 13; qtd in Herman 2011, 265). Similarly, as the review in the *Daily Telegraph* suggested, each reader had to 'carve' his or her own *Umwelt* out of the fictional environment Joyce created in his 'Work in Progress'.

The Inverness *Courier* (8 May 1931) stressed that, although the fragment was part of Joyce's 'much debated experimental "Work in Progress"', 'this is an episode, complete in itself' (UBC 47: 2147). The *Daily Sketch* (8 May 1931) called *Haveth Childers Everywhere* 'both a book and a portent' by 'the pet of highbrows' and doubted whether 'Mr. Joyce's unoculated thuggeries' would ever become a best-seller (UBC 46: 930). The West Lancashire *Evening Gazette* (Blackpool; 8 May 1931) quoted a few short passages in 'the jargon of Mr. James Joyce' and concluded that 'there is still something to be said for sticking to the general rules of whatever game one may be playing' (UBC 68: 2035).

On 9 May, the London *Star* focused on the price of the volume: 'Some time ago, when a famous London publisher offered to issue "Work in Progress" at three guineas a time, Joyce refused an almost fabulous sum in advance royalties. Instead, he went to another publisher and offered the book on the condition that they published it in short sections and at a shilling a time. And the publishers (Messrs. Faber & Faber) had the courage and the good sense to agree that [. . .] it wouldn't be fair to the public to ask three guineas for a book of which only one in ten thousand readers know[s] what it means'. And the experiment had more than justified itself, for *Haveth Childers Everywhere* was 'selling like hot cakes at a shilling a time' (UBC 69: 2034). On the same day (9 May 1931), the Nottingham *Guardian* reported that, after the 'incoherent tangle of syllables' called *Anna Livia Plurabelle* had 'run into three printings', Joyce 'ha[d] been at it again'. Judging from his new 'grotesque caricature of English prose' called *Haveth Childers Everywhere*, 'the author's fertility of verbal expedient show[ed] no decline' (UBC 68: 2032). 'Gibberish in Excelsis' was the heading of a short article in the *Irish News* (Belfast; 9 May 1931) with the laconic ending: 'some find mental pabulum in Joyce. There is no accounting for tastes' (UBC 68: 2036).

The *Birmingham Post* ('Mr. Joyce's Play on Words', 9 May 1931) discussed *Haveth Childers Everywhere* as a 'companion volume' to *Anna Livia Plurabelle*, another volume 'alleged to be complete in itself'. After reading it, 'there remains on the mind a certain confused impression of knowingness, of grotesque and other elements bewilderingly intermingled, of enthusiasm and enormous energy bombinating'. On every page, there was 'evidence of Mr. Joyce's delight in words for their own sake', and yet it was impossible 'to shake off the conviction that Mr. Joyce is on a wrong tack' (UBC 14: 924).

Every day, another newspaper spent at least a short article on the one-shilling publication. The London *Sunday Express* ('Queer Words', 10 May 1931) suggested that *Haveth Childers Everywhere* might be 'a satirical reflection of the cacophony of modern life'. To the quoted question 'Who can tell their tale' the review replied 'Who, indeed, if not Mr. Joyce?' But it concluded that, since it was good to 'know something of modern tendencies in the arts', this was a cheap investment: 'here is a good shilling sample of literary experimentation' (UBC 47: 2149).

The *Evening Standard* (11 May 1931) categorized the one-shilling publication as a 'pamphlet', in which 'Mr. Joyce takes the English language in his teeth and shakes it like a rat' (UBC 46: 2164). The Glasgow *Daily Record* (11 May 1931) reported that Joyce was visiting London, but 'not in the hope or desire of personal publicity' for 'he sincerely dislikes that'.

Echoing the *Star*'s comments on the idea of publishing 'Work in Progress' at 'a shilling a time', the announcement concluded: 'Purchasers, even if they cannot understand their bobsworth, get more than a bob's worth of pleasure out of trying to do so' (UBC 69: 2033). The Southport *Guardian* (16 May 1931) noted that, even though the episode – 'it is stated' – was complete in itself, its 'burblings' were 'difficult of comprehension' (UBC 46: 926). The London *Sunday Referee* (17 May 1931) 'discovered that the only way to read Joyce is to do so in a hot bath on an empty stomach and to read him backwards in a mirror', thanking Joyce for his 'Throothly Intertarment': 'My dear Joyce, a thousand thinkabuddies for a terooly kinsome laffenhour! I am most ernst intarnidued and give you gransiderlies!' (UBC 46: 927).

A week after the publication of *Haveth Childers Everywhere*, several newspapers were still writing about it. On Thursday, 14 May 1931, the *Daily Mail* (in the section 'Looking at Life') admitted it seemed impossible to discover what Joyce's neologisms meant, but was certain that 'there are several mild vulgarities hidden among them' (UBC 46: 921). In the *Yorkshire Evening Post* (Leeds, 15 May 1931), Norah Hoult wrote that *Haveth Childers Everywhere* was 'said to be complete in itself' but added that she had to take the publishers' word for it, because she 'read Mr. Joyce through a glass darkly' (UBC 46: 923).

The Inverness *Courier* (19 May 1931) revisited *Haveth Childers Everywhere* after its short announcement of 8 May, this time devoting a proper review to the publication and wondering 'Does he attempt to write in terms of the mind's rapid movement from one association to another?' Even though the question expressed incomprehension and frustration, it did indicate a recognition of the work's cognitive stakes, as well as an unwillingness to appreciate the mind's fickle mutability. The absence of a proper blurb was interpreted as a symptom in and of itself: 'Whatever his purpose may be, it would appear to be hidden, even from the usually enthusiastic minds of the literary experts employed by Messrs Faber and Faber, for instead of the usual publishers'"blurb", they content themselves with the bald statement that "this, like Anna Livia Pluribelle [sic] (No. 15 in the Criterion Miscellany), is an episode complete in itself"'. Again, this statement did not seem to convince the reviewer: it was 'good to learn that it is an episode complete in itself, but what the episode is remains a mystery' (UBC 14: 925).

The Glasgow *Herald* (25 May 1931) was of the opinion that it would not do dismissing 'Work in Progress' as 'pedantry in excelsis without first trying a fall with its difficulties'. After an attempt to tell the story and reconstruct the plan of the book (by means of the fragments available at the time), the review explained that 'Mr Joyce has worked on the principle of a palimpsest: one meaning, one set of symbols is written over another'. Applied to the workings of the mind, this principle of a palimpsest comes remarkably close to Dennet's 'multiple drafts model'. The fragment *Haveth Childers Everywhere* illustrated the Joycean method 'in all its intricacies', but from a linguistic point of view, Joyce made use of words 'with unpardonable liberty' (UBC 14: 920). The Manchester *City News* (30 May 1931) did not bother to discuss 'The New Prose'; it just quoted an appropriately selected passage 'From "Haveth Childers Everywhere"', opening with 'Things are not as they were' (UBC 47: 916).

The Yorkshire *Evening Press* ('Typing Artist's 226 Words a Minute', 1 June 1931) featured a remarkable article on Miss Stella Willins, a New York typist who was not only 'pretty, witty, and self-possessed', but also 'the world's woman champion typist'. She gave an impressive demonstration at the York Railway Institute, and afterwards she was presented with a page of *Haveth Childers Everywhere*. When it was shown to her, 'Miss Willins blinked. "You may as well ask me to type Sanskrit", she said. [. . .] "I hope it doesn't mean anything it shouldn't"'. The result of the test was that she had typed the page at a speed of nearly 100 words a minute, less than half the speed at which she had typed the memorized speed test (226 words a minute). The article was inconclusive as to what this result was supposed to prove; probably it just proved what the reporter explained at the outset: that *Haveth Childers Everywhere* 'reads like nonsense [. . .] always on the point of deviating into sense, and therein lies the difficulty, for so many of the words begin like English words and end like nothing on earth' (UBC 47).

In the Yorkshire *Daily Post* (Leeds, 2 June 1931) Francis Watson reviewed *Haveth Childers Everywhere* together with *The Diabolical Principle and The Dithyrambic Spectator* (Chatto and Windus) by Wyndham Lewis, who 'is under no delusions about his mission as a critic': 'He sees himself as the implacable enemy of insignificant shams in modern literature'. Especially in the essay 'The Diabolical Principle' Lewis castigates 'the New Stein Age' of the *transition* circle, its 'cult of revolt' and its 'childishness posing as novelty'. According to Watson, Lewis's 'chief virtue as a pamphleteer' was his fundamental respect for 'the earnest, balanced worker'. The link with Joyce is made by means of an unwittingly ironic 'transition' to the second book to be reviewed: 'Mr. Lewis's respect for the honest worker extends, of course, to James Joyce'. The latter's method was described as 'photographing the thought-stream as it exists when the unconscious is on the point of merging in the conscious'. The focus on the workings of the mind was potentially interesting, but the photography metaphor suggested a static rather than dynamic treatment of cognition, which the review did not develop. So, the promising idea of discussing Lewis and Joyce together resulted disappointingly in a tepid review instead of the anticipated clash of intellects (UBC 14: 918).

A month after *Everyman* had reported on the publication of *Haveth Childers Everywhere*, several letters to the editor started appearing. F. B. Cargeege (11 June 1931) had bought a copy, after reading about it in *Everyman*, and now wanted to 'protest against such drivel being foisted on us as literature': 'How is it that a publisher of repute can publish this rubbish of Joyce's? How is it he is referred to, and quoted by serious journals, even by EVERYMAN, without condemnation? Are there really people who imagine they can read this jargon? I simply do not believe it. Is it an amazing literary hoax? Or is it a crazy experiment indulged in by a literary humbug, and, by some strange freak, allowed to get a foothold by the critics who have not the honesty or courage to oppose it?' (UBC 14: 2185).

On 25 June 1931, Michael Petch responded to Cargeege's claim that *Haveth Childers Everywhere* had been 'foisted on "us"'. Petch, who said he started reading Joyce in the trenches, now wrote a remarkable defence of his work: 'Reliance on phrases clouds the intellect. Respectably married adjectives beget Victorian families of clichés, while an enfranchised imagination will grow athletic and inventive at exercise. If language is to be a living thing there must be innovations in grammar, spelling and syntax' (qtd in Deming 1977 [1970], vol. II, 545). And on 2 July 1931, *Everyman* published another letter to the editor by John H.S. Rowland, who had thought of Joyce 'as one of the more extreme innovators of our time', but a perusal of *Anna Livia Plurabelle* and *Haveth Childers Everywhere* had led him 'to wonder whether, after all, Joyce is not enjoying a great joke at the expense of the literary critics of the world', for it seemed certain to him that 'in this mad-looking jargon of his, a great literary artist is being lost' (UBC 33: 878).

The *Church Times* (19 June 1931) was irritated by the language of *Haveth Childers Everywhere*, which was 'mere, rather unpleasant, nonsense': 'It is not English, it is not anything' (UBC 46: 912). According to the Sheffield *Independent* (22 June 1931) the newest addition to the Criterion Miscellany served 'to exemplify the catholicity of the series': 'None of Mr. Joyce's writings is exactly "easy" to read, and "Haveth Childers Everywhere" would seem as difficult as anything he has written' (UBC 47: 884). The *John O'London Weekly* (27 June 1931) wondered whether Joyce's fragments were 'Rubies or Rubbish?' The only comprehensible sentence in *Haveth Childers Everywhere* was the editors' explanation that 'This, like "Anna Livia Plurabelle", is an episode, complete in itself, from Mr. Joyce's much-discussed "Work in Progress"'. After quoting six lines, the article concluded: 'If this is not enough, you can buy thirty-six complete printed pages of plu-perfect modernity for a silly shilling' (UBC 46: 915). The Manchester *Guardian* ('T.M.M.', June 1931) referred to the same comprehensible sentence about the completeness of the episode: 'Well, it may be so, complete and an episode, but on a superficial reading it resembles much more nearly Dr. Johnson's definition of an essay – an undigested piece'. Although this remark was intended as negative criticism, it was actually appealing from a cognitive perspective because it suggested a view of cognition in terms of constant digesting and peristaltic motion. But the Manchester *Guardian* preferred to see Joyce's 'essay' in terms of a literary *in*digestion. Admittedly, there was 'a kind of ribald rhythm in the work that lingers in the mind making all thought grotesque', but 'who haveth childers and why it is difficult to say' (UBC 14: 889).

Chapter 7

The Mime of Mick, Nick and the Maggies

Of all the subscribers to *transition*, one of the most loyal readers of Joyce's instalments was the Dutch publisher Carolus Verhulst, who revived the journal in 1932 (see Chapter 3). Peter de Voogd notes that in the copies of the first 13 numbers of *transition* that have been preserved in Verhulst's library, only those gatherings containing Joyce's texts have been cut (de Voogd 2013, 234). The first issue of *transition* published by his Servire Press (*transition* 21), was the one that contained a 'Homage to James Joyce' (March 1932; see Chapter 3). It came at a moment when Joyce could use a boost. Lucia's mental health was one of the reasons why it became increasingly difficult for Joyce to finish his book. On his fiftieth birthday (2 February 1932), Lucia threw a chair at her mother and a few months later she became catatonic and was diagnosed with schizophrenia (Ellmann 1983, 651; Shloss 2003, 215–9; Birmingham 2014, 244). As Kevin Birmingham puts it, 'Joyce's life was falling apart' (2014, 288). But he still had the support of fans such as Carolus Verhulst, as is evidenced by the 'Homage to James Joyce' in *transition* 21.

Peter de Voogd pays due attention to *transition*'s typography as an aspect of modernism too often neglected. As he points out, the house style of the Servire Press was inspired by De Stijl and 'based on the Dutch "New Typography" created by typeface designers such as Cesar Domela-Nieuwenhuis, Theo van Doesburg, and S. H. de Roos' (de Voogd 2013, 233). A tinge of chauvinism was part of Verhulst's mission as a publisher, as a page-long advertisement for his own company in *transition* 21 illustrates. It opens with the word 'PRINTING' in large sans serif letters, followed in smaller font by: 'THE EIGHTH ART / 500 YEARS OLD / CRADLED IN HOLLAND / AT THE HAGUE WE HAVE / STATUES TO PRINTERS / OUR PRINTERS ARE ARTISTS'. As a sort of motto, the following statement preceded the Servire Press's address: 'IN OPTICAL DELIGHT / A PAGE CAN COMPETE / WITH A PAINTING'. The company presented itself explicitly as 'PRINTERS TO MODERNS' and advertised its expertise: 'SPECIALISTS / IN / EDITIONS DE LUXE / ALL ART PRINTING / AT PLEASING PRICES'.

The change did not go unnoticed in the Dutch press. J.F. Otten in the *Nieuwe Rotterdamsche Courant* (*NRC*, 20 April 1932) opened his review with a discussion not of the magazine's content, but of the takeover by the 'Dutch publishing house Servire' and its decision to pay more attention to its outward appearance.[1] The

---

[1] 'Het is een goed denkbeeld geweest van de Hollandsche uitgeverij Servire om het Engelsche tijdschrift Transition, destijds in Parijs in bescheiden kleedij en formaat verschijnend, in nieuwen vorm uit te geven' (*NRC*, 20 April 1932).

review also drew attention to the new subtitle: 'An International Workshop for Orphic Creation'. The subtitle reflected the preoccupations of both the editor in chief and the publisher. While Jolas was preoccupied by his notion of a 'metaphysical language' and the 'revolution of the word', 'Verhulst was into esoteric theories' (de Voogd 2013, 239). The Servire Press used its first issue of *transition* to announce the publication of the so-called 'Transition Series / under the direction of / Eugene Jolas'. The first number in the series was Jolas's own book, *The Language of Night: A Study of the Orphic Word*. A short blurb proclaimed that the 'crisis of language through which we are passing' was largely due to the intrusion of the mythological form of expression by 'a reactionary sociological form', as an alternative to which Jolas offered 'his conception of a metaphysical language' (*transition* 21). It is characteristic of the importance Verhulst attached to printing as 'the eighth art' that the advertisement also mentions the bibliographical and even typographical details such as the font: 'Set up in Neuzeit Grotesk, 64 pages, size 13 × 19 cm. Printed on Japanese Vellum, in Propandora paper cover. Limited edition of 550 copies'.

In the second issue published by the Servire Press (*transition* 22) Joyce's 'Continuation of a Work in Progress' stood out typographically because it was completely set in bold sans serif font, in constrast with the preceding text by Eugene Jolas and Georges Pelorson ('Hysteriette of la Cosmosa') and the following texts by Eugene Jolas ('The Primal Personality'), Stuart Gilbert ('Dichtung and Diction'), and Carola Giedion-Welcker ('Die Funktion der Sprache').

The text of Joyce's instalment in *transition* 22 was published separately by the Servire Press as *The Mime of Mick, Nick and the Maggies*. This time, the impulse for the separate publication was Lucia Joyce, who designed illuminated letters, which she and her father called 'lettrines'. According to Neil Pearson, 'Joyce convinced himself that the lettrines had artistic as well as therapeutic value, and scenting the possibility of a career for Lucia at last, he touted her work to artists, illustrators and designers. He found no takers: only when he offered them attached to his own work did anybody show even a passing interest' (Pearson 2007, 417). Joyce sent the lettrines to the composer, Herbert Hughes, who was editing *The Joyce Book* (published by Oxford University Press in 1933, containing settings of *Pomes Penyeach* by 13 different composers). They were returned with the excuse that the type had already been set.

He then sent the lettrines to Caresse Crosby. The plan was to make a de luxe facsimile edition of Joyce's handwritten *Pomes Penyeach*, each poem opening with a lettrine by Lucia. But the plan never materialized, at least not in this set-up with Caresse Crosby.

Eventually, Joyce found Jack Kahane willing to undertake the enterprise and co-publish it with Desmond Harmsworth, on condition that Joyce would underwrite the production costs and find subscribers for the expensive edition of only 25 copies (and six *hors commerce*), printed on Japan nacrepaper, costing 1,000 French francs or £12 a piece. It was published in September 1932 by The Obelisk Press, Paris, and Desmond Harmsworth Ltd, London. The title page mentions explicitly that the 'Initial letters [are] designed and illuminated by Lucia Joyce'. In retrospect,

Kahane wrote he was 'never really proud of it' (Kahane 1939, 244), and Neil Pearson describes how difficult it was to get a mere 25 copies sold: 'Despite Joyce's best efforts the 25 copies sold slowly: a prospectus issued by harmsworth in the autumn of 1932 notes that five copies remained unsubscribed, and Kahane was still advertising the book for sale in Paris as late as 1936' (Pearson 2007, 419). Joyce sent 1000 francs to Kahane to send on to Lucia as an 'ego-boosting "royalty"' (419) and he also bought two copies to be deposited at the British Library and the Bibliothèque Nationale, as Carol Loeb Shloss notes (Shloss 2003, 241). The art critic Louis Gillet, whose daughter Dominique was a good friend of Lucia, wrote about the lettrines in a review for the *Revue des deux mondes*, and so did the Paris art critic Fritz Vanderpyl by the end of 1932, in an essay called 'Pulchritudo tam Antiqua et tam Nova: Les Lettrines de Lucia Joyce'.[2]

This essay prompted Carolus Verhulst to contact Joyce on 28 December 1932 with the proposal to publish a de luxe edition of (a fragment from) his work with illuminations by his daughter: 'Verhulst would finance the edition himself, and he proposed royalties of ten per cent to be paid to Lucia and thirty per cent to Joyce' (Shloss 2003, 244). Joyce liked the idea, but B.W. Huebsch did not agree. No more fragments were to be published before the completion of 'Work in Progress', which Huebsch had contracted to publish. And in London, Faber and Faber briefly considered bringing out a limited edition themselves, but eventually decided against it, so 'it took two months of active negotiation to work out the terms for Servire's publication of the *Mime* fragment' (244).

The text opens with a 'lettrine' and the narrative of the episode is framed as a play. Following the presentation of the programme and *dramatis personae* of 'The Mime of Mick, Nick and the Maggies', the children's games start with Glugg (the Devil), who is asked a riddle. After a second failed attempt to answer a riddle, the rainbow or flower girls dance and sing in praise of Chuff (Shaun as Angel).[3] The flower girls try to seduce Chuff, turning toward their sun and exposing their genitals in floral fashion: 'the tot of all the tits of their understamens is as open as he can posably she and is tournesoled straightcut or sidewaist, accourdant to the coursets of things feminite, towooerds him in heliolatry' (*Mime* 36–7; *FW* 236–7). The answer to the riddles is 'heliotrope', as Joyce explained to Frank Budgen (*LI* 406), so by turning (Gr. *tropein*) toward sunny Shaun (Gr. *helios*), the Maggies give away the answer by performing it. Meanwhile, night falls and 'It darkles, all this our funnominal world' (*Mime* 48–9). The struggle between light and darkness underlines the theme of the riddles, the apparently unstoppable human urge to solve them and create a sense of certainty by naming the phenomenal world, but not without the nominalist recognition that our concepts are mere labels. The Devil is

---

[2]   In *Mercure de France*; see Shloss 2003, 244–5; also published in *transition* 22, 131 (February 1933).

[3]   See letter to Harriet Shaw Weaver, 22 November 1930 (*LI* 295); see also letters to Harriet Weaver 21 May, 7 June, 15 July 1926.

asked a third riddle, but again fails to answer. The parents arrive and take the boys home. Issy seems to stay behind, in her capacity as 'That little cloud' which 'still hangs isky'. As HCE shuts the door of the pub, the bang is followed by a thundering noise (another thunderword), and the noise of applause: 'Byfall. / Upploud!' (*Mime* 75). That is how the mime ends: 'The play thou schouwburgst, Game, here endeth. The curtain drops by deep request' (75). It is followed only by the children's prayer before going to bed: 'Loud, heap miseries upon us yet entwine our arts with laughters low! / Ha he hi ho hu. / Mummum' (77).

As to the 'bibliographical code' (McGann 1991) of the edition, it is remarkable that Verhulst did not choose his favourite sans serif Neuzeit Grotesk typeface – the archetype of a modernist font – to print this text by his favourite modernist author, as he did for the version in *transition* 22. Instead, he chose a serif Grotius typeface, which can hardly be called modernist, as Peter de Voogd points out, 'but Verhulst thought it fitted Lucia's decorative lettrines better' (de Voogd 2013, 244). The Colophon at the back of the book explicitly mentioned that the initial letter, the tailpiece and the cover were 'specially designed for these editions by Miss Lucia Joyce'. By 'these editions' were meant the 1,000 copies on 'Old Antique Dutch' and the 29 copies on 'Simili Japon' by Van Gelder Zonen, bound in parchment and signed by both James and Lucia Joyce.

The limited edition of 29 copies served to reflect the 29 leap year girls as incarnations of Issy, the daughter figure in 'Work in Progress'. Katarzyna Bazarnik notes that 'the special limitation [of 29 copies] represents her multiple personality' (Bazarnik 2007).

That Lucia was now making an alphabet of lettrines for a planned edition of *A Chaucer A.B.C.* (announced in *transition* 27; see Figure 7.1) must have struck Joyce as an eerie materialization of the alphabet of 29 letters he wrote during the preparation of *transition* 6 (first in notebook VI.B.19, page [12],[4] and then on an A5 piece of paper, probably as a gift to Sylvia Beach), opening with Joyce's siglum for Issy: '[Issy]'s alphabet of 29 letters (she^Izzy is born on last day of February of a leap year) – ada / bet / celia / daisy / ena / fretta / giselda / hilda / ita / jess / katty / lou / maomi / nanny / opal / pearl / queenie / ruth / susie / tottie / una / vera / wanda / xenia / yvalyna / zita / psita / thita / and Mee' (UB JJC VI.J.4).

The copyright page of the *Mime* mentions 1933 as the year of publication, but the edition did not appear until June 1934 (Norburn 2004, 166). On 30 November 1933, Carolus Verhulst sent the opening pages of the *Mime* to Sylvia Beach, which she returned on 13 December 1933, as he had requested, adding: 'The printing is very handsome and it promises to be a lovely edition. I would be delighted to act as agent for it. I am sorry that it is quite impossible for me, in my present

---

[4] Added to the first copy of the first set of galley proofs of *transition* 6 (BL MS 46473, f. 204), as Luca Crispi notes in the Buffalo catalogue of the James Joyce Collection (UB JJC VI.J.4).

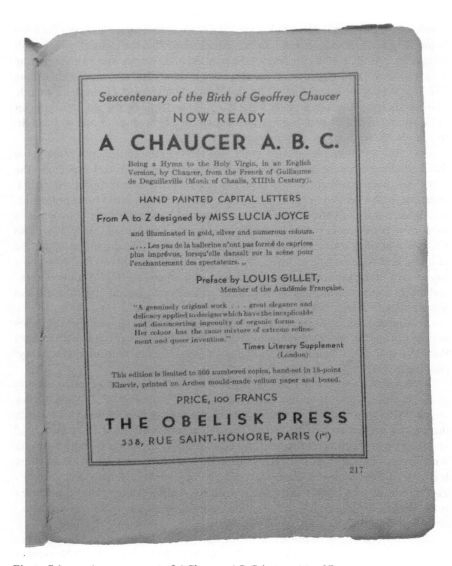

Figure 7.1   Announcement of *A Chaucer A.B.C.* in *transition* 27

circumstances, to buy any of the copies outright. A certain number of them, say one hundred, might be sent to me on consignment' (UB JJC XII: Beach to Verhulst, folder 2). Verhulst managed to make agreements with Faber and Faber in the UK, Gotham Book Mart in the US and the Messageries Dawson in France: the 1,000 copies were issued under these three imprints besides that of the Servire Press (Norburn 2004, 166).

Verhulst naturally made use of *transition* to advertise the edition, inserting a handout in *transition* 23,[5] which mentioned that the *Mime* was the first separate instalment of 'Work in Progress' in 'many years'. The expression 'many years' was not quite accurate (Peter de Voogd even calls it 'nonsense'; 244) for *Two Tales* had been published only two years earlier. Still, *Two Tales* was a partial reprint of *Tales Told* and it had indeed been a while since a new fragment had appeared in book format since the first publication of *Haveth Childers Everywhere* (1930).

More publicity was made in subsequent issues. At the back of *transition* 26, Gotham Book Mart (51 West 47th Street, New York) advertised '*The Mime of Mick, Nick and the Maggies* by James Joyce' as 'a fragment of Work in Progress', explicitly mentioning the 'cover and tail piece by Lucia Joyce' (available in two formats: an 'edition limited to 300 copies for America. Wrappers – \$3.50' and a 'Super de luxe edition limited to twenty-five copies on Japan paper, signed by both author and illustrator. Handsomely bound – \$15.00').

The advertisement also briefly described the piece as a 'fairy tail'[sic]: 'In this cosmological fairy tail, the poet presents his visions of the childhood of mankind, lifting the local elements into universal relationships of Swiftian humor and magic symbolism' (see Figure 7.2).

After the publication of *The Mime of Mick, Nick and the Maggies* by the Servire Press, it was not until 1937 that the text was revised and prepared for *Finnegans Wake*. As Sam Slote notes, the draft history beyond *The Mime* is relatively straightforward: 'two sets of corrected pages were prepared – one in autograph overlay and one with typed overlay – for the printer of *Finnegans Wake*. Then, in early 1938 Joyce was sent the galley proofs, and in late 1938 he was sent the page proofs' (Slote 2007, 188). Although this trajectory was straightforward, the text changed significantly. So, while the special limitation of 29 copies of *The Mime* may represent Lucia's multiple personalities, as Katarzyna Bazarnik suggests, another form of mental multiplicity was still at play: the idea of the mind as a palimpsest (see Chapter 6) or the 'multiple drafts model'. While realizing that his own daughter's mental state was increasingly being regarded as 'out of the ordinary', Joyce carried on writing a work that makes cognitive mutability and variation thematic as a form of what is considered the 'ordinary' functioning of the extended mind.

Immediate Reception: Press Clippings

On 6 January 1934, the Liverpool *Post* reported that Faber and Faber announced another fragment of Joyce's 'Work in Progress' – 'about which we have heard so much during the decade that has elapsed since the publication of *Ulysses*' – was

---

[5]   'The handout with which Verhulst advertised the *Mime* and which he inserted in *transition*, 23, was set in the Futura Schmalfett, one of the bold variants of Paul Renner's Futura and part of the house style of Servire' (de Voogd 2013, 244).

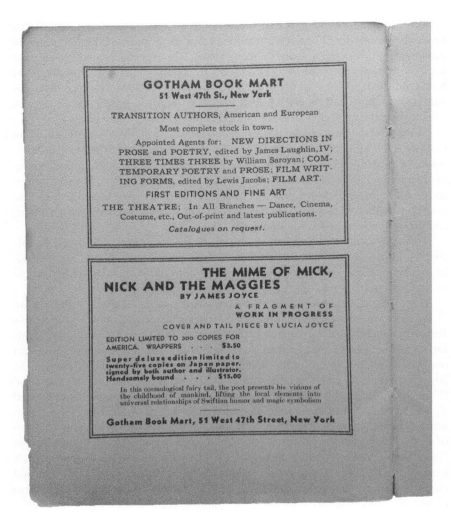

Figure 7.2   Advertisement for *The Mime of Mick, Nick and the Maggies* in *transition* 26

forthcoming, 'under the characteristically queer title' *The Mime of Mick, Nick and the Maggies*. The announcement also mentioned that the pages were 'illuminated by Miss Lucia Joyce, the author's daughter' (UBC 69).[6]

G.W. Stonier indicated that there seemed to be no end to 'Work in Progress'. In his review in the *New Statesman and Nation* 8 ('Joyce without End', 22 September

---

[6]   On 24 January, (almost literally) the same announcement appeared in the Southport *Guardian*; UBC 69: 1373).

1934, 364) he was of the opinion that *The Mime of Mick, Nick and the Maggies* was 'not as good as *Anna Livia Plurabelle*', but that it still was 'a fair specimen of its author's prose'. Again, the performative quality of Joyce's language was hinted at, a language that consisted of 'animated words', which require 'the sort of acuteness which will spot a *double entendre*'. But this was not an insurmountable difficulty for the reader, according to Stonier: 'If a music-hall audience can appreciate sexual jokes in this way, there is no reason why educated readers should not be capable of catching the allusions, historical and topical, which are embedded in *Work in Progress*' (qtd in Fargnoli 2003, 342).

A few years after the Servire Press edition came out, a passage from *The Mime* was reprinted in 'A Phoenix Park Nocturne', *Verve* 1.2 (March–June 1938) (cf. *FW* 244.13–246.02; Crispi and Slote 2007, 492).

With regard to the pre-book publications in general, Peter de Voogd notes that 'All of these pre-publications of *Finnegans Wake* differ significantly from the final text which appeared in 1939; Joyce was in the habit of adding to and drastically changing his text the moment he got it in proofs, much to the chagrin of printers and publishers' (244). There is, however, a significant difference between the *Mime* and the other pre-book publications. In general, Joyce kept adding more text, but not in equal measure. In the case of the *Mime*, the number of words added is more than ten times higher than in the case of the other pre-book publications (simply in terms of quantity, without counting corrections or substitutions). So, all the pre-book publications grew, but the *Mime*'s growth was atypical for a separate pre-book publication: *Anna Livia Plurabelle* grew with ca 290 words; *The Mookse and the Gripes* with only ca 20 words; *The Ondt and the Gracehoper* with ca 100 words; *Haveth Childers Everywhere* with ca 50 words; *The Mime of Mick, Nick and the Maggies* with ca 4,000 words; *Storiella* (and *The Muddest Thick*) with ca 270 words. Of all the separately published fragments, *The Mime* is the text that expanded most spectacularly after the pre-book publication (see Appendix 3 for a critical apparatus). Within the context of the accretive revision process of 'Work in Progress' / *Finnegans Wake*, the pattern seems to be that Joyce was generally less inclined to keep adding more text to fragments that had already been published as separate booklets than to other parts of *Finnegans Wake*. To that pattern, the *Mime* would be the exception confirming the rule.

Chapter 8
Storiella as She Is Syung

Anna Livia Plurabelle and *Haveth Childers Everywhere* represented the mother and father figures of 'Work in Progress' as Katarzyna Bazarnik suggests: 'As if to match the parental figure, Joyce brought out their offspring: *Two Tales of Shem and Shaun, The Mime of Mick, Nick and the Maggies* and *Storiella as She Is Syung*' (Bazarnik 2007). *Storiella* had appreared in *transition* 23 (see Chapter 3). When the next instalment appeared in *transition* 26 (cf. *FW* 309–31) the name of James Joyce in the 'Contributors' section (of *transition* 26) was not followed by a short bio – he needed no introduction. Instead, the following explanation was given with regard to Joyce's work and its progress:

> The fragment of James Joyce's 'Work in Progress' which appeared in TRANSI-
> TION No. 23 (February 1935), 'Opening and Closing Pages of Part II, Section
> II', will be published in book form early in 1937, under the title of 'Storiella as
> she is Syung', by the Corvinus Press, London. This edition, which will be limited
> to 150 hand-printed copies, will include reproductions in color of two illuminated
> lettrines by Lucia Joyce.
>
> No further fragments of 'Work in Progress' will be published in book form,
> as the book will appear in its entirety some time in 1937, probably some six
> months after the issuance of the trade edition of 'Ulysses' in Great Britain. One
> thousand de luxe copies of 'Ulysses' were published in London by John Lane on
> October 3, 1936.
>
> (*t26* 5)

As Stacey Herbert points out, Joyce 'made use of limited editions in part to circum-vent censorship' and 'he took an increasing interest in shaping the material form of his books, choosing type, layout and binding design as integral elements of the work' (Herbert 2009, 3). Of these pre-book publications, *Storiella* is by far the most luxuriant edition.

In their collation and bibliographic description, Slocum and Cahoon (58–9) pay due attention to its large format (32.3 × 26 cm); its untrimmed edges and gilt top edge; the handmade paper, watermarked 'unbleached Arnold'; its explicit statement on the text and the decoration on page 45 (see Figure 8.1; 'This book comprises the opening and closing pages of part II: section II of "Work in Prog-ress". The illuminated capital letter at the beginning is the work of Lucia Joyce, the author's daughter'); the binding in flexible orange vellum, gilt stamped (see Plate 8), contrasting sharply with the plain gray-green slip case in which it was issued.

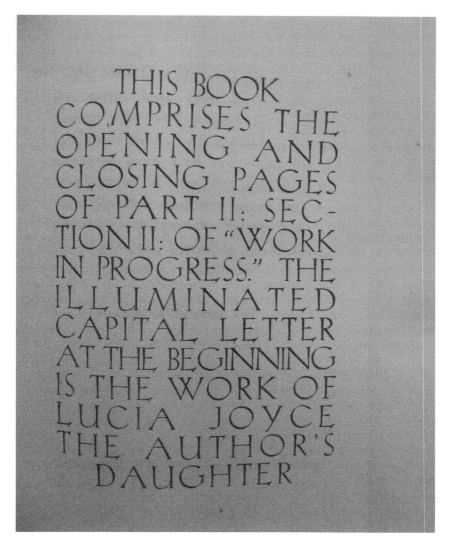

THIS BOOK COMPRISES THE OPENING AND CLOSING PAGES OF PART II: SECTION II: OF "WORK IN PROGRESS." THE ILLUMINATED CAPITAL LETTER AT THE BEGINNING IS THE WORK OF LUCIA JOYCE THE AUTHOR'S DAUGHTER

Figure 8.1   Statement on page 45 of *Storiella as She Is Syung*

The statement in *transition* 26 was not entirely correct, for the edition's print run was actually 175 (numbered) copies, 25 of which were signed by the author (plus one extra copy, lettered 'A', printed on a white Japanese mulberry paper and reserved for the printer).

The beautiful edition was printed and published by Lord Carlow of the Corvinus Press. In the early 1930s, as an officer in the Auxiliary Air Force, George

Lionel Seymour, Viscount Carlow (1907–44), had become interested in collecting books and in March 1936, he had established the Corvinus Press, named after the bibliophile King Matthias Corvinus of Hungary.[1] Joyce sent the text of *Storiella* with Lucia's 'initial' to Carlow on 22 July 1936 (*LIII* 386) and the book was published in October 1937 (Nash and Flavell 1994, 48).

As to the content of *Storiella*, David Hayman explained in 1963 that Joyce initially thought to open chapter II.2 with a passage that begins with the word: 'Scribbledehobbles are ~~at~~ ^{bent on} their pensums' (*FDV* 148). In 1966, Hayman called it an 'abortive passage': 'Whereas the other passages were written quickly, almost off the top of the author's head, this piece was the product of much preparation and thought. It was painfully elaborated in 1932 from extensive notes which appear to have been taken six years earlier in the *Scribbledehobble* notebook' (Hayman 1966, 107). This notebook was edited by Thomas E. Connolly (Evanston: Northwestern University Press, 1961) and was named after its opening word, 'Scribbledehobble'. Joyce literally *com-posed* the passage, putting it together by means of a 'recombination' (*FW* 614.35) of entries he found in the notebook: starting with the word '**scribbledehobble**' on the first page, he found the words '**trifid tongue**' and '**S P dove without gall**'[2] on page 2; and on page 3 a reference to Euclid: '**dulcarnon = 2 horned**, 47th prop of Euclid or **Alexander**'s **2 horn heads**' and '**to pulfer turnips**' (Connolly 1961, 5–8; the words in bold typeface were used in the first draft). As Luca Crispi shows, these entries were then assembled 'in a very craftsmanlike manner' (Crispi 2007, 227) in the first writing layer of the first draft:

> **Scribbledehobbles** are at their pensums. **Trifid tongue** and **dove without gall** to solve **dulcarnon**'s ~~dire~~ ~~twohorned~~ twohornedheaded dilemma what stumped bold **Alexander** and drove him **to pulfer turnips**.
>
> (*FDV* 148; emphasis added)

To this first writing layer, Joyce then started incorporating overlay additions, for which again he drew from the *Scribbledehobble* notebook. On page 8 he found 'T **reads his nails**'; on pages 12–3 'Kathleen's **mind a jackdaw's nest**'; on page 13 '**others work or woofor** T' and a passage about Issy who '**tears up letters**'; and on page 14 the entry '**backslapper gladhander**' (Connolly 1961, 12–18):

> **Scribbledehobbles** are ~~at~~ ^{bent on} their pensums ^{reading nails & biting lips}. **Trifid tongue** ^{others woo & work for the backslapper gladhander} and **dove without gall** ^{and she whose mind's a jackdaw's nest of tearing up letters she never wrote} to solve **dulcarnon**'s ~~dire~~ ~~twohorned~~ twohornedheaded dilemma what stumped bold **Alexander** and drove him **to pulfer turnips**.
>
> (*FDV* 148; emphasis added)

---

[1]   In a period of nine years, the press published 58 titles, until Lord Carlow died on a secret diplomatic mission to Yugoslavia in 1944.

[2]   Referring to Saint Patrick. 'Dubh-Gall' is the Gaelic term for Danish Viking.

David Hayman points out that half of the first draft is thus derived from the note-book: 'Of the 266 words in the completed first draft approximately 132 can be traced directly to the notes' (Hayman 1966, 110). The 'scribbledehobble' notes were reconfigured into the draft of 'Scribbledehobbles' and this is 'how they grew', to use Hayman's organic metaphor (1966, 107). Luca Crispi employs a – perhaps more appropriate – constructive metaphor, emphasizing the way Joyce 'creatively constructed the first draft' (Crispi 2007, 227): 'During the next three years he continued to refine, elaborate, and amplify this technique of transferring and juxtaposing lexical elements and textual fragments, eventually coming to rely upon it to compose and structure, among other compositions, the newer "Storiella" sections' (228).

As to the question why Joyce chose to 'hammer his raw material into a useful object practically without the intervention of the creative imagination', Hayman speculates that 'he was not interested in this passage though he felt obliged to complete the lessons chapter' (1966, 112):

> in 1932 Joyce, being in a none-too-creative state of mind, turned to a chore he had put off for seven years, looked for the easiest possible solution to the difficult problem of structuring an important chapter. The process of writing and revision with the aid of the Scribbledehobble notes brought with it needed inspiration and perhaps enthusiasm. As a result he was able, among other things, to conceive the textbook format, develop the 'Storiella' and through the dismemberment and reconstitution of the central pages highlight Issy's role as a female force.
>
> (117)

Whether Joyce 'was not interested in this passage' is arguable, but it is again strik-ing how well both the formal aspects of this text and its composition process match the content of the piece, expressing the difficulty the children experience doing their homework, including their writing or composition assignment. As so often in 'Work in Progress', there is a performative quality to the painful elaboration of the 'pensums', which is again relevant to '4e cognition' (the embedded, embodied, extended, enactive mind). Joyce's remarkably mechanical composition process may have originated in a 'none-too-creative state of mind', but it also served as a model of the mind, a model that helped him shape the fictional minds of his char-acters. This does not imply that Joyce consciously adhered to a particular philsophi-cal paradigm and had a systematically defined concept of the mind before he gave shape to these fictional minds. Nor does it imply a direct analogy between the author and his characters in the sense that the children would have to be read as alter egos of the writer. The passage merely illustrates a corrrelation on a more abstract level, a congruity in terms of a common model of the (extended) mind. The act of writing has a similar function both in the writer's real-life situation and in the simulated situation within the narrative. Especially when the mind is in a 'none-too-creative state', in Hayman's terms, it tends to rely more heavily on its *Umwelt*. This enactive process applies both to the worldmaker's and to his characters'*Umwelt*. The children *have to* write; writing is their pensum. No wonder that they are in a 'none-too-creative state of mind' as well. So their writing starts as a mere scribble and it does not proceed swiftly, but hobbles along. Whatever they can find in their immediate environment is used as a direct stimulus.

Joyce performs the role of what Wyndham Lewis disparagingly called the behaviourist 'tester', examining the act of writing and starting from its most mechanical aspects, not unlike the way Louise Barrett describes it in terms of enactive cognition: 'Think of the way that we use Post-it notes, Memory Sticks, notebooks, computer files, whiteboards, books, and journals to support our written work [. . .] All of these behaviors reflect a habit of simplifying what would otherwise be cognitively demanding tasks – a habit that is now all-pervasive and underscores just how much of routine human cognition is enacted in the context of environmental supports' (219). Barrett's conclusion is that 'the real "problem-solving machine" is not the brain alone, but the brain, the body, and the environmental structures that we use to augment, enhance, and support internal cognitive processes' (219).

So, when Hayman writes that this piece was written 'practically without the intervention of the creative imagination', the question rises what creative imagination *is*. It is not because Joyce had no clear preconceived idea or intention to write this passage, that its writing was unimaginative. As Sally Bushell notes, intention is an 'ongoing event within the process' (Bushell 2009, 54), which is 'constantly being changed and redirected by the unintentional contexts with which it engages' (61). One could also read 'Scribbledehobbles' and its development into *Storiella* as a fairly truthful study of creative imagination as part of the workings of the embedded, embodied, enactive, extended/extensive mind. In David Herman's terms, Joyce is an '*Umwelt* researcher' and in order to examine the *Umwelt* of the children's (fictional) minds at work, Joyce drew upon his experience with his own *Umwelt*, of which notebooks were an integral part. 'Scribbledehobbles' may have been written without 'creative imagination' if this notion is understood in Hayman's conception of the term, but not if 'creative imagination' is something that extends beyond the brain and if it involves interaction with external source texts, with notes and multiple drafts, with publishers and with criticism. And on the diegetic level, the writing of the pensums are a simulation of this cognitive model, enacting what Crémieux called the hesitations, the errors, the sketches, the multiple drafts of the mind (UBC 33: 1018; see Chapter 3).

From this cognitive perspective, it is quite appropriate that it took several drafts to arrive at a narrative, the story of *Storiella as She Is Syung*. 'Joyce saw fit after six revise-and-complete drafts to chop it [the "Schribledehobbles" passage] into kindling, preserving intact only the first page or so, discarding a large segment and using most of the remainder in Issy's footnotes' (Hayman 1966, 107). The boys' identification with their history lesson in 'Scribbledehobbles', and Issy's lessons in seduction only gradually developed into *Storiella*'s instruction in 'gramma's grammar' (*S*[28]): 'mind your genderous towards his reflexives such that I was to your grappa' (*S*[28]). The 'Scribbledehobbles' dissolved into Issy's footnotes, which became the female foil for the boys' marginalia to the mysteries of sexuality –

thus creating the mirror image of the triangular relationship visualized at the end of the fable of the Mookse and the Gripes, where Nuvoletta was hovering above and between her brothers. As David Hayman points out, it is 'in the order of things that [Issy's] sexual awakening should precede and balance theirs' (116).

In *transition* 23, the boys' marginalia were in italics on the left-hand side, and in bold black sans serif typeface on the right. The Corvinus Press edition shows no sans-serif typeface; instead, the marginalia on the right are in red, bold typeface. In *Finnegans Wake*, this was changed again: no sans serif, no colour, no bold typeface, but capitals. Later on, after the publication of *Finnegans Wake*, Joyce explained to Frank Budgen that the classbook's marginalia by the twins 'change sides at half time' (end July 1939; *LI* 406). The turning point seems to be thematized in the marginalia themselves, on the page with the Euclidian diagram, where the right-hand marginalia 'why my as likewise whis his' suggests their interchangeability. Before this moment in the text, the right-hand marginalia are more Shaunish in nature, characterized by what Beckett called the 'loutishness of learning' and by what Joyce (with reference to the piece in *transition* 6) had called the 'know-all''voice of The Enemy' (*LI* 257–8). After the diagram, this pontificating voice shifts to the left-hand side with its italicized marginalia. In *Storiella*, this shift is not as easily recognizable, because the 'triangle' episode is not part of this publication. While the playful, Shemmish marginalia of the 'opening pages' of chapter II.2 end with '*Puzzly, puzzly, I smell a cat*' (in italics on the 'left bank'; *S*36]), the last Shaun-ish marginalia (red and bold on the right) deal with serious business: the '**Panoptical purview of political progress and the future presentation of the past**' (*S*[32–3]). The first marginalia of the 'closing pages' do sound differently: now, the italics on the left are more serious ('*Service superseding self*'; '*Catastrophe and Anabasis*'; *S*[37]) whereas the red, bold marginalia on the right sound more playful: '**Euchre risk, merci buckup, and mind who you're pucking, flabby**'.

After the 'opening pages', closing with 'Erin's hircohaired culoteer' (*S*[36]), the body of the text continues with the 'closing pages' of chapter II.2: 'Thanks eversore much, Pointcarried!' (*S*[37]). The children look back on a day of the medieval universities' lower and upper divisions of the seven liberal arts, the triv-ium (grammar, rhetoric and logic) and quadrivium (arithmetic, geometry, astron-omy and music). And, *en passant*, Joyce makes a reference to the *Dial*:

> But while the dial are they doodling dawdling over the mugs and the grubs? Oikey, Impostolopulos? Steady steady steady steady steady studiavimus. Many many many many many many manducabimus. We've had our day at triv and quad and writ our bit as intermidgets. Art, literature, politics, economy, chemistry, human-ity, &c.
>
> ([39–40])

The reference to the *Dial* and the remark that the children have 'writ [their] bit' are only a few of the numerous instances of what James S. Atherton has called the book's 'awareness of itself as a "work in progress"' (1959, 59). This metafictional quality also shows on the next page of *Storiella*: 'Tell a Friend in a Chatty Letter the Fable of the Grasshopper and the Ant' (*S*[41]). The allusion is in the first place to Aesop, but with the explicit mention of the 'Friend' (as opposed to 'The Enemy') it already 'prefigures' the fable of the Ondt and the Gracehoper. Within the structure of *Finnegans Wake*, this is a form of 'foreshadowing', for the fable only appears in Book III; but in the history of the pre-book publications, it is a retroactive reference to what had already been written, emphasizing the constant feedback loop between the new pre-book publications and the 'text produced so far' (Flower and Hayes 1981, 370; see Introduction).

Against the background of the mention of this fable and its self-referential function in *Storiella*, another fable becomes relevant again: Swift's fable of the spider and the bee, the Ancients and the Moderns, in *The Battle of the Books*. In general, Joyce's method is that of the bee in that he relies heavily on 'found objects' – and the composition of 'Scribbledehobbles' is one of the most extreme examples of his reliance on these verbal *objets trouvés*, as David Hayman and Luca Crispi have shown. This is not only relevant to genetic critics and researchers interested in the invention and production of the storyworld; it has consequences for the evocation of the workings of the fictional mind *in* that storyworld as well – and of the mind *as* a storyworld, a 'Storiella', or Dennett's 'narrative selfhood' (418), for which the web of intertextuality is perhaps an adequate metaphor. As discussed in Chapter 4, Dennett suggested that telling stories is one of the human being's basic tactics of self-protection and self-definition, comparable to a spider's tactic of spinning webs – but not without the immediate disclaimer that, unlike a spider, a human being does not 'exude' its web (416). A more adequate metaphor for the intertextual quality of stories is that of the roaming bee, as Swift already suggested centuries ago: in the *Battle of the Books*, the bee draws the spider's attention to the fact that it is an illusion to think that it spins its web out of its own entrails. The spider may have wanted to build its own web 'with [its] own hands, and the materials extracted altogether out of [its] own person', as Swift puts it (Swift 1986, 112), but the Ancients point out that the spider also feeds on insects and the 'vermin of its age', otherwise it would not be able to make its web. If storytelling is so fundamental that it shapes our 'narrative selfhood' and if human consciousness is the product of tales told, it is fitting that the story of the pre-book publications of 'Work in Progress' ends with *Storiella*, the personification of narrative selfhood.

Conclusion
In the Wake of 'Work in Progress'

In the previous chapters, I have suggested a reading of 'Work in Progress' as a simulation of the human mind at work, an evocation not so much of a dream or of 'the unconscious' but of human consciousness, including its default mode network. From a cognitive perspective, the relationship between 'Work in Progress' (the production process) and *Finnegans Wake* (the final product) can be regarded as paradigmatic of the workings of the human mind in terms of Dennett's 'multiple drafts model' and what Mark Rowlands calls '4e cognition' (the embedded, embodied, extended, enactive mind). The way in which the workings of Joyce's extended mind served as a model of the mind as evoked in 'Work in Progress' explicitly includes the interaction with notebooks and drafts, with the cultural and material circumstances of the production process, the publication history and the immediate reception – or what Jerome McGann has called 'the double helix of a work's reception history and its production history' (16).

Regarding the reception history, it is symptomatic that the number of reviews of the separately published pre-book publications dwindle gradually. Robert Deming's edition of the critical heritage reflects this pattern; in his selection, the number of reviews decreases from almost 20 reviews of *Anna Livia Plurabelle*, to half a dozen of *Tales Told*, two reviews of *Haveth Childers Everywhere*, one of *The Mime* and none of *Storiella*. The same trend can be observed in the newspaper clippings archive at the University at Buffalo. By the second half of the 1930s, the hostility in the press had died down and made room for relative indifference, but it was Joyce's *perception* of his environment as being increasingly hostile to his project that had an immediate impact on the final years of 'Work in Progress', as analysed by Geert Lernout. In these years, Joyce could rely on Paul Léon, whom Stuart Gilbert described as Joyce's 'permanently attached slave' (1993, 34). As Joyce's 'mostly unpaid secretary', one of his main jobs was 'to shield Joyce from an outside world that the author had begun to perceive as hostile', even though this outside world included several people who still considered themselves to be Joyce's friends (Lernout 2013, 5), notably his British and American publishers, T.S. Eliot and B.W. Huebsch, two key players in the other strand of McGann's double helix, the production history.

As early as 1931, Joyce had signed a contract with Faber and Faber in London and Viking Press in New York. When Joyce was in London for his wedding (on 4 July, his father's birthday), T.S. Eliot wrote him a letter (6 July 1931) reassuring him that there was 'no question about our wanting to publish the book' and making a few very concrete suggestions:

> So far as we can see from the data available, we could certainly offer an advance of £300 on the book from 190,000 to 200,000 words to be published at a guinea: there is no need to stipulate the number of words – the only point is that if you particularly wished it to be published at a lower price we should have to reconsider the advance. We could pay the advance in either of two ways (1) £100 on signing contract, £100 on delivery of manuscript, and £100 on publication; or (2) £150 on signing contract and £150 on publication. This is on a royalty of 15% up to 5000 copies and 20% after that. Furthermore, if you agreed to the publication of a limited signed edition, we should suggest a further 100 signed copies to be sold at £5:5:- each. (We think that a small number of signed copies at a high price would be better than a larger number at a lower price). On this we could offer a straight 20% royalty. Our Sales Manager thinks that 100 copies at five guineas could surely be subscribed before publication, which means that on publication of the limited edition (which, as well as being signed, would be rather more elaborately produced than the ordinary edition), you would be entitled to a further £100 besides the £300 on the ordinary edition.
>
>   (UB JJC XI: Eliot to Joyce, folder 18)

Eliot called this 'a basis for negotiation' and suggested he would come and 'have a talk', since Joyce was staying close by at Campden Grove in Kensington. On 13 July, Joyce wrote to Sylvia Beach that 'In addition to Faber's offer for W I P (£400 advance of 15% royalties rising to 20%) and Viking Press (£600 of 15% royalties) Harcourt Brace cabled yesterday they would pay £600'. After these figures in the opening sentence, he put her under time pressure: 'As I have to decide within a few days, pending two other American offers and two English ones, will you please let me know your views? Are you interested in publishing this book yourself?' He did explain the reasons for his haste: '1st interest in this book is now at the crest and if I do not bind people by contract they may cool off in a year or so. 2nd all the people concerned are here on the spot. 3rd I have had an enormous lot of worry lately which I could have coped with better if I had not been left in the lurch for money' (*JJSB* 173). Apart from the rather malicious way of presenting himself as a poor victim, left without assistance when he needed it most ('left in the lurch'), he did have a point with regard to his first reason: he was right about the interest in his 'Work in Progress' being 'at the crest'. From that moment onwards, the interest would only wane. And his intuition to 'bind people by contract' turned out to be perfect timing. Perhaps this is also part of what Wyndham Lewis called Joyce's 'shoppy' nature (1993 [1927], 88). In a cynical sense, Joyce certainly showed 'a true craftsman's impartiality' (88) in that he was open to any offer, and his courtesy letter to Beach, asking her if she was interested in publishing 'Work in Progress' herself after having confronted her with the bigger companies' offers first, cannot really be seen as a gentle gesture of loyalty. What drove him at that moment was the advance money. He was even trying to find a new publisher for *Our Exagmination* and managed to convince T.S. Eliot to write a letter to Beach in this regard. Eliot did not know how to formulate the offer and he clearly had more scruples than Joyce. Because Eliot felt that the draft of his letter was longwinded he sent it to Joyce (on 17 July 1931), asking him for suggestions: 'The difficulty is that Miss Beach herself could get nothing out of it, unless you forewent your own 10%; and you know already how little profit a pamphlet brings. The appeal to her has to be to her public spirit and devotion to your work etc., and I don't know her well enough to know how to make that appeal' (UB JJC XI, folder 19). No one knew better how to make such an appeal than Joyce, and when the letter was ready, he advanced a copy of it to Sylvia Beach without further ado (19 July 1931; *JJSB* 173).

In the accompanying letter, he announced that 'there will be an English and an American contract [for 'Work in Progress'] both amounting to an advance of 15% of £1250 about 160,000 frs'. The contract stipulated that they were to publish the book simultaneously in both a general trade edition and a limited, signed edition. The text would be set by Faber and Faber, and printed both in the UK and the US, for reasons of copyright. At that point, the two publishers evidently assumed that the work was as good as ready, since most of parts I and III had already appeared in *transition*. In August, Faber and Faber started setting up two pages in 11 types,[1] and a letter of 19 November 1931 gives a good impression of how seriously Eliot and his co-editors at Faber and Faber were taking what they presumed to be the imminent publication of 'Work in Progress': 'Herewith is the revised specimen which I mentioned and which I ought to have sent you some days ago. You will see that this setting appears to bring the book up not to 526 pages, but to 598. I therefore very much hope that you will be satisfied with this expansion, for as I said, any further increase must substantially increase both the bulk and the price, and decidedly throws out our estimates' (UB JJC XI: Eliot to Joyce, folder 21). Five days later, Eliot again urged Joyce to send Part I as soon as possible, for they were 'quite ready to start setting up',[2] and another three weeks later he wrote that 'the printers will really be glad to tackle "Work in Progress" as soon as the manuscript is available' (UB JJC XI: Eliot to Joyce, folder 23). On 16 March 1932, Eliot

---

[1]   In a P.S. to his letter of 20 August 1931, T.S. Eliot wrote to Joyce: 'Owing probably to my not having explained your wishes fully enough to de la Mare he has not had the whole of those pages of Transition set up yet. What he has done is to have two pages set up in eleven different types. These specimens we have ready. I suggest that you should look over these eleven different specimens and pick out the most likely ones so that we may have more pages set up' (UB JJC XI, folder 20).

[2]   'We found that the next largest size would mean a book of probably 800 pages, and I explained that such a size would be very unwieldy, and furthermore could not be published at one guinea. It merely happens that the first of these two specimen pages is more heavily inked than the second. We are quite ready to start setting up, and should be glad to have Part I as soon as you can send it' (24 November 1931, UB JJC XI: Eliot to Joyce, folder 22).

tried again: 'This letter is merely to ask whether there is any likelihood of our soon having the first part of W.I.P. to send to the printers' (folder 29).

What Eliot did not know was that within months after signing the contract – as early as 23 October 1931 – Joyce had made Paul Léon write a letter to Pinker, his literary agent, with a postscript stating that Joyce had 'at present no communication to make to either his English or American publishers concerning the date of completion of Work in Progress' (qtd in Lernout 2013, 7). So, when Joyce told Sylvia Beach he was trying to 'bind people by contract' there was a rather malevolent aspect to his 'business strategy'. He was not intent on delivering his manuscript soon. In fact, the advance money, meant to encourage the author to finish his manuscript, seems to have had the opposite effect. To some extent, Joyce's creative productivity in the following years can be expressed in quantitative terms, as Geert Lernout suggests: whereas Joyce filled some five notebooks per year in 1930 and 1931, the number dropped to only one notebook after he signed the contract.[3] This situation lasted until 1936, when he 'took up work seriously once more' and decided to 'make a real effort to finish the book' (Lernout 2013, 8–9). But then, while the galley proofs for books I and III were going back and forth to Paris, Joyce suddenly interrupted his work to prepare *Storiella* in the Corvinus Press's expensive limited edition. So, Eliot had to start sending the same kind of requests for parts of the manuscript as in 1931: 'When I last saw you in Paris you promised to let me have a page of type to indicate what you would like better of Work in Progress than the specimen pages which you had from us. [. . .] So if you have anything to send will you please send it to Richard de la Mare' (21 August 1936; UB JJC XI: Eliot to Joyce, folder 36). Joyce's replies to his publishers – usually through Paul Léon – were often curt and blunt, and his conduct vis-à-vis the patient publishers shows a pattern: 'In his relationship with Viking and Faber & Faber, Joyce was consistently mean' (Lernout 2013, 29). In *transition* 26, the book's publication 'in its entirety' had been announced for 'some time in 1937' (see Chapter 8), but in the end, it would take until 4 May 1939 for the book to come out (Norburn 2004, 186).

* * *

The bleak picture of these last years of 'Work in Progress', leading up to the publication of *Finnegans Wake*, only shows Joyce the (business)man, not Joyce the virtuoso writer. The latter did produce a masterpiece, but not without the help of dozens of collaborators and 'the continually more and less intermisunderstanding minds of the anticollaborators' (*Cr* 505), such as amanuenses, typists, publishers, printers, critics and journalists. And as the previous chapters have shown, the 628-page text of *Finnegans Wake* is not as monolithic as it may seem. Not only did it grow out of a set of short vignettes, sections and fragments, in many ways it also remained an amalgam of sections. Several of these sections are still recognizable

---

[3]   The only exception was 1933 with two notebooks (Lernout 2013, 7).

in the final version of the text. Joyce self-confidently claimed that they would 'fuse of themselves' (9 October 1923; *LI* 204), and they are undeniably integrated very skilfully in *Finnegans Wake*, but they also function separately. In that sense, 'Work in Progress' has its own publication history.

From the perspective of a contemporary author, the pre-book publications might appear to be the literary equivalent of 'exuviae', referring to the skin that is shed every year by animals such as snakes and scorpions. When the skin is shed, a new one has already been developing underneath. This is the image Paul Valéry employed to describe his view on his literary work, that is, from the author's point of view. Once a work was published, Valéry regarded it as dead skin. In the meantime, he had moved on. And that was more important to him, the development of the poet and his work in progress. Valéry's interest was not in the skin, but in the mind that left it behind. At first sight, this image may seem applicable to James Joyce, working on his 'work in progress' *par excellence*. It took him 17 years to complete this work, composed of numerous interconnecting narrative units. In Valéry's case, the shed skin may have been a somewhat denigrating term for pre-book publications, but the attention Valéry paid to the way in which the skin was shed does indicate that the act of pre-publishing was not seen as mere collateral damage.[4] The effort, time and money that went into the disposing of this skin contradicted the 'throwaway' gesture suggested by the aesthetic theory behind it. While the surrealists were publishing throwaways (pamphlets as disposable pieces of art; see Chapter 6), Valéry and Joyce chose to publish expensive collectors' items with small fine arts presses.

---

[4]   Ellmann mentions that Joyce liked Valéry's 'Ébauche d'un serpent' ('Sketch of a Serpent'; Ellmann 1983, 702), especially the opening lines: 'Parmi l'arbre la brise berce / la vipère que je vêtis' (Valéry 2007, 104) – in the translation by Peter Dale: 'About the boughs the breeze alleys / And lulls the viper I invest' (105). By means of the verb 'vêtir', Valéry starts his poem with a reference to the serpent's disposable skin. In July 1924, Joyce took excerpts from Paul Valéry's poem 'Ébauche d'un serpent' in notebook VI.B.05.113–115. These excerpts also occur on the first two of a set of four separate notesheets, apparently torn from a mathematics exercise book, preserved at the National Library of Ireland (MS 36,639/2/B; for a more detailed discussion of these notes, see Van Hulle 2011). The poem 'Ébauche d'un serpent' was first published in *La Nouvelle Revue Française* (nr. 94; 1 July 1921). In February 1922 it was published separately as a book by Éditions de la Nouvelle Revue Française with the title *Le Serpent* (no longer as an 'ébauche' or 'sketch'). A few months later (June 1922) it appeared as part of the collection of poetry *Charmes*, with its original title 'Ébauche d'un serpent'. When *Le Serpent* was again published separately in 1926 in an expensive deluxe edition (with lithographs by Jean Marchand and decorations by Sonia Lewitska), Valéry's idea that any publication is merely like a snake's disposable skin was visualized by 'investing' the poem with a snakeskin cover. Joyce received a copy of *Le Serpent* from Valéry, with the dedication 'À James Joyce. Paul Valéry' and an ink drawing of a serpent, biting its own tail, 'encircling the title on the half-title page, with the note: "Je mords ce que je puis!"' ('I bite whatever I can!'; Connolly 1955, 41).

In Joyce's case, however, it seems more difficult to present the pre-book publications of 'Work in Progress' / *Finnegans Wake* as 'exuviae'. There is an interesting tension between the avant-garde nature of Joyce's 'work in progress' and the way parts of it were presented to the public. At the same time, the one-shilling re-publications of *Anna Livia Plurabelle* and *Haveth Childers Everywhere* by Faber and Faber complicate the publication pattern. The 'exuviae' metaphor only applies insofar as each pre-book publication was just an instantiation of the work in progress, and as the work went on, multiple versions of the same fragment were published. But a closer look at each of these instantiations shows that it is hardly appropriate to compare these texts with dead skin. As Carola Giedion-Welcker[5] duly pointed out in September 1929 (see Chapter 5), if Joyce's texts of 'Work in Progress' can be compared to a skin at all, it is a *living* skin. Whereas the English language, 'abstracted to death' according to Beckett, had become a 'rigid and exhausted form' ('eine erstarrte und erschöpfte Form'), Joyce turned this 'passive carrier of spiritual content' into an 'actively functioning mediator of cognition'. Thus, in his texts, a lifeless wrapper changes into 'a vibrating skin' ['eine vibrierende Haut'] (671). And from this organic metaphor, Giedion-Welcker abruptly shifted to that of a precision instrument, calling Joyce's verbal skin a 'seismograph of the enclosed organism'. But precisely the seismograph's sensitivity to vibrations qualifies the 'enclosed'-ness of the textual 'organism' as it suggests an interplay with the surroundings – a 'work in progress' like a living organism, sensitive to its material and cultural environment, which notably included the numerous critical responses, as the previous chapters have shown.

In this book, I have tried to read 'Work in Progress' in terms of enactive cognition and the extended mind, starting from Clark and Chalmers' example of Otto's notebook (see Introduction), in which they also refer to the skin: 'Otto carries a notebook around with him everywhere he goes. When he learns new information, he writes it down. When he needs some old information, he looks it up. For Otto, his notebook plays the role usually played by a biological memory. [. . .] The information in the notebook functions just like the information constituting an ordinary non-occurrent belief; it just happens that this information lies *beyond the skin*' (Clark and Chalmers 2010, 33–4; emphasis added). Being an active notebook-user himself, Joyce intuitively acknowledged the workings of this extended mind, which informs his 'Work in Progress'. As I have argued, this work is not *about* a cognitive process – to paraphrase Samuel Beckett – it *is* that cognitive process itself. When Beckett called Joyce a 'biologist in words' (Beckett 1972 [1929], 19), this could usefully be interpreted as a biologist in von Uexküll's sense: the storyworlds in the tales told of Shem, Shaun, Issy, HCE and ALP 'constitute a staging ground for procedures of *Umwelt* construction', as David Herman put it, and Joyce can be regarded as an *Umwelt* researcher (Herman 2011, 266; see Chapter 3). The model

---

[5]   'Work in Progress: Ein sprachliches Experiment von James Joyce', *Neue Schweizerische Rundschau* (September 1929), 658–71; UBC 33: 1184.

for this literary exploration was based on the worldmaker's own *Umwelt*, Joyce's world as enacted through the interplay with his cultural and material circumstances and the way he experienced them. In that sense it is important to take the material circumstances of the pre-book publications – both their production process and their immediate reception – into account since they are part and parcel not only of the author's extended mind, but also of the workings of the 'fictive imagination' at work in *Finnegans Wake*, shedding new light on what Atherton called the book's 'awareness of itself as a "work in progress"' (1959, 59).

Appendix 1
Survey of Pre-Book Publications

The publication history of 'Work in Progress' consists of dozens of pre-book publications of separate fragments, which can be presented from different perspectives, according to different parameters. The following surveys arrange the pre-book publications according to:

1. the chronology and material aspect (1.1. contributions to books and periodicals; 1.2. separate books);
2. the place in the narrative sequence of *Finnegans Wake*.

1. Pre-book Publications Arranged According to Chronology and Material Aspect

1.1. Contributions to Books and Periodicals

In their *Bibliography of James Joyce*, John J. Slocum and Herbert Cahoon make a difference between the 'Books and Pamphlets' (section A), 'Contributions to Books' (section B), and the 'Contributions to Periodicals' (section C). The relevant items in the latter two sections (pages 76–8; 99–106) bear the following titles:

'From Work in Progress', *transatlantic review*, Paris, 1.4 (April 1924), 215–23 [*FW* 383–398.30] (Slocum and Cahoon 1971 [1953], 100; C.62)

'Fragment of an Unpublished Work', *The Criterion*, London, III.12 (July 1925), 498–510 [*FW* 104–125] (C.64)

'A New Unnamed Work', *Two Worlds*, New York, I.1 (September 1925), 45–54 [*FW* 104–125] (C.65)

'From Work in Progress', *Contact Collection of Contemporary Writers* (Paris: Contact Editions, 1925): 133–6 [*FW* 30–4] (B. 7)

'From Work in Progress', *Navire d'Argent*, Paris, II.5 (October 1925), 59–74 [*FW* 196–216] (C.66)

'Extract from Work in Progress', *This Quarter*, Milan, I.2 (Autumn–Winter 1925–26), 108–23 [*FW* 169–95] (C.67)

'A New Unnamed Work', *Two Worlds*, New York, I.2 (December 1925), 111–14 [*FW* 30–4] (C.65)

'A New Unnamed Work', *Two Worlds*, New York, I.3 (March 1926), 347–60 [*FW* 196–216] (C.65)

'A New Unnamed Work', *Two Worlds*, New York, I.4 (June 1926), 545–60 [*FW* 169–95] (C.65)

'A New Unnamed Work', *Two Worlds*, New York, II.5 (September 1926), 35–40 [*FW* 383–99] (C.65)

'Opening Pages of a Work in Progress', *transition* 1 (April 1927), 9–30 [*FW* 3–29] (C.70)

'Continuation of a Work in Progress', *transition* 2 (May 1927), 94–107 [*FW* 30–47] (C.70)

'Continuation of a Work in Progress', *transition* 3 (June 1927), 32–50 [*FW* 48–74] (C.70)

'Continuation of a Work in Progress', *transition* 4 (July 1927), 46–65 [*FW* 75–103] (C.70)

'Continuation of a Work in Progress', *transition* 5 (August 1927), 15–31 [*FW* 104–25] (C.70)

'Continuation of a Work in Progress', *transition* 6 (September 1927), 87–106 f. [*FW* 126–68] (C.70)

'Continuation of a Work in Progress', *transition* 7 (October 1927), 34–56 [*FW* 169–95] (C.70)

'Continuation of a Work in Progress', *transition* 8 (November 1927), 17–35 [*FW* 196–216] (C.70)

'Continuation of a Work in Progress', *transition* 11 (February 1928), 7–18 [*FW* 282–304] (C.70)

'Continuation of a Work in Progress', *transition* 12 (March 1928), 7–27 [*FW* 403–28] (C.70)

'Continuation of a Work in Progress', *transition* 13 (Summer 1928), 5–32 [*FW* 429–73] (C.70)

'Continuation of a Work in Progress', *transition* 15 (February 1929), 195–238 [*FW* 474–554] (C.70)

'Continuation of a Work in Progress', *transition* 18 (November 1929), 211–36 [*FW* 555–90] (C.70)

'A Muster from Work in Progress', in *transition stories: Twenty-three stories from 'transition', selected and edited by Eugene Jolas and Robert Sage* (New York: Walter V. McKee, 1929), 177–91 [seven excerpts, corresponding to *FW* 30–34.29; 76.33–78.6; 65.5–33; 454.26–455.29; 413.3–24; 23.16–26; 74.13–19] (B.11)

'From "Tales Told of Shem and Shaun: Three Fragments from Work in Progress" by James Joyce', in *Imagist Anthology* (London: Chatto & Windus: 1930), 121–22; and (New York: Covici, Fried, 1930), 177–79 [*FW* 417.24–419.10] (B.12)

'From Work in Progress', *New Experiment*, Cambridge, UK, 7 (Spring 1931), 27–9 [*FW* 3–29] (C.79)

'Continuation of a Work in Progress', *transition* 22 (February 1933), 49–76 [*FW* 219–59] (C.70)

'The Mime of Mick, Nick and the Maggies', *Les Amis de 1914* 2.40 (23 February 1934), 1 [*FW* 258.25–259.10, excerpt reprinted from *transition* 22] (Crispi and Slote 2007, 492)

'Work in Progress', *transition* 23 (July 1935), 109–29 [*FW* 260–75; 304–8] (C.70)

'Work in Progress', *transition* 26 (February 1937), 35–52 [*FW* 309–31] (C.70)

'A Phoenix Park Nocturne', *Verve* 1.2 (March–June 1938): 26 [*FW* 244.13–246.02, reprinted from *The Mime of Mick Nick and the Maggies*] (Crispi and Slote 2007, 492)

'Fragment from Work in Progress', *transition* 27 (April–May 1938), 59–78 [*FW* 338–55] (C.70)

1.2. Books

Among the relevant items categorized under 'Books and Pamphlets' (section A) by Slocum and Cahoon, all but one item (the first edition of *Anna Livia Plurabelle*) mention 'Work in Progress' in the title or subtitle:

Anna Livia Plurabelle by James Joyce with a Preface by Padraic Colum (New York: Crosby Gaige, 1928) (A.32)

Anna Livia Plurabelle: Fragment of Work in Progress by James Joyce (London: Faber and Faber, 1930) (A.33)

Tales Told of Shem and Shaun: Three Fragments from Work in Progress by James Joyce (Paris: The Black Sun Press, 1929) (A.36)

Two Tales of Shem and Shaun: Fragments from Work in Progress by James Joyce (London: Faber and Faber, 1932) (A.37)

Haveth Childers Everywhere: Fragment from Work in Progress by James Joyce (Paris and New York: Henry Babou and Jack Kahane / The Fountain Pess, 1930) (A.41)

Haveth Childers Everywhere: Fragment from Work in Progress by James Joyce (London: Faber and Faber, 1931) (A.42)

The Mime of Mick, Nick and the Maggies: A Fragment from Work in Progress (The Hague: The Servire Press, 1934) (A.43)

Storiella As She Is Syung: A Section of 'Work in Progress' by James Joyce (London: Corvinus Press, 1937) (A.46)

The fragments printed for copyright purposes are all explicitly called volumes or parts of *Work in Progress*:

Work in Progress Volume 1 (New York: Donald Friede, 1927 [actual publication date 9 January 1928]) (A.30)

Work in Progress Part 11 and 12 (July 1928) [reprinted from *transition* 11 and 12] (A.31)

Work in Progress Part 13 (August 1928) [reprinted from *transition* 13] (A.34)

Work in Progress Part 15 (February 1929) [reprinted from *transition* 15] (A.35)

Work in Progress Part 18 (January 1930) [reprinted from *transition* 18] (A.38)

2. Pre-Book Publications Arranged According to the Narrative Structure of *Finnegans Wake*

2.1 Narrative Structure of Finnegans Wake *and Pre-Book Publications*

Book	Ch.	FW
I	*1*	
		3–29 *transition 1 (Apr. 1927): 9–30.*
		3–29 *New Experiment, Cambridge, UK, 7 (Spring 1931): 27–9.*
		'A Muster from Work in Progress' in: transition stories, ed. Eugene Jolas and Robert Sage (1929)
	2	
	§1	30–34 *Contact Collection (Contact Editions, 1925): 133–36. ('Here Comes Everybody')*
		30–34 *Two Worlds 1.2 (Dec. 1925): 111–14.*
		30–47 *transition 2 (May 1927): 94–107.*
	3	
		48–74 *transition 3 (June 1927): 32–50.*
	4	
		75–103 *transition 4 (July 1927): 46–65.*
	5	
		104–125 *The Criterion 3, no. 12 (July 1925): 498–510.*
		104–125 *Two Worlds 1.1 (Sep. 1925): 45–54.*
		104–125 *transition 5 (Aug. 1927): 15–31.*
	6	
		126–168 *transition 6 (Sep. 1927): 87–106f.*
	§3	152–159 *'The Mookse and the Gripes' in* **Tales Told of Shem and Shaun (Black Sun Press, 1929)**
	§3	152–159 *'The Mookse and the Gripes' in* **Two Tales of Shem and Shaun (Faber and Faber, 1932)**
	7	
		169–195 *This Quarter (Nov. 1925): 108–23.*
		169–195 *Two Worlds 1.4 (June 1926): 545–60.*
		169–195 *transition 7 (Oct. 1927): 34–56.*
	8	
		196–216 *Le Navire d'Argent (Oct. 1925): 59–74.*
		196–216 *Two Worlds 1.3 (Mar. 1926): 347–60.*
		196–216 *transition 8 (Nov. 1927): 17–35.*
		196–216 ***Anna Livia Plurabelle (Crosby Gaige, Oct. 1928)***
		196–216 ***Anna Livia Plurabelle (Faber and Faber, 1930)***

Book	Ch.	FW
II	*1*	
		219–259 *transition 22 (Feb. 1933): 49–76.*
	(end)	258–259 *Les Amis de 1914 2, no. 40 (23 Feb. 1934)*
		219–259 **The Mime of Mick, Nick and the Maggies (Servire Press, 1934)**
	§5	244–246 *Verve 1.2 (March 1938): 26.*
	2	
	§8	282–304 *transition 11 (Feb. 1928): 7–18.*
	§8	282–304 *'The Triangle' or 'The Muddest Thick That Was Ever Heard Dump' in* **Tales Told of Shem and Shaun (Black Sun Press, 1929)**
	§1–3, 9	260–275, 304–308 *transition 23 (July 1935): 109–29.*
	§1–3, 9	260–275, 304–308 **Storiella as She Is Syung (Corvinus Press, 1937)**
	3	
	§1	309–331 *transition 26 (Feb 1937): 35–52.*
	§4–5	338–355 *transition 27 (May 1938): 59–78.*
	4	
	§2	383–398 *transatlantic review 1, no. 4 (Apr. 1924): 215–23 ('Mamalujo').*
	§2	383–398 *Two Worlds 2.5 (Sep. 1925): 35–40.*
III	*1*	
		403–428 *transition 12 (March 1928): 7–27.*
	§C	414–419 *'The Ondt and the Gracehoper' in* **Tales Told of Shem and Shaun (Black Sun Press, 1929)**
	§C	414–419 *'The Ondt and the Gracehoper' in* **Two Tales of Shem and Shaun (Faber and Faber, 1932)**
	§C (fragments)	*Imagist Anthology 1930, ed. R. Aldington (Chatto and Windus, 1930)*
	2	
		429–473 *transition 13 (Summer 1928): 5–32.*
	3	
		474–554 *transition 15 (Feb. 1929): 195–238.*
	§B	532–554 **Haveth Childers Everywhere (Fountain Press, 1930)**
	§B	532–554 **Haveth Childers Everywhere (Faber and Faber, 1931)**
	4	
		555–590 *transition 18 (Nov. 1929): 211–36.*
IV		

Appendix 2

Anna Livia Plurabelle and *Haveth Childers Everywhere*: Variants between the first editions and the '1-shilling' editions by Faber and Faber

Variants between the first edition of *Anna Livia Plurabelle* (Crosby Gaige, 1928) and the Faber and Faber '1-shilling' edition.

ALP, Crosby Gaige			ALP, Faber and Faber		
Page	Line	Variant	Page	Line	Variant
3	1–3	O / tell me about / Anna Livia! I want to hear all about Anna Livia.	5	1–4	O / tell me about / Anna Livia! I want to hear all / about Anna Livia.
6	4	spliced.	6	19	spliced?
6	8	isthmass?	6	22	isthmass.
6	9	another!	6	22	another.
9	17	Srue	8	12	Sure
10	8	setting	8	19	sittang
10	9	drummm	8	20	drommen
10	17	huneseself	8	26	hunselv
13	2	mouth.	9	27	mouth!
17	11	*made is as*	12	2	*made's as*
19	11	agapó	13	1	agapo
24	4	A froth-dizzying	15	6	Afroth-dizzying
24	15–6	Anna-na Poghue's	15	15	Anna-na-Poghue's
25	7	picts	15	22	pickts
30	7	around	18	4	round
30	17	Grimmfather.	18	12	Grimmfather!
31	18	really!	18	28	really.
34	11	Affluence-Ciliegia	20	6	Affluence, Ciliegia
35	15	weights!	20	23	weights?
41	7	edereider'making	23	14	edereider making
42	8	chipping	23	29–30	Chipping
43	2	Gipsy Lee:	24	9	Gipsy Lee;
43	3	Guardsman:	24	10	Guardsman;

ALP, Crosby Gaige			ALP, Faber and Faber		
Page	Line	Variant	Page	Line	Variant
43	5	strong:	24	11	strong;
43	7	MacFarlane:	24	12–3	MacFarlane;
43	10	Mmarriage:	24	15	Mmarriage;
43	11	Johnny Walker Beg:	24	16	Johnny Walker Beg;
43	13	O' Dea:	24	17	O'Dea;
43	14	Tombigby:	24	19	Tombigby;
43	16	Hartigan:	24	20	Hartigan;
43	18	Clonliffe:	24	21	Clonliffe;
44	1	Skibereen:	24	23	Skibereen;
44	3	jackeen:	24	24	jackeen;
44	4	Teague O'Flanagan:	24	25	Teague O'Flanagan;
44	5	Jerry Coyle:	24	25	Jerry Coyle;
44	6	Mackenzie:	24	26	Mackenzie
44	12	eye to	25	1	eye, to
44	15	Patsy Presbys:	25	3	Patsy Presbys;
44	18	Biddy:	25	6	Biddy;
45	1	Mobbely:	25	7	Mobbely;
45	2	tearorne:	25	7	tearorne;
45	5	Helen Arhone:	25	9	Helen Arhone;
45	6	Lawless:	25	10	Lawless;
45	8	pitcher:	25	12	pitcher;
45	9	Puckaun:	25	12	Puckaun;
45	9	a potamus	25	13	apotamus
45	10	Dunne:	25	13	Dunne;
45	17	frey:	25	19	frey;
46	2	Twimjim:	25	21	Twimjim;
46	7	pillow:	25	25	pillow;
46	8	brooch:	25	26	brooch;
46	9–10	warmingpan:	25	27	warmingpan;
46	11	Meagher:	25	28	Meagher;
46	13	fractions:	25	30	fractions;
46	14	Betty Bellezza:	26	1	Betty Bellezza;
46	17	boy:	26	3	boy;
47	1	Rubiconstein:	26	4	Rubiconstein;
47	3	Victor Hugonot:	26	6	Victor Hugonot;
47	5	Cleaner:	26	7	Cleaner;
47	5	Hosty:	26	8	Hosty;
47	9	Infanta:	26	10	Infanta;
47	9	tolast	26	11	to last
47	10	ashpit:	26	11	ashpit;

(Continued)

ALP, Crosby Gaige			ALP, Faber and Faber		
Page	Line	Variant	Page	Line	Variant
47	12	Ferry:	26	13	Ferry;
47	14	Gough:	26	15	Gough;
47	16	Lawrence a	26	16	Lawrence; a
48	3	Kane:	26	20	Kane;
48	5	Post:	26	22	Post;
48	6	Nolan:	26	23	Nolan;
48	7	Vance:	26	24	Vance;
48	8	Meretrix:	26	25	Meretrix;
48	9	Dunboyne:	26	25	Dunboyne;
48	12	Where-is-he?:	26	28	Where-is-he?;
48	13–4	swash, Yuinness	26	28–9	swash Yuinness
49	2	around:	27	4	around;
51	11	*dito Faciasi*	28	9	*dito: Faciasi*
51	11	*Omo.*	28	10	*Omo!*
51	11–2	*Omo fu fó.*	28	10	*E omo fu fó.*
51	15	(Sheridens)	28	12	(Sheridan's)
51	15	Old House by the Coachyard	28	12–3	*Old House by the Coachyard*
51	16	(J)	28	13	(J.)
51	16	On Woman	28	13	*On Woman*
51	16 to 17	Ditto on the Floss.	28	14	*Ditto on the Floss.*
53	6	send-us-pray!	29	4	Send-us-pray!
57	16	Mac Dougal	31	9	MacDougal
59	7	Before! Before!	32	1	*Befor! Bifur!*
61	3	Tell me tale	32	27	*Telmetale*

Variants between the first edition of *Haveth Childers Everywhere* (Babou and Kahane/The Fountain Press, 1930) and the Faber and Faber '1-shilling' edition.

Babou and Kahane / Fountain Press			Faber Edition		
Page	Line	Variant	Page	Line	Variant
13	3	off!	7	25	off.
14	16	paviour); to	8	21	paviour) to
15	1–2	flowers searchers	8	23	flowers, searchers
15	11	forhim	9	1	for him
15	17	ajavelin	9	5	a javelin
16	1	highflyet	9	7	highflyer
16	15	oer	9	19	o'er
16	18	ecelesensy	9	21	ecclesency

Babou and Kahane / Fountain Press			Faber Edition		
Page	Line	Variant	Page	Line	Variant
17	11	Noksagt Per	9	30	Noksagt! Per
24	8–9	harroween	13	8	haroween
25	11	Improbable!	13	24	Inprobable!
33	16	Meludd	17	22	Me ludd
38	18	soakey	20	4	soakye
39	6	eyes?	20	10	eyes!
42	4	german	21	21	German
42	17	roe's	22	1	Roe's
43	13	night soil	22	12	nightsoil
43	15	excentric	22	13	eccentric
44	1	rhumatic	22	16	rhuematic
44	10	water tap	22	23	watertap
44	10	yards	22	24	yards'
45	18	dunplings,	23	14	dumplings,
46	2	five storied	23	16	fivestoried
46	17	goodmens' field,	23	28	Goodmens' Field
47	4	come they	24	1–2	come, they
47	10	childrens' childrens'	24	7	children's children's
47	15	Tolbris a	24	10	Tolbris, a
48	13	Foulkes's	24	23	Foulke's
49	5	walk not!). Quo	24–5	30 to 1	walk not! Sigh lento, Morgh!) Quo
51	12–3	world turned	26	7	world, turned
52	1	chivily crookcrook	26	12–3	chivilycrookcrook
55	18	twas	28	11	'twas
56	14	best of taste	28	22	best taste
60	3	O'Conee	30	12	O'Connee
61	15	St Pancreas	31	8	St. Pancreas
62	18	slaphung,	31	24	slapbang,
62	18	drapier-cutdean	31	24–5	drapier-cut-dean[1]
63	8–9	Mrs Dattery and	32	1	Mrs Dattery,
64	5	panes all	32	13	panes, all
64	6	Duanna, dwells,	32	14–5	Duanna dwells,
64	16	*pelves ad hombres sumus:*	32	23	*pelves ad hombres sumus:*[2]
65	15	elskede my	33	6	elskede, my
66	6	stelas	33	13	stellas
66	7	reders,	33	14	readers,
66	12	camels	33	19	camels'
68	18	tellforths'	34	21	tellforth's

1 In the Faber edition, the first hyphen coincides with a line break.
2 In the Faber edition, the colon is italicized.

Appendix 3

Variants between the Pre-Book Publications and the Text of *Finnegans Wake* (London: Faber and Faber; New York: Viking, 1939)

Anna Livia Plurabelle

Comparison with *Finnegans Wake* (1939)

Published by Crosby Gaige

New York
October 1928

page	ALP (Crosby Gaige)	page.line	Finnegans Wake (1939)
4	rwusty	196.17	wrusty
5	walking rat	197.04	walking wiesel rat
5	all. Qu'appelle	197.08	all? Qu'appelle
5	Earlyfouler? Or	197.08	Earlyfouler. Or
5	Tvistown, on	197.09	Tvistown on
6	Merrimake? Was	197.10–11	Merrimake? Who blocksmitt her saft anvil or yelled lep to her pail? Was
6	spliced. For	197.13	spliced? For
6	isthmass? O	197.15–17	isthmass. She can show all her lines, with love, license to play. And if they don't remarry that hook and eye may. O
6	doll when	197.20–21	doll, delvan first and duvlin after, when
6	shadda, past	197.24–25	shadda, (if a flic had been there to pop up and pepper him!) past
7	pie! In	197.29–30	pie! Not a grasshoop to ring her, not an antsgrain of ore. In
8	kalled	198.07	kaldt
8	backwater	198.11	bakvandets
8	around to	198.11–12	around, nyumba noo, chamba choo, to
8	Well, that's	198.13	Yssel that
9	dextro. A	198.15	dextro! A
9	care, the	198.16–17	care, sina feza, me absantee, him man in passession, the
9	phthat? Tell	198.18–19	phthat? Emme for your reussischer Honddu jarkon! Tell
9	for	198.23	par
9	now out	198.23	now in conservancy's cause out

page	ALP (Crosby Gaige)	page.line	*Finnegans Wake* (1939)
9	Srue	198.27	Sure
9	never heard	198.27–28	never now heard
10	causeway, setting sambre	198.32–34	causeway and deathcap mushrooms round Funglus grave and the great tribune's barrow all darnels occumule, sittang sambre
10	benk	198.34	sett
10	drummm, his	198.35	drommen, usking queasy quizzers of his ruful continence, his
10	handset	199.01	handsetl
10	hunseself	199.05	hunselv
11	child, in	199.12	child, Wendawanda, a fingerthick, in
11	eygs and	199.16	eygs, yayis, and
12	Si-kiang	199.19	Sikiang
12	shinkobread for	199.19–20	shinkobread (hamjambo, bana?) for
12	graters and	199.21–22	graters while her togglejoints shuck with goyt and
12	his towering	199.23	metauwero
12	or	199.28	ov
13	mouth. And	199.31	mouth! And
13	all kinds	200.05	her femtyfyx kinds
14	then	200.08	after
14	waterglucks? You'll	200.08–09	waterglucks or Madame Delba to Romeoreszk? You'll
14	below in	200.14	below like Bheri-Bheri in
14	teesing	200.16	teasing
15	I did. And do.	200.22	Bedouix but I do!
16	cushingloo! I	200.36–201.02	cushingloo, that was writ by one and rede by two and trouved by a poule in the parco! I
17	*pound*	201.14	*dace*
17	*horsemeat*	201.15–16	*horsebrose*
17	*made is*	201.17	*made's*
17	*offwith*	201.18	*off with*
18	vet. Well,	201.23–25	vet. That homa fever's winning me wome. If a mahun of the horse but hard me! We'd be bundukiboi meet askarigal. Well,
18	bywanbywan	201.29–30	bywan bywan, making meanacuminamoyas
19	agapó	202.07	agapo
19	diveline? Linking	202.08–10	diveline? Casting her perils before our swains from Fonte-in-Monte to Tidingtown and from Tidingtown tilhavet. Linking

(Continued)

page	*ALP* (Crosby Gaige)	page.line	*Finnegans Wake* (1939)
20	I always want to know	202.15	I'm elwys on edge to esk
20	upper	202.16	vardar
20	Nuancee? She	202.21	Nuancee! She
20	way backwards	202.22–23	waybashwards
20	says	202.23	sid
21	jumnpad	202.26	jumpnad
21	her. She	202.26	her and how it was gave her away. She
22	Collin? Neya	203.12–14	Collin? Or where Neptune sculled and Tritonville rowed and leandros three bumped heroines two? Neya
22	nen and nos	203.14	nen, nonni, nos
24	A froth-dizzying	203.27–28	Afroth-dizzying
24	Maass! He	203.31–32	Maass! But the majik wavus has elfun anon meshes. And Simba the Slayer of his Olga is slewd. He
24	never to, never to, never	203.36	niver to, niver to, nevar
25	since. O	204.03–04	since. That was kissuahealing with bantur for balm! O
25	picts	204.07	pickts
26	and feefee fiefie fell	204.16	and, feefee fiefie, fell
26	name. And	204.21–22	name, Mtu or Mti, sombogger was wisness. And
28	sculling	205.06	cruisery
28	flushcoloured	205.08–09	flushcaloured
28	Kehoe's	205.09–10	Keown's
28	drawers	205.12	drawars
28	you. Where	205.13	you! Where
28	yet. Garonne	205.14–15	yet. I amstel waiting. Garonne
30	burning	205.28	cammocking
30	around	205.32	round
30	local with	205.32–33	local as the peihos piped und ubanjees twanged, with
30	owned, that	205.36	owned that
31	she'd	206.05	she's
31	bag	206.09	zakbag
31	mailbag	206.10	mailsack
31	off one of her swapsons	206.10–11	with the lend of a loan of the light of his lampion, off one of her swapsons
32	Terry	206.19	Tirry
32	while. If	206.21	while! If
32–33	more./ First	206.28–29	more. And pooleypooley./ First
33	fall	206.29	fal

page	*ALP* (Crosby Gaige)	page.line	*Finnegans Wake* (1939)
33	islets	206.35	eslats
33	dun quincecunct allover	206.35	dun, quincecunct, allover
34	sent	207.11	sendred
34	Affluence-Ciliegia	207.12	Affluence, Ciliegia
35	nerthe. Oceans	207.22–23	nerthe. Not for the lucre of lomba strait. Oceans
35	mussel	207.23	mosel
35	ladyfair	207.25	lady fair
35	all, but	207.29	all but
37	she had to keep the sun from spoiling her wrinkles	208.10–11	for the sun not to spoil the wrinklings of her hydeaspects
38	ffiffty Irish	208.26	ffiffty odd Irish
39	saft	208.32	mush
39	dobelong	208.33	dobelon
40	deaconess	209.06	archdeaconess
40	says	209.07	sedges
40	baggyrhatty? And	209.10–12	baggyrhatty? Just the tembo in her tumbo or pilipili from her pepperpot? Saas and taas and specis bizaas. And
40	promise. I'll	209.15	promise I'll
41	here careero	209.21	here, careero
41	wich	209.21	which
41	edereider'making	209.22	edereider, making
41	Reims, then	209.25–26	Reims, on like a lech to be off like a dart, then
42	youths and maidens	209.32–33	juvenile leads and ingenuinas, from the slime of their slums and artesaned wellings
42	vielo	209.34	Vielo
42	chipping	209.36	Chipping
43	Lee: a cartridge	210.07	Lee; a cartridge
43	Guardsman: for sulky	210.08	Guardsman; for sulky
43	strong: a cough	210.09	strong; a cough
43	MacFarlane: a jigsaw	210.10–11	MacFarlane; a jigsaw
43	Mmarriage: a brazen	210.12	Mmarriage; a brazen
43	Beg: a paper	210.13	Beg; a paper
43	Dea: a puffpuff	210.14	Dea; a puffpuff
43	Techer	210.15	Techertim
43	Tombigby: waterleg	210.15	Tombigby; waterleg
43	Hartigan: a prodigal	210.16–17	Hartigan; a prodigal

(Continued)

page	*ALP* (Crosby Gaige)	page.line	*Finnegans Wake* (1939)
43	Clonliffe: a loaf	210.18	Clonliffe; a loaf
44	Tim	210.18	Val
44	Skibereen: a jauntingcar	210.19	Skibereen; a jauntingcar
44	jackeen: a seasick	210.20–21	jackeen; a seasick
44	O'Flanagan: a louse	210.22	O'Flanagan; a louse
44	Coyle: slushmincepies	210.23	Coyle; slushmincepies
44	Mackenzie: a hairclip	210.23–24	Mackenzie; a hairclip
44	vipercatcher's	210.27	viper catcher's
44	Presbys: a reiz	210.27–28	Presbys; a reiz
44	Biddy: two	210.29	Biddy; two
45	Mobbely: for Saara	210.30	Mobbely; for Saara
45	tearorne: a pretty	210.31	tearorne; a pretty
45	Arhone: a	210.32	Arhone; a
45	Lawless: for Kitty	210.33	Lawless; for Kitty
45	pitcher: a putty	210.34	pitcher; a putty
45	Puckaun: a potamus	210.35	Puckaun; an apotamus
45	Dunne: a	210.35	Dunne; a
46	Bravo; penteplenty	211.07	Bravo: penteplenty
46	pillow: for Nancy	211.09	pillow; for Nancy
46	brooch: for Dora	211.10	brooch; for Dora
46	warmingpan: a pair	211.11	warmingpan; a pair
46	Meagher: a hairpin	211.11–12	Meagher; a hairpin
46	fractions: an old	211.13	fractions; an old
46	Bellezza: a bag	211.14	Bellezza; a bag
46	Fitz: a *Missa*	211.14	Fitz; a *Missa*
46	boy: a Rogerson	211.15–16	boy; a Rogerson
47	Rubiconstein: three	211.16–17	Rubiconstein; three
47	Hugonot: a stiff	211.18	Hugonot; a stiff
47	Cleaner: a hole	211.19	Cleaner; a hole
47	Hosty: two	211.20	Hosty; two
47	Infanta: a letter	211.22	Infanta; a letter
47	tolast	211.22	to last
47	ashpit: the heftiest	211.22–23	ashpit; the heftiest
47	Ferry; spas	211.24	Ferry; spas
47	Gough: a change	211.25	Gough; a change
47	Lawrence a guillotine	211.26	Lawrence; a guillotine
48	aC_3	211.29	a C_3
48	Nolan: a stonecold	211.32	Nolan; a stonecold
48	Vance: all lock	211.32	Vance; all lock
48	Meretrix	211.33	Merreytrickx
48	Where-is-he?: whatever	211.36	Where-is-he?; whatever

page	*ALP* (Crosby Gaige)	page.line	*Finnegans Wake* (1939)
49	knocking around: and	212.05	knocking around; and
49	Mosel	212.08	Maassy
50	tub. All	212.21–22	tub. And Hibernonian market. All
50	Clane. The	212.25	Clane! The
51	*dito Faciasi*	212.34	*dito: Faciasi*
51	*Omo*	212.34	*E omo*
51	(Sheridens)	213.01	(Sheridan's)
51	House by the Coachyard	213.01	*House by the Coachyard*
51	Mill (J)	213.02	Mill (J.)
51	On Woman with Ditto on the Floss	213.02	*On Woman* with *Ditto on the Floss*
52	since	213.15	senne
53	send-us-pray	213.19	Send-us-pray
55	sound	214.10	zswound
56	madammangut	214.19	Madammangut
57	lavender	214.28	lavendier
58	trinkettoes. And	215.13	trinkettoes! And
59	Before! Before!	215.18–19	Befor! Bifur!
59	Elvenland? Teems	215.22	Elvenland! Teems
60	Tom	215.33	Thom
60	the	215.33	thim
61	Tel me tale	216.03	Telmetale

Tales Told of Shem and Shaun Published by Black Sun Press

Paris

Comparison with *Finnegans Wake* (1939) August 1929

page	*Tales Told* (Black Sun Press)	page.line	*Finnegans Wake* (1939)
The Mookse and The Gripes			
1	Eins within a space	152.16–18	Gentes and laitymen, fullstoppers and semicolonials, hybreds and lubberds! Eins within a space
2	ways. As	152.30–31	ways. / As
2	immortal. He	152.34–35	immortal. / He
2	*thee!* And	153.08–09	*thee!* / And
5	Rot	154.13	Rots
5–6	*you* barbarousse	154.23	*you,* barbarousse

(Continued)

page	*Tales Told* (Black Sun Press)	page.line	*Finnegans Wake* (1939)
6	him. *Culla*	154.29	him! *Culla*
6	Mookse	154.30	Mooksey
7	*or*	155.05	or
10	Mookse.	156.20	Mookse the pius.
10	Gripes,	156.21	Gripes the gregary,
11	shimmers was	157.08	shimmers, was
11	Mrs Moonan	157.15	Mrs. Moonan
12	emanations, stood	157.19	emanations stood
13	Mrs Cornwallis-West	157.33–34	Mrs. Cornwallis-West
13	obliviscent. I	158.04–05	obliviscent. / I
14	grasyaplaina	158.19	Grasyaplaina
14	Echo	158.20	echo
15	bushop's	158.30	boshop's
16	Missisliffi), there	159.13	Missisliffi) there
16	those who	159.14	those crylove fables fans who

The Muddest Thick That Was Ever Heard Dump [The Triangle]

All the marginalia and footnotes in *Finnegans Wake* were added after the pre-book editions. This comparison focuses on the variants in the body of the text.

17	A flink dab was	282.07–08	A flink dab for a freck dive and a stern poise for a swift pounce was
17	boy	282.10	bird
17	First by observation	282.12	First, by observation
17	cheekchaps	282.14	cheekadeekchimple
17	upwithem. And	282.17–18	upwithem. Holy Joe in lay Eden. And
18	reciting of them up	282.24	reciting of them, hoojahs koojahs, up
18	caiuscounting	282.29	caius-counting
18	scale of piff puff pive poo,	282.30	scale of pin puff pive piff, piff puff pive poo,
18	He could find by practice	283.09–10	He could find (the rakehelly!) by practice
19	achers	283.19	archers
19	alegobrew. O	283.24–25	alegobrew. They wouldn't took bearings no how anywheres. O
19	jerrybly! Show	283.26–32	jerrybly! Worse nor herman doror-rhea. Give you the fantods, seemed to him. They ought to told you every last word first stead of trying every which way to kinder smear it out poison long. Show
19	Brickbaths. A	284.04	Brickbaths. The family umbroglia. A
20	∞ find,	284.11	∞, find,

page	*Tales Told* (Black Sun Press)	page.line	*Finnegans Wake* (1939)
20	then, Big Wheeler	284.24–25	then, Aysha Lali-pat behidden on the footplate, Big Whiggler
20	presents to us an ottomantic	284.26–28	presents to us (tandem year at lasted length!) an otto-mantic
20	so long as pictorial summer,	284.29	so long as, gad of the gidday, pictorial summer,
20	but, if this	285.01	but (lenz alack lends a lot), if this
20	order	285.02	redor
20	enviolated, the zitas	285.02–03	enviolated by a mierelin roundtableturning, like knuts in maze, the zitas
20	dart, with	285.04	dart with
20	their muddle, while	285.05–09	their muddle, like a seven of wingless arrows, hodgepadge, thump, kick and hurry, all boy more missis blong him he race quickfeller all same hogglepiggle longer house blong him, while
21	beem the	285.10–11	beem (he wins her hend! he falls to tail!) the
21	and the losed farce	285.11–12	and (uhu and uhud!) the losed farce
21	erroroots, MPM	285.12–15	erro-roots, twalegged poneys and threehandled dorkeys (madahoy, morahoy, lugahoy, jog-ahoyaway) MPM
21	aquilavant to kaksi-toista	285.16–17	aqualavant to (Cat my dogs, if I baint dingbushed like everything!) kaksitoista
21	volts yksi to the finish	285.21–22	volts yksi, allahthallacamellated, caravan series to the finish
21	ballycleevers	285.25–26	bully-clavers
21	Evening World	285.27	Evenine's World
21	com-prendered. The aximones.	285.28–29	comprendered. Inexcessible as thy by god ways. The aximones.
21	neuralgiabrown. Equal to = soahc.	286.01–02	neuralgiabrown. / Equal to = aosch.
21	bagdad, as I know and you know yourself and the arab in the street knows better nor anymeade or persan, comic cuts always were	286.04–09	bagdad, after those initials falls and that primary taincture, as I know and you know yourself, begath, and the arab in the ghetto knows better, by nexus, nor anymeade or persan, comic cuts and series exerxeses always were
22	adieu adroit adieu atout atous	286.13	adieu atout atous
23	beginning. Anny	287.06–07	beginning, big to bog, back to bach. Anny

(Continued)

page	*Tales Told* (Black Sun Press)	page.line	*Finnegans Wake* (1939)
23	I guess. Mux	287.08–13	I guess. A.ɪ. *Amnium instar.* And to find a locus for an alp get a howlth on her bayrings as a prisme O and for a second O unbox your compasses. I cain but are you able? Amicably nod. Gu it! So let's seth off betwain us. Prompty? Mux
23	all	287.16	whole
23	(for Dolph,	287.18	(for – husk, hisk, a spirit spires – Dolph,
23	stone	287.19	stoan
23	*letitia*	287.22	*letitiae*
23	*carnium spectantes*	287.22	*carnium, spectantes*
23	*sapientam*	287.25	*sapientiam*
24	univarsity	287.30	Univarsity
24	he would smilabit	288.05	he druider would smilabit
24	he would, so prim,	288.05–06	he, to don't say nothing, would, so prim,
24	ungles, retelling	288.06–08	ungles, trying to undo with his teeth the knots made by his tongue, retelling
24	math hour a reel	288.08	math hour, long as he's brood, a reel
24	hexenshoes; and,	288.12–13	hexenshoes, in fine the whole damning letter; and,
25	time off	288.14	time, off
25	unguished P.T.	288.17	unguished. P.T.
25	Mr Dane!	288.19	Mr. Dane!
25	laudhavemiseries	288.25	landhavemiseries
25	for our people	288.27–28	for our massangrey if mosshungry people
26	steeplechange back to their	289.07–08	steeplechange back once from their ophis workship and twice on sundises, to their
26	curefully to his continental's	289.11–12	curefully to the interlooking and the under-lacking of her twentynine shifts of his continental's
26	(t.a.W.) let drop	289.13–14	(t.a.W.), sick or whole, stiff or sober, let drop
26	eitherways, as priesto as puddywhack, coal on : and, talking of missions	289.15–18	eitherways, in their own lineal descendance, as priesto as puddywhack, coal on and, as we gang along to gigglehouse, talking of molniacs' manias and missions
26	blameall in that world to say to his privates	289.19–20	blameall in that medeoturanian world to say to blessed by Pointer the Grace's his privates

page	*Tales Told* (Black Sun Press)	page.line	*Finnegans Wake* (1939)
26	when, so to put it, conn the shaughraun;	289.21–23	whenso to put it, *disparito, duspurudo, desterrado, despertieu,* or, saving his presents for his own onefriend Bevradge, Conn the Shaughraun;
27	pretty elisabess	289.25	pretty Lady Elisabbess
27	tell (Love.	289.26	tell love.
27	sudd-enly) and	289.29	suddenly), and
27	when now in what niche	289.29–290.01	when now, uncrowned, decepterd, in what niche
27	lauschening, a time	290.08	lauschening a time
27	Devine Foresygth)	290.10–11	Devine Fore-sygth and decretal of the Douge)
27–28	day-light	290.12	day light
28	the totterer, doubling back, in nowtime, *O alors!,*	290.16–18	the totterer, the four-flights-the-charmer, doub-ling back, in nowtime, bymby when saltwater he wush him these iselands, *O alors!,*
28	we shall say	290.20	wen shall say
28	lampblick to pure	290.22	lampblick, to pure
28	hornest girls to buy	290.22	hornest girls, to buy
28	*mon foie*	290.23	*par jure*
28	for simper and	290.23	for simper, and
28	come messes, come	290.25	come messes; come
28	title Grindings	290.28	title, Grindings
29	whowhowho?	291.04	whowghowho?
29	iseuladed	291.05	inseuladed
29	ages tipped to console	291.08	ages of our timocracy tipped to console
29	Staneybooter	291.11	Staneybatter
30	street ondown – for merry	291.17–20	street ondown, through, for or from a foe, by with as on a friend, at the Rectory? Vicarage Road? Bishop's Folly? Papesthorpe?, after picket fences, stonewalls, out and ins or oxers – for merry
30	analvse	291.21	analyse
30	moustaches into	291.23–24	mous-taches, Dammad and Groany, into
30	*tuffluff*	291.24	*tuff, tuff*
30	diarmee aud	291.28	diarmee and
30	yondest heaven	292.02–03	yondest (it's life that's all chokered by that batch of grim rushers) heaven
31	and an you could peep	292.12–13	and, an you could peep

(Continued)

page	*Tales Told* (Black Sun Press)	page.line	*Finnegans Wake* (1939)
31	thoughtsam what	292.15–16	thoughtsam (was you, that is, decontaminated enough to look discarnate) what
31	laggin too, not only that but searchlighting pharahead	292.18–20	laggin too, longa yamsayore, not only that but, search lighting, beached, bashed and beaushelled *à la Mer* pharahead
31	faturity your own	292.20	faturity, your own
31	convolvulis would	292.20–21	convolvulis pickninnig capman would
31	equally so the crame of it is that,	292.22–23	equally so, the crame of the whole faustian fustian, whether your launer's lightsome or your soulard's schwearmood, it is that,
31	lark to you that no mouth	292.25–26	lark to you symibellically that, though a day be as dense as a decade, no mouth
31	in half a sylb onward	292.27–28	in half a sylb, helf a solb, hold a salb, onward
31	lurking down	292.28–29	lurking gyrographically down
31	gogoing ot whisth	292.29–30	gogoing of whisth
32	sternly how you must, how, draw	292.30–31	sternly how – Plutonic loveliaks twinnt Platonic yearlings – you must, how, in undivided reawlity draw
32	Your parn! (and in truth he had albut list himself, so had he gazet in the lazily	293.01–11	Your parn! You, you make what name? (and in truth, as a poor soul is between shift and shift ere the death he has lived through becomes the life he is to die into, he or he had albut – he was rickets as to reasons but the balance of his minds was stables – lost himself or himself some somnione sciupiones, soswhitchoverswetch had he or he gazet, murphy come, murphy go, murphy plant, murphy grow, a maryamyria-meliamurphies, in the lazily
32	DVbLIn) Given	293.12–13	DVbLIn, 'twas one of dozedeams a darkies ding in dewood) the Turnpike under the Great Ulm with Mearingstone in Fore ground). Given
32	eye	294.01	yeye
33	Fig,	294.03	Fig.,
33	Lambday. Modder	294.04	Lambday: Modder
33	anchore. I	294.05	anchore, I
33	take this in! With Olaf	294.06–08	take this in! One of the most murmurable loose carollaries ever Ellis threw his cookingclass. With Olaf

page	*Tales Told* (Black Sun Press)	page.line	*Finnegans Wake* (1939)
33	discobely! You've	294.12–13	discobely! After Makefearsome's Ocean. You've
33–34	*Bene!* But it's not alover yet. The mystery	294.26–28	*Bene!* But, thunder and turf, it's not alover yet. One recalls Byzantium. The mystery
34	sing now	294.30	sing, as I think, now
34	istherdie and forivor	295.02	istherdie forivor
34	night and a day. In effect, I remumble, purr lil murrerof myhind, so she used indeed. Faithful departed. Rest in peace! What a wonderful	295.03–16	night of thoughtsendyures and a day. As Great Shapesphere puns it. In effect, I remumble, from the yules gone by, purr lil murrerof myhind, so she used indeed. When she give me the Sundaclouths she hung up for Tate and Comyng and snuffed out the ghost in the candle at his old game of haunt the sleepper. Faithful departed. When I'm dreaming back like that I begins to see we're only all telescopes. Or the comeallyoum saunds. Like when I dromed I was in Dairy and was wuckened up with thump in thudderdown. Rest in peace! But to return. What a wonderful
34	sleeve, Now	295.18	sleeve. Now
34	all fours. Watch! Allow, allow! Hop lala!	295.21–24	all fours, as my instructor unstrict me. Watch! And you'll have the whole inkle. Allow, allow! Gyre O, gyre O, gyrotundo! Hop lala!
34	accomplasses! *Beve!* Now, there's tew	295.27–29	accomplasses! You, allus for the kunst and me for omething with a handel to it. *Beve!* Now, as will pressantly be felt, there's tew
34	bicirculars dunloop	295.30–31	bicirculars, mating approxemetely in their suite poi and poi, dunloop
34	Lucihere!	295.32	Lucihere.!
35	quatsch, and I think	296.02	quatsch, vide pervoys akstiom, and I think
35	suqeez the limon	296.03	suqeez in the limon
35	punctum but	296.03	punctum, but
35	likelong to mack	296.04–05	likelong, by Araxes, to mack
35	go and mick	296.08	go, Airmienious, and mick
35	end. With a geing	296.10–11	end. Where your apexojesus will be a point of order. With a geing

(Continued)

page	*Tales Told* (Black Sun Press)	page.line	*Finnegans Wake* (1939)
35	are you right? Ay, I'm right here, Nickel, and I'll write. But it's the muddest thick that was ever heard dump. Now join	296.14–24	are you right? Do you think you can hold on by sitting tight? Well, of course, it's awful angelous. Still I don't feel it's so dangelous. Ay, I'm right here, Nickel, and I'll write. Singing the top line why it suits me mikey fine. But, yaghags hogwarts and arrahquinonthiance, it's the muddest thick that was ever heard dump since Eggsmather got smothered in the plap of the pfan. Now, to compleat anglers, beloved bironthiarn, and hushtokan hishtakatsch, join
35	especious. Like pah. I peh.	296.28	especious. The Nike done it. Like pah, I peh.
35	pokestiff	296.29–30	poke stiff
35	geomater. Hissss! Arrah, go on!	297.01–04	geomater. And if you flung her headdress on her from under her highlows you'd wheeze whyse Salmonson set his seel on a hexen-gown. Hissss!, Arrah, go on!
35	Fin for fun?	297.04	Fin for fun!
35	shower but let's have at it!	297.05–06	shower like a son of Sibernia, but let's have at it!
36	hem at the spidsiest	297.08–09	hem and jabote at the spidsiest
36	done before) the maidsapron	297.10–11	done before since fillies calpered. Ocone! Ocone!) the maidsapron
36	nearmear	297.15	near mear
36	is dark. And light your mech. And this	297.15–16	is dark. Lob. And light your mech. Jeldy! And this
36	redneck, mygh and thy, discinet and isoplural in its sixuous parts, midden wedge	297.17–23	redneck. For addn't we to gayatsee with Puhl the Punkah's bell? mygh and thy, the living spit of dead waters, fastness firm of Hurdlebury Fenn, discinct and isoplural in its (your sow to the duble) sixuous parts, flument, fluvey and fluteous, midden wedge
36	triagonal delta plain	297.24	triagonal delta, fiho miho, plain
36	pluvaville, the no niggard	297.25–26	pluvaville, (hop the hula girls!) the no niggard
36	threeingles, the constant of fluxion and allaph	297.27–32	threeingles, (and why wouldn't she sit cressloggedlike the lass that lured a tailor?) the constant of fluxion, Mahamewetma, pride of the province and when that tidled boare rutches up from the Afrantic, allaph

page	*Tales Told* (Black Sun Press)	page.line	*Finnegans Wake* (1939)
36	you see it is her her. Quicks	298.02–04	you see it is her. And if you could goaneggbetter we'd soon see some raffant scrumala riffa. Quicks
36	Quef! For,	298.05–08	Quef! So post that to your pape and smarket. And you can haul up that languil pennant, mate. I've read your tunc's dismissage. For,
36	littlenest	298.08	littlenist
36	magnetude or let it	298.09	magnetude or again let it
37	mantissa-minus	298.20–21	mantissa minus
37	umdescribables shrinks	298.32–33	umdescribables (one has thoughts of that eternal Rome) shrinks
38	Qued? O, dear me, look at that now! I'm glad	299.03–05	Qued? Mother of us all! O, dear me, look at that now! I don't know is it your spictre or my omination but I'm glad
38	My Lourde! My Lourde! And a superpbosition! Quoint a quincidence! As Ollover	299.06–09	My Lourde! My Lourde! If that aint just the beatenest lay I ever see! And a superpbosition! Quoint a quincidence! O.K. *Omnius Kollidimus.* As Ollover
38	Cromleck said	299.09–10	Kromwall sayed
38	grannyamother. But you're	299.10–13	grannyamother. Kangaroose feathers. Who in the name of thunder'd ever belevin you were that bolt? But you're
38	vou	299.14	you
38	domefool! You must	299.16–17	domefool! Where's your belested loiternan's lamp? You must
38	braindbox	299.18–19	brain-box
38	puncture. Luck! Well,	299.20–21	puncture. So he done it. Luck! See her good. Well,
38	lovely! Vely lively entirely. So analytical plausible. It will be a lozenge to me all my lipe. Ever thought about Guinness's? Want	299.22– 300.01	lovely! We like Simperspreach Hammeltones to fellow Selvertunes O'Haggans. When he rolls over his ars and shows the hise of his heels. Vely lovely entiley! Like a yangsheepslang with the tsifengtse. So analytical plausible! And be the powers of Moll Kelly, neighbour topsowyer, it will be a lozenge to me all my lauffe. More better twofeller we been speak copperards. Ever thought about Guinness's? And the regrettable Parson Rome's advice? Want
38	police? You	300.01	police. You
38	unugol	300.05	wanigel

(Continued)

page	*Tales Told* (Black Sun Press)	page.line	*Finnegans Wake* (1939)
39	gayet that he would	300.09–11	gayet that when he stop look time he stop long ground who here hurry he would
39	lothst, word. with	300.11	lothst word, with
39	slidepage, would	300.14	slidepage of de Vere Foster, would
39	such is spanish	300.16–17	such a spanish
39	chuthor with his muffetee	300.19–25	chuthor for, while that Other by the halp of his creactive mind offered to deleberate the mass from the booty of fight our Same with the holp of the bounty of food sought to delubberate the mess from his corructive mund, with his muffetee
39	trigamies pursuiting	300.26–27	trigamies and spirals' wobbles pursuiting
39	taughtropes. Es war	301.01–02	taughtropes. (Spry him! Call a blood-lekar! Where's Dr Brassenaarse?) Es war
41	pascol's candle	302.03	pascol's kondyl
41	Thirst. Blott.	302.09–10	Thirst. From here Buvard to dear Picuchet. Blott.
41	Now, (brush your	302.11–12	Now, (peel your eyes, my grins, and brush your
41	complete, (Can you write	302.19–23	complete, (Exquisite Game of in-spiration! I always adored your hard. So could I too and without the scrope of a pen. Ohr for oral, key for crib, olchedolche and a lunge ad lib. Can you write
41	Intrieatedly	302.24	intrieatedly
42	pardonsky!,	303.01	pardonsky!
42	regard!,	303.10	regard!
42	L'Arty	303.13	L'arty
43	fruit and Kevvy too just loves his puppadums!) after all his paraboles	303.17–19	fruit and, my Georgeous, Kevvy too he just loves his puppadums, I judge!) after all his autocratic writings of paraboles
43	pergaman do for the blessted selfchuruls smarter	303.23–24	pergaman hit him where he lived and do for the blessted selfchuruls, what I think, smarter
43	length he measured	303.27–28	length, you one bladdy bragger, by mercystroke he measured
43	earth? could	303.28–29	earth anyway? could
43	adder's way our frankson who, to be plain, was misocain.	303.30–33	adder's badder cadder way our frankson who, to be plain, he fight him all time twofeller longa kill dead finish bloody face blong you, was miscocain.
43	Loves deathhow simple!	304.03	Formalisa. Loves deathhow simple!

page	*Tales Told* (Black Sun Press)	page.line	*Finnegans Wake* (1939)
The Ondt and the Gracehoper			
45	a jog	414.22	ajog
45	hoppy, on	414.22	hoppy on
45	everlastings	414.29	everlistings
46	if he was not done doing that, improbably he	414.35	if he
46	deborah, (seven	415.04	deborah (seven
46	three-furts	415.05	threefurts
46	o' shooker	415.06	o'shouker
46	taon!) and	415.08	taon!), and
46	aprils to, the ra	415.11	aprils, to the ra
47	pszinging. *Satyr's*	415.14	pszinging *Satyr's*
47	*Humbly*	415.14	*Hombly*
47	*Dumbly*	415.15	*Dombly*
47	Omniboss perhops	415.17	Omniboss, perhops
47	fog for	415.21	fog, for
47	Pou! Ptah!	415.27	Pou! Pschla! Ptuh!
48	nether this	415.31–32	nether, thon sloghard, this
49	contrited, I	416.19–20	contrited with melanctholy. Meblizzered, him sluggered! I
49	voracioused	416.24	vorasioused
50	branches off	416.25–26	branches, off
50	twicylched	416.30	twicycled
50	lugly tournedos	416.34	lugly whizzling tournedos
50	Boraborayellers blohablasting	416.34–35	Boraborayellers, blohablasting
50	coppeehouses with	416.36	coppeehouses, playing ragnowrock rignewreck, with
50	knew his	417.03–04	knew, not a leetle beetle, his
50	entymology promptly	417.04–05	entymology asped nissunitimost lous nor liceens but promptly
50	buzzer and	417.06–07	buzzer, tezzily wondering wheer would his aluck alight or boss of both appease and
51	themselves it	417.09	themselves, these mouschical umsummables, it
51	Ondt prostrandvorous	417.11	Ondt, prostrandvorous
51	babooshkees, with	417.12–13	babooshkees, smolking a spatial brunt of Hosana cigals, with

(Continued)

page	*Tales Told* (Black Sun Press)	page.line	*Finnegans Wake* (1939)
51	aristotaller) as	417.16	aristotaller), as
51	Libido with	417.17	Libido, with
51	tutties up the large	417.20	tutties up the allabroad length of the large
51	smalls. Emmet	417.20–21	smalls. As entomate as intimate could pinchably be. Emmet
51	host, was	417.24	host, a spiter aspinne, was
52	myre, sans	417.33–34	myre, after his thrice ephemeral journeeys, sans
52	feather weighed	417.34	featherweighed
52	gravitates. A	418.01–05	gravitates. Let him be Artalone the Weeps with his parisites peeling off him I'll be Highfee the Crackasider. Flunkey Footle furloughed foul, writing off his phoney, but Conte Carme makes the melody that mints the money. *Ad majorem l.s.d.! Divi gloriam.* A
52	threshold? Haru!	418.05	threshold. Haru?
52	wideheight! Haru!	418.08	wideheight. Haru!
53	*onn*	418.10	*on*
54	*Aqileone*	418.27	*Aquileone*
54	*heal,*	418.36	*heal.*

Haveth Childers Everywhere   Published by Babou and Kahane & Fountain Press

Comparison with *Finnegans Wake* (1939)

Paris and New York
June 1930

page	*HCE* (Babou and Kahane)	page.line	*Finnegans Wake* (1939)
8	Dashe, in Kissilov's	532.21	Dashe, and with Any of my cousines in Kissilov's
9	clad. I should her have awristed	532.26–27	clad. Yet, as my acquainters do me the complaisance of apprising me, I should her have awristed
9	Passe, handicapped	532.34	Passe, with awards in figure and smile subsections, handicapped
10	dainty spekin	533.06	dainty, spekin
10	prentice serving	533.07	prenticeserving
10	Dolekey bishopregionary	533.08	Dolekey, bishopregionary

page	*HCE* (Babou and Kahane)	page.line	*Finnegans Wake* (1939)
11	numborines why	533.15	numborines, why
11	tunis	533.16	tunies
11	Hoardpayns	533.20	hoardpayns
11	aw!) gleeglom	533.22	aw!), gleeglom
12	coner and	533.24	coner, and
12	broad church	533.27	broadchurch
12	clairaudience as this is as	533.31	clairaudience, as this is, as
12	Hiemlancollin Pimpim's	533.33	Hiemlancollin. Pimpim's
12	forninehalf Shaun	533.34	forninehalf. Shaun
14	justness I	534.13	justness, I
14	Weston inc.	534.16	Weston, Inc
14	tix	534.17	tixtim
14	paviour); to my nonesuch	534.23	paviour) to my nonesuch
15	flowers searchers	534.25	flowers, searchers
15	is by	534.28	is, by
15	forhim	534.31	for him
15	Tower. Steck	534.35	Tower! Steck
15	ajavelin	534.35	a javalin
16	highflyet	534.36	highflyer
16	fig	534.36	jig
16	charger Pferdinamd	535.09	charger, Pferdinamd
16	Yeddonot	535.09	yeddonot
16	oer	535.10	o'er
16	ecelesensy	535.12	ecclesency
17	Noksagt Per	535.19	Noksagt! Per
17	Shugon	535.20	shugon
18	Colonel	535.36	colonel
19	Krumlin	536.10	krumlin
20	mugnum. He would	536.16	mugnum, he would
20	tis naught).	536.18	'tis naught.)
20	neberls mest	536.19	neberls, mest
21	prisons	536.24	prisonce
22	you indeed to goodness that	537.02	you, indeed to goodness, that
22	when as Sigismond	537.08	when, as Sigismond
22	pattern	537.10	Pattorn
23	even as	537.14	even, as

(Continued)

page	HCE (Babou and Kahane)	page.line	Finnegans Wake (1939)
23	time	537.18	times
23	prebellic when	537.18–19	prebellic, when
24	cootcops	537.23	cootcoops
24	Blawlawnd-via- Brigstow	537.24–25	Blaw-lawnd-via-Brigstow
24	be) would	537.28	be), would
24	harroween	537.28	haroween
24	Wake	537.34	Weck
25	Improbable!	538.05	Inprobable!
25	I do not credit one word of it.	538.06–07	I do not credit one word of it from such and suchess mistraversers.
25	outings, cent	538.09	outings: cent
26	One line, with with!	538.20	One line with with!
27	youngsters	538.25	youngsteys
28	and minhatton testify	539.02	and, minhatton, testify
28	A. G. whom	539.06	A. G., whom
28	lessons as	539.09	lessons, as
28	think if	539.10	think, if
29	athacleeath	539.17	Athacleeath
29	starrimisty	539.21	starrymisty
29	thollstall for	539.22	thollstall, for
30	siegewin with Abbot Warre to blesse on	539.27	siegewin, with Abbot Warre to blesse, on
30	whencehislaws	539.29–30	Whencehislaws
30	kingsinnturns T. R. H.	539.31	kingsinnturns, T. R. H.
30	Hathed here	539.33	Hathed, here
30	Skat and Skuld	539.35	skat and skuld
31	oppedemics the	539.36	oppedemics, the
31	river called of Ptolemy the Libnia Labia runneth	540.07	river, called of Ptolemy the Libnia Labia, runneth
31	*Ersed*	540.11	*ersed*
32	Things	540.13	– Things
32	whistle, here Tyeburn	540.15	whistle. Here Tyeburn
32	see yea	540.16	see, yea
32	giant, Estoesto!	540.17	giant. Estoesto!
33	Rothmere's	540.25	rothmere's
33	Jonathans wild	540.28	Jonathans, wild
33	Thank you besters!	540.29	Thank you, besters!
33	Meludd	540.34	Me ludd
33	Firebugs good	540.35	Firebugs, good

page	*HCE* (Babou and Kahane)	page.line	*Finnegans Wake* (1939)
34	well worth	541.06	wellworth
34	ontreachesly	541.08	outreachesly
35	Gambelden	541.13	Gambleden
36	Warschouw	541.23	warschouw
36	Slobodens	541.26	slobodens
36	murmel, but	541.31–32	murmel but
36	whinninared	541.32	whinninaird
37	spudully	542.01	spudfully
38	folksfiendship enmy	542.18	folksfiendship, enmy
39	eyes? Mr Answers	542.26	eyes! Mr Answers
39	esausted: I	542.30	esausted; I
41	This missy my taughters, and these man my son	543.15–16	This missy, my taughters, and these man, my son
41	house that	543.18	house, that
42	german	543.25	German
42	Big-man-up-in-the-sky	543.30	Big-man-up-in-the-Sky
42	roe's	543.33	Roe's
43	hall-way	544.03	hallway
43	night soil	544.07	nightsoil
43	excentric	544.07–08	eccentric
43	clugstrump	544.09	clumpstump
44	rhumatic	544.10	rheumatic
44	feasable	544.12	feasible
44	water tap	544.15	watertap
44	yards run	544.16	yards' run
45	servants, lieabed	544.29–30	servants, outlook marred by ne'er-do-wells using the laneway, lieabed
45	dunplings	544.35	dumplings
46	five	544.36	five-
46	semi-detached	545.01	semidetached
46	lodging house	545.03	lodginghouse
46	goodmens' field	545.10–11	Goodmen's Field
47	I have expected, all, let them all come they	545.13	I could have expected, all, let them all come, they
47	commanded upon	545.15	commanded, upon[3]
47	heirs firmly	545.19	heirs, firmly
48	wrecks. Struggling	545.23–24	wrecks. / Struggling
48	livramentoed milles	545.24	livramentoed, milles

(Continued)

page	*HCE* (Babou and Kahane)	page.line	*Finnegans Wake* (1939)
48	Lo I	545.25	Lo, I
48	hope: in seralcellars louched I bleakmealers on	545.27	hope, in seralcellars louched I bleakmealers: on
48	Foulkes's	545.31	Foulke's
49	obstain. Clayed	546.01	obstain! Clayed
49	wake not! walk	546.01	wake not, walk
49	walk not!). Quo warranto	546.01–02	walk not! Sigh lento, Morgh!). *Quo warranto*
49	etoiled flappant	546.06	etoiled, flappant
49	Coleopter	546.07	coleopter
49	partifesswise blazond	546.07–08	partifesswise, blazoned
49	potent	546.10	portent
50	it repassing	546.11	it, repassing
50	or	546.18	of
50	journeymanright, and	546.20	journeymanright and
51	Kore !	546.28	Fore!
51	friends. I	546.29	friends! I
51	world turned	546.31	world, turned
51	men Earalend	546.32	men of Earalend
51	Blackwater	546.33	Black Water
51	Poole	546.34	Pool
52	my goods waif, as I, chiefly endmost, hartyly	547.04	my mmummy goods waif, as I, chiefly endmost hartyly
52	Fluvia iddle	547.05	Fluvia, iddle
53	jealousy, and	547.15–16	jealousy, ymashkt, beyashmakt, earswathed, snoutsnooded, and
53	Rivierside Drive	547.19	rivierside drive
53	there by	547.21	there, by
53	puntpole and	547.23–24	puntpole, the tridont sired a tritan stock, farruler, and
54	hallthundered, Heydays	547.29	hallthundered; Heydays
54	singular iday	547.34	singular, iday
54	What	547.36	what
54	bulls!) from	548.01	bulls!): from
54	Livland hoks	548.01	Livland, hoks
55	music goosegaze	548.03	music: goosegaze
55	canzoned, and	548.04	canzoned and
55	twas	548.13	'twas
56	clene, and, had	548.15	clene and had

page	*HCE* (Babou and Kahane)	page.line	*Finnegans Wake* (1939)
56	lay, and	548.19	lay and
56	ande	548.26	and
57	Sparrow's loomends day, lumineused	548.27	Sparrow's, loomends day lumineused
57	*Sourire d'Hiver,* and	548.29	*Sourire d'Hiver* and
57	King's	548.35	king's
57	olos	548.35	oloss
57	Soll leve! with	549.01	Soll leve!): with
58	hoist!): for	549.05	hoist: for
58	Prince	549.07	prince
58	flashnose	549.13	Flashnose
59	Tarred	549.15	tarred
59	block through	549.16	block, through
59	ampire from	549.16	ampire, from
59	Waterford's	549.18–19	Wexterford's
59	bellomport. When	549.22	bellomport: when
59	due	549.25	dues
60	sadly feeling	549.27	sadly, feeling
60	O'Conee	549.28	O'Connee
60	thougts	549.30	thoughts
60	Adam duffed	549.33	Adam, duffed
60	Guinass exposant	549.34	Guinnass, exposant
61	Hes	550.04	He's
61	Collegtium	550.06	collegtium
61	And	550.08	– And
61	St Pancreas	550.13	Saint Pancreas
62	Shallots	550.15	shallots
62	uliv's	550.18	Uliv's
62	and my	550.22	and, my
62	esquirial with	550.24	esquirial, with
62	librariums I	550.25	librariums, I
62	slaphung	550.26	slapbang
62	drapier-cutdean	550.27	drapier-cut-dean
63	Pi ten	550.31	Pieter
63	ballast. In our	551.01	ballast: in our
63	Elenders	551.02	elenders
63	ghoasts. She	551.03	ghoasts: she
64	Duanna, dwells	551.06	Duanna dwells
64	littlered ridinghats	551.08	littlerit reddinghats

(Continued)

page	HCE (Babou and Kahane)	page.line	*Finnegans Wake* (1939)
64	traemen, *pelves*	551.13	traemen: *pelves*
64	prostitute: let	551.14	prostitute; let
65	brothers, Chau	551.15	brothers; Chau
65	will; who	551.17	will: who
65	shall in	551.22	shall, in
65	adams all	551.22	adams, all
65	alive. My tow	551.22	alive: my tow
65	elskede my	551.24	elskede, my
66	stelas	551.30	stellas
66	reders	551.31	readers
66	sevendialed	551.32	sevendialled
66	12	551.33	twelve
66	camels	551.34	camels'
66	oi	551.35	Oi
66	Migreawis	552.02–03	Mifgreawis
67	covenanters	552.06	covennanters
67	Shemites retrace!	552.09	Shemites, retrace!
67	Farrel	552.12	Farrell
67	gentes!) keep	552.14	gentes!), keep
68	booth	552.15	Booth
68	ewigs I	552.20	ewigs, I
68	piggiesknees my sweet coolocked my	552.21	piggiesknees, my sweet coolocked, my
68	sixton, clashcloshant duominous	552.24	sixton clashcloshant, duominous
68	tellforths'	552.26	tellforth's
69	pewmillieu christous	552.28	pewmillieu, christous
69	babazounded ollguns	552.28	babazounded, ollguns
69	wholesail	552.35	wholehail,
69	blessing where	552.35–36	blessing, where
70	oyir; and	553.04	oyir: and
70	turrisses	553.11	turisses
70	statuesque	553.12	statuesques
70	templeogues the	553.12	templeogues, the
71	phoenix and	553.25	phoenix: and
71–72	plurabelle wigwarming wench (speakeasy!)	553.26	plurabelle, wigwarming wench, (speakeasy!)
72	parading (hearsemen	553.31	parading, (hearsemen
72	nuptiallers get	553.32	nuptiallers, get
72	Hosseyeh	553.35	Hoseyeh
72	king's	553.36	King's

page	*HCE* (Babou and Kahane)	page.line	*Finnegans Wake* (1939)
73	gents aroger	554.03	gents, aroger
73	damsels	554.03–04	damsells
73	softsidesaddled covertly	554.04	softsidesaddled, covertly
73	Shjelties and Skewbald	554.06	shjelties and skewbald

3 The 1939 Viking Press edition reads: 'commanded. upon', but what looks like a full stop is most probably a broken comma.

The Mime of Mick Nick and the Maggies Published by The Servire Press & Faber and Faber

Comparison with *Finnegans Wake* (1939)

The Hague & London
June 1934

page	*The Mime* (The Servire Press)	page.line	*Finnegans Wake* (1939)
1	(Bar and conveniences always open.)	219.03	(Bar and conveniences always open, Diddlem Club douncestears.)
1	With nightly redistribution of parts and players and daily dubbing of ghosters under the distinguished patronage	219.03–10	Entrancings: gads, a scrab; the quality, one large shilling. Newly billed for each wickeday perfumance. Somndoze massinees. By arraignment, childream's hours, expercatered. Jampots, rinsed porters, taken in token. With nightly redistribution of parts and players by the puppetry producer and daily dubbing of ghosters, with the benediction of the Holy Genesius Archimimus and under the distinguished patronage
1	Falias. Messoirs	219.11	Falias, Messoirs
1	Sennet. The mime of Mick, Nick and the Maggies, featuring:	219.13–21	Sennet. As played to the Adelphi by the Brothers Bratislavoff (Hyrcan and Haristobulus), after humpteen dumpteen revivals. Before all the King's Hoarsers with all the Queen's Mum. And wordloosed over seven seas crowdblast in certelleneteutoslavzendlatinsoundscript. In four tubbloids. While fern may cald us until firn make cold. *The Mime of Mick, Nick and the Maggies*, adopted from the Ballymooney Bloodriddon Murther by Bluechin Blackdillain (authorways 'Big Storey'), featuring:

(Continued)

page	*The Mime* (The Servire Press)	page.line	*Finnegans Wake* (1939)
1	Mr Seumas	219.22	Mr. Seumas
2	who has been divorced	219.24–220.01	who, when the tabs go up, as we discover, because he knew to mutch, has been divorced
2	St Bride's	220.03	St. Bride's
2	acidulateds) a	220.04	acidulateds), a
2	her, form the guard	220.05–06	her, their pet peeve, form with valkyrienne licence the guard
2	Mr Sean	220.11	Mr. Sean
2	wrestles with	220.13	wrestles for tophole with
3	caps or something	220.14–15	caps or puds or tog bags or bog gats or chuting rudskin gunerally or something
3	both brought	220.16	both carried off the set and brought
3	(Miss Corrie Corriendo, bring the babes, she mistributes mandamus monies)	220.18–21	(Miss Corrie Corriendo, Grischun scoula, bring the babes, Pieder, Poder and Turtey, she mistributes mandamus monies, after perdunamento, hendrud aloven entrees, pulcinellis must not miss our national rooster's rag)
3	house to	220.22	house, playing opposite to
3	Mr Makeall	220.23	Mr. Makeall
3	and topper, the	220.25–26	and topper, coat, crest and supporters, the
3	everlasting, is engaged in entertaining in his customhouse	220.28–36	everlasting, but throughandthoroughly proconverted, propounded for cyclological, is, studding sail once more, jibsheets and royals, in the semblance of the substance for the membrance of the umbrance with the remnance of the emblence reveiling a quemdam supercargo, of The Rockery, Poopinheavin, engaged in entertaining in his pilgrimst customhouse at Caherlehome-upon-Eskur those statutory persons
4	St Patricius'	221.01–02	St. Patricius'
4	the annuary). a bundle	221.02–03	the annuary, coldporters sibsuction), a bundle
4	civics inn quest of outings, who are more sloppily served by	221.04–05	civics, each inn quest of outings, who are still more sloppily served after every cup final by
4	(Mr Knut Oelsvinger, imitation of flatfish, torchbearing supperaape, bad halfsovereign, rolly pollsies, Glen of the Downs, o.s.v.)	221.06–09	(Mr. Knut Oelsvinger, Tiffsdays off, wouldntstop in bad, imitation of flatfish, torchbearing supperaape, dud halfsovereign, no chee daily, rolly pollsies, Glen of the Downs, the Gugnir, his geyswerks, his earsequack, his lokistroki, o.s.v.)

page	*The Mime* (The Servire Press)	page.line	*Finnegans Wake* (1939)
4	a spoilcurate and butt of	221.09–11	a scherinsheiner and spoilcurate, unconcerned in the mystery but under the inflounce of the milldieuw and butt of
4	palmer Madam	221.13	palmer teaput tosspot Madam
4	kook-and-general.	221.14–17	kook-and-dishdrudge, whitch believes wanthingthats, whouse be the churchyard or whorts up the aasgaars, the show must go on. / Time: the pressant.
4	Pageant of History worked up by Messrs Thud	221.18–20	Pageant of Past History worked up with animal variations amid everglaning mangrovemazes and beorbtracktors by Messrs. Thud
4	blunder	221.21	Blunder
5	Coldlimbeina	221.25	Coollimbeina
5	Mr T. M. Finnegan	221.27	Mr. T. M. Finnegan
5	Morgen. The crack	221.30–35	Morgen. Bosse and stringbag from Heteroditheroe's and All Ladies' presents. Tree taken for grafted. Rock rent. Phenecian blends and Sourdanian doofpoosts by Shauvesourishe and Wohntbedarft. The oakmulberryeke with silktrick twomesh from Shop-Sowry, seedsmanchap. Grabstone beg from General Orders Mailed. The crack
5	gods, The	221.36	gods. The
5	pit, accidental	222.01	pit. Accidental
5	L'archet	222.02	L'Archet
5	Laccorde. To start	222.02–03	Laccorde. Melodiotiosities in purefusion by the score. To start
5	barely say	222.03	hirtly bemark
6	respectively, O	222.08	respectively: O
6	Nitscht. The whole thugogmagog to be wound up by a Magnificent	222.11–17	Nitscht. Till the summit scenes of climbacks castastrophear, *The Bearded Mountain* (Polymop Baretherootsch), and *The River Romps to Nursery* (Maidykins in Undiform). The whole thugogmagog, including the portions understood to be oddmitted as the results of the respective titulars neglecting to produce themselves, to be wound up for an afterenactment by a Magnificent
6	lost-to lurning	222.25	lost-to-lurning
7	hoof and jarrety.	222.31	hoof and jarrety: athletes longfoot.
7	after. with	222.34	after, with

(Continued)

page	*The Mime* (The Servire Press)	page.line	*Finnegans Wake* (1939)
7	agnois	223.03	agnols
8	the signics	223.03–04	the airish signics
8	helpabit could	223.04–05	helpabit from an Father Hogam till the Mutther Masons could
8	Butup tighty	223.08–09	But, the monthage stick in the melmelode jawr, I am (twintomine) all thees thing. Up tighty
8	O holytroopers?	223.11	O holytroopers? Isot givin yoe?
8	stulpled glee	223.12	stulpled, glee
8	Came	223.19	came
9	brains the	223.26	brains, the
9	feinder. / He askit	223.26–29	feinder. / The howtosayto itiswhatis hemustwhomust worden schall. A darktongues, kunning. O theoperil! Ethiaop lore, the poor lie. He askit
9	johntily. / With	223.33–34	johntily. The skand for schooling. / With
9	either. / Ah ho!	223.34–224.09	either. / Item. He was hardset then. He wented to go (somewhere) while he was weeting. Utem. He wished to grieve on the good persons, that is the four gentlemen. Otem. And it was not a long time till he was feeling true forim he was goodda purssia and it was short after that he was fooling mehaunt to mehynte he was an injine ruber. Etem. He was at his thinker, aunts to give (the four gentlemen) the presence (of a curpse). And this is what he would be willing. He fould the fourd; they found the hurtled stones; they fell ill with the gravy duck: and he sod town with the roust of the meast. Atem. / Towhere byhangs ourtales. / Ah ho!
10	antiets	224.12	antlets
10	poker, please : so that Glugg	224.15–16	poker, please? And bids him tend her, lute and airly. Sing, sweetharp, thing to me anone! So that Glugg
10	murder	224.18	morrder
10	nearly	224.19	mearly
11	trapadour sinking	224.25	trapadour, sinking
11	bellas here	224.28–29	bellas, here
11	two own, though	224.33	two though
11	gracious: O	224.34–35	gracious: Mi, O
12	ensembled though	225.03	ensembled, though

page	*The Mime* (The Servire Press)	page.line	*Finnegans Wake* (1939)
12	Otherwised they	225.05–06	Otherwised, holding their noises, they
12	private he	225.06	private, Ni, he
13	Montagnone	225.15	Mountagnone
13	spoke,	225.19	spokes
16	shoddyshoes quicked	226.24	shoddyshoes, quicked
16	luvium	226.35	Luvium
16	eons	226.36	Eons
17	dies	226.36	Dies
17	the	227.03	she
17	Magrievy	227.06	Megrievy
17	least this	227.09	least, this
18	forsekeme-nought	227.16	foresake-me-nought
18	vicereversi	227.19	vicereversing
18	arbour, virid	227.20–21	arbour, treerack monatan, scroucely out of scout of ocean, virid
18	racked	227.21	rocked
18	diviun	227.22	divlun
19	Gille	227.30	Gillie
19	Macisaac	227.33	MacIsaac
19	shameleast, imbretelated, himself	227.34–36	shameleast, tel a Tartaran tastarin toothsome tarrascone tourtoun, vestimentivorous chlamydophagian, imbretallated himself
19	over from	228.01	over to the Machonochie Middle from
19	Allwhile preying in his mind he swure. Cross	228.03–05	Allwhile, moush missuies from mungy monsie, preying in his mind, son of Everallin, within himself, he swure. Macnoon maggoty mag. Cross
19	where absolution. He take skiff with three shirts and a wind, the bruce, the coriolano and the ignacio. Mum's	228.06–15	where from yank islanders the petriote's absolution. Mocknitza! Genik! He take skiff come first dagrene day overwide tumbler, rough and dark, till when bow of the shower show of the bower with three shirts and a wind, pagoda permettant, crookolevante, the bruce, the coriolano and the ignacio. From prudals to the secular but from the cumman to the nowter. Byebye, Brassolis, I'm breaving! Our war, Dully Gray! A conansdream of lodascircles, he here schlucefinis. Gelchasser no more! Mischnary for the minestrary to all the sems of Aram. Shimach, eon of Era. Mum's

(Continued)

page	*The Mime* (The Servire Press)	page.line	*Finnegans Wake* (1939)
20	sheolmastress. He wholehog himself care of	228.17–19	sheolmastress. And Unkel Silanse coach in diligence. Disconnection of the succeeding. He wholehog himself for carberry banishment care of
20	Mrs Gloria	228.20	Mrs. Gloria
20	recorporated, by	228.20	recorporated, (prunty!) by
20	to catch	228.21–22	to hail a hurry laracor and catch
20	that tarry	228.22	that absendee tarry
20	years. From	228.24	years. Right for Rovy the Roder. From
20	O'Tuli. Euro	228.25	O'Tuli, Euro
20	cashel with	228.26–27	cashel where every little ligger is his own liogotenente with
20	He would fire off his farced epistol to the hibruws. No more turdenskaulds!	228.29–36	He would, with the greatest of ease, before of weighting midhook, by dear home trashold on the raging canal, for othersites of Jorden, (heave a hevy, waterboy!) make one of hissens with a knockonacow and a chow collegions and fire off, gheol ghiornal, foull subustioned mullmud, his farced epistol to the hibruws. From Cernilius slomtime prepositus of Toumaria to the clutch in Anteach. Salvo! Ladigs and jointuremen! No more turdenskaulds!
20	Farther	229.01	farther
20	Wild primates not stop him .	229.01–02	Wild primates not stop him frem at rearing a writing in handy antics.
21	Inklenders. For	229.03–05	Inklenders. And daunt you logh if his vineshanky's schwemmy! For
21	them, she,	229.09–10	them, malady of milady made melodi of malodi, she,
21	arrant. For	229.11–12	arrant. To Wildrose La Gilligan from Croppy Crowhore. For
21	He would	229.17	Maleesh! He would
21	world how	229.17–19	world of Leimuncononnulstria (and what a strip poker globbtrottel they pairs would looks!) how
23	himself first	230.02	himself, first
23	and over	230.03	and, besouns thats, over
23	they eggspilled	230.04–05	they provencials drollo eggspilled
23	domum because	230.06	domum (osco de basco de pesco de bisco!) because
23	was in	230.07	was an omulette finas erbas in

page	*The Mime* (The Servire Press)	page.line	*Finnegans Wake* (1939)
23	ark and he could not join the flood	230.07–09	ark finis orbe and, no master how mustered, mind never mend, he could neither swuck in nonneither swimp in the flood
23	accoster as	230.11–12	accoster her coume il fou in teto-dous as
23	waters, Mondamoiseau	230.14	waters, making goods at mutuurity, Mondamoiseau
24	Armentières. He	230.15–17	Armentières. Neblonovi's Nivonovio! Nobbio and Nuby in ennoviacion! Occitantitempoli! He
24	sanctuaries so	230.17–18	sanctuaries maywhatmay mightwhomight so
24	herslF	230.22	herslF
24	silence while	230.23	silence, while
24	hehave	230.23	he, being brung up on soul butter, have
24	tears, for	230.24	tears for
24	Arty, reminiscensitive, dreaming	230.26–27	Tholedoth, treetrene! Zokrahsing, stone! Arty, reminiscensitive, at bandstand finale on grand carriero, dreaming
24	Sator's	230.28	Sators
25	germane faces	230.33	germanefaces
25	ekonome world.	230.35–231.04	ekonome world. Remember thee, castle throwen? Ones propsperups treed, now stohong baroque. And oil paint use a pumme if yell trace me there title to where was a hovel not a havel (the first rattle of his juniverse) with a tingtumtingling and a next, next and next (gin a paddy? got a petty? gussies, gif it ope?), while itch ish shome.
25	— My God, alas, that dear olt tumtum home/ Whereof in youthfood port I preyed / Amook the verdigrassy convict vallsall dazes. / And cloitered for amourmeant in thy / boosome shede!	231.05–08	*— My God, alas, that dear olt tumtum home / Whereof in youthfood port I preyed / Amook the verdigrassy convict vallsall dazes. / And cloitered for amourmeant in thy boosome shede!*
25	ecstasy, herepong	231.09–10	ecstasy (for Shing-Yung-Thing in Shina from Yoruyume across the Timor Sea), herepong
25	errooth	231.11	errorooth

(Continued)

page	*The Mime* (The Servire Press)	page.line	*Finnegans Wake* (1939)
25	wisdom as	231.11–15	wisdom (who thought him a Fonar all, feastking of shellies by googling Lovvey, regally freytherem, eagelly plumed, and wasbut gumboil owrithy prods wretched some horsery megee plods coffin acid odarkery pluds dense floppens mugurdy) as
25–26	years, he shall not forget it.	231.19–21	years, from their roseaced glows to their violast lustres, he shall not forget-it that pucking Pugases.
26	Howlsbawls	231.21	Holihowlsballs
26	unheardh	231.22	unheardth
26	esercizian	231.27	esercizism
26	He threwed	231.28–29	And it was so. And Malthos Moramor resumed his soul. With: Go Ferchios off to Allad out of this! An oldsteinsong. He threwed
26	hornypipe. Lookery	231.31–34	hornypipe. The hopjoimt jerk of a ladle broom jig that he learned in locofoco when a redhot turnspite he. Under reign of old Roastin the Bowl Ratskillers, readyos! Why was that man for he's doin her wrong! Lookery
26	coal. The worst is over. Wait! For	232.01–07	coal. And may his tarpitch dilute not give him chromitis! For the mauwe that blinks you blank is mostly Carbo. Where the inflammabilis might pursuive his comburenda with a pure flame and a true flame and a flame all toogasser, soot. The worst is over. Wait! And the dubuny Mag may gang to preesses. With Dinny Finneen, me canty, ho! In the lost of the gleamens. Sousymoust. For
27	When a	232.09	When (pip!) a
27	them on	232.10	them (pet!) on
27	waves, a	232.11	waves, (call her venicey names! call her a stell!) a
27	forecotes. And	232.13–14	forecotes. Isle wail for yews, O doherlynt. The poetesser And
27	leste. Hers	232.16	leste. A claribel cumbeck to errind. Hers
27	whingeywilly. Stop	232.24	whingeywilly! Stop
28	dot! Like	232.27–29	dot! Old cocker, young crowy, sifadda, sosson. A bran new, speedhount, outstripperous on the wind. Like
28	one, or	232.29	one or
28	off, gotten	232.33	off, doubledasguesched, gotten

page	The Mime (The Servire Press)	page.line	Finnegans Wake (1939)
28	capers letting	233.03	capers, letting
29	cam	233.13	can
30	nunsibelli	233.25	nunsibellies
30	— Get.	233.27	— Asky, asky, asky! Gau on! Micaco! Get!
30	And he did a get and slink his hook away. For	233.28–32	Ping an ping nwan ping pwan pong. / And he did a get, their anayance, and slink his hook away, aleguere come alaguerre, like a chimista inchamisas, whom the harricana hurries and hots foots, zingo, zango, segur. To hoots of utskut, urqurd, jamal, qum, yallah, yawash, yak! For
30	chew	233.33	ciappacioppachew
30	engelsk as	233.33–34	engelsk, melanmoon or tartatortoise, tsukisaki or soppisuppon, as
30	your cow	233.34	your cheesechalk cow
30	spanich. He	233.34–234.01	spanich. Makoto! Whagta kriowday! Gelagala nausy is. Yet right divining do not was. Hovobovo hafogate hokidimatzi in kamicha! He
30	Showpanza. could	234.06	Showpanza, could
31	anybroddy have	234.06–07	anybroddy which walked this world with eyes whiteopen have
31	sinelab? How he stud theirs mookst kevinly, inwreathed	234.08–14	sinelab? Of all the green heroes everwore coton breiches, the whitemost, the goldenest! How he stud theirs with himselfs mookst kevinly, and that anterevolitionary, the churchman childfather from tonsor's tuft to almonder's toes, a haggiography in duotrigesumy, son soptimost of sire sixtusks, of Mayaqueenies sign osure, hevnly buddhy time, inwreathed
31	priestessd, with	234.15–17	priestessd, their trail the tractive, and dem dandypanies knows de play of de eyelids, with
31	spritties they went peahenning around him in	234.18–20	spritties, lusspillerindernees, they went peahenning a ripidarapidarpad around him, pilgrim prinkips, kerilour kevinour, in
31	excited, allauding	234.21	excited rpdrpd, allauding
31	perfume praypuffs	234.24	perfume most praypuffs

(Continued)

page	*The Mime* (The Servire Press)	page.line	*Finnegans Wake* (1939)
31	(shall we help you to rigolect a bit?)	234.25–26	(shllwe help, now you've massmuled, you to t'rigolect a bit? yismik? yimissy?)
31	fairhaired	234.27	fairhailed
31	everyone the	234.27–28	everyone, asfar as safras durst assune, the
32	Meanings: We	234.29–30	Meanings: Andure the enjurious till imbetther rer. We
32	impures so tell that old bellows upthe tumtum ergan and	234.30–33	impures, (and your liber as they sea) we certney like gurgles love the nargleygargley so, arrahbeejee, tell that old frankay boyuk to bellows upthe tombucky in his tumtum argan and
32	O the singing.	234.34	O, the singing!
32	Adelphus.	234.35	Adelphus!
32	goholden,	234.36	goholden!
32	they've	234.36	They've
32	head. As	235.03–04	head. May thine evings e'en be blossful! Even of bliss! As
32	A pause. Then:	235.06–08	A pause. Their orison arises misquewhite as Osman glory, ebbing wasteward, leaves to the soul of light its fading silence (allahlah lahlah lah!), a turquewashed sky. Then:
33	nicest in	235.15–16	nicest and boskiest of timber trees in
33	nebohood. We'll	235.16–21	nebohood. Oncaill's plot. Luccombe oaks, Turkish hazels, Greek firs, incense palm edcedras. The hypsometers of Mount Anville is held to be dying out of arthataxis but, praise send Larix U' Thule, the wych elm of Manelagh is still flourishing in the open, because its native of our nature and the seeds was sent by Fortune. We'll
34	welcome. Lady	235.31–32	welcome. While the turf and twigs they tattle. Tintin tintin. Lady
34	Lemonade	236.03	Le Monade
35	Marmela. He's	236.06–07	Marmela. Luisome his for lissome hers. He's
35	till Easter	236.07–08	till Cantalamesse or mayhope till Rose Easter
35	Day. The	236.08–09	Day. So Niomon knows. The
35	adin. So	236.10–12	adin. We'll sing a song of Singlemonth and you'll too and you'll. Here are notes. There's the key. One two three. Chours! So
35	trough	236.20	through

page	*The Mime* (The Servire Press)	page.line	*Finnegans Wake* (1939)
37	peepers, as	237.04–06	peepers, (meaning Mullabury mesh, the time of appling flowers, a guarded figure of speech, a variety of perfume, a bridawl, seamist inso one) as
37	Lovelyt! / — Enchainted,	237.09–11	Lovelyt! / And they said to him: / — Enchainted,
37	salutant	237.12	salutamt
37	mails, send	237.14–18	mails, bag, belt and balmybeam, our barnaboy, our chepachap, with that pampipe in your putaway, gab borab, when you will be after doing all your sightseeing and soundhearing and smellsniffing and tastytasting and tenderumstouchings in all Daneygaul, send
37	adorables, a	237.18–19	adorables, thou overblaseed, a
37	ceive from	237.19–20	ceive, chief celtech chappy, from
38	among us. The Great	237.30–34	among us! The rains of Demani are masikal as of yere. And Baraza is all aflower. Siker of calmy days. As shiver as shower can be. Our breed and better class is in brood and bitter pass. Labbeycliath longs. But we're counting on the cluck. The Great
38	we, toutes	237.35–36	we (to be slightly more femmiliar perhips than is slickly more then nacessory), toutes
38	(you appreciate?) from you. We	238.02–11	(you appreciate?) so as to be very dainty, if an isaspell, and so as to be verily dandydainty, if an ishibilley, of and on, to and for, by and with, from you. Let the hitback hurry his wayward ere the missive has time to take herself off, 'twill be o'erthemore willfully intomeet if the coming offence can send our shudders before. We ſeem to have being elſewhere as tho' th' had paſs'd in our ſuſpens. Next to our shrinking selves we love sensitivas best. For they are the Angèles. Brick, fauve, jonquil, sprig, fleet, nocturne, smiling bruise. For they are an Angèle's garment. We
39	yes, the	238.12–14	yes, for sold long syne as we shall be heing in our created being of ours elvishness, the
39	promisus you	238.15	promisus as at our requested you

(Continued)

page	*The Mime* (The Servire Press)	page.line	*Finnegans Wake* (1939)
39	and draw	238.16–17	and, though if whilst disrobing to the edge of risk, (the bisifings in idolhours that satinfines tootoo!) draw
39	time! How	238.18–19	time! You don't want to peach but bejimboed if ye do. Perhelps. We ernst too may. How
39	years! Bashfulness	238.20	years till the myriadth and first become! Bashfulness
39	her! List!	238.21–23	her! Talk with a hare and you wake of a tartars. That's mus. Says the Law. List!
39	finnishfurst. Herzog	238.24	finnishfurst, Herzog
39	ravin have good three chancers after Bohnaparts. Eer's	238.25–31	ravin, my coosine of mine, have mour good three chancers, weothers, after Bohnaparts. The mything smile of me, my wholesole assumption, shes nowt mewithout as weam twin herewithin, that I love like myselfish, like smithereens robinsongs, like juneses nutslost, like the blue of the sky if I stoop for to spy's between my whiteyoumightcallimbs. How their duel makes their triel! Eer's
39	jennyjos. Will	238.33–34	jennyjos. Caro caressimus! Honey swarns where mellisponds. Will
39	yourself. We	238.35–36	yourself. Teomeo. Daurdour. We
39	all so	238.36–239.01	all here in Gizzygazelle Tark's bimboowood so
40	but we	239.03–04	but, master of snakes, we
40	change	239.04	sloughchange
40	allsee your quick. It's	239.05–09	allsee for deedsetton your quick. By the hook in your look we're eyed for aye were you begging the questuan with your lutean bowl round Monkmesserag. And whenever you're tingling in your trout we're sure to be tangled in our ticements. It's
40	ores. No	239.12	ores. Then shalt thou see, seeing, the sight. No
40	mennage! Vania,	239.13–14	mennage! A her's fancy for a his friend and then that fellow yours after this follow ours. Vania,
41	maidfree. So	239.22–23	maidfree. Methanks. So much for His Meignysthy man! And all his bigyttens. So
41	Cherie	239.25	Chérie
41	helds	239.30	bears

page	*The Mime* (The Servire Press)	page.line	*Finnegans Wake* (1939)
41	way oaths	239.30–32	way (mearing unknown, a place where pigeons carry fire to seethe viands, a miry hill, belge end sore footh) oaths
41	lucisphere. Lonedom's	239.34	lucisphere. Helldsdend, whelldselse! Lonedom's
42	party. For	240.02–03	party. No honaryhuest on our sposhialiste. For
42	memory do. He dooly	240.07–12	memory schemado. Nu mere for ever siden on the stolen. With his tumescinquinance in the thight of his tumstull. No more singing all the dags in his sengaggeng. Experssly at hand counterhand. Trinitatis kink had mudded his dome, peccat and pent fore, pree. Hymserf, munchaowl, maden, born of thug tribe into brood blackmail, dooly
42	He proform penance. He make polentay rossum out	240.13–18	He, by bletchendmacht of the golls, proforhim penance and come off enternatural. He, selfsufficiencer, eggscumuddher-in-chaff sporticolorissimo, what though the duthsthrows in his lavabad eyes, maketomake polentay rossum, (Good savours queen with the stem of swuith Aftreck! Fit for king of Zundas) out
42	lovabilities. He make	240.20–21	lovabilities, appeal for the union and play for tirnitys. He, praise Saint Calembaurnus, make
42	breast	240.21	breastsack
42	flint	240.23	Flinn the Flinter
42	him. He relation	240.24–27	him. He go calaboosh all same he tell him out. Teufleuf man he strip him all mussymussy calico blong him all same he tell him all out how he make what name. He, through wolkenic connection, relation
43	Andrum, pure blood Jebusite. Intrance	240.27–29	Andrum, parleyglutton pure blood Jebusite, centy procent Erserum spoking. Drugmallt storehuse. Intrance
43	A. A., possible sooth to say notwithstanding he	240.30–31	A. A., in peachskin shantungs, possible, sooth to say, notwithstanding far former guiles and he
43	considerable, to	240.31–32	considerable, by saving grace after avalunch, to
43	true his	240.35–36	true what chronicles is bringing his

(Continued)

page	*The Mime* (The Servire Press)	page.line	*Finnegans Wake* (1939)
43	say he coaxyorum offering candid	241.01–03	say short again akter, even while lossassinated by summan, he coaxyorum a pennysilvers offarings bloadonages with candid
43	Spinisters'	241.03	Spinshesses
43	pecuniarity spectacularly on	241.05–06	pecuniarity ailmint spectacularly in heather cliff emurgency on
43	rhodomantic lie	241.08	rhodomantic not wert one bronze lie
43	he walk	241.09	he, greyed vike cuddlepuller walk
43	funts. How	241.10–12	funts. Of so little is her timentrousnest great for greeting his immensesness. Sutt soonas sett they were, her uyes as his auroholes. Kaledvalch! How
44	ambersandalled. A mish he	241.15–16	ambersandalled, after Aasdocktor Talop's onamuttony legture. A mish, holy balm of seinsed myrries, he
44	everybody he	241.17–18	everybody what is found of his gients he
44	know	241.18	knew
44	Wikingson with	241.18–19	Wikingson, furframed Noordwogen's kampften, with
44	brisees, have	241.20–21	brisees, what naver saw his bedshead farrer and nuver met his swigamore, have
44	ignomen of	241.21	ignomen from prima signation of
44	and how	241.22–23	and, adcraft aidant, how
44	forsunkener, all	241.24	forsunkener, dope in stockknob, all
44	tommy	241.25	tammy
44	ratkins. They	241.25–28	ratkins. The kurds of Copt on the berberutters and their bedaweens! Even was Shes whole begeds off before all his nahars in the koldbethizzdryel. No gudth! Not one zouz! They
44	Calumdonia. In his contrary this	241.30–242.01	Calumdonia. As is note worthies to shock his hind! Ur greeft on them! Such askors and their ruperts they are putting in for more osghirs is alse false liarnels. The frockenhalted victims! Whore affirm is agains sempry Lotta Karssens. They would lick their lenses before they would negatise a jom petter from his sodalites. In his contrary and on reality, which Bichop Babwith bares to his whitness in his *Just a Fication of Villumses*, this
44	Mr Heer	242.01	Mr. Heer

page	The Mime (The Servire Press)	page.line	Finnegans Wake (1939)
44	Neelson, laxtleap	242.01–02	Neelson, of sorestate hearing, diseased, formarly with Adenoiks, den feed all lighty, laxtleap
45	velvet sidden mangy years and	242.06–08	velvet on geolgian mission senest mangy years his rear in the lane pictures, blanking same with autonaut and annexes and
45	a babyboy	242.08	a daarlingt babyboy
45	bucktooth coming	242.08–09	bucktooth, the thick of a gobstick, coming
45	so nursely at	242.09–10	so nerses nursely gracies to goodess, at
45	gunnfodder. That	242.10–12	gunnfodder. That why ecrazyaztecs and the crime ministers preaching him mornings and makes a power of spoon vittles out of his praverbs. That
45	feminister, with	242.13–14	femorniser, for a trial by julias, in celestial sunhat, with
45	biss. Old	242.16–18	biss, young shy gay youngs. Sympoly far infusing up pritty tipidities to lock up their rhainodaisies and be nice and twainty in the shade. Old
45	altfrumpishly falls	242.19–20	altfrumpishly like hear samhar tionnor falls
45	weal! A	242.21	weal! Revelation! A
45	badder, his	242.23	badder and a whorly show a parfect sight, his
46	goosemother, woman	242.25–26	goosemother, laotsey taotsey, woman
46	about. Meet	242.26–27	about. You sound on me, judges! Suppose we brisken up. Kings! Meet
46	logs	242.29	sawlogs
46	standing. His	242.30–31	standing. Psing a psalm of psexpeans, apocryphul of rhyme. His
46	Coolley-Couley	242.36	Cooley-Couley
46	elefents	243.01	elskerelks'
46	(he take a rap	243.03	(magrathmagreeth, he takable a rap
47	forty	243.04	fiertey
47	mytinbeddy? Yet	243.06–08	mytinbeddy? Schi schi, she feightened allsouls at pignpugn and gets a pan in her stummi from the pialabellars in their pur war. Yet
47	sole and	243.10	sole, her zoravarn lhorde and givnergenral, and

(Continued)

page	*The Mime* (The Servire Press)	page.line	*Finnegans Wake* (1939)
47	him so	243.12	him, oz her or damman, so
47	chickenbrooth	243.13	checkenbrooth
47	feed	243.15	nutre
47	almsdish when	243.15–18	almsdish, giantar and tschaina as sieme as bibrondas with Foli Signur's tinner roumanschy to fishle the ladwigs out of his lugwags, like a skittering kitty skattering hayels, when
47	day. The	243.20	day. Winden wanden wild like wenchen wenden wanton. The
47	bite she would delicate	243.21–25	bite and plug his baccypipes and renownse the devlins in all their pumbs and kip the streelwarkers out of the plague and nettleses milk from sickling the honeycoombe and kop Ulo Bubo selling foulty treepes, she would make massa dinars with her savuneer dealinsh and delicate
47	Mary's	243.27	Megan's
48	hat like	243.28–29	hat from Alpoleary with a viv baselgia and a clamast apotria like
48	princess to	243.29	princess or woman of the grave word to
48	Crucis, on	243.31–32	Crucis, with an ass of milg to his cowmate and chilterlings on
48	quaqueduxed and	243.33	quaqueduxed for the hnor of Hrom and
48	Orelli to	243.34–35	Orelli that gave Luiz-Marios Josephs their loyal devouces to
48	tattling!/ But	244.01–03	tattling! Backwoods, be wary! Daintytrees, go dutch! / But
48	moon. And the	244.04–08	moon. Bring lolave branches to mud cabins and peace to the tents of Ceder, Neomenie! The feast of Tubbournigglers is at hand. Shopshup. Inisfail! Timple temple tells the bells. In syngagyng a sangasongue. For all in Ondslosby. And, the
48	haste 'tis	244.09	haste, 'tis
48	darkles, all	244.13	darkles, (tinct, tint) all
49	marshpond is	244.14	marshpond by ruodmark verge is
49	tide. We	244.14–15	tide. Alvemmarea! We
49	koud. Where	244.17	koud. Drr, deff, coal lay on and, pzz, call us pyrress! Ha. Where
49	within. Huzoor	244.19	within. Haha. Huzoor

page	*The Mime* (The Servire Press)	page.line	*Finnegans Wake* (1939)
49	Hands. Nought	244.20–26	Hands. Tsheetshee. Hound through the maize has fled. What hou! Isegrim under lolling ears. Far wol! And wheaten bells bide breathless. All. The trail of Gill not yet is to be seen, rocksdrops, up benn, down dell, a craggy road for rambling. Nor yet through starland that silver sash. What era's o'ering? Lang gong late. Say long, scielo! Sillume, see lo! Selene, sail O! Amune! Ark!? Noh?! Nought
49	fields. In	244.28–29	fields. Tranquille thanks. Adew. In
49	silent. The	244.30–32	silent. ii. Luathan? Nuathan! Was avond ere a while. Now conticinium. As Lord the Laohun is sheutseuyes. The
49	Aurore. No	244.33–245.03	Aurore. Panther monster. Send leabarrow loads amorrow. While loevdom shleeps. Elenfant has siang his triump, *Great is Eliphas Magistrodontos* and after kneeprayer pious for behemuth and mahamoth will rest him from tusker toils. Salamsalaim. Rhinohorn isnoutso pigfellow but him ist gonz wurst. Kikikuki. Hopopodorme. Sobeast! No
49–50	lights! When	245.04–05	lights! Brights we'll be brights. With help of Hanoukan's lamp. When
50	and warnerforth's	245.08	and wextward warnerforth's
50	now the	245.09–10	now with robby brerfox's fishy fable lissaned out, the threads simwhat toran and knots in its antargumends, the
50	about feriaquintaism and if	245.11–13	about Junoh and the whalk and feriaquintaism and pebble infinibility and the poissission of the hoghly course. And if
50	harker to	245.14	~~harker~~ horker to
50	ribber he	245.14–15	ribber, save the giregargoh and dabardin going on in his mount of knowledge (munt), he
50	night? It	245.16–17	night? Es voes, ez noes, nott voes, ges, noun. It
50	sirut	245.19	~~sirut~~ strut
50	musketeering. But	245.20–22	musketeering. Brace of girdles, brasse of beauys. With the width of the way for jogjoy. Hulker's cieclest elbownunsense. Hold hard! And his dithering dathering waltzers of. Stright! But

(Continued)

page	*The Mime* (The Servire Press)	page.line	*Finnegans Wake* (1939)
50	wenderer, here lurks no iron	245.24–25	wenderer, while Jempson's weed decks Jacqueson's Island, here lurks, bar hellpelhullpulthebell, ~~no~~ none iron
50	Thunderation! Were	245.26–27	Thunderation! You took with the mulligrubs and we lack mulsum? No sirrebob! Great goodness, no! Were
50	Last, here's	245.28–30	Last, (our duty to you, chris! royalty, squat!) how matt your mark, though luked your johl, here's
51	ratification your	245.31–32	ratification by specification of your
51	Mr Knight	245.32	Mr. Knight
51	Kate homeswab	245.34	Kate, homeswab
51	number. De	245.35–36	number. Where Chavvyout Chacer calls the cup and Pouropourim stands astirrup. De
51	whoopee week	246.01	Whoopee Weeks
51	Gorey. Housefather calls enthreateningly. Ansighosa	246.04–10	Gorey. Between the starfort and the thornwood brass castle flambs with mutton candles. Hushkah, a horn! Gadolmagtog! God es El? Housefather calls enthreateningly. From Brandenborgenthor. At Asa's arthre. In thundercloud periwig. With lightning bug aflash from afinger. My souls and by jings, should he work his jaw to give down the banks and hark from the tomb! Ansighosa
52	plague	246.14	palashe
52	Myles. Ready. Now	246.19–20	Myles. And lead raptivity captive. Ready. Like a Finn at a fair. Now
52	them. Childs	246.21	them. Ninan ninan, the gattling gan! Childs
52	wilds. And	246.22	wilds. 'Twastold. And
52	merchand. For	246.23–26	merchand. The horseshow magnete draws his field and don't the fillyings fly? Educande of Sorrento, they newknow knowwell their Vico's road. Arranked in their array and flocking for the fray on that old orangeray, Dolly Brae. For
52	twain, since	246.27	twain, bartrossers, since
53	tenzones. For	246.33	tenzones. Bettlimbraves. For
53	Jeremy, the	246.36	Jeremy, the chastenot coulter, the
54	Teapotty. / He	247.15–17	Teapotty. / Kod knows. Anything ruind. Meetingless. / He

page	*The Mime* (The Servire Press)	page.line	*Finnegans Wake* (1939)
54	Santalto cursing	247.20	Santalto, cursing
54	deletious. An	247.20–22	deletious to ross up the spyballs like exude of margary! And how him it heaviered that eyerim rust! An
54	wound? It	247.23–25	wound? Soldwoter he wash him all time bigfeller bruisy place blong him. He no want missies blong all boy other look bruisy place blong him. Hence. It
54	him	247.25–26	the chastenot
57	fect. When	248.26–27	fect. I've a seeklet to sell thee if old Deanns won't be threaspanning. When
58	cockle. But	249.01–02	cockle. When here who adolls me infuxes sleep. But
59	prospiodes	249.15	prosplodes
59	her. Oh	249.19–20	her. The boy which she now adores. She dores. Oh
60	Misha, but	249.29	Misha but
60	Toffey-Tough	249.29	Toffey Tough
61	hushy. little	250.11	hushy, little
61	roohish cleany	250.11	roohish, cleany
61	Grandicellies al stay	250.12	Grandicellies, all stay
61	befour! When	250.12–13	befour! For you've jollywelly dawdled all the day. When
62	O. For	250.30–31	O. And what do you think that pride was drest in! Voolykins' diamondinah's vestin. For
63	duff, the few fly the farbetween! Attilad!	250.34–251.01	duff, a marrer of the sward incoronate, the few fly the farbetween! We haul minymony on that piebold nig. Will any tubble dabble on the bay? Nor far jocubus? Nic for jay? Attilad!
63	Cet	251.01	Get
63	oblious of	251.04–05	oblious autamnesically of
63	proprium, the	251.05–06	proprium, (such is stockpot leaden, so did sonsepun crake) the
63	light, he	251.07	light, apophotorejected, he
63	Blackarss. given	251.11–12	Blackarss, given
64	lerningstoel and	251.22	lerningstoel, and
64	difficult, but	251.25	difficult but
65	thou. / As	251.34–36	thou. / But listen to the mocking birde to micking barde making bared! We've heard it aye since songdom was gemurrmal. As

(Continued)

page	The Mime (The Servire Press)	page.line	Finnegans Wake (1939)
65	parry! / — Now	252.04–07	parry! Dvoinabrathran, dare! The mad long ramp of manchind's parlements, the learned lacklearning, merciless as wonderful. / — Now
66	ago. / The bivitellines, obscindgemeinded	252.13–16	ago. / And each was wrought with his other. And his continence fell. The bivitellines, Metellus and Ametallikos, her crown pretenders, obscindgemeinded
66	know who	252.19–20	know twigst timidy twomeys, for gracious sake, who
66	in but	252.27	in, not for pie, but
67	Stop. / Creedless	252.31–33	Stop. Who is Fleur? Where is Ange? Or Gardoun? / Creedless
67	crownless	252.33	, croonless
67	haughty. He	252.33–35	haughty. There end no moe red devil in the white of his eye. Braglodyte him do a katadupe. A condamn quondam jontom sick af a suckbut! He
67	spendthrifts. Nor	253.08–09	spendthrifts, no thing making newthing wealthshowever for a silly old Sol, healthytobedder and latewiser. Nor
68	what and	253.13	what, bite simbum, and
69	namely, the	253.23–25	namely, since ever apart that gossan duad, so sure as their's a patch on a pomelo, this yam ham in never live could, the
69	ejaculation of urine	253.27	ejaculations of aurinos
69	thumbtonosery, one	253.28–29	thumbtonosery (Myama's a yaung yaung cauntry), one
69	But, god	253.33	But, vrayedevraye Blankdeblank, god
69	recompounded, how	253.35–36	recompounded, an isaac jacquemin mauromormo milesian, how
69	him?	253.36	him, moreblue?
69	pitssched as	254.01	pitssched for an ensemple as
69	Rurle	254.02	Rurie
69	Cleaver, Orion	254.02–03	Cleaver, those three stout sweynhearts Orion
70	the product	254.04	the, Ipse dadden, product
70	anyone, or	254.05–06	anyone, your brutest layaman with the princest champion in our archdeaconsy, or
70	clippings, for	254.07–08	clippings, which the chroncher of chivalries is sulpicious save he scan, for
70	again while	254.09–11	again as John, Polycarp and I renews eye-to-eye ayewitnessed and to Paddy Palmer, while

page	*The Mime* (The Servire Press)	page.line	*Finnegans Wake* (1939)
70	inturned?/ The	254.14–15	inturned? So Perrichon with Bastienne or heavy Humph with airy Nan Ricqueracqbrimbillyjicqueyjocqjolicass? How sowesthow, *dullcisamica*? A and aa ab ad abu abiad. A babbel men dub gulch of tears. / The
71	em in	254.27	em, par Mahun Mesme, in
71	phrases	254.28	phases
71	aspire. For	254.32–34	aspire. And insodaintily she's a quine of selm ashaker while as a murder of corpse when his magot's up he's the best berrathon sanger in all the aisles of Skaldignavia. As who shall hear. For
71	man, shoehanded	254.35–255.01	man, prince of Bunnicombe of wide roadsterds, the herblord the gillyflowrets so fain fan to flatter about. Artho is the name is on the hero, Capellisato, shoehanded
71	Hold! / Why	255.03–05	Hold! / Yet stir thee, to clay, Tamor! / Why
71	wareabouts: If	255.08	wareabouts. If
72	sire. Even	255.12–22	sire. The wing of Moykill cover him! The Bulljon Bossbrute quarantee him! Calavera, caution! Slaves to Virtue, save his Veritotem! Bearara Tolearis, *procul abeat*! The Ivorbonegorer of Danamaraca be, his Hector Protector! Woldomar with Vasa, peel your peeps! And try to saviourise the nights of labour to the order of our blooding worold! While Pliny the Younger writes to Pliny the Elder his calamolumen of contumellas, what Aulus Gellius picked on Micmacrobius and what Vitruvius pocketed from Cassiodorus. Like we larnt from that Buke of Lukan in Dublin's capital, Kongdam Coombe. Even
72	licence. And	255.23–24	licence. Nor a duckindonche divulse from bath and breakfast. And
72	Mr John	255.26	Mr. John
72	as	255.27	at
72	consort, weighing	255.29–31	consort, foundling filly of fortyshilling fostertailor and shipman's shopahoyden, weighing

(Continued)

page	*The Mime* (The Servire Press)	page.line	*Finnegans Wake* (1939)
73	to the rescue	256.01–02	with your hokey or mehokeypoo
73	pullets. Their	256.02–03	pullets. That's where they have wreglias for. Their
73	thinkling, while Bier	256.04–07	thinkling (and not one hen only nor two hens neyther but every blessed brigid came aclucking and aclacking), while, a rum a rum, the ram of all harns, Bier
73	pleaders, is	256.08–09	pleaders, Mas marrit, Pas poulit, Ras ruddist of all, though flamifestouned from galantifloures, is
73	go./ 'Tis	256.11–16	go. Halome. Blare no more ramsblares, oddmund barkes! And cease your fumings, kindalled bushies! And sherrigoldies yeassymgnays; your wildeshaweshowe moves swiftly sterneward! For here the holy language. Soons to come. To pausse. / 'Tis
73	bee, Fine's	256.18–19	bee, with jaggery-yo to juju-jaw, Fine's
74	Grammaires and	256.20–21	Grammaires and bothered parsenaps from the Four Massores, Mattatias, Marusias, Lucanias, Jokinias, and
74	of your	256.30–31	of the scores and crores of your
74	valuations on	256.31–32	valuations in the pice of dinggyings on
74	cloud still	256.33	cloud, a nibulissa, still
74	cries	256.33	sulks
74	me. What	256.34–257.01	me. Caspi, but gueroligue stings the air. Gaylegs to riot of us! Gallocks to lafft. What
74	While they jeerilied along about	257.03–10	While, running about their ways, going and coming, now at rhimba rhomba, now in trippiza trappaza, pleating a pattern Gran Geamatron showed them of gracehoppers, auntskippers and coneyfarm leppers, they jeerilied along, durian gay and marian maidcap, lou Dariou beside la Matieto, all boy more all girl singoutfeller longa house blong store Huddy, whilest nin nin nin nin that Boorman's clock, a winny on the tinny side, ninned nin nin nin nin, about
75	like auld	257.12–14	like (You'll catch it, don't fret, Mrs Tummy Lupton! Come indoor, Scoffynosey, and shed your swank!) auld
75	to bold	257.16–17	to (The nurse'll give it you, stickypots! And you wait, my lasso, fecking the twine!) bold

page	*The Mime* (The Servire Press)	page.line	*Finnegans Wake* (1939)
75	of illed	257.19–21	of (You're well held now, Missy Cheekspeer, and your panto's off! Fie, for shame, Ruth Wheatacre, after all the booz said!) illed
75	bakin for Wold	257.22–24	bakin with a pinch of the panch of the ponch in jurys for (Ah, crabeyes, I have you, showing off to the world with that gape in your stocking!) Wold
75	who was	257.25–26	who, in deesperation of deispiration at the diasporation of his diesparation, was
75	Lukkedoerendunand urraskewdy- looshoofermoypor tertooryzooysph- alnabortansa kroidverjkapakkapuk	257.27–28	Lukkedoerendunandurraskewdy- looshoofermoyportertooryzooysph-alna bortansporthaokansakroidverjkapakkapuk
75–76	request. / For	257.32–258.20	request. / Uplouderamain! / Gonn the gawds, Gunnar's gustspells. When the h, who the hu, how the hue, where the huer? Orbiter onswers: lots lives lost. Fionia is fed up with Fidge Fudgesons. Sealand snorres. Rendningrocks roguesreckning reigns. Gwds with gurs are gttrdmmrng. Hlls vlls. The timid hearts of words all exeomnosunt. Mannagad, lammalelouh, how do that come? By Dad, youd not heed that fert! Fulgitudes ejist rowdownan tonuout. Quoq! And buncskleydoodle! Kidoosh! Of their fear they broke, they ate wind, they fled; where they ate there they fled; of their fear they fled, they broke away. Go to, let us extol Azrael with our harks, by our brews, on our jambses, in his gaits. To Mezouzalem with the Dephilim, didits dinkun's dud? Yip! Yup! Yarrah! And let Nek Nekulon extol Mak Makal and let him say unto him: Immi ammi Semmi. And shall not Babel be with Lebab? And he war. And he shall open his mouth and answer: I hear, O Ismael, how they laud is only as my loud is one. If Nekulon shall be havonfalled surely Makal haven hevens. Go to, let us extell Makal, yea, let us exceedingly extell. Though you have lien amung your posspots my excellency is over Ismael. Great is him whom is over Ismael and he shall mekanek of Mak Nakulon. And he deed. / Uplouderamainagain! / For

(Continued)

page	*The Mime* (The Servire Press)	page.line	*Finnegans Wake* (1939)
76	spoken and the	258.20–22	spoken in tumbuldum tambaldam to his tembledim tombaldoom worrild and, moguphonoised by that phonemanon, the
76	habitations. Thou	258.27–28	habitations. And nationglad, camp meeting over, to shin it, Gov be thanked. Thou
76	thereby that	258.30–31	thereby, even Garda Didymus and Garda Domas, that
76	bodemen, Pray-your-Prayers	258.34–35	bodemen, the cheeryboyum chirryboth with the kerry-bommers in their krubeems, Pray-your-Prayers
76	Tom./ O	258.36–259.03	Tom. / Till tree from tree, tree among trees, tree over tree become stone to stone, stone between stones, stone under stone for ever. / O

Storiella as She Is Syung   Published by Corvinus Press

—

Comparison with *Finnegans Wake* (1939)   October 1937

Note: The 1937 edition of *Storiella as She Is Syung* has no page numbers. To refer to the appropriate pages in this edition, this table cites the first (fw) and last (lw) word on the page in question. The first entry for example indicates that the page of which the first word is 'As' and the last word is 'beard' (denoted 'As.beard') shows a change from 'AS WE THERE' to 'As we there' in the 1939 edition of *Finnegans Wake*. Furthermore, the line numbers of the footnotes are transcribed as follows: '260.f1' indicates a change in line1 of the footnotes on page 260 in *Finnegans Wake* (1939). An added footnote is preceded by a superscripted F (as in 'thunder [F]').

Section (fw.lw)	*Storiella* (Corvinus Press)	page.line	*Finnegans Wake* (1939)
As.beard	AS WE THERE	260.01	As we there
As.beard	**Sic**	260.04	**Sic.**
As.beard	Herod was	260.f1–2	Herod with the Cormwell's eczema was
As.beard	Snuffler I'd	260.f2–3	Snuffler whatever about his blue canaries I'd
Whence. arounds	*Menily*	260.09	*Menly*
Whence. arounds	**Universal**	260.13	**Universal.**
Whence. arounds	fear. And	260.15	fear! And

Section (fw.lw)	*Storiella* (Corvinus Press)	page.line	*Finnegans Wake* (1939)
Whence. arounds	heppnessised	261.f1	happnessised
and.her	mosoleum, Length	261.13	mosoleum. Length
and.her	*Barbar*	261.14	*Barbar.*
and.her	Longfellow's Lodgings	261.f3	Kellywick, Longfellow's Lodgings
and.her	Co Mahogany	261.f4	Co. Mahogany
and.her	Bhing said	261.f6	Bhing, said
Cross. Begge	Knock.	262.06 (f1–2)	Knock.^F yussive smirte and ye mermon answerth from his beelyingplace below the tightmark, Gotahelv!
Cross. Begge	*Thsight*	262.11–15	*Swing the banjo, bantams, bounce-the-baller's blown to fook./ Thsight*
Cross. Begge	thunder.	262.12 (f4)	thunder. ^F A goodrid croven in a tynwalled tub.
Cross. Begge	Pickardstown. Or	262.21–23	Pickardstown. And that skimmelk steed still in the ground-loftfan. As over all. Or
Tickets. cimadoro	spicerobed	263.06	incenstrobed
Tickets. cimadoro	same.	263.16 (f2–5)	same. ^F We dont hear the booming cursowarries, we wont fear the fletches of fightning, we float the meditarenias and come bask to the isle we love in spice. Punt.
tight. Swords	perishers. Wone	265.20–23	perishers, Tytonyhands and Vlossyhair, a kilolitre in metromyriams. Presepeprosapia, the parent bole. Wone
tight. Swords	tavern	265.23 (f8–9)	tavern ^F Tomley. The grown man. A butcher szweched him the bloughs and braches. I'm chory to see P. Shuter.
tight. Swords	soup-plate	265.f3	soupplate
tight. Swords	C.P.	266.f3	B.B.
The. Inishmacsaint	castle	266.03	Castle

(Continued)

Section (fw.lw)	*Storiella* (Corvinus Press)	page.line	*Finnegans Wake* (1939)
The. Inishmacsaint	it. But	266.04	it! But
The. Inishmacsaint	barrabelowther, past	266.10–11	barrabelowther, bedevere butlered table round, past
The. Inishmacsaint	upsturts. The	266.13–15	upsturts. Here we'll dwell on homiest powers, love at the latch with novices nig and nag. The
The. Inishmacsaint	doll.	266.18 (f5)	doll. F Ravens may rive so can dove deelish.
The. Inishmacsaint	Here till	266.20–21	Here (the memories framed from walls are minding) till
The. Inishmacsaint	gambit, lead	266.26	gambit, (that buxom bruzeup, give it a burl!) lead
lead.manger	time.	267.f5	time but I thinks more of my pottles and ketts.
The.pullovers	nereids	267.24	Nereids
The.pullovers	fore	267.29	or
The.pullovers	sexappealing	268.02	sex appealing
The.pullovers	one the	268.f1	one, the
your.out	difference	269.15 (f3)	difference F If she can't follow suit Renée goes to the pack.
your.out	Zeus the	269.18	Zeus, the
lumpsum.hell	limberlimbed	270.08	limber-limbed
O'MaraFarrell. gymnufleshed	*O'MaraFarrell.*	270.25	*O'Mara Farrell.*
O'MaraFarrell. gymnufleshed	ga, ga of	270.31	ga, ga, of
O'MaraFarrell. gymnufleshed	torskmester	271.04 (f1–2)	torskmester F All his teeths back to the front, then the moon and then the moon with a hole behind it.
O'MaraFarrell. gymnufleshed	rompers	271.05 (f3)	rompers F Skip one, flop fore, jennies in the cabbage store.
blow.yourself	be. As	271.22	be to have to have been to will be. As
blanks.see	statesmen Brock	272.25	statesmen, Brock
banks.see	bawls.	273.02 (f1)	bawls. F Shake eternity and lick creation.
the.now	*Cowe's*	273.13	*Kine's*
the.now	Sir	273.f8	sir

Section (fw.lw)	*Storiella* (Corvinus Press)	page.line	*Finnegans Wake* (1939)
hitheris. please	Hegerite	274.10 (f2)	Hegerite ᶠ If I gnows me gneesgnobs the both of him is gnatives of Genuas.
hitheris. please	M. Potter	274.f3	Mr Potter
gosongingon. warcheekeepy	te	274.31	to
gosongingon. warcheekeepy – Service. know	Erin's hircohaired culoteer. Thanks eversore much	275.01– 02–304.05	Erin's hircohaired culoteer. [*The Triangle*] Thanks eversore much
Service.know	delph.	304.26	delph. ᶠ If I'd more in the cups that peeves thee you could cracksmith your rows tureens.
retorting. sacrifice	Keane. Biddy	305.19	Keane! Biddy
he.Gusty	hush. Bide	305.25	hush! Bide
he.Gusty	do. The law	305.25	do! The law
he.Gusty	Impostolopulos?	306.10 (f1)	Impostolopulos? ᶠ The divvy wants that babbling brook. Dear Auntie Emma Emma Eates.
he.Gusty	*Saul. / Aristotle.*	306.17	*Saul. Aristotle.*
many.things	manducabimus.	306.12 (f2)	manducabimus. ᶠ Strike the day off, the nightcap's on nigh. Goney, goney gone!

Bibliography

Abbott, H. Porter. 1996. *Beckett Writing Beckett: The Author in the Autograph*. Ithaca and London: Cornell University Press.
————. 2004. 'Narrative'. In *Palgrave Advances in Samuel Beckett Studies*, edited by Lois Oppenheim, 7–29. Houndmills, Basingstoke: Palgrave Macmillan.
Atherton, James S. 1959. *The Books at the Wake: A Study of Literary Allusions in James Joyce's 'Finnegans Wake'*. London: Faber and Faber.
Aubert, Jacques. 1985. Introduction to 'Anna Lyvia Pluratself', 417–18. *Cahiers de l'Herne: James Joyce*. Paris: L'Herne,
Banta, Melissa and Oscar A. Silverman. 1987. *James Joyce's Letters to Sylvia Beach*. Oxford: Plantin Publishers.
Barrett, Louise. 2011. *Beyond the Brain: How Body and Environment Shape Animal and Human Minds*. Princeton and Oxford: Princeton University Press.
Barry, Peter. 1980. 'The Enactment Fallacy'. *Essays in Criticism* 30.2: 95–104.
Bazarnik, Katarzyna. 2007. 'Joyce, Liberature and Writing of the Book'. *Hypermedia Joyce Studies* 8.2. hjs.ff.cuni.cz/archives/v8_2/essays/bazarnik.htm.
Beach, Sylvia. (1953) 1980. *Shakespeare and Company*. Lincoln and London: University of Nebraska Press.
————. 2010. *Letters*, edited by Keri Walsh. New York: Columbia University Press.
Beckett, Samuel et al. (1929) 1972. *Our Exagmination Round His Factification for Incamination of Work in Progress*. Norfolk, Connecticut: New Directions.
Begnal, Michael H. 1969. 'The Fables of *Finnegans Wake*'. *James Joyce Quarterly* 6.4: 357–67.
Begnal, Michael H. and Grace Eckley. 1975. *Narrator and Character in 'Finnegans Wake'*. Lewisburg: Bucknell University Press.
Benjamin, Walter. 1991. *Das Passagen-Werk. Gesammelte Schriften Band V:1*. Frankfurt am Main: Suhrkamp.
Bernaerts, Lars, Dirk De Geest, Luc Herman and Bart Vervaeck, eds. 2013. *Stories and Minds: Cognitive Approaches to Literary Narrative*. Lincoln and London: University of Nebraska Press.
Birmingham, Kevin. 2014. *The Most Dangerous Book: The Battle for James Joyce's* Ulysses. New York: The Penguin Press.
Blakemore, Gregory. 2013. 'Reexamining Enactivism'. *Aporia* 23.1: 37–48.
Brown, Dennis. 2000. 'James Joyce's Fable of the Ondt and the Gracehoper: "Othering", Critical Leader-Worship and Scapegoating'. *Wyndham Lewis Annual* 7: 32–42.
Bushell, Sally. 2009. *Text as Process: Creative Composition in Wordsworth, Tennyson and Dickinson*. Charlottesville and London: University of Virginia Press.

Cadbury, Bill. 2007. '"The March of a Maker": Chapters I.2–4'. In *How Joyce Wrote 'Finnegans Wake': A Chapter-by-Chapter Genetic Guide*, edited by Luca Crispi and Sam Slote, 66–97. Madison: The University of Wisconsin Press.

Clark, Andy. 2012. 'Embodied, Embedded, and Extended Cognition'. In *The Cambridge Handbook of Cognitive Science*, edited by Keith Frankish and William M. Ramsey, 275–91. Cambridge: Cambridge University Press.

Clark, Andy and David J. Chalmers. 1998. 'The Extended Mind'. *Analysis* 58: 10–23.

———. 2010. 'The Extended Mind'. In *The Extended Mind*, edited by Richard Menary, 27–42. Cambridge, MA: MIT Press.

Conley, Tim. 2014. '"Cog it out": Joyce on the Brain'. *Joyce Studies Annual* 2014: 25–41.

Conley, Tim, ed. 2010. *Joyce's Disciples Disciplined: A Re-Exagmination of the 'Exagmination' of 'Work in Progress'*. Dublin: University College Dublin Press.

Connolly, Thomas E. 1955. *The Personal Library of James Joyce: A Descriptive Bibliography*. Buffalo, NY: The University of Buffalo.

Connolly, Thomas E., ed. 1961. *James Joyce's 'Scribbledehobble': The Ur-Workbook for 'Finnegans Wake'*. Evanston, IL: Northwestern University Press.

Conover, Anne. 1989. *Caresse Crosby: From Black Sun to Roccasinibalda*. Santa Barbara: Capra Press.

Crispi, Luca. 2007. 'Storiella as She Was Wryt: Chapter II.2'. In *How Joyce Wrote 'Finnegans Wake': A Chapter-by-Chapter Genetic Guide*, edited by Luca Crispi and Sam Slote. Madison: The University of Wisconsin Press, 214–49.

Crispi, Luca and Stacey Herbert. 2003. *In Good Company: James Joyce & Publishers, Readers, Friends*. An Exhibition of McFarlin Library's Special Collections. Tulsa: The University of Tulsa.

Crispi, Luca and Sam Slote, ed. 2007. *How Joyce Wrote 'Finnegans Wake': A Chapter-by-Chapter Genetic Guide*. Madison: The University of Wisconsin Press.

Crosby, Caresse. 1953. *The Passionate Years: An Autobiography*. New York: The Dial Press.

Crowley, Ronan. 2015. 'Dial M for Marianne: The *Dial*'s Refusals of 'Work in Progress', *Genetic Joyce Studies* 15 (Spring 2015), www.geneticjoycestudies.org

Damasio, Antonio. 2012. *Self Comes to Mind: Constructing the Conscious Brain*. London: Vintage Books.

Deane, Vincent, Daniel Ferrer and Geert Lernout, eds, 2001. *James Joyce's* Finnegans Wake *Notebooks at Buffalo*. Turnhout: Brepols.

Deming, Robert H., ed. (1970) 1977. *James Joyce: The Critical Heritage*, 2 volumes. London and Henley: Routledge and Kegan Paul.

Dennett, Daniel C. 1991. *Consciousness Explained*. London: Penguin.

———. 2014. *Intuition Pumps and Other Tools for Thinking*. London: Penguin.

Deppman, Jed. 2007. 'A Chapter in Composition: Chapter II.4'. In *How Joyce Wrote 'Finnegans Wake': A Chapter-by-Chapter Genetic Guide*, edited by Luca Crispi and Sam Slote, 304–46. Madison: The University of Wisconsin Press.

de Voogd, Peter. 2013. 'Modernism and the Art of Printing: *transition* and Carolus Verhulst'. In *Modernism Today*, edited by Sjef Houppermans, Peter Liebregts, Jan Baetens and Otto Boele, 237–46. Amsterdam and New York: Rodopi.

Douglas, James. 1922. 'Beauty – and the Beast'. *Sunday Express* (28 May).

Eagle, Chris. 2014. '"Stuttistics": On Speech Disorders in *Finnegans Wake*'. In: *Literature, Speech Disorders, and Disability: Talking Normal*, edited by Chris Eagle, 82–99. New York: Routledge.

Edwards, Paul. 2000. *Wyndham Lewis: Painter and Writer*. New Haven and London: Yale University Press.

Ellmann, Richard. 1983. *James Joyce*. New and Revised Edition. Oxford: Oxford University Press.

Eliot, T.S. 2011. *The Letters of T.S. Eliot. Vol. 2, 1923–1925*, edited by Valerie Eliot and Hugh Haughton. New Haven and London: Yale University Press.

Fargnoli, A. Nicholas, ed. 2003. *James Joyce: A Literary Reference*. New York: Carroll and Graf.

Ferrer, Daniel. 2007. 'Wondrous Devices in the Dark: Chapter III.4'. In *How Joyce Wrote 'Finnegans Wake': A Chapter-by-Chapter Genetic Guide*, edited by Luca Crispi and Sam Slote, 410–435. Madison: The University of Wisconsin Press.

———. 2011. *Logiques du brouillon: Modèles pour une critique génétique*. Paris: Seuil.

Ferrer, Daniel and Jacques Aubert. 1998. 'Anna Livia's French Bifurcations'. In *Transcultural Joyce*, edited by K.R. Lawrence, 179–86. Cambridge: Cambridge University Press.

Fitch, Noel Riley. 1985. *Sylvia Beach and the Lost Generation: A History of Literary Paris in the Twenties and Thirties*. New York and London: Norton.

Fordham, Finn. 2010. *I Do, I Undo, I Redo: The Textual Genesis of Modernist Selves*. Oxford: Oxford University Press.

Fuse, Mikio. 2007. 'The Letter and the Groaning: Chapter I.5'. In *How Joyce Wrote 'Finnegans Wake': A Chapter-by-Chapter Genetic Guide*, edited by Luca Crispi and Sam Slote, 98–123. Madison: The University of Wisconsin Press.

Flower, Linda and John R. Hayes. 1981. 'A Cognitive Process Theory of Writing'. *College Composition and Communication* 32.4: 365–87.

Genette, Gérard. 1980. *Narrative Discourse*. Oxford: Blackwell.

Gilbert, Stuart. 1993. *Reflections on James Joyce: Stuart Gilbert's Paris Journal*, edited by Thomas Staley and Randolph Lewis. Austin: University of Texas Press.

Gillet, Louis. 1931. 'M. James Joyce et son nouveau Roman Work in Progress', *Revue des Deux Mondes* lxxxiv (August 1931): 928–39.

Glasheen, Adaline. 1971. 'Rough Notes on Joyce and Wyndham Lewis', *A Wake Newsletter* VIII.5 (October 1971): 67–75.

Gottschall, Jonathan. 2012. *The Storytelling Animal: How Stories Make Us Human.* New York: Houghton Mifflin Harcourt.

Guerard, Albert J. (1958) 2006. 'The Journey Within'. In Joseph Conrad, *Heart of Darkness*, edited by Paul B. Armstrong, 326–36. New York and London: Norton Critical Editions.

Hart, Clive. 1967. 'His Good Smetterling of Entymology'. *A Wake Newslitter* IV.1 (Feb. 1967): 14–24.

Hayman, David. 1966. '"Scribbledehobbles" and How They Grew', edited by Jack P. Dalton and Clive Hart, *Twelve and a Tilly: Essays on the Occasion on the 25th Anniversary of 'Finnegans Wake'* 107–18. Evanston: Northwestern University Press.

———. 1990. *The 'Wake' in Transit.* Ithaca and London: Cornell UP.

———. 1998. 'Enter Wyndham Lewis Leading Dancing Dave: New Light on a Key Relationship'. *James Joyce Quarterly* 35.4/36.1 (Summer–Fall 1998): 621–32.

———. 2007. 'Male Maturity or the *Pub*lic Rise & Private Decline of HC Earwicker: Chapter II.3'. In *How Joyce Wrote 'Finnegans Wake': A Chapter-by-Chapter Genetic Guide*, edited by Luca Crispi and Sam Slote, 250–303. Madison: The University of Wisconsin Press.

Herbert, Stacey. 2009. 'Composition and Publishing History of the Major Works: An Overview'. In *James Joyce in Context*, edited by John McCourt, 3–16. Cambridge: Cambridge University Press.

Herman, David. 2011. 'Re-Minding Modernism', In *The Emergence of Mind: Representations of Consciousness in Narrative Discourse in English*, edited by David Herman, 243–71. Lincoln: University of Nebraska Press.

———. 2013. *Storytelling and the Sciences of Mind.* Cambridge, MA: The MIT Press.

Higginson, Fred H. 1960. *Anna Livia Plurabelle: The Making of a Chapter.* Minneapolis: University of Minnesota Press.

Hogan, Patrick Colm. 2013. *How Authors' Minds Make Stories.* Cambridge: Cambridge University Press.

Hutchins, Edwin. 2000. 'Cognition, Distributed'. In *International Encyclopedia of the Social and Behavioral Sciences*, edited by Neil Smelser and Paul Baltes, 2068–72. Amsterdam: Elsevier.

Hutto, Daniel D. and Erik Myin. 2013. *Radicalizing Enactivism: Basic Minds without Content.* Cambridge, MA: The MIT Press.

Joyce, James. 1931. 'Anna Livie Plurabelle', translated by Samuel Beckett, Ivan Goll, Eugene Jolas, James Joyce, Paul Léon, Adrienne Monnier, Alfred Péron and Philippe Soupault. *Nouvelle Revue française* 19.212: 633–46.

———. 1963. *A First-Draft Version of 'Finnegans Wake'*, edited by David Hayman. Austin, TX: University of Texas Press.

————. (1930) 1985. 'Anna Lyvia Pluratself', translated by Samuel Beckett and Alfred Péron, 418–21. *Cahier de l'Herne: James Joyce*. Paris: L'Herne.

————. 2000. *A Portrait of the Artist as a Young Man*. London: Penguin Classics.

————. 2002. *Finnegans Wake*, translated by Erik Bindervoet and Robbert-Jan Henkes. Amsterdam: Athenaeum-Polak & Van Gennep.

————. 2002b. *The 'Finnegans Wake' Notebooks at Buffalo: Notebook VI.B.29.* Turnhout: Brepols.

————. 2014. *Brouillons d'un baiser: Premiers pas vers* Finnegans Wake, edited by Daniel Ferrer, translated by Marie Darrieussecq. Paris: Gallimard.

Joyce, James and C.K. Ogden. 1935. 'Anna Livia Plurabelle', *transition* 21: 259–62.

Kahane, Jack. 1939. *Memoirs of a Booklegger*. London: M. Joseph.

————. 2010. *Memoirs of a Booklegger*. S.l.: Obolus Press.

Kahler, Erich von. 1973. *The Inward Turn of Narrative*, translated by Richard and Clara Winston. Princeton: Princeton University Press.

Klein, Scott W. 1994. *Fictions of James Joyce and Wyndham Lewis: Monsters of Nature and Design*. Cambridge: Cambridge University Press.

Landuyt, Ingeborg. 1999. *'Words in Distress': A Genetic Investigation into James Joyce's Early 'Work in Progress'*. PhD dissertation, University of Antwerp.

Leavis, F.R. 1952. *The Common Pursuit*. London: Chatto and Windus.

Leijten, Mariëlle, Sven de Maeyer and Luuk van Waes. 2011. 'Coordinating Sentence Composition with Error Correction: A Multilevel Analysis', *Journal of Writing Research* 2.3: 331–63.

Lernout, Geert. 1999. 'Beginning Again', *James Joyce Quarterly* 36.4: 984–6.

————. 2001. 'Introduction to V.B.29'. In: James Joyce, *The 'Finnegans Wake' Notebooks at Buffalo: Notebook VI.B.29*. Turnhout: Brepols.

————. 2007. 'The Beginning: Chapter I.1'. In *How Joyce Wrote 'Finnegans Wake': A Chapter-by-Chapter Genetic Guide*, edited by Luca Crispi and Sam Slote, 3–48. Madison: The University of Wisconsin Press.

————. 2013. 'Finishing a Book Without Title: The Final Years of "Work in Progress"'. In *Joyce Studies Annual*, edited by Moshe Gold and Philip Sicker, 3–32. New York: Fordham UP.

Lewis, Wyndham. (1928) 1965. *The Childermass*. London: John Calder.

————. (1926) 1989. *The Art of Being Ruled*, edited by Reed Way Dasenbrock. Santa Rosa: Black Sparrow Press.

————. (1927) 1993. *Time and Western Man*, edited by Paul Edwards. Santa Rosa, Black Sparrow Press.

Litz, A. Walton. 1964. *The Art of James Joyce: Method and Design in* Ulysses *and* Finnegans Wake. Oxford: Oxford University Press.

Malafouris, Lambros. 2013. *How Things Shape the Mind: A Theory of Material Engagement*. Cambridge, MA, and London: MIT Press.

Mayoux, Jean-Jacques. 1965. *Joyce* (Series: La Bibliothèque idéale). Paris: Gallimard.

McArthur, Ian. 1976a. 'A Textual Study of III.3 – Part I'. *A Wake Newslitter* XIII.3: 43–8.

———. 1976b. 'A Textual Study of III.3 – Part II'. *A Wake Newslitter* XIII.5 (October 1976): 85–92.

McCourt, John, ed. 2009. *James Joyce in Context*. Cambridge: Cambridge UP.

McGann, Jerome J. 1991. *The Textual Condition*. Princeton, NJ: Princeton University Press.

McMillan, Dougald. 1975. *Transition 1927–38: The History of a Literary Era*. Amsterdam: Meulenhoff / Calder and Boyars.

Mecsnóber, Tekla. 2014. 'A Notion of Joyce's Time: Interpreting the Diacritics of *Finnegans Wake* 124.8–12', *Genetic Joyce Studies* 14. www.geneticjoycestudies.org.

Meisel, Perry. 2006. 'Psychology'. In *A Companion to Modernist Literature and Culture*, edited by David Bradshas and Kevin Dettmar, 79–91. Oxford: Blackwell.

Menary, Richard. 2007. 'Writing as Thinking'. *Language Sciences* 5: 621–32.

———. 2010. 'Introduction'. In *The Extended Mind*, edited by Richard Menary, 1–25. Cambridge, MA, and London: MIT Press.

Meyers, Jeffrey. 1980. *The Enemy: A Biography of Wyndham Lewis*. London and Henley: Routledge & Kegan Paul.

Michaud, Gerald Albert. 1973. *The Casus of the Ondt and the Gracehoper*. PhD Dissertation, Saint Louis University.

Moore, Marianne. 1997. *The Selected Letters of Marianne Moore*, edited by Bonnie Costello, Celeste Goodridge and Cristanne Miller. New York: Knopf: Distributed by Random House.

Moses, Belle. 1910. *Lewis Carroll in Wonderland and at Home*. New York and London: D. Appleton & Co.

Mullin, Katherine. 2008. 'Joyce through the Little Magazines', in *A Companion to James Joyce*, ed. Richard Brown, 374–89. Malden, MA, and Oxford: Blackwell.

Nash, Paul W. and A. J. Flavell. 1994. *The Corvinus Press: A History and Bibliography*. Aldershot, Hants: Scolar Press.

Nashe, John. 2006. *James Joyce and the Act of Reception: Reading, Ireland, Modernism*. Cambridge: Cambridge University Press.

Noë, Alva. 2004. *Action in Perception*. Cambridge: MIT Press.

———. 2006. 'Experience without the Head'. In *Perceptual Experience*, edited by T.S. Gendler and J. Hawthorne, 411–33. Oxford: Oxford University Press.

Norburn, Roger. 2004. *A James Joyce Chronology*. Houndmills, Basingstoke: Palgrave Macmillan.

Ogden, C.K. 1929. 'Preface'. In James Joyce, *Tales Told of Shem and Shaun*, i–xv Paris: The Black Sun Press.

———. (1931) 1994. *Debabelization, with a Survey of Contemporary Opinions on the Problem of a Universal Language*. In *C.K. Ogden and Linguistics*, volume II, edited by W. Terrence Gordon, 227–66. London: Routledge/Thoemmes Press.

O'Keeffe, Paul. 2000. *Some Sort of Genius: A Life of Wyndham Lewis*. London: Jonathan Cape.

O'Neill, Patrick. 2013. *Impossible Joyce: Finnegans Wakes*. Toronto: University of Toronto Press.

Ortner, Hanspeter. 2000. *Schreiben und Denken*. Tübingen: Niemeyer.

Pearson, Neil. 2007. *Obelisk: A History of Jack Kahane and the Obelisk Press*. Liverpool: Liverpool University Press.

Poli, Bernard J. 1967. *Ford Madox Ford and the Transatlantic Review*. Syracuse, NY: Syracuse University Press.

Quigley, Megan M. 2004. 'Justice for the "Illstarred Punster": Samuel Beckett and Alfred Péron's Revisions of "Anna Lyvia Pluratself"', *JJQ* 41 (Spring 2004): 469–87.

Rabaté, Jean-Michel. 2007. 'The Fourfold Root of Yawn's Unreason: Chapter III.3'. In *How Joyce Wrote 'Finnegans Wake': A Chapter-by-Chapter Genetic Guide*, edited by Luca Crispi and Sam Slote, 384–409. Madison: The University of Wisconsin Press.

Raichle, Marcus E. and Abraham Z. Snyder. 2007. 'A Default Mode of Brain Function: A Brief History of an Evolving Idea'. *Neuroimage* 37.4: 1083–90.

Rose, Danis. 1995. *The Textual Diaries of James Joyce*. Dublin: The Lilliput Press.

Rowlands, Mark. 2010. *The New Science of the Mind: From Extended Mind to Embodied Phenomenology*. Cambridge, MA, and London: The MIT Press.

Schork, R.J. 2007. 'Genetic Primer: Chapter I.6'. In *How Joyce Wrote 'Finnegans Wake': A Chapter-by-Chapter Genetic Guide*, edited by Luca Crispi and Sam Slote, 124–41. Madison: The University of Wisconsin Press.

Senn, Fritz. 1966. 'Insects Appalling'. In *Twelve and a Tilly: Essays on the Occasion of the 25th Anniversary of 'Finnegans Wake'*, edited by Jack P. Dalton and Clive Hart, 36–39. London: Faber and Faber.

Shloss, Carol Loeb. 2003. *Lucia Joyce: To Dance in the Wake*. New York: Picador.

Sigler, Amanada. 2014. 'In Between the Sheets: Sexy Punctuation in American Magazines', in *Doubtful Points: Joyce and Punctuation*, edited by Elizabeth M. Bonapfel and Tim Conley, *European Joyce Studies* 23, 43–66. Amsterdam: Brill.

Slocum, John J. and Herbert Cahoon. (1953) 1971. *A Bibliography of James Joyce*. Westport, Connecticut: Greenwood Press.

Slote, Sam. 2000. 'The Prolific and the Devouring in "The Ondt and the Gracehoper"'. *Joyce Studies Annual* 11: 49–65.

———. 2001. 'Sound-Bite against the Restoration'. *Genetic Joyce Studies* 1.

———. 2007. 'Blanks for When Words Gone: Chapter II.1'. In *How Joyce Wrote 'Finnegans Wake': A Chapter-by-Chapter Genetic Guide*, edited by Luca Crispi and Sam Slote, 181–213. Madison: The University of Wisconsin Press.

Soupault, Philippe. 1931. 'A propos de la traduction d'Anna Livia Plurabelle'. *Nouvelle Revue française* 19.212: 633–6.

Spoo, Robert. 2013. *Without Copyrights: Piracy, Publishing, and the Public Domain*. Oxford: Oxford University Press.

Swift, Jonathan. 1986. *A Tale of a Tub and Other Works*, edited with an Introduction by Angus Ross and David Woolley. Oxford: Oxford University Press.

Thompson, Evan. 2007. *Mind in Life: Biology, Phenomenology, and the Sciences of Mind*. Cambridge, MA: Harvard University Press.

Travers Smith, Hester. 1923. *Psychic Messages from Oscar Wilde*. London: T. Werner Laurie.

Uexküll, Jakob von. (1934) 1957. 'A Stroll through the Worlds of Animals and Men: A Picture Book of Invisible Worlds'. In *Instinctive Behavior: The Development of a Modern Concept*, edited and translated by Claire H. Schiller, 5–80. New York: International Universities Press.

Valéry, Paul. 1921. 'Ébauche d'un serpent'. *Nouvelle revue française* 94: 5–17.

———. 1922. 'Ébauche d'un serpent'. In *Charmes ou Poèmes*, 59–73. Paris: Éditions de la Nouvelle revue française.

———. 2007. *Charms, and Other Pieces*, translated by Peter Dale. London: Anvil Press Poetry.

Van Hulle, Dirk. 1999. *Textual Awareness: A Genetic Approach to the Late Works of James Joyce, Marcel Proust, and Thomas Mann*. PhD Dissertation, University of Antwerp.

———. 2004. *Textual Awareness: A Genetic Study of Late Manuscripts by Joyce, Proust and Mann*. Ann Arbor: University of Michigan Press.

———. 2008. *Manuscript Genetics: Joyce's Know-How, Beckett's Nohow*. Gainesville: University Press of Florida.

———. 2009. 'Writing Sequence of the 'Guiltless' Notebook'. *Genetic Joyce Studies* 9. www.geneticjoycestudies.com/guiltless/index.html.

———. 2011. 'Valéry's Serpent and the *Wake*'s Genesis: Toward a Digital Library of James Joyce'. *James Joyce Quarterly* 47:3: 427–44.

———. 2013. 'Modernism, Mind, and Manuscripts'. In *A Handbook of Modernism Studies*, edited by Jean-Michel Rabaté, 225–38. Oxford and Malden, MA: Wiley-Blackwell.

Van Mierlo, Wim. 2007. 'Shaun the Post: Chapters III.1–2'. In *How Joyce Wrote 'Finnegans Wake': A Chapter-by-Chapter Genetic Guide*, edited by Luca Crispi and Sam Slote, 347–83. Madison: The University of Wisconsin Press.

Van Waes, Luuk, Mariëlle Leijten and Daphne van Weijen. 2009. 'Keystroke Logging in Writing Research: Observing Writing Processes with Inputlog'. *GFL German as a Foreign Language* 2.3: 41–64.

Varela, Francisco J., Evan Thompson and Eleanor Rosch. 1991. *The Embodied Mind: Cognitive Science and Human Experience*. Cambridge, MA, and London: The MIT Press.

Vico, Giambattista. 1961. *The New Science of Giambattista Vico*, trans. T.G. Bergin and M. H. Fisch. New York: Doubleday.

Wasserstrom, William. 1963. 'Marianne Moore, *The Dial*, and Kenneth Burke', *Western Humanities Review* 17.3: 249–62.

Williams, William Carlos. 1927. 'A Note on the Recent Work of James Joyce', *transition* 8: 149–54.

Woolf, Virginia. 1992. *Mrs Dalloway*. London: Penguin Classics.

———. 1994. *The Essays of Virginia Woolf*. Vol. 4, edited by Andrew McNeillie. London: Hogarth.

Index

For Product Safety Concerns and Information please contact our EU
representative GPSR@taylorandfrancis.com Taylor & Francis Verlag GmbH,
Kaufingerstraße 24, 80331 München, Germany

Printed and bound by CPI Group (UK) Ltd, Croydon, CR0 4YY
08/05/2025
01864359-0002